ROMANOV RELATIONS

ROMANOV RELATIONS

THE PRIVATE CORRESPONDENCE OF TSARS ALEXANDER I, NICHOLAS I AND THE GRAND DUKES CONSTANTINE AND MICHAEL WITH THEIR SISTER QUEEN ANNA PAVLOVNA

1817–1855

Edited by S. W. Jackman

Assisted by Bèrangère Steel

MACMILLAN

First published 1969 by
MACMILLAN AND CO LTD
Little Essex Street London WC2
and also at Bombay Calcutta and Madras
Macmillan South Africa (Publishers) Pty Ltd Johannesburg
The Macmillan Company of Australia Pty Ltd Melbourne
The Macmillan Company of Canada Ltd Toronto
Gill and Macmillan Ltd Dublin

Printed in Great Britain by
ROBERT MACLEHOSE AND CO LTD
The University Press Glasgow

Dedicated by permission to
His Royal Highness
Prince Willem-Alexander of the Netherlands
Prince of Orange-Nassau

Contents

List of Illustrations

The author and publishers wish to thank the Director of the Royal House Archives, The Hague, for kindly giving permission to reproduce all the photographs except the sketch of Tsar Nicholas I, which is reproduced by permission of the Mansell Collection.

Acknowledgements

I ACKNOWLEDGE the gracious permission of Her Majesty the Queen of the Netherlands, as owner of the copyright, to print the letters of Queen Anna Pavlovna in this book, and also the letters of Tsar Alexander I, Tsar Nicholas I, the Grand Duke Constantine and the Grand Duke Michael which are in Her Majesty's possession in the Royal House Archives in The Hague. I thank the Director of the Thuringian State Archives in Weimar for permission to publish the letters of Queen Anna Pavlovna and her family which are part of the collected papers of the Grand Duchess Sophie of Saxe-Weimar.

In editing any collection of this nature there are many who aid both directly and indirectly in bringing the work to a satisfactory conclusion. To all who have assisted me in my task I am most grateful.

I acknowledge with special thanks the many kindnesses of Mr Egbert Pelinck, the Director of the Royal House Archives in The Hague. He and his colleagues Mr A. J. Ubels and Mr A. F. Ubels (Jr), Archivists in the Royal House Archives, were very patient and most helpful in resolving many of my queries. Jonkheer Ir. P.F.O.R. Sickinghe, the former Director of the Royal House Archives, gave me much help and assistance during the early stages of the project.

Mrs George Shelton undertook to decipher the somewhat obscure and rather involved handwriting of the Grand Duke Constantine and thus made it possible for the letters to be included. Without her help it is doubtful if these letters would have been transcribed.

My research assistant, Mrs Christopher Heaman, utilised her extensive knowledge of the Russian and French languages to assist not only in the translation of the letters but also in preparing the material for many of the biographical notes.

I should like to add my thanks to the following: Mr and Mrs Michael Blair, Dr Daisy Lichtenberger, Francisca Hayman-Noé, Mr A. J. Whitfield, Mr Nicholas van der Vliet, Prince Nicholas Abkazi, The Director of the Lenin Library in Moscow, Mr Richard Steel, Dr Charlotte S. M. Girard, Mr Dean Halliwell and Mrs William Rodney.

Miss Caroline Hobhouse of Macmillan and Co. constantly encouraged and aided me in the preparation of the manuscript for the printer. To her and to my publishers I am most grateful.

My uncle, Mr E. Tatton Anfield, made it possible for me to devote much of my time to this project by assuming obligations which otherwise would have been mine. I am most appreciative of everything he has done for me now and in the past.

The typing of the manuscript was done by various hands, but two persons in particular should be noted. Mrs Reid, who worked on the original drafts, and Mrs A. J. Whitfield, who typed the final version *in toto*. Both Mrs Reid and Mrs Whitfield coped with many difficulties, and for all of their efforts on my behalf I cannot thank them enough.

Cornelus and Elizabeth Willems of Amsterdam are in many ways the true progenitors of this book. They have been most generous – nay more, lavish – in their hospitality when I invited myself on numerous occasions to stay with them. In their company and under their guidance, I have made numerous expeditions to see places and to look at artifacts concerned with Queen Anna Pavlovna and her world. They have given many valuable suggestions which have improved the text, and from them I have learned much Dutch history. I am deeply indebted to them for all of their help.

By leaving to the last my colleague Bérangère Steel, it is to emphasise her particular role. She undertook to transcribe from the French originals the majority of the letters included in this book. She aided in the translation and helped in so many ways that it is impossible to enumerate them all. She is truly the co-editor of this volume and it has been wonderful to work with her in this capacity.

S. W. JACKMAN

Fête du régiment des Lanciers de la garde de S.M. l'Empereur de la Russie

Victoria, British Columbia
13 February 1969

Introduction

IF a census of the Romanov family had been taken shortly after the accession of Tsar[1] Nicholas II in 1894, the figures would have added up to a respectable total. There were numerous members of the imperial dynasty itself, all direct descendants of Tsar Nicholas I; there were the Oldenburgs and the Leuchtenbergs – foreign princes who had married into the Romanov family and had become Russians; there were the Yurievskis, who were connected with the imperial line by virtue of being descended from Tsar Alexander II and his second wife Princess Catherine Dolgoruky; and there were legions of cousins among the many European royal houses. A century earlier, however, when Tsar Paul came to the throne, the Romanov family had been relatively small in contrast with most other reigning families. At the end of the eighteenth century the imperial family consisted of Tsar Paul, his wife the Tsarina Maria Feodorovna, and their children the Grand Dukes Alexander, Constantine, Nicholas and Michael, and the Grand Duchesses Alexandra, Helena, Catherine, Maria and Anna. There were no Romanov cousins; in the previous generation the family had consisted of Tsar Peter III, who had no brothers or sisters – and what few relations they had were either very distant or connections of the Tsarina or of the late Empress Catherine. The consequence of this was that the Russian imperial family were to be generally more intimate throughout their lives and to retain stronger ties with each other than might normally be expected. There was a further complication in that the elder sons of Tsar Paul had largely been educated by the Empress Catherine II and this caused some polarisation within the family itself; the divisions were in part chronological, with one group consisting of Alexander, Constantine, Alexandra, Helena, Catherine and Maria and the other consisting of Anna, Nicholas and Michael. For example, there was a difference of seventeen years between Alexander and his sister Anna. Despite these further problems it may generally be accepted that they faced the world as a united group and as one united family with common interests.

The Grand Duchess Anna Pavlovna was born in 1795, two years

[1] Tsar and Emperor are used interchangeably throughout the text, as are Tsarina and Empress.

before her father succeeded her grandmother the Empress Catherine II as ruler of Russia. Unlike the elder children, she was to be brought up in close proximity to her parents, a pattern to be repeated with her younger brothers Nicholas and Michael. Her mother, Maria Feodorovna supervised her education and appointed a Swiss governess, Mlle de Sybourg – known to the family as 'Bourcis' – as her teacher. The young princess learnt to read, write, and speak fluent French, German, and Russian; she was taught music and painting, the rudiments of mathematics and science, and was well grounded in religion. Indeed, it may be noted that all members of the Romanov family of that generation were as well if not better educated than many other scions of royal houses.

After her father became Tsar the imperial family resided in the Winter Palace at St Petersburg and at Tsarskoe Selo, but they passed much time at Gatchina too. Here life was more informal and intimate, a much better environment for the natural development of the young.

Tsar Paul is an enigmatic figure. Much that has been written about him has been calumnious. He was born in 1754 and was educated under the supervision of the Empress Elizabeth with Panin as his tutor. He was not unintelligent and acquired a fluency in French, German, and Russian and was well acquainted with the ideas of the Enlightenment. He first married Princess Wilhelmina of Hesse in 1773, who died in childbirth. Then he married Princess Sophia Dorothea of Württemberg in 1776. During his mother's reign he had no political power and lived much in retirement. He was very interested in the army, and drilled and organised his own soldiers in the manner of Frederick the Great of Prussia, whom he greatly admired. It was long thought that Catherine II intended to nominate her grandson Alexander Pavlovich to succeed her, but this did not occur, largely through the influence of Alexander's tutor, La Harpe, who refused to support the project and warned the boy of the possibility of his father's exclusion from the throne. This timely intervention caused the Tsarevich to become more intimate with his elder sons to prevent the Empress from using them as pawns. Paul was a believer in the absolutist system, a system based on law and duty in which discipline and loyalty were the highest of virtues. He abhorred the principles of the French Revolution and dreamt of a mystical union of monarch and people.

Tsar Paul became the ruler of Russia in November 1796. Initially he was mild and generous; there were no proscriptions, a number of persons were released from gaol, and his government seemed orderly and purposeful. On 5 April 1797, his coronation day, he promulgated a new law of succession which made the crown hereditary in the House of Romanov, thus repealing the law of 1722 which allowed the sovereign to choose his own successor. If his domestic administration was sensible, however, his foreign policy tended to be erratic. He made war on France, interfered with the sovereign order of the Knights of Malta which precipitated a disruption in Anglo-Russian relations, and, following the *coup d'état* of Brumaire 18, 1798, altered his French policy completely with an eye to joining his former enemy in an alliance. This new policy projected the dismemberment of Turkey and Russian annexation of Constantinople, Bulgaria, Rumelia and Moldavia. India was to be invaded, and a force of some 23,000 Cossacks was dispatched southward under the command of Vasili Orlov, who was, unfortunately, not provided with any maps of the country he was to conquer. These hare-brained schemes, combined with increasingly harsh regulations for the administration of the army and tyrannical behaviour towards the nobility, resulted in a plot to depose the Tsar.

Tsar Paul had become highly suspicious of his entourage; there were rumours that he intended to arrest his two elder sons and to place his wife in a convent. Paranoic in his actions, he refused to live in the Winter Palace and resided instead in the security of the Michael Palace. On the night of 11 March 1801 (Old Style) a group of nobles and officers gained entrance to his quarters and in the ensuing scuffle Tsar Paul was murdered. Immediately thereafter his son Alexander was proclaimed his successor. Tsarina Maria Feodorovna accepted the *coup*, for there was little she could do otherwise, but thereafter she rarely lived in the capital and made Gatchina her home and the centre of her court.

The murder of Tsar Paul united the imperial family still more since they all felt they owed their continued existence to Alexander. He was for them not only their brother and their sovereign but also their saviour. They all deferred to his wishes on every occasion; only Tsarina Maria Feodorovna was in a position to offer alternative suggestions and plans. She did this not infrequently, and Tsar Alexander generally paid heed to her advice. The violent end of their father's life was an awful warning to the imperial family for the rest of their days. They never forgot it although they spoke and wrote of him rarely, but the shadow of the events at the Michael Palace was always there, even when life was at its best.

The Grand Duchess Anna Pavlovna resided with her mother at Gatchina. Here she was an observer of the various convolutions and involutions of her brother's actions. Her first introduction to the international scene was a brief one. In 1809 Napoleon was contemplating remarriage after his divorce from Josephine, and, following a meeting with the Tsar at Erfurt, he asked Alexander for his sister

Anna's hand. Tsar Alexander had seemed favourably inclined to the idea, but back in St Petersburg other opinions were heard, including those of Tsarina Maria Feodorovna, who was violently opposed to the proposal. The Russian court did not give an immediate answer, but early in 1810 Tsar Alexander wrote to Napoleon asking him to defer the question for two years since the Grand Duchess was only fifteen. This was a polite form of refusal. The letter crossed one from Napoleon, who, apparently anticipating the Tsar's refusal, wrote to withdraw his request as he had proposed instead to the Archduchess Marie Louise of Austria.

International rather than matrimonial matters were to be the concern of Tsar Alexander for the next half-dozen years, and it was not until after the defeat of Napoleon that he took up the question of finding a husband for his sister. In the interim, life for Anna Pavlovna continued much as it always had; she lived with her mother and participated in the usual round of court functions. She was the confidante of her young brothers Nicholas and Michael. The three young people had formed themselves into a club which they called the Triopathy, and as a sign of membership they wore special rings – an extra ring had been given to their mother, who was a kind of honorary member – and wrote to each other constantly. When her brothers joined the army, following the outbreak of war with France, the Triopathy continued but in a more limited manner. Even so, their intimacy did not diminish, and each informed the other of their daily activities by means of the post.

Following Napoleon's abdication in April 1814 Tsar Alexander could now turn his attention to more private and family matters, and the question of a husband for his sister the Grand Duchess Anna Pavlovna could be considered anew. Several German princes were proposed but after investigation were rejected. Following Alexander's visit to London it was rumoured that the Duke of Clarence, later William IV, was interested in an alliance with the Tsar's sister. This came to nothing, however, probably partly because the Prince Regent and his guest were not sympathetic – the Tsar and his sister the Grand Duchess Catherine had been too friendly with the Whigs – and partly because it is unlikely that the Duke of Clarence's intentions were considered to be serious. Moreover, the Duke of Clarence was a younger son; his brother the Prince Regent, his niece the Princess Charlotte, and his brother the Duke of York stood between him and the throne; this was not the sort of husband envisaged by the Tsar of Russia for his sister.

One of the decisions made by the Powers at Vienna was to unite both parts of the Netherlands into one single state under the rule of the House of Orange. The reason behind this decision was sensible enough: to create a viable buffer state in the north-east to help contain France within her borders as determined by the treaty of peace. The Netherlands as a state would combine the commerce of the north with the industry of the south and as such the prosperity of all seemed to be ensured. The sovereign of the new kingdom was to be the Prince of Orange. He had long been in exile but had returned to The Hague in November 1813, and soon after had been invited to resume his authority. His powers were somewhat limited in theory but in practice he was the chief executive of the state. The government of the new Kingdom of the Netherlands was similar to the state set up by the Dutch themselves. There was a constitution called 'The Fundamental Law', which the sovereign agreed to uphold, and there was a legislature of two chambers called the States-General. To continue the historic association of the House of Orange with the Netherlands the heir to the throne bore the title of Prince of Orange.

King William I had two sons; the elder, William, Prince of Orange, was born in 1792, more than two years before his parents went into exile. He had served in the British army in Spain, at Quatre-Bras and at Waterloo, and had considerable reputation as a soldier. Indeed, so much had his fellow-countrymen appreciated his military prowess that after Waterloo they presented him with the estate and palace of Soestdijk.

As Protestant prince, a British field officer, and member of a family connected with the House of Hanover, he was a logical choice as husband to the Princess Charlotte, the daughter of the Prince Regent and heiress to the British throne. But Princess Charlotte did not wish to marry the Prince of Orange; indeed, she actually refused to accept him and ran away from her father's house to join her mother, from whom her father was estranged. It took considerable persuasion to convince her to return to her own home. She was certain that the Prince Regent was promoting the match in order to get her out of England since he was jealous of her popularity. She asserted that the Prince of Orange was ugly – which was certainly not true, for all of his portraits show him to have been quite handsome; and that he had an unpleasant character – which was equally false, since he was generous, warm-hearted and considerate. Moreover, she had decided that she would not reside in the Netherlands under any circumstances, and this created an impossible situation since the Prince of Orange himself was committed to his own countrymen. Certainly, it would have been illogical for the Prince to accept the idea that he could not reside in his own country and have his wife with him; once Princess Charlotte became queen changes would occur, but for the time being a residence in the Netherlands was essential and natural.

Negotiations were broken off. Prince William did not seem to take the rebuff too severely, and indeed he too might well have had reservations about the obstinate and self-willed English princess. If they had married, and she had survived, complications would undoubtedly have ensued. With his gay and insouciant, but nevertheless proud, nature he could hardly have relished his role as Prince Consort. Two reigning sovereigns in tandem was not altogether practical; in the Netherlands he would have been king and she his wife, in England she would have been queen and he only her husband. He returned home from London with the Order of the Garter and the Order of the Bath but still unwed.

In the shifting pattern of alliances in the European system after Waterloo, the Netherlands held a more prominent place than it had in the late eighteenth century. In order to counterbalance some of his erstwhile allies, Tsar Alexander decided that a closer relationship with the Low Countries would advance Russian policy. The Tsar had met the Prince of Orange in London in 1814 and had found him personable and sensible. The Prince was still a bachelor, heir to a throne, and was certainly eligible as a husband for the Grand Duchess Anna Pavlovna. A marriage between the sister of the Tsar and the Prince of Orange would be one of considerable lustre and rather more prestige than might have been expected under the circumstances. Indeed, Anna Pavlovna was later to be always acutely conscious of the favour that she and her family had conferred upon the House of Orange through this act. She never failed to recall that she was of imperial birth, the daughter of an emperor and a grand duchess in her own right. During the crises of later years, when there was a chance that the House of Orange might fall, she insisted that despite everything she was and would always be – whatever title was conferred or removed – Her Imperial Highness the Grand Duchess Anna Pavlovna.

Once the matter had been put in train, negotiations moved swiftly, and by the end of 1815 a marriage contract had been signed. Anna Pavlovna was to have a dowry of one million roubles from the Tsar; the King of the Netherlands agreed to pay 5 per cent interest on this money and to give her supplementary sums in addition. The contract further stipulated that Anna Pavlovna was to be allowed to remain a member of the Russian Church, although it was understood that any children resulting from the marriage would be brought up as communicants of the Dutch Reformed Church. In 1816 the Prince of Orange travelled to St Petersburg for the wedding. The festivities were conducted with lavish splendour and the bridegroom, with his taste for luxury and elegance, vastly enjoyed his stay in the Russian capital. He became a great favourite of Tsar Alexander and his brothers the Grand Dukes Constantine, Nicholas and Michael – an intimacy that was to continue as long as they lived – and gained the approbation of his mother-in-law the Dowager Empress. The young couple remained in Russia for about six months and then began the journey back to the Netherlands.

It was difficult for the Grand Duchess to leave her family with whom she had such close ties and to depart from her homeland. Moreover, it was obvious that in all likelihood she would have little chance to see any of them for a number of years. The leave-taking was a very final act indeed. To assist the young bride in her new country, and to give her one companion from her youth, the Dowager Empress Maria Feodorovna persuaded Mlle de Sybourg to leave St Petersburg and go to the Netherlands. 'Bourcis' was to be a great comfort to Anna Pavlovna throughout the years to come and a great friend to all the family.

On their arrival in The Hague the Prince and Princess of Orange took up residence in a house on the Voorhout which King William had occupied earlier. The Princess of Orange was given an exceedingly warm welcome by the Netherlanders and was greeted in a very friendly manner by her husband's relations.

Her father-in-law, King William I, was a straightforward man, shrewd and perceptive, deeply interested in financial and industrial matters. His manner was old-fashioned and, though conscious of his position as king, he lacked the graciousness and ease that were necessary to the role. In public he was affable enough and was generally liked by his subjects, particularly in the northern provinces, for he was more at home in The Hague than in Brussels; yet his court was a great contrast to the splendours of St Petersburg. Queen Wilhelmina, who was a sister of King Frederick William III of Prussia, was most charming and pleasant, with a candid and friendly manner and a sympathetic and understanding character. Universally popular, everyone spoke of her with affection and respect. The other two members of the family were the Dowager Princess of Orange, herself a Prussian princess and mother of King William I, and Princess Louise, the widow of the Duke of Brunswick and sister of King William I. These ladies were somewhat formidable but not necessarily disagreeable; they were conservative and staid with the outlook of an earlier age. Neither was particularly overwhelmed by the pretensions of the Romanov dynasty, each being more than satisfied with her own position.

The younger generation was represented by Prince Frederick and Princess Marianne. Prince Frederick – known to the family as Fritz – was five years younger than the Prince of Orange. He was a good soldier, very popular with all classes, and throughout his entire life he remained on good terms with all members of his family. Indeed, he spent considerable effort attempting to resolve the various family difficulties that arose from time to time. Princess Marianne played no part in court life. She was only six years old when her brother married.

Although physically far from her family in Russia, the young Princess of Orange quickly established the old intimacy anew by means of a stream of letters home. Naturally her earliest letters were to her mother, the Dowager Empress Maria Feodorovna. This stern and unbending woman had a strong sense of duty and fulfilled her obligations without any difficulties whatsoever; she expected and exacted considerable deference from everyone, including her family – only the old Countess Lieven, her lady-in-waiting, was really a confidante – but she remained vitally concerned for the welfare of her children. They in turn respected her opinions, sought her advice and revered her as a model of character and intellect. Anna Pavlovna wrote to her mother about twice a week; thus, the Dowager Empress was well informed on events in the Netherlands. Anna wrote fewer letters to Tsar Alexander I – the head of the family – for there was an understanding that he would see all letters written to his mother, should they contain matters of political significance, or if his sister requested advice and counsel from her relations. As Tsar, Alexander's position was a special one; not only was he the eldest of the family but he was also the Emperor. In this modern age it is perhaps hard to comprehend the deference given to a reigning monarch; his opinions were accepted without challenge and he was above criticism. Any letter written to him directly by his family, while affectionate enough in tone, was very formal and without the ease of manner that was characteristic of the correspondence of the other members of the dynasty with each other.

In contrast, the letters between Anna Pavlovna and her brother the Grand Duke Constantine Pavlovich were far more open and casual. The Grand Duke was almost a generation older than his sister, and he occupied a position somewhere between that of a doting father and a brotherly comrade. Constantine resembled his father Tsar Paul in character and interests. The army was his first love – he was a ruthless and rigid disciplinarian – and he regarded his Polish troops with great affection; he made the soldiers under his command into a highly efficient body of men. Yet he was subject to sudden and violent rages; it is said that his anger was so fierce that men feared for their lives, and on one occasion a group of officers which had incurred his wrath actually committed suicide, convinced that he would have ordered them to be shot. Constantine was well educated and spoke Polish as well as Russian, German and French. He had married Julia Henrietta – a sister of Leopold, Prince of Saxe-Coburg, later King of the Belgians, and Victoria, Duchess of Kent, mother of Queen Victoria – but the marriage was not a success. They were unsympathetic towards each other, and Constantine's irregular way of life, licentiousness and numerous affairs caused the marriage to collapse. Julia Henrietta left Russia in 1801 and never returned. Constantine does not appear to have been unduly distressed, and as early as 1803 he suggested that the marriage should be dissolved. At that time he wished to espouse Princess Janetta Antinova Chetvertinskoi, the sister of Princess Maria Antinova Naryshkin – long the mistress of Tsar Alexander I – but the Dowager Empress opposed the plan. After this decision was made Constantine lived for a number of years with Mlle Friedrichs, a French actress, and by her he had a natural son, Paul Constantinovich Aleksandrov. Nevertheless, Constantine and his wife met from time to time in western Europe, and in 1814 there was actually talk of a reconciliation, but nothing came of it.

With the re-creation of the Kingdom of Poland by the Congress of Vienna, under Russian control and with Tsar Alexander as king, the Grand Duke Constantine was appointed viceroy. He lived in the Belvedere Palace in Warsaw in considerable state, and was accompanied by Mlle Friedrichs to the Polish capital where their relationship continued. In due course, however, Constantine fell madly in love with the Countess Jeannette Grudzinska, a member of a distinguished Polish family. As virtuous as she was beautiful, however, the countess resolutely refused to become the Grand Duke's mistress even after he had parted from Mlle Friedrichs, and it was not until 1820, after Constantine had been divorced, that they were able to marry, and then only after it had been decreed that any issue of the union were not eligible to succeed to the throne. It was at this time that Constantine renounced his rights to the throne as heir to Tsar Alexander; but his decision was not made public, and the tragic events of the Decembrist revolt, following the death of Tsar Alexander, were in part the consequence of the failure of the imperial family to make known the new state of affairs. Jeannette Grudzinska was made a princess, but she was not received in St Petersburg by the imperial family until after Constantine's death.

Constantine has an odious reputation. Posterity has accepted the general impression of certain of his contemporaries that he was a tyrant and a maniac. It is true that he was a military martinet, but so were many other men of his generation. Queen Victoria's father, the Duke of Kent, was recalled from Gibraltar because of his excessively severe military discipline; the Duke of Cumberland insisted on the most rigid attention to parade-ground drill; and the Duke of Wellington himself, who was never thought to be exacting, always believed in the lash to keep soldiers under control. Constantine is generally portrayed as an illiterate oaf, a boor and a bully. Yet in his correspondence with his sister quite another side of his character emerges; he appears as an understanding, sympathetic, generous, candid, honourable and witty man, intelligent, and far more perceptive about his family and the world than he is thought to have been.

With the Grand Duke Nicholas Pavlovich – later Tsar Nicholas I – Anna Pavlovna was very much of an equal. They were close in age – she was a year his senior – and he had been a member of the Triopathy. Posterity has also not been very generous in its judgement of Nicholas. Although he is thought not to have lacked private virtues, in his public life he is considered to have been a despot, a martinet, a man of limited outlook and no feeling whatsoever for the masses. Born in 1796, the Grand Duke Nicholas was educated under the careful supervision of his mother. After Alexander, he may well have been her favourite child. He spoke Russian, French, German and English, was grounded in the classics, and was taught economics, law and political science; nevertheless, he early indicated that he had no real interest in what he chose to call 'abstractions'. His view of life may be summed up as follows: 'Sound morals are the best theory of law, they must be present in the heart of every man, irrespective of any abstraction, and must be based on religion.' Indeed, his life was to be guided by three words: orthodoxy, autocracy and nationality. He was keenly interested in the army, and a great expert on drill and technique. Fond of music, he played the flute, patronised the opera and, to a degree, was a balletomane. He had considerable artistic talent, showing an aptitude for painting, and collected pictures assiduously.

In 1814 Nicholas joined the army, and, after Napoleon's abdication, travelled extensively. He admired the discipline of Prussia, allied himself to the House of Hohenzollern and in 1817 married Princess Charlotte – daughter of King Frederick William III and the beautiful Queen Louise – who, when she joined the Orthodox Church, took the name of Alexandra Feodorovna. Alexander, their eldest son, was born in 1818 and was joined over the years by a number of other children.

The youthful intimacy of Anna Pavlovna and Nicholas was a bond that united them for the rest of their lives. They were to correspond with great frequency and to turn to each other in times of crisis or distress. Nicholas was Anna's ally and confidant. He was always tremendously generous to her, giving her magnificent presents, supporting her financially and rewarding her servants; he rarely denied any of her requests.

The youngest of the brothers, the Grand Duke Michael Pavlovich, had also been a member of the Triopathy. As the baby of the family he was always treated with considerable indulgence and was referred to as 'cadet'. In a family noted for its interest in military affairs,

Michael was outstanding in his mastery of military drill but, despite his abilities, he was not popular in the army because of his pedantry and severity, for he too had a violent temper. Greatly attached to his brother Constantine, he emulated him in every way, even to his clothes, and often visited Warsaw and stayed with the viceroy. A gay charmer and somewhat indolent, he was rather feckless and certainly selfish. His marriage to Princess Charlotte of Württemberg, known in Russia as the Grand Duchess Helene, was not successful. Michael found her salons tedious and she, being too intelligent and refined, found the army barracks distasteful. In an effort to improve his poor health the Grand Duke travelled extensively, and was apparently not a very good correspondent as news of him and his activities generally came from others. However, despite his failings, he was always regarded affectionately and was often the object of concern.

At the time of Anna Pavlovna's marriage only two of her four sisters were still living: the Grand Duchesses Maria Pavlovna and Catherine Pavlovna. The elder of the two, the Grand Duchess Maria, was the wife of Duke Charles Frederick of Saxe-Weimar. She was a talented woman, and her court was the centre of considerable intellectual and cultural life. She and her youngest sister Anna were extremely friendly and over the years they met and corresponded frequently. In due course their families were to be brought more closely together through the marriage of Anna's daughter, the Princess Sophie, with Maria's son Prince Charles Alexander. With her other sister, Catherine, Anna was not particularly intimate. Catherine's first husband was George, Duke of Oldenburg, and they lived at Tver. After she became a widow she returned to St Petersburg where she became the confidante of Tsar Alexander; she accompanied him on his campaigns and travels between 1813 and 1815, and was with him on a visit to London in 1814. Although clever, she was extremely autocratic in behaviour and alienated many people as a result. In 1816 Catherine married King William of Württemberg, who divorced his wife in order to make this alliance – but she died three years later. She had three children, two sons by her first marriage and a daughter by the second. This daughter was to marry William, the eldest son of Anna Pavlovna. The antipathy between Catherine and her youngest sister was to have unfortunate results, because Anna Pavlovna saw in Catherine's daughter many of the traits that had displeased her in the sister. Hence, relations between Princess Sophie and her mother-in-law were never very amiable. The Queen of Württemberg and the Princess of Orange corresponded only rarely, and generally only on the most formal of terms.

The flow of letters between the imperial family in Russia and the Princess of Orange continued unceasingly until Anna's death in 1865.

Apart from her husband and children, her Russian relations and their activities were her chief interest. Anna Pavlovna lived in the Netherlands for nearly half a century, but she never ceased to consider herself Russian and a Romanov.

The parliament and the court were located alternatively in The Hague and Brussels. King William I lived in the royal palace in The Hague with a summer palace, Het Loo, at Apeldoorn. He had a state residence in Brussels and a country home at Laeken near by. His son and daughter-in-law had a palace at The Hague and their country house Soestdijk. They also had a palace in Brussels where they spent part of every year. The Prince of Orange was lively and sociable; he enjoyed parties, soirées, concerts and the theatre, and he surrounded himself with a vivacious court of young people. Indeed, the palace in Brussels was the social centre of the Netherlands; even though it was not as grand as St Petersburg, it was certainly more sophisticated than the king's court in The Hague. Anna Pavlovna felt very much at ease in this urbane society, preferring it to the bourgeois world of the Dutch. Her good looks, elegance, style and affability were more appreciated, she felt, by the citizens of Brussels. In addition, her husband had a wider scope for his talents in the south and greater independence; his abilities were recognised and his aims understood. In The Hague he was distinctly second to his father, being merely the sovereign's eldest son and first subject.

Although King William was willing to grant his son considerable powers, he never permitted him much authority to carry out decisions. This was to lead to difficulties, particularly in spheres in which the Prince of Orange felt that he had some expertise; the problem was exacerbated by virtue of the fact that the Prince of Orange was more popular in many circles than his father was, and this was not liked by the king. From the very first, Anna Pavlovna was intensely loyal to her husband and in letters home to her family always presented matters from his point of view. On several occasions the young couple were at odds with King William, and there were some unfortunate scenes; in the end, however, the differences were generally resolved, if not entirely, at least satisfactorily so that no permanent rift in family relations resulted. These problems in part indicated not only a clash of personalities but also a decided difference in outlook between the generations.

In 1817, in Brussels, a son, William, was born to the Prince and Princess of Orange and was christened in the Protestant church. Four other children were to follow: Alexander in 1818, Henry in 1820, Casimir in 1822, and Sophie in 1825. Of the five children, four reached maturity, although Alexander was to die a young man. Casimir did not live a year.

When the Grand Duke Constantine obtained imperial permission to espouse the Countess Grudzinska, the project had the approbation of his sister Anna as well, since she desired his happiness. She did not realise that he had surrendered his rights to the throne and continued to regard him as Tsarevich – a title he continued to use even after his brother Nicholas had come to the throne – and as Tsar Alexander's heir. Nowhere in the correspondence is there any indication that Constantine intimated that such might not be the case. However, he does declare that since Nicholas has children the succession is assured. In the light of later events it might well have been more sensible had the matter been made clear from the start, but even when the decision finally did become known upon Alexander's death, Anna Pavlovna only saw in it one further proof of the disinterestedness of Constantine's behaviour, and she salutes him as 'the Bayard of the family'.

One of Anna Pavlovna's greatest desires was to return to her homeland for an extended stay, but King William was not enthusiastic about the plan and made difficulties. There were further complications about the children, but these were resolved when Bourcis agreed to remain in the Netherlands in charge of the nursery. Finally, in 1824, the visit became possible and there was a Romanov reunion in St Petersburg. Anna Pavlovna recaptured the joys of her youth, the Triopathy was reconstituted, and the court life at Gatchina, Tsarskoe Selo and the Winter Palace seemed exactly as it had been in 1816. This was the last time that the old circle was together, for Alexander died at Taganrog in December 1825.

The news of Tsar Alexander's death was sent to his sister in the Netherlands. She wrote immediately to her brother Constantine hailing him as 'Emperor', but when she learned the true state of affairs she conveyed her compliments to her brother Nicholas while still regarding Constantine as the titular head of the family. The news of the Decembrist Revolt, the military revolt to give Russia a constitution, horrified her. To all the Romanovs it must have brought to mind the awful events of March 1801. The death of Tsar Alexander, who was thereafter referred to by the family as 'our Angel', was followed by that of his wife the Empress Elizabeth – a somewhat shadowy figure and one apparently not excessively mourned by the family – and then, in 1828, by that of 'Mama', the Dowager Empress Maria Feodorovna. This succession of doleful events, coupled with the new regime in St Petersburg, in many ways loosened the ties with the past. Although Anna Pavlovna turned to her husband and children for consolation, her affection for her surviving brothers was nevertheless undiminished.

Life in the Netherlands for the Prince and Princess of Orange continued in its familiar pattern. They moved from one residence to another, spending the seasons in different houses and in various parts of the country. The court functions, the balls, the opera and the theatre saw the Prince and Princess in their accustomed places. The Prince of Orange still preferred Brussels to The Hague, and the worldliness of the former was in sharp contrast with the simplicity of the latter. However, the charms of Brussels had been somewhat dimmed because the Princess of Orange's magnificent jewelry had been stolen while she was in residence in the southern capital. The jewels, many of them gifts from her family in Russia, were of great value and their loss to the Princess severe. Yet another catastrophe also befell the Prince and Princess in Brussels; the palace in which they lived was destroyed by fire, the royal family and their attendants only just managing to escape the flames. All of their possessions were lost. In addition to these more personal tragedies, the population of Brussels was no longer as affectionately inclined toward the Prince and Princess of Orange as in the past. Governmental policy, by which they were inevitably associated, was such that the ruling house was becoming less popular.

To a superficial observer the union of the Dutch and the Belgians seemed harmonious, but in fact there were many difficulties. The linguistic differences between the Walloons and the Dutch did not make communications easy; the royal family involved itself in religious controversy and further gave its approbation to the Protestant elements in the country; the general conservatism of the monarchy and its resistance to change did little to bind together the various factions in the state. For too long had the Low Countries had a separate history; the decisions of Vienna, while laudable enough in aim, were simply not workable.

In 1830 the adage 'When Paris sneezes, France catches a cold' might have been extended to read 'When France catches a cold, Europe gets pneumonia', for events in France were to be the catalyst which caused the Belgian revolt. On 28 July 1830 Charles X was overthrown and was forced to abdicate, and the Bourbons, who had been restored in 1814, were unable to resist the forces of change. Legitimacy as a principle suffered a severe blow. The events in Paris disturbed the various chancelleries considerably but there was no indication that the trouble would spread beyond France. Certainly there was no indication of an uprising in Belgium, and indeed the signs pointed the other way, for the situation seemed to be very calm since King William had agreed shortly before to repeal some of his more obnoxious legislation which had rankled with his Belgian subjects.

Revolutions occur in the most amazing ways, but Belgium has the unique distinction of beginning its struggle for independence in an opera house. To honour King William, a festival had been planned with music and fireworks; the fireworks were countermanded as being possibly provocative but the musical programme was allowed to continue. On 23 August 1830 a gala performance of Daniel Auber's opera *La Muette de Portici* was presented at the Théâtre de la Monnaie. The opera tells the story of Masaniello, who rebels against King Philip IV of Spain. One aria in particular, 'Amour Sacré de la Patrie', received tumultuous applause:

> For a slave what peril counts,
> Better death than live in chains,
> Off the yoke that stifles us,
> Perish aliens at our hands.
> Holy love of native land,
> Give me courage, give me pride!
> To my country, life I owe,
> And she owes me liberty!

This aria was to become the tocsin. After the performance, many of the audience and other citizens in Brussels began to wander about the streets; crowds gathered; and suddenly shops were broken into and houses burned. A violent mood seemed to have been unleashed, and since many of the rioters were from the unemployed it seemed as if a proletarian revolt was in full force. The burgomaster was out of town, and the garrison was too small to take control. Fearful that radical sentiment would dominate and that property and lives would be seriously endangered, the more conservative elements in the city the next day enrolled in the civic guard to maintain order, setting up a commission to rule the city. The news of the outburst in Brussels soon spread and similar demands for freedom were heard in other towns throughout the southern provinces.

King William, at his palace in The Hague, did not act precipitately, for such was not his way; had the Prince of Orange been resident in Brussels at the time it is unlikely that the revolt would have become so serious, but unfortunately he too was in the north. The government decided that the Prince should be sent with six thousand troops to occupy the city. The Prince of Orange had no desire to shed blood; he was personally still popular in the south and did not wish to lose his popularity by any rash act. Instead of marching into the city, therefore, he offered to act as a mediator with the King in The Hague. King William, who often said 'Night is the best counsellor', agreed merely to call the States-General to see if the difficulties could be resolved. To indicate still further that he was not unduly perturbed by the situation, he calmly proceeded with the ceremonies arranged for the marriage of the Princess Marianne and Prince Albert of Prussia.

Nevertheless, the situation in Brussels had to be settled. The insurgents continued in control of the city and, as the days passed, increasingly radical groups came to the fore. On 20 September an extremist faction took power and seized the town hall. Prince Frederick, who had been placed in charge of the troops outside the city, now indicated that he would reoccupy the town. On 23 September the Dutch army marched into Brussels with the bands playing the overture to *La Muette de Portici*. There was no sign of opposition. Once the royal palace was reached, the town would be theirs. Unfortunately an error was made, and, instead of proceeding straight on, the soldiers halted in a park. With their targets thus lined up for them, the rebels began to shoot from all directions. Prince Frederick recognised his danger, but there was little that he could do and, rather than risk the loss of his entire army, he withdrew. For the moment it appeared that the revolution had triumphed.

As earlier, the example of Brussels emboldened other rebels to threaten violence and the Dutch retreated on all fronts. Few lives were lost, for both sides really wished to proceed with caution. The rebels simply wanted the garrisons out, the army simply wanted to make such terms as would guarantee the safety of lives and property. Only in Antwerp was there any real trouble: here the insurgents broke the armistice, unleashing a retaliatory bombardment. Unfortunately, the destruction in Antwerp did much to bring sympathy for the revolutionary cause and to undermine Orange support.

The situation in the southern provinces was now getting out of control and the Powers decided to take a hand. Since the kingdom was the creation of decisions taken at Vienna, the Powers felt they had a special interest in the case. Moreover, in accordance with the policies evolved by the Holy Alliance, direct intervention in the affairs of European states was permitted. A meeting of the interested parties and representatives of the Powers was arranged to convene in London. Meanwhile, Russia, Austria and Prussia all gave signs of sending in troops to restore order. The rebellions in central Italy distracted Austrian attention, however, and the Polish revolution immobilised the Russians. Since the Prussians would only act in concert, it was therefore left to the English and the French to resolve the question.

Had the Duke of Wellington remained Prime Minister, it is likely that the House of Orange would have continued to rule, but with a changed administrative arrangement. However, the Whigs under Lord Grey had taken office and they were not committed to the principle of legitimacy, although they too initially did not disavow the House of Orange entirely and would probably have supported the Prince of Orange as ruler of Belgium. Once the Belgian national congress had voted the deposition of the Orange family, the only way the

Prince could have taken power was by force, and the Whigs refused to countenance such a course of action.

In an effort to preserve the authority of the House of Orange the Prince went to London to represent his father, but was rather coolly received by the English. Unknown to him, Anna Pavlovna had sent her entire fortune to Prince Lieven, the Russian Ambassador to the Court of St James, in an attempt to aid her husband and to promote a counter-revolt. Considerable sums were expended, but nothing came of the projected restoration.

On 20 December 1830 the plenipotentiaries dissolved the Kingdom of the Netherlands and, in January 1831, set up two protocols which were to be the basis of separation. The Dutch accepted them, but the Belgians refused. Palmerston summed up the situation nicely: 'Everyone agrees in saying the Belgians are mad. It is a waste of effort arguing with them.' The French minister Sebastiani confirmed this statement: 'The Belgians have no ideas except mad ones; they had better take care, or other people may think in the same way.' The Belgians now proceeded to act even more madly, electing various princes to their vacant throne, princes who for various obvious reasons were bound to be vetoed by the English or the French. Finally, some sanity descended on the assembly in Brussels and it elected Leopold of Saxe-Coburg as king. The conference gave him its blessing, and with this approbation a new protocol to determine the basis for separation. This time it was the Belgians who accepted and the Dutch who did not.

King William now decided to take the matter into his own hands, and on 2 August 1831 he ended the armistice. Leopold and his advisers were taken completely by surprise. The Dutch army crossed the frontier, meeting minimal resistance. The Belgians, who had done so well the year before, believed that they could do so again, but this time the story was very different. The Prince of Orange severely defeated the Belgians at Hasselt on 8 August. Leopold regrouped his troops near Louvain, but once more the Dutch defeated his army and he was almost captured himself by some Dutch cavalrymen. To rescue the beleaguered Belgians, Louis-Philippe sent in the French army on 9 August, and three days later all hostilities ceased. The Dutch retired very slowly to their own territory and the Ten Days' Campaign was ended. The Dutch had recovered some of their lost prestige; the new Belgian kingdom had survived only because of the assistance given by France, supported by England. Again the Powers attempted to settle the matter; new protocols were drawn up, but King William refused to consider them and continued to occupy Antwerp.

The patience of the delegates at the London Conference seemed inexhaustible. A year went by but no settlement was reached. Finally, in November 1832, a combined Anglo-French naval force blockaded the Dutch coast, and a Franco-Belgian army besieged Antwerp. The siege of Antwerp was war at its most gentlemanly, and after a month the Dutch forces, under Chasse, withdrew with full honours. The naval blockade had some effect, for King William signed another armistice in May 1833. But he did not and would not recognise the new state and it took six more years before a final agreement was reached.

On 19 April 1839 King William agreed to the Twenty-Four Articles which had been drawn up in 1831. King Leopold had remade his army and had appointed a number of Polish officers, much to the fury of Tsar Nicholas and his sister, but Leopold knew that even this new army could not risk a new war. Belgium was lost irretrievably to the House of Orange, but King William kept part of Luxembourg, initially claimed by the Belgians. The province of Limburg was partitioned, and the national debt divided. Everyone was pleased when the question was finally resolved; even Tsar Nicholas had at last lost patience with King William. Nevertheless it was a severe blow to the pride of the Dutch, and King William's increasing unpopularity with his fellow-countrymen was in large part a result of these events.

Anna Pavlovna had never wavered in her support of her husband. In August 1831, to demonstrate her loyalty, she had sent her husband a portrait bearing the inscription 'Plutôt une cabane avec mon Guillaume que de souscrire au deshonneur'. She kept her family in Russia posted of the situation almost daily, and the tone of her letters becomes increasingly emotional. She is buoyed up to the heights by Hasselt and Louvain and cast down by the French invasion and the later siege of Antwerp.

Tsar Nicholas could do little but offer moral assistance. His emissaries in London did everything in their power to maintain his sister and her husband, but to no avail. He was not able to send troops to help them since he had problems closer to home; on 29 November 1830 a small group of cadets and students invaded the Belvedere Palace in Warsaw, hoping to capture Constantine and his staff. There was some violence; a number of Polish officials and some officers were killed, but Constantine managed to escape. The revolt might have been put down, but Constantine chose to withdraw from Warsaw rather than use force. The conservative elements in Poland condemned the rebellion, but the radicals rebuffed them and took over, establishing a provisional government. The erstwhile viceroy was extremely reasonable and promised not to attack the capital without notice and even offered a free pardon for all of the insurgents. Indeed, he went further in permitting any Polish soldiers who had accompanied him out of the city to return, while he and his Russian troops retired behind the Russian frontier. Such conciliatory behaviour did not find favour in St Petersburg, and the Tsar refused to receive any Polish emissaries officially. In February 1831 General Diebitsch attacked the Poles and, after severe losses on both sides, the Russians were victorious. Before he could consolidate his victory, however, Diebitsch died of cholera, and it was not until September 1831 that Warsaw finally surrendered to Paskevich.

In the meantime, Constantine had retired to Vitebsk with his wife, who, although she was Polish, remained loyal to her husband. Constantine caught cholera and died on 15 June 1831. Surprisingly enough Anna Pavlovna did not indulge in excessive emotionalism upon learning of his death, undoubtedly because she herself was at the moment involved personally and directly in the Belgian revolution. Her letter to Tsar Nicholas is almost cool and detached. Obviously, however, her brother's death had its effect and she turned more than ever to Nicholas for support in the years to come. Constantine's widow, the Princess Grudzinska, was invited by Tsar Nicholas to come to St Petersburg – at long last she was officially received by the imperial family – and she agreed to do so. On arrival she shut herself up in her suite at Tsarskoe Selo and saw virtually no one, with the exception of Count Benckendorf, who realised that her distress was not only personal but also national, since she mourned both her husband and her country. She died on 15 November 1831, and was buried in the Roman Catholic church at Tsarskoe Selo.

With the restoration of Russian authority in Poland and the armistice with Belgium, life for Tsar Nicholas and Anna Pavlovna returned to some degree of normality. The Princess of Orange wished to have the pleasure of seeing her brother once more and after many difficulties a meeting was arranged in 1835. She had a happy but brief reunion with the Tsar at Dux in Bohemia. In 1839 Anna Pavlovna had a further contact with her Russian relations when her nephew the Tsarevich Alexander Nicolaievich was her guest and celebrated his twenty-first birthday at her house. With the passing years her own family, Russian and Dutch alike, meant more and more to her.

The Prince and Princess of Orange continued to represent the more progressive elements in the Netherlands. The old King favoured no change in the government. After his wife's death in 1837 he became increasingly isolated from society and lived largely removed from political reality. His Belgian policy had been a fiasco, the finances of the state were in a parlous way, and reform was essential. Throughout the country there was growing discontent with the situation.

The children of Anna Pavlovna were now starting to lead their own lives. Prince William, the eldest son, was very much in the shadow of his popular father. The young prince was not particularly outgoing or easy in manner, and in public he was inclined to be brusque. In 1834 he had visited his uncle Tsar Nicholas in St Petersburg, and in 1836 he accompanied his father and his brother Alexander on a journey to England. He continued these tours, and during a visit to the court at Stuttgart fell in love with his cousin Princess Sophie and insisted upon marrying her. His mother was very displeased about this for she felt that, at nineteen, he was too young, and she did not greatly approve of the marriage of cousins. More particularly, she had always disliked Sophie's mother, the Grand Duchess Catherine, and transferred her hostility to the daughter. Despite this maternal opposition, the marriage took place on 18 June (Waterloo Day) 1839. The young couple were received enthusiastically by everyone except Anna Pavlovna, who greeted her daughter-in-law in a cold and formal manner despite Tsar Nicholas's advice to receive Sophie cordially and mould her to a proper standard. Relations between the Princess of Orange and her daughter-in-law were never easy, and in later years they met only on state occasions.

The younger children found more approbation from their parents. Prince Alexander was sent to the University of Leiden in 1835, and was joined there by his elder brother William a year later. In 1836 Prince Alexander was in London and was briefly considered as a possible husband for Princess Victoria, but nothing came of it. Princes of the House of Orange seemed to be ill-fated in their matrimonial prospects with English princesses in the nineteenth century. Another flurry was caused when a proposal was made to marry Alexander to the young Spanish queen, Isabella II, but the idea of a Hispano-Netherlands match was too extreme in view of the history of both countries. Moreover, the religious differences were such that they could not be bridged. In 1839 Alexander went to St Petersburg where he received a cordial welcome. He did not take an active part in public life since his health did not permit it.

The youngest son, Prince Henry, had entered the Dutch navy in 1832 and made a number of voyages as a cadet and as an officer. He visited Scandinavia, England, Russia, Ireland and Spain; in 1835 he crossed the Atlantic and travelled to the Antilles and Surinam before sailing up to New York, where he was warmly received. From October 1836 to July 1838 he was in the East Indies and was rarely on shore for long until after 1847. Princess Sophie, the youngest child, continued to be her parents' darling, but was now becoming a definite young lady.

In 1840 William and Anna Pavlovna finally came into their own.

The King had grudgingly accepted some reforms which had been forced upon him. He realised that he had lost his popularity, that he was out of touch and that the only sensible thing was to retire. This was a wise decision because the last remnants of his popularity vanished when he announced that he intended to marry the Countess Henriette d'Oultremont, a lady-in-waiting to the late Queen. The lady was unobjectionable in manner and decorum, but she was a Belgian and a Roman Catholic, two inexcusable offences at that moment in the Netherlands. On 7 October 1840 King William I abdicated, taking the title Duke of Nassau. Soon afterward he and his new wife left the country. He lived in retirement in Berlin, in his palace Unter den Linden, or on his estates in Silesia. He reappeared on occasion in the Netherlands, and one of his few and rare public appearances was at the christening of his first great-grandson William. He died on 12 October 1843, and was buried in the Netherlands.

The first notable event of the new reign was the swearing-in of the sovereign. The ceremony prescribed in the Dutch constitution replaces a formal coronation and it took place in the New Church at Amsterdam on 28 October 1840. It was an occasion of great solemnity and splendour – the sort of event which Queen Anna Pavlovna loved – and she described it in great detail to her brother the Tsar. Under the new monarchs, court life took on a rather more formal tone than it had had in the previous reign; indeed, it was more elegant than before or even since that time, but King William II remained his charming and agreeable self, being affable and easy at all times. Queen Anna Pavlovna, always conscious of her imperial background, expected and exacted considerable deference from everyone.

As Princess Sophie grew to maturity, a number of suitors appeared: the Prince de Joinville, son of Louis-Philippe, wished to marry her but was rejected for political and religious reasons, and numerous German princelings hovered about, hoping to be accepted. The choice finally fell upon Prince Charles Alexander, son of the Grand Duke of Saxe-Weimar and Anna Pavlovna's sister, the Grand Duchess Maria. Prince Charles Alexander was thus Princess Sophie's first cousin, but in this instance Queen Anna Pavlovna's antipathy to the marriage of near relations does not seem to have been revived. The wedding took place in 1842, and although Charles and Sophie resided in Weimar, they made frequent visits to the Netherlands and were always very welcome.[1]

[1] After Queen Anna Pavlovna's death her daughter the Princess Sophie inherited many of her possessions including part of her private papers. These papers, including many of her letters, were placed in the Grand Ducal House Archives – now the Thuringian State Archives – and this accounts for the collections being divided.

The reign of King William II was one in which many and long-overdue changes occurred. When he came to the throne, the national finances were in a deplorable state but after 1844 this problem was, if not completely resolved, at least on the way to a solution. In the same year constitutional changes were proposed but were not immediately put into effect. Indeed, the general unrest in the country resulting in part from the potato famine of 1845–6 made King William rather more conservative than he had been initially.

For the House of Orange the year 1848 was crucial, not only in the public but also in private. In late 1847 William and Anna's second son, Prince Alexander, had gone to Madeira for his health. He did not improve significantly, however, and soon alarming reports were dispatched to his parents. His younger brother Prince Henry was sent out to see him and bring him back home. All was in vain, for on 20 February 1848 Prince Alexander died at the age of twenty-nine. The family was crushed. Queen Anna Pavlovna retired to Soestdijk, King William never again was completely happy, and the Prince of Orange did not allow his own birthday – 19 February – to be celebrated for many years. The death of 'the golden prince' opened the fateful year.

Even before word of the Prince's death had reached The Hague, news of the revolution in Paris was reported everywhere. The abdication of Louis-Philippe on 24 February 1848 was a sign of the times. King William II was a man of sense and perception. He recognised very quickly that if concessions were not made to resolve the discontent that was rife in his own country, he too might face an open revolt. Suddenly and quite without warning – there is a tradition that he took the decision after receiving a letter from his daughter Sophie in Weimar commending a conciliatory policy – the King called for revisions in the constitution. A special commission was appointed, under the leadership of the liberal statesman Rudolf Thorbecke, and in October the revisions received royal assent. The new constitution was much more liberal than the old and it created a democratic kingdom. Much credit must be given to King William for his timely cognisance of the course of events. Other sovereigns, less prescient than he, had to abdicate or were driven from their thrones and only returned accompanied by foreign troops.

King William's last public appearance was to open the States-General on 13 February 1849; on this occasion he expressed anew his intention of accepting the revised constitution. Already there were signs that he was in poor health, and he died at his favourite residence, Tilburg – his headquarters from 1830 to 1839 – on 17 March 1849.

For Anna Pavlovna the loss of her husband was overwhelming;

this, in conjunction with the death a year earlier of their son, and the political upheavals all over Europe, caused the widowed Queen to retire from public life. Never again did she occupy The Hague palace on the Kneuterdyck. One major problem remained to be settled: the resolution of the late King's debts, which were discovered to be enormous. Queen Anna Pavlovna realised that all of her husband's assets, including the palace at Soestdijk, would have to be sold at auction. Since this particular residence had such personal associations for the family, having been given to William by the Dutch nation after Waterloo, she asked the Tsar if she might use part of her personal fortune to buy it for herself. He readily agreed, and thus Soestdijk remained in the possession of the House of Orange. The magnificent picture collection which King William had built up over the years and which was hung in the 'Gothic Chamber' of the palace on the Kneuterdyck was purchased for 173,823 guilders by Tsar Nicholas, who had long admired it. The departure of this superb collection to the Hermitage in St Petersburg was a real loss to the Netherlands.

Dowager Queen Anna Pavlovna occupied herself with her church and her charities. She made several trips to Russia to see her brother and his family, her last visit occurring after Tsar Nicholas's death early in 1855, and extending from November of that year to June 1856. The outbreak of the Crimean War distressed her greatly, for she was unable to be neutral, and her Russian sympathies were apparent.

In her old age Queen Anna Pavlovna leaned on her son Prince Henry and his wife Princess Amalia of Saxe-Weimar for comfort and support. She saw her daughter, the Princess of Saxe-Weimar, for extended periods each year, but the Princess had her own family and life elsewhere. Anna's relations with King William III and Queen Sophie did not greatly improve; formal deference was paid to the Dowager Queen by the new sovereigns, but not much more. She continued to be on good terms with her brother-in-law Prince Frederick, but she had no patience with her sister-in-law, Princess Marianne, and probably never really approved of her divorce from Prince Albert. On 1 March 1865 Queen Anna Pavlovna died; she was the last of the family of Tsar Paul, her sister Maria having died in 1859. The funeral service was conducted by her private chaplaius according to the rites of the Russian Orthodox faith to which she had remained devoted all her life. She was buried next to her husband in Delft.

What sort of woman was Anna Pavlovna? Her letters to her family indicate certain very distinct traits. First, she had a good mind, a perceptive eye and a shrewd comprehension of the world at large. If she tended to interpret things with a view towards enhancing her own position, she nevertheless observed clearly and was able to express herself precisely and with much animation. She had a real fund of common sense, and this enabled her to keep her perspective. To be sure, in moments of stress she became highly emotional, but these occasions were rare; generally she kept herself under control, for an excessive display of sentiment was not to be admired. Second, she was always conscious of her position as a member of an imperial family, and anyone who failed to give her the respect and deference which this position entailed found her an implacable enemy. *Lèse-majesté*, however slight, was, to her, a serious offence. Third, she was devoted to her family and its interests. She could be critical of any and every member and often was, but she never hesitated to keep family interests to the fore. Her affection for her husband was constant, though at times she was obviously displeased and distressed by some of his activities. She recognised all of his good points, and these outweighed his faults. She was critical of her eldest son – and here she was very like Queen Victoria – but her disapproval arose largely because she wanted William to shine. Her models were her brothers, Tsars Alexander and Nicholas, and her husband King William, and the young prince found it hard to live up to the perfection of these idealised individuals. Her consistent affection for her Russian relatives is obvious. Tsar Alexander, 'our Angel', is more than mortal, as, indeed, is her mother the Dowager Empress Maria Feodorovna; Tsar Nicholas was her greatest friend and confidant, and he never failed her.

How do her chief correspondents emerge from the letters? As indicated above, the Grand Duke Constantine appears very differently in his letters from the customary view of him. He is sharp, witty, perceptive and knowledgeable. Not uncritical of his family, he assesses his own character shrewdly. He is able to give good advice, but does not do so gratuitously. Neither a tyrant nor a monster, he is rather a good, kindly and affectionate elder brother.

Tsar Nicholas, too, consistently shows the better side of himself. It is clear that he was very family-minded and held all of his close relatives in great affection. His concern and interest in all of their many activities is engaging. He feels close to his sister and obviously enjoys her letters, but at times grows impatient with her and is inclined to bring her back to reality. Basically he can deny her nothing: he was always acceding to her many requests – and as far as she was concerned, Russia seemed to be a bottomless well. Tsar Nicholas bestowed orders upon her and decorations upon her servants, rescued her finances and sent her costly presents. With all this, he could never understand why the world did not see him as he saw himself – 'a slave to duty' and 'the friend of all the world'. He was mystified by the lack of appreciation the world showed towards him. The behaviour of the Poles, the Austrians, the English, the Belgians and French seemed to him gross ingratitude. Tsar Nicholas always felt that he was working for the welfare and interests of all civilised people and not just for Russia alone. Only his family was truly perceptive, since its members never questioned his actions and his sister supported him consistently. None of the darker aspects of Tsar Nicholas appear in the letters. Perhaps, in the case of both Constantine and Nicholas, these letters redress the balance. To a certain extent, historians do not always see nor understand the Russian side of affairs, and the West looks at things largely through its own coloured spectacles.

The letters also illustrate other aspects. They present a view of political events from the inside as seen by a member of a closed circle, and the view they give of the Belgian revolt differs from that commonly held outside the Netherlands. Moreover, they indicate how very limited the royal world actually was; for example, there is practically no mention of anyone except other members of this world. People as people hardly exist; subjects were to listen and obey; and when non-royals do appear it is largely in the character of devoted court attendants such as Everard the doctor, Mlle de Sybourg the governess, or essential governmental personalities, but all in a limited fashion.

Another thing which seems to emerge from the correspondence is that royal persons rarely had much real personal enjoyment. They took their duties seriously and their pleasures likewise. They never seem to have thought that their position allowed them to act purely for their own delight. On the other hand, they all felt they were much overworked. King William II seems to have been one of the very few who enjoyed his public duties; for the rest, these tasks were an onerous burden that had to be borne. Anna Pavlovna found her duties exhausting and loved to retire to her private family circle; Tsar Nicholas frequently comments on his great pleasure at being with his family at 'the Cottage', away from the capital.

The correspondence between Anna Pavlovna and her brothers indicates that the Romanov family in the nineteenth century had great *élan* and verve, a sense of style and an awareness of their role in history. The letters show the imperial family in a different light from that which is customary. The traditional viewpoint is, as a consequence, challenged or modified – the Romanovs are not unfeeling tyrants or maniacs, but rather they are people of sentiment and feeling. In their own eyes they sought to do their duty and fulfil their obligations; posterity must judge if they succeeded. At all events, the Romanovs were always interesting and, as people, never dull.

Note on the method of editing the correspondence

The letters were originally written in French and in translating them every effort has been taken to maintain the style and flavour of the originals. Since the correspondents were not writing for publication, paragraphing and punctuation were somewhat casual; in order to make the whole more readable I have seen fit to assume the usual editorial role in these matters. In preparing the letters for publication I have sometimes omitted the formal salutations and conclusions since they add little to the text, but, in order to show the original form of the letters, I have retained some of them.

Family letters are probably best not given all of the trappings of scholarship. Too many footnotes, brackets, *sic*, &c., are irritating and they add little to the sense of the text. Therefore, I have not burdened the reader with these things. In an effort to explain the state of affairs current when the letters were written, I have subdivided the correspondence into chapters and given a brief outline of the politics of the period covered. A *dramatis personae* has been provided to give short biographical sketches about the majority of the individuals mentioned in the text. The Romanovs were as addicted to family names used in the intimate circle as was Queen Victoria, and these names have been explained in the *dramatis personae* for clarity. The letters often have two dates – particularly those written from Russia – this is because the Julian Calendar was still in effect in Russia while the Gregorian Calendar was used elsewhere. The use of the double dating prevented confusion since otherwise it would seem that replies were written before the original letters were indited.

Every effort has been made to keep the correspondence orderly and generally it has been possible to do this, since the Royal House Archives in The Hague and the Thuringian State Archives in Weimar together preserved the mass of the correspondence. However, it is clear that some letters have not survived and others which may well have done so were not available for me. However, the bulk of the correspondence was such that significant matters under discussion by the writers generally is carried through by a topical correlation.

Dramatis Personae

ADOLPH OF NASSAU (1817–1905) was Duke of Nassau from 1839 to 1866. In the Austro-Prussian war of 1866 he sided with Austria and his lands were annexed by Prussia; later he did receive some settlement as compensation. Upon the death of King William III of the Netherlands in 1890 he succeeded to the Grand Duchy of Luxembourg. He married Adelaide of Anhalt-Dessau. His sister Marie married Herman of Wied. They were to be the parents-in-law of Princess Marie, the daughter of Prince Frederick, the brother of King William II of the Netherlands.

ALEXANDER OF ORANGE (1818–48), the second son of King William II and Queen Anna Pavlovna. He was named after his uncle Emperor Alexander I of Russia, the oldest brother of Queen Anna Pavlovna. As a boy he lived a relatively unsophisticated life; when he was sixteen he began to study at the University of Leiden where he was joined the next year by his elder brother William. Early he was known to be in poor health but this did not seem to limit his activities and he was very fond of sport. He was to found a 'Hawking Club'. In 1836 he made a visit to London accompanied by his father and his elder brothers; there was some talk of a marriage between the youthful Princess, later Queen, Victoria but nothing came of it. He was also mentioned at one time as a candidate for the hand of Queen Isabella II of Spain but he and his family were disinclined toward a Roman Catholic alliance and the whole saga of Hispanic-Dutch history was certainly inauspicious for the project. At another time an alliance with the House of Orleans was mooted but this too was still-born. In 1838 he visited his uncle the Emperor Nicholas I in St Petersburg; he travelled in Italy in 1846 and here he met Pope Pius IX, who was much charmed by the young man. Prince Alexander's health gradually worsened and his medical advisers ordered him to remove himself from The Hague and to live in a warmer climate. In late 1847 he went to Madeira. However, he did not improve and he died on 20 February 1848. He was immensely popular and attractive as a person – he was referred to as 'the golden prince' and from all contemporary reports this flattering phrase was correct. His family were desolated by his death and for many years his elder brother William would not permit his own birthday to be celebrated (19 February), since it coincided so closely with the anniversary of Prince Alexander's death.

ALBERT OF PRUSSIA (1809–72), the youngest son of King Frederick William III and his wife the famous beauty, Queen Louise. He was the brother of the Empress Alexandra Feodorovna (*née* Princess Charlotte), the wife of Emperor Nicholas I. He married his cousin Marianne, the daughter of King William I of the Netherlands, in 1830. There were three children, Charlotte (1831–55), Albert (1837–1906) and Alexandrine (1842–1906). He and his wife separated in 1845, in 1849 there was a divorce, but as this did not have the approbation of the King of Prussia he could not re-marry. In 1853 the consent of the King of Prussia was given to the divorce and Albert married Rosalie von Rauch, the daughter of the Prussian Minister of War. This marriage was morganatic and the lady was given the title of Countess of Hohenau.

ALEXANDER OF ORANGE (1851–84), the second surviving son of King William III and Queen Sophie. He was the last Prince of Orange until our own day. He was very much attached to his mother throughout all of his life. He was very nervous and shy and suffered from chronic ill-health. He was very unhappy after his mother and elder brother died and he virtually became a recluse thereafter. He does not seem to have approved of his father's second marriage and he was disinclined to have much to do with his stepmother and may very well have seen his half-sister Wilhelmina practically not at all. During the last year of his life he virtually never left his residence. His eccentricities coupled with his melancholy nature isolated him from his future subjects. He died of typhoid fever. With his death the male line of the House of Orange was extinct.

ALEXANDER NICOLAIEVICH (1818–81), Emperor Alexander II of Russia and known to his family as Sasha. He was the oldest son of Emperor Nicholas. He was brought up very simply and his education, which was supervised by his parents, was entrusted to an outstanding Russian poet and humanist, Vasili Zhukovsky. His schooling over, he toured Russia and, in 1838, Europe. He passed his twenty-first birthday at the Dutch court as the guest of his aunt Anna Pavlovna. During his tour of Europe he fell in love with Princess Marie of Hesse-Darmstadt, to whom, after some parental opposition – there were some rumours in court circles that the Princess was illegitimate although the Grand Duke recognised her as his daughter – he eventually became betrothed and finally married. After his father's death in 1855 his liberal education bore fruit – principally in the liberation of the serfs in 1861, and he gained the sobriquet 'Tsar Liberator'. His enthusiasm for reform waned later in his reign as had been the case in the time of his uncle, Emperor Alexander I, because of violent revolutionary activity on the part of Nihilists and Anarchists. Three attempts were made on his life before the final successful one. His domestic life was complicated because he and his wife grew apart, especially after her health began to decline; he turned to Catherine Dolgoruky for affection and she became his mistress and they had several children. After the Empress died in 1880 Emperor Alexander married Catherine Dolgoruky morganatically and conferred on her the title of Princess Yurievskaya.

ALEXANDER PAVLOVICH (1777–1825), Emperor Alexander I of Russia, was the eldest son of Emperor Paul. Alexander was the favourite of his grandmother, the Empress Catherine II, who claimed him as a child and supervised his upbringing, and consequently he saw little of his parents. He was educated by a Swiss tutor, La Harpe, a disciple of Rousseau, and in the early part of his reign he gave promise of a liberal regime – particularly after the semi-tyrannical reign of his father, whom he succeeded as a result of a *coup*. Originally he opposed Napoleon but later became his ally; the Russo-French alliance collapsed and Napoleon invaded Russia in 1812. Alexander, following the fall of Napoleon in 1814, was to be enthusiastically welcomed in the European capitals and these included Paris. He made a visit to London accompanied by his sister Catherine Pavlovna, but the visit was not an unqualified success. The populace greeted him favourably, but the court and government found their Russian guests difficult. It was here in London that Alexander got to know William, who later married Anna Pavlovna, the Emperor's younger sister. At the Congress of Vienna Poland was united with the Russian Empire and Alexander became king of a constitutional Poland. He appointed his brother and heir, the Grand Duke Constantine, as Viceroy of Poland. Alexander gradually became less liberal and more devout and mystical; he fell under the influence of the Baroness de Krudener. He founded the Holy Alliance with Austria and Prussia, and, largely under Metternich's influence, his subsequent policies were extremely reactionary. In person he was very tall and handsome, elegant and personable, affable and charming. He married Louise of Baden, who took the name Elizabeth when she joined the Russian Church. Initially the marriage was a romantic idyll but this euphoric state did not last and the Emperor had many amatory adventures. Two daughters were born to the royal couple in 1799 and 1806, but both died in infancy. In 1804 Maria Naryshkin became his mistress and there were several children of this liaison. This situation lasted until about 1819 when

Alexander became more and more pious. Alexander and his wife were reconciled by 1824 and the journey to Taganrog in the autumn of 1825 was made for her health. The final romantic *mise en scène* ended with the Emperor's death on 1 December 1825. All of his family had great affection for Alexander and held him also in considerable awe since he was *the* Emperor. After his death his family, following the example of his widow, always referred to him as 'Our Angel'.

ALEXANDRA FEODOROVNA (1798–1860), the wife of Emperor Nicholas I, known as Alexandrine, was born Charlotte of Prussia and daughter of King Frederick William III and Queen Louise. The marriage was probably made for diplomatic reasons but it was also a love match and the couple were ideally happy for many years. They had a large family. The empress enjoyed her husband's confidence in affairs of state but herself had no real political leanings, being merely the obedient admiring echo of her husband's views. Her chief interests were in domestic affairs, dancing, balls and jewels. After 1841 she was largely an invalid – the death of her daughter Alexandrine was a terrible blow. She and her sister-in-law Anna Pavlovna were united in their affection for the Emperor Nicholas.

ALEXANDRA JOSIFVNA was the daughter of the Duke of Saxe-Altenburg and she married Constantine Nicolaievich, the son of Emperor Nicholas I, in 1848. There were five children, Nicholas Constantinovich, Constantine Constantinovich, Dimitri Constantinovich, Olga Constantinova and Vera Constantinova.

ALEXANDRA NICOLAIEVNA (1825–44) – known to the family as Alexandrine – was the youngest daughter of Emperor Nicholas I. She married Frederick of Hesse-Cassel in 1843 and died in childbirth in July 1844.

ALEXANDRA PAVLOVNA (1783–1801), the daughter of Emperor Paul and sister of Emperors Alexander I and Nicholas I, was betrothed in 1786 to Gustavus Adolphus IV of Sweden. The negotiations broke down when the Russian court refused to allow the princess to change her religion. The Romanov dynasty were very firm on this matter and all imperial princesses who married outside the country continued to be members of the Russian Orthodox Church. In 1799 Alexandra Pavlovna married the Austrian Archduke Joseph, the Archduke Palatine, but this was a very unhappy household. The princess did not feel at home with the Habsburgs. She died in childbirth in 1801.

AMALIA OF SAXE-WEIMAR (1830–72) was the daughter of Duke Bernard of Saxe-Weimar. She married Prince Henry of Orange in 1853. The marriage was a very happy and successful one, but there were no children.

ANNA PAVLOVNA (1795–1865), the youngest daughter of Emperor Paul I, married the Prince of Orange in 1816. They had five children. Anna Pavlovna was a very definite personality, as her letters indicate. She was devoted to her family – both in Russia and in the Netherlands – and constantly sought to promote their interests and their happiness. She was somewhat imperious in nature and very conscious of her imperial heritage. She expected great deference from all classes of society. During the nine years that she and her husband reigned the court life in The Hague was very formal and rather grander than it had been previously or has been since. She was very attached to all things Russian and never wavered from her national church. She had definite likes and dislikes – one object of her antipathy was her daughter-in-law Sophie, the wife of William. For her favourites and protégés nothing was too good; she continuously importuned her brother Nicholas for orders, ribands and pensions and she was often successful. Her brothers she held in vast respect and affection, and for Nicholas, in particular, she allowed her emotions full play. After she became a widow she played no real role in public affairs, devoting herself to religion and charity. Her son Henry and his wife made their home with her much of the time. She made several trips to Russia in the course of her life and travelled extensively elsewhere. She died in 1865 and was buried beside her husband in Delft.

PETER ARRIENS (1791–1860), Dutch naval officer, entered the service in 1802. In 1830 he was appointed to supervise the naval education of Prince Henry. He commanded several of the ships in which the prince served as a cadet and later as an officer. Arriens and the prince were in close contact for eleven years. Arriens retired as a vice-admiral in 1843.

JULIA FEODOROVNA BARANOVA (1789–1864), *née* Adlerberg, was a friend of the imperial family. She married Count Trofim Baranov and supervised the education of a number of noble children. She was appointed Grand Mistress of the Court and was very much part of the life both in St Petersburg and Tsarskoe Selo. Her brother Vladimir Adlerberg was a lifelong confidant of Emperor Nicholas.

AUGUSTIN DANIEL BELLIARD (1769–1832), a French officer who was appointed French Ambassador to Brussels.

ALEXANDER CHRISTOFOROVICH BENCKENDORF (1783–1844), of a Baltic family, he served in the Russian army, joining in 1806, and finally becoming a general. In 1826 Emperor Nicholas appointed him Head of the Third Department, in which capacity he was Chief of the Secret Police. In spite of his job he was personally very popular. He was a friend and confidant of Emperor Nicholas and accompanied him on the Turkish campaign and frequently on his travels.

BERNARD OF SAXE-WEIMAR (died 1862), father-in-law of Prince Henry 'the Seafarer' of Orange, entered Dutch service in 1815 and in 1830 he was appointed 'Stathalter' of Luxembourg, to be succeeded later in this post by Prince Henry. During the Belgian revolution he served in the army; in 1849 he led a military expedition against Bali in the East Indies; he had been appointed commander-in-chief in the East Indies in 1848 and held this command until 1853 when he retired and lived in The Hague.

ANDREI VON BUDGBERG (1820–81), a Russian diplomat who held various posts in Frankfurt, Berlin, Vienna and Paris. He retired in 1868 in order to call out Baron von Meyendorff in a duel. After the affair of honour was over he was reinstated in governmental service and became a Privy Councillor.

STRATFORD CANNING, 1ST VISCOUNT STRATFORD DE REDCLIFFE (1786–1880), educated at Eton and King's College, Cambridge, he entered the diplomatic service in 1807 and the next year was appointed first secretary at Constantinople, becoming Minister-plenipotentiary in 1810. He negotiated the Treaty of Bucharest in 1812 between Russia and Turkey, thereby freeing the Russian army on the Danube for an attack on Napoleon. He held various other diplomatic posts until 1825 when he was sent as Ambassador to Constantinople. He worked for Greek independence; after Navarino the embassy was withdrawn. In 1831 he was appointed to St Petersburg but Emperor Nicholas I refused to receive him. When not abroad on diplomatic missions he sat as an M.P. in the Commons. From 1842 to 1858 he was once more in Constantinople and gained extraordinary influence over the Sultan which he used to improve the lot of the Sultan's Christian subjects. In the dispute between Russia and Turkey over the Holy Places he took a very pro-Turkish line and his anti-Russian sentiments undoubtedly helped to bring about the Crimean War. He resigned in 1858 and lived thereafter in retirement.

GIOVANNI ANTONIO, COUNT CAPO D'ISTRIA (1776–1831), was born on Corfu and studied medicine in Padua and Venice. In 1807 he entered the Russian service and in 1813, as envoy to Switzerland, he aided in framing the Swiss constitution. In 1816 Emperor Alexander I appointed him Minister of Foreign Affairs, a post which he held until 1822 when the Emperor accepted Metternich's proposal for a conference to discuss Greek affairs. (This violated a principle adhered to since the days of Empress Catherine II that no outside influence was permitted in Turkish affairs.) He had always favoured Greek independence – hoping, of course, that Empress Catherine's 'Greek Project', or something like it, would be effected by Russia – and he supported the liberation movement. He was elected president of the Greek national party in 1827 but he soon became unpopular because of the strict discipline he enforced on the insurgents. He was assassinated at Nauplia by a former adherent.

CATHERINE PAVLOVNA (1788–1819), daughter of Emperor Paul and sister of Anna Pavlovna, married Duke George of Oldenburg in 1809; they resided in Tver where he was the governor of the province. Interested in literature, science and history, she had a salon and attracted Karamzin the historian, among others, into her circle. She was politically active and in 1812 organised her peasants into a militia which took part in a number of battles. When discontent against Alexander was at its height a plot is said to have existed to overthrow the Emperor and replace him by his sister Catherine. Nevertheless, Alexander was passionately devoted to her and after the death of her husband she accompanied him on his campaigns and travels in 1813–15. She was with him on his visit to England in 1814 when she alienated many by her autocratic manner. In 1816 she married King William I of Württemberg. She had two sons by her first marriage and one daughter by her second. Her daughter, Sophie, married William the son of Anna Pavlovna.

CHARLES OF PRUSSIA (1801–83), the third son of King Frederick William III, was the brother of the Empress Alexandra Feodorovna, the wife of Emperor Nicholas I, and grandfather of Princess Marie, the wife of Prince Henry 'the Seafarer' of Orange. He served in the Prussian army and in 1854 he became Master-General of the Ordnance. He was a patron of the arts and an avid collector of pictures and weapons.

CHARLES ALEXANDER OF SAXE-WEIMAR (1818–1901), the son of Grand Duke Charles Frederick and the Grand Duchess Marie Pavlovna. He married his cousin Princess Sophie of Orange in 1842. He succeeded his father as Grand Duke in 1853; his only son predeceased him in 1894 and he was succeeded by his grandson William. Charles Alexander was an intellectual and maintained a court with many savants and artists; he was a liberal and a democrat and often out of sympathy with the policies of King William I of Prussia.

PETER ALEXANDROVICH CHICHERIN (1778–1841), a Russian military officer, was Adjutant-General and General of Cavalry in the reign of Emperor Nicholas I.

CONSTANTINE NICOLAIEVICH (1827–92), 'Costy', the second son of Emperor Nicholas I, entered the naval service. He early became an active proponent of Pan-Slavism and frequented the salon of his aunt the Grand Duchess Helene, who was the patroness of the movement. He was interested in reform, in literature and in science – in sum he wished to modernise his country. In 1848 he married Alexandra of Saxe-Altenburg. During the many years of his naval career he made notable attempts to modernise the Russian fleet. He was also the President of the State Council for sixteen years during the reign of his brother Emperor Alexander II. He retired from public life upon the accession of his nephew Alexander III.

CONSTANTINE PAVLOVICH (1778–1831), the second son of Emperor Paul, was educated by his grandmother Empress Catherine II and was to be part of her great 'Greek Project', viz. the promotion of Russian influence in Turkey and the ultimate re-location of an Orthodox empire in Constantinople. He was named Inspector-General of all Cavalry by his father and retained this title until his death. He was on better terms with Emperor Paul than his brother Alexander; upon the latter's accession in 1801 Constantine continued in high favour and never lost his position of power. He was violent-tempered and somewhat unstable but he could be most charming and gallant when he chose. He was intensely loyal and very family-minded. In 1796 he married Julia Henrietta of Saxe-Coburg (1781–1860), the aunt of Queen Victoria, but the marriage was unsuccessful, there were no children, and it was dissolved by imperial decree on 12 May 1820. He then married, morganatically, Joanna Grudzinska (1781–1831). In his youth he was thought to be wild and licentious, he sired at least one illegitimate child – a son called Paul – but as he grew older he became more easy and calm. In 1815, when Poland was an autonomous kingdom under Emperor Alexander, Constantine was named viceroy; he also bore the title Tsarevich, as heir to the throne, and even after his brother Nicholas's succession he continued to use it. He did not like the constitution but obeyed orders and supported it; the Polish army he made into a model force. He had given up his rights to the throne when he married the Princess Grudzinska and warmly and loyally supported his brother Nicholas. The Polish revolt of 1830 seems to have taken him by surprise and he withdrew from Warsaw with the Russian troops. The rebels soon became entrenched. He died of cholera at Vitebsk on 15 June 1831. His wife died a few months later.

GEORGES D'ANTHES was born in Alsace in 1812 and educated at St-Cyr. He and his family were legitimists and after the Revolution of 1830 he emigrated from France. He became a protégé of Prince William of Prussia, who supported him when he decided to enter the Russian army. In 1834 he was appointed to the Imperial Guards. He was extremely handsome and elegant and a beau-sabreur. He attracted the attention of the Dutch Minister van Heeckeren, who became his patron and who in due course formally adopted him in 1836. d'Anthes was much attracted to Natalie Goncharova, who married the poet Pushkin. The affair was well known in St Petersburg, and Pushkin called out d'Anthes, but a reconciliation of sorts followed. d'Anthes then married Catherine Goncharova, the sister of his former mistress. Pushkin's honour was still unsatisfied and the matter was further exacerbated with a series of anonymous letters. d'Anthes and Pushkin met on the field of honour 27 January 1837 (O.S.) and Pushkin was wounded and died two days later. d'Anthes was arrested by the Russian authorities, dismissed from the army – Nicholas regretted having to do this – and exiled from Russia. After some years of a semi-nomadic existence d'Anthes entered the service of Emperor Napoleon III. He finally became a senator and died at an advanced age. He always protested his innocence in the Pushkin affair and claimed that his actions had not been properly understood. There are a number of mysteries about Pushkin's death which have never been resolved and d'Anthes may, indeed, have been a pawn. Certainly the whole affair did little to popularise the Dutch in Russia since d'Anthes was the adopted son of the ambassador.

JEAN VICTOR DE CONSTANT REBECQUE (1773–1850), a German, entered the French army, emigrated to England and became tutor to the Prince of Orange (later King William II). When the prince joined the British army and was ordered to Spain, de Constant accompanied him. After 1814 he entered Dutch service and in due course became the Quarter-Master General of the army. During the Belgian revolution he served on the staff of the Prince of Orange; in 1837 he retired from the army. For his long and devoted service to the royal family and to his adopted country he was ennobled and awarded the title of baron.

IVAN IVANOVICH DIEBITSCH (1785–1831) was born in Silesia and served in the cadet corps in Berlin until transferred to Russia to join his father. He served with distinction against Napoleon – as a cadet he had gained approbation for his studies – and after a short period of disfavour, occasioned by the displeasure of Arakcheev, the chief military councillor of Emperor Alexander, he was appointed Chief of Staff with a seat in the State Council and the Council of Ministers. He accompanied Emperor Alexander on all of his travels and was present when the Emperor died at Taganrog. Almost his first duty to the new Emperor was to report the facts on the army conspiracy – the Decembrist Revolt – and his zeal in arresting the leaders ensured him of Nicholas's lifelong trust. He was in charge of the Russian army in the Turkish war of 1828–9. After the revolt occurred in Poland he was placed in command of the army, but he was singularly ineffective in quelling the revolution. He died of cholera during the campaign and was succeeded by Ivan Feodorovich Paskevich. In appearance Diebitsch was short, fat and ugly with an explosive temperament – he was nicknamed 'Samovar'.

HENRY DEMBINSKI (1791–1864), a Polish officer, educated in Vienna, joined the army of the Grand Duchy of Warsaw. After the creation of 'the Congress Kingdom' he lived in Poland. He played an active role in the Polish army during the rebellion of 1830 and succeeded Skrznecki as Commander-in-Chief. After the fall of Warsaw he fled and led a nomadic existence. He organised Mehemet Ali's army in Syria. In 1849 he joined the revolutionary forces in Hungary; he was given a senior command but accomplished little. Following the failure of the Hungarian revolt he fled to Turkey once more.

VASILI ANDREEVICH DOLGORUKY (1804–68), a member of a very distinguished noble family, entered the army and happened to be on guard at the Winter Palace during the Decembrist Revolt. He remained loyal to the dynasty and in due course received the confidence of Nicholas I. In 1848 he joined the Ministry of War and in 1853 he became *the* Minister of War. His health declined and he resigned in 1856. In due course he recovered his health and he was appointed Head of the Third Department and Chief of Gendarmes.

HENRIETTE D'OULTREMONT (1792–1864), the second wife of King William I, was the daughter of Ferdinand d'Oultremont, a Belgian, and Johanna Hartsinck of Amsterdam. She became known as Princess d'Oultremont after her marriage to King William in 1841. The King's decision to marry a second time was very unpopular because Mlle d'Oultremont was a Belgian and a Roman Catholic; there was no scandal and the princess was recognised by many to be an excellent woman of impeccable character, but her origin and her religion made public acceptance impossible. The princess and the King lived in Berlin until his death.

Empress Elizabeth of Russia (1779–1826), born Louise of Baden, married Alexander when he was fifteen and she was fourteen. Initially the marriage was idyllical but in due course the royal couple drifted apart. Empress Elizabeth – beautiful and virtuous – bore her husband two daughters but they both died young; the lack of children as a tie was one of the reasons for the failure of the marriage. The Empress lived very quietly. By Russian custom the Dowager Empress had precedence as long as she lived, and Alexander's mother Empress Marie played a more prominent role than the young Empress. Alexander and his wife were reconciled early in the 1820s and by 1824 were once again the happy couple of their youth. Empress Elizabeth's health was the reason for the fatal journey to Taganrog in 1825 when Alexander died. After his death, it was she who coined the phrase 'Our Angel' when referring to Alexander, and this was to be used by all of the family. Empress Elizabeth continued at Taganrog for four months and then on her return journey died at Bebo on 15 May 1826. She was not much liked, apparently, by the Romanov family, and they did not seem to mourn her death.

Alexei Petrovich Ermolov (1772–1861), army officer, served under Alexander in the campaigns 1805–7 and 1812–14. He took charge of the army in the Crimea in 1817; he quelled several minor rebellions in the area and assumed executive powers to pacify the countryside. However, he was not very effective and in 1826 Emperor Nicholas I recalled him and replaced him with Paskevich. Ermolov retired from active service in the army in 1827 and was appointed to the Council of State, but he really took little part in public life and was virtually in retirement until his death a number of years later.

Ernst Casimir of Orange (1822–22), the fourth son of King William II and Queen Anna Pavlovna. He lived only five months and was a sickly child from birth. Apparently he was very frail and suffered from water on the brain.

Dr Everard was the court physician to Queen Anna Pavlovna and her family in the Netherlands. He was very much the confidant and devoted servitor. He was sent to Madeira during the last illness of Prince Alexander. He is referred to frequently in the correspondence since all of the family were concerned about their health. For his many services to Anna Pavlovna Emperor Nicholas gave Everard a Russian order.

Baroness Fagel was the *grande maîtresse* of the court of Anna Pavlovna in 1824.

Charles Louis Ficquelmont (1777–1857) came from Lorraine. He emigrated in 1792, was a strong legitimist, and fought with the British in Spain in 1812. He rose to the rank of Major-General. He entered the Austrian diplomatic service and served in several diplomatic posts including that of ambassador to Sweden. In 1829 he was sent to St Petersburg where he remained for ten years; he was much liked by Emperor Nicholas, who greatly regretted his departure. He returned to Vienna and worked with Prince Metternich, whom he served loyally, and he was entrusted with several special missions, e.g. the annexation of Cracow. After the revolution of 1848 he was appointed Foreign Minister to replace Metternich, then he was made Minister President but was soon forced into retirement. The fall of Metternich really meant the end of his career.

Frederick of Orange (1797–1881), brother of King William II, known to the family as 'Fritz', was born in Berlin and as a youth served in the Prussian army. After the restoration he joined the Dutch army. In the war with Belgium he played a prominent role and was reckoned an able and gallant commander. He continued to serve in the Dutch army during his brother's and nephew's reigns. He was a candidate for the Greek throne in 1829. Earlier – in 1825 – he married Louise of Prussia and they had four children, Louise (1828–71), who married Charles XV of Sweden, William (1833–4), Frederick (1836–1846) and Marie (1841–1910), who married William of Wied. (Marie was one of the princesses considered suitable for Albert Edward of England, but she was rejected because she was not thought to be beautiful enough.) Frederick, 'The Nestor of the Oranges', was very popular with everyone and he was often called upon to act as mediator in family disputes. His wife and King William III were not always sympathetic since the latter's pro-French policies did not appeal to the patriotic sentiments of the Prussian princess. However, at no time were there any difficulties between Frederick and his nephew. Frederick provided an historical touch to the christening of Princess, later Queen, Wilhelmina in 1880 since he himself was the last survivor of the family of the Stathalter Prince.

Frederick William III of Prussia (1770–1840), the great nephew of Frederick the Great, was a rather weak and temporising sovereign. His indecisive policies against Napoleon, 1805–7, were disastrous, culminating in the battles of Jena and Auerstadt with Napoleon virtually destroying the Prussian armies. The Treaty of Tilsit completed Prussia's humiliation. With the overthrow of Napoleon in 1814 Prussia was restored and gained new territories, but Frederick William was really passive. His policies were directed either by Hardenburg or Stein or Metternich. Frederick William married Louise of Mecklenburg-Strelitz. They had a large family – one daughter married Emperor Nicholas I, another married Frederick of Orange and a son married Marianne of Orange. He was the father of King Frederick William IV and King William I – later Emperor William I.

FREDERICK WILLIAM IV OF PRUSSIA (1795–1861), the eldest son of Frederick William III, succeeded to the throne in 1840. His policies were often contradictory and unrealistic and his attitude toward the revolution of 1848 was vacillating and feeble. He granted a constitution to his people in 1848; he refused the imperial crown from the Frankfurt assembly in 1849. His indecision led Austria to reassume authority in Germany, and Prussia was forced at Olmutz to accept a secondary role. In the 1850s his policies were more conservative and more in harmony with the restored order in Europe; they were supported by his brother-in-law Emperor Nicholas. In 1857 he became insane, and the next year his brother William became regent. He married Elizabeth of Bavaria but they had no children.

STEPHEN MAURICE GÉRARD (1773–1852), French soldier – count and marshal – took part in the wars of the revolution and the empire. After the fall of Napoleon he continued in the army. In the 'Ten Days' War' and its aftermath he played a prominent role, capturing Antwerp in 1832. Under Louis-Philippe he was Minister of War and President of the Council (1834) and Grand Chancellor of the Legion of Honour (1836). Napoleon III made him a senator in 1852.

JOANNA GRUDZINSKA (1781–1831), later Princess Lowicz, known to the family as 'Jeannette', was the second wife of the Grand Duke Constantine. They were married in 1820; the marriage, however, was morganatic and the princess was not received by the imperial family in St Petersburg. The princess, being Polish herself, was much distressed at the events of 1830 but she supported her husband rather than her countrymen. She accompanied him when he withdrew and was with him at his death in Vitebsk in June 1831. She was invited by

Emperor Nicholas to St Petersburg and lived in retirement in Tsarskoe Selo; she survived her husband only a few months.

NICHOLAS DMITRIEVICH GURIEV (1789–1849), Russian diplomat and Privy Councillor, held a number of posts as ambassador, viz. The Hague, Rome, Naples and Vienna. He was not a favourite of Anna Pavlovna.

HALIL was an envoy of the Turkish sultan. He was sent to St Petersburg in February 1830 to try and persuade Emperor Nicholas to modify the terms of the Treaty of Adrianople. He was quite successful – the Turkish indemnity was reduced and the Russian occupation of the Danubian principalities very much shortened. It was at this time that the Turkish delegation gave up their traditional eastern costume and wore instead a uniform and a fez – an outfit designed by the Sultan – which gave them a more modern and more European appearance.

HELENE (1806–73), wife of Grand Duke Michael Pavlovich and sister-in-law of Emperor Nicholas I, was the daughter of Paul of Württemberg – as a Württemberg princess she was called Charlotte – and cousin of Sophie, who married King William III. She was educated in Paris and was much interested in scholarship and the arts. Personally she was extremely charming, affable and very popular but her marriage to Michael was not a happy one; he preferred the barracks and she the salon. She had liberal ideas – she freed her serfs in 1859 – and she put them into practice. She became a widow in 1849 after twenty-five years of marriage; there were five daughters born but only one, Catherine (1827–76), survived infancy.

HENRY OF ORANGE (1820–79), known as 'the Seafarer', was the third son of William II and Anna Pavlovna. He entered the navy in 1832 and for the next twenty years he travelled extensively with the fleet. He visited Scandinavia, Russia, England, Iceland, Spain, Surinam, the Antilles, the U.S.A., South America and the East Indies. He was devoted to the navy and was an extremely competent officer. He was twice married, first, in 1853, to Amalia, the daughter of Bernard of Saxe-Weimar, and secondly, in 1878, to Marie of Prussia. Both of these marriages were extremely happy; unfortunately Henry left no descendants. After the death of King William II in 1849 Henry and his wife spent much time with Queen Anna Pavlovna; he was her favourite surviving son and she leaned on him for company. He and his brother King William III were on very good terms and he acted as one of the king's confidants. For many years Henry was the 'Stathalter' of Luxembourg – he succeeded his father-in-law, Bernard of Saxe-Weimar. He was present at the ceremony when King William III espoused Emma of Waldeck-Pyrmont in 1879 and at that time was named Admiral of the Fleet. He died a week later. His second wife married Henry of Saxe-Altenburg in 1885 and died in 1888.

Login Loginovich Heyden (born 1806), a Russian nobleman, was of Westphalian origin. He entered the navy and in due course became one of the senior admirals in the Russian fleet.

Paul Dimitrevich Kiselev (1788–1872), Russian nobleman and army officer, fought in the French campaign wherein he gained great distinction. He was a personal friend of Pestel, the leader of the Decembrists, and for a time was himself suspected of being involved, but he was cleared in due course. In the Turkish war he commanded the armies on the left bank of the Danube and after the Treaty of Adrianople was signed he was made President of Moldavia and Wallachia. He was extremely effective in setting up the government and his 'Organic Statute' later formed the basis of the Romanian constitution. He was placed in charge of the peasants by Nicholas – there were projects to improve their lot, but nothing came of them. He was appointed ambassador to France; this was his last governmental post and he resigned in 1862 and retired to private life.

Victor Pavlovich Kochubey (1768–1834) was brought up in England where he became imbued with liberal principles. He was a friend of the Empress Catherine II and entered government service in her reign. He was initially in the diplomatic service but transferred to the home department. He was an intimate of Alexander I, who made Kochubey a senator in 1801. He was Minister of the Interior in Alexander's reign; under Nicholas he was President of the Council of State and Committee of Ministers. For his many services to his country he was given the title of prince.

Vladimir Alexeevich Kornilov (1806–54) trained in the corps of sea cadets and took part in the Battle of Navarino. In 1849 he was chief of staff of the Black Sea Fleet; he took part in the Battle of Sinope. He was active in the defence of Sevastopol, where he won the admiration of all concerned. He was killed in action at Sevastopol on 5 October 1854.

Voin Andreevich Korsakov (died 1871), Rear-Admiral, was the director of the naval corps.

Peter Borisovich Kozlovsky (1783–1840), Russian nobleman and diplomat, served in numerous ambassadorial posts including

Stuttgart and Turin. He wrote a volume of memoirs. He was well known in court society and a noted wit.

MATVEI IVANOVICH LAMSDORFF (1745–1828), of Baltic origin coming from Courland, he was an army officer and in due course rose to the rank of Major-General. He was director of the cadet corps in 1799; in the next year Emperor Paul I appointed him to supervise the education of the Grand Dukes Nicholas and Michael. He had no real qualifications as an educator and had been given his post only because he had the support and approbation of Empress Maria Feodorovna. His educational theory, if it can be so called, was to thwart the wishes and inclinations of his charges completely; he frequently had recourse to severe corporal punishment to enforce his wishes. He accompanied the princes on their travels after 1814. His duties ended in 1817 when Nicholas married. He was given honours, decorations and a munificent pension. He retired from St Petersburg in 1822 on account of deafness and age.

NICHOLAS MATVEEICH LAMSDORFF (1803–77), the son of Nicholas's tutor, entered his court duties as a page and in due course became an aide-de-camp. He fought in the Turkish War in 1829 and then later was sent as an emissary to Warsaw, Dresden, Leipzig, Weimar, Frankfurt, Brussels and The Hague to report to the various members of the family on the Treaty of Adrianople. As an army officer he was noted for his punctilliousness and devotion to duty. He was staff officer at the famous parade and manœuvres at Kalisch in 1835. He was appointed to the War Ministry, then he became Director of the Forest and Land Survey Institute, finally holding other equally important court posts. He retired in 1857.

LEOPOLD OF SAXE-COBURG-SAALFELD (1790–1865), the first King of the Belgians and 'the dear uncle' of Queen Victoria and Prince Albert, was the fourth son of Duke Francis. In 1816 Leopold married Charlotte, the only daughter of the Prince Regent; this happy marriage ended when Charlotte died in childbirth in 1817. Leopold continued to live in England, but travelled widely on the Continent. In 1830 he was elected King of Greece, but declined the throne when his stipulations were not accepted. The next year he was elected King of the Belgians and had the support of England and France. He married as his second wife Marie Louise, the daughter of Louis-Philippe. His early years as King of the Belgians were not easy, but in due course he was able to consolidate his power. He was an extremely wise and able sovereign, hard-working and industrious. He promoted the interests of his family – his nephew Albert married Queen Victoria and his nephew Ferdinand married Queen Maria II of Portugal. The Coburg family in due course were related to all of the principal royal houses in Europe.

CHARLOTTE CARLOVNA LIEVEN (1743–1828), 'the Countess', *née* Kaarlov, she married Baron Lieven, a Livonian. In 1783 she was appointed *gouvernante* and supervised the early education of the imperial family; in 1794 she became a Lady of the Bedchamber and in 1789 was raised to the rank of countess. She was a confidante of Empress Marie, the wife of Emperor Paul, and she remained in her service until her death. She had a privileged position and did not hesitate to use her authority to keep the younger members of the family in order; they all submitted to her demands since they held her in great affection. In 1825, on the occasion of the coronation of Nicholas, she was created Princess. Her second son Christopher was the ambassador to London and the husband of the famed Dorothy Lieven. She had little formal education and it was said that although conversant with German, Russian and French, she spoke no language properly.

CHRISTOPHER ANDREEVICH LIEVEN (1777–1838), the son of Charlotte, Princess Lieven, Lady-in-waiting to Empress Marie, was a diplomat. For many years he was ambassador to London. In 1834 he was recalled and became tutor to the Tsarevich Alexander Nicolaievich. His wife Dorothy was one of the great figures of European politics and undoubtedly her position assisted him in his diplomatic duties. After his retirement to Russia he and his wife parted company and she lived in Paris.

DOROTHY LIEVEN (1785–1857), *née* Benckendorff; left an orphan at an early age, her education was supervised by the Empress Marie, who had been a friend of her mother. In 1800 she married Count Christopher Lieven and when she accompanied him to London in 1812 she became a great favourite. She developed a passion for politics and intrigue, in due course she became a close friend of Prince Metternich – it was rumoured that she was his mistress – but later turned against him. There were stories current during the Congress of Vienna that she was also the mistress of other European statesmen. During the Regency and reign of George IV she was an *habituée* of the court and exercised considerable influence. She was a great friend of Lord Grey of the 'Reform Bill', and one of her chief confidantes was Lady Emily Lamb, later Lady Palmerston. Dorothy Lieven claimed that she had suggested Palmerston to Grey for the Foreign Office and hence was much aggrieved when Palmerston's policies opposed her own. In

1834 her husband was recalled to Russia; she was much distressed at leaving London, but she went with him. However, she soon became bored in St Petersburg and went to live in Paris; in due course she and her husband had a formal separation. She became 'the Egeria' of Guizot, and during the reign of Louis-Philippe she was very powerful. During the Crimean War she was forced to leave Paris, but finally Napoleon III allowed her to return and she died there. She was a famous correspondent and many of her letters have been published.

Paul Petrovich Liprandi (1796–1864), a Russian army officer, took part in the campaigns of 1813–14, the Turkish War of 1828–9 and the suppression of the Polish revolution in 1830. In 1853–4 he commanded a division in Wallachia, and during the Crimean War he particularly distinguished himself at the Battle of Balaclava.

Sergei Grigorevich Lomonosov (died 1857), Russian diplomat, was for a time Russian ambassador to the Netherlands.

Louis-Philippe (1773–1850), son of Philippe Égalité, duc d'Orléans, served in the French army but later emigrated. For a brief time he lived in the United States and later lived in England. After the Restoration in 1814 he returned to France. In 1830 following the July Revolution he became King of the French. He reigned from 1830 to 1848; during his reign he was opposed by the Republicans, the Bonapartists and the Legitimists. Initially, he was an ally of Great Britain but after 'the Spanish Marriages Affair' the *entente* was broken and he was increasingly isolated. During the Belgian revolution he hoped to make some political capital from it and perhaps even hoped to annex the country. He was forced instead to co-operate with England and had to appear to favour an independent Belgium. His reign became less popular and after his refusal to moderate the electoral law a revolution broke out and he was forced to abdicate in favour of his grandson. However, a republic was proclaimed and the Orléans dynasty was overthrown. He died in exile at Claremont, in England, in 1850. He married Maria Amalia of Naples and had eight children. His daughter Louise married Leopold of Saxe-Coburg.

Louise of Orange (1770–1819), the sister of King William I of the Netherlands, married Charles George August (1766–1806), the Hereditary Prince of Brunswick. She lived in The Hague. She was quite content with her position as a member of the House of Orange and was unimpressed by the pretensions of Anna Pavlovna and the Romanovs.

Louise of Prussia (1776–1810), the beautiful daughter of Charles of Mecklenburg-Strelitz, married Frederick William of Prussia in 1790. Her beauty, virtue and patriotism made her very popular; she used all of her influence to persuade her vacillating husband to make war against Napoleon. After the defeats at Jena and Friedland she was unable to persuade Napoleon to soften the terms imposed on Prussia at Tilsit. She had seven children: her youngest, Albert, married Marianne of Orange; her eldest daughter, Charlotte, married Emperor Nicholas I; and her youngest daughter married Frederick of Orange.

Louise of Prussia (1808–70), the daughter of King Frederick William III and Queen Louise, married Frederick of Orange (1797–1888) in 1825. They had four children, Louise (1828–71), William (1833–4), Frederick (1836–46) and Marie (1841–1910). She did not frequent the court of her nephew King William III of the Netherlands because she disliked his pro-French policies. She was always very loyal to her native country and remained pro-Prussian in her outlook all of her life.

Maria Alexandrovna (1824–80), wife of Emperor Alexander II, known to the family as 'Marie Alexander' was a princess of Hesse-Darmstadt. She met Alexander when he toured Europe and he fell in love with her – she was only fourteen when they first became acquainted – and they were not betrothed until 1840. Emperor Nicholas and his wife were somewhat disapproving of the engagement – there were rumours about the legitimacy of the princess – but were finally won over. Marie and her husband were initially very happy – they had six children – Alexander, Vladimir, Alexis, Serge, Paul and Marie. The last married the Duke of Edinburgh, the second son of Queen Victoria; the Edinburghs in due course succeeded to the Duchy of Saxe-Coburg. Empress Marie's health declined and for some years prior to her death she was very much of an invalid. Her husband's relations with her became very formal – he found consolation in the company of Catherine Dolgoruky, whom he married after Marie's death.

Maria Feodorovna (1759–1828), *née* Sophia Dorothea of Württemberg, was the second wife of Emperor Paul I. They had a large family – two of the sons ultimately succeeded to the throne. She saw little of her older children, who were educated under the supervision of the Empress Catherine II. The younger children, Anna Pavlovna, Nicholas Pavlovich and Michael Pavlovich, were, however, her special charges and she had a more intimate life with them. She was an honorary member of 'the Triopathy' as a consequence. After the death of her husband she retired to live at Gatchina and Povlovsk. For a brief moment after the *coup* against her husband it appeared as if she aspired to the sovereign power but did not press her claims. She had considerable influence over Alexander I. She was somewhat cold and formal and required a high standard of action and behaviour from her family and her entourage. She tended to outshine the wives of Alexander and Nicholas and held pride of place in court life. She did not much favour Constantine's remarriage and probably did a good deal to bring about the renunciation of his rights. She was held in great respect by all her children and they always turned to her for counsel and advice. Her death in 1828 was much mourned by the imperial family.

Maria Louisa Victoria of Saxe-Coburg (1786–1861), the sister of King Leopold I of the Belgians and of Julia, who married the Grand Duke Constantine, was twice married. Her first husband was the Prince of Leiningen, her second husband was Edward, Duke of Kent. By her first marriage she had two children, Charles and Feodor, and by the second one, Victoria, later Queen of England. She was widowed soon after her daughter Victoria's birth and lived a retired life in Kensington Palace. She, like all her family, was politically ambitious and hoped to have some authority upon her daughter's accession, but this was not to be. Relations between Queen Victoria and the Duchess were not good and it was only after the Queen's marriage to her cousin Albert of Saxe-Coburg that they improved. In her later years the Duchess was the beloved 'Grandmamma' and her death in 1861 caused Queen Victoria to refer to herself – and she was forty-one – as 'a poor orphan child'.

Maria Nicolaievna (1819–76), the daughter of Nicholas I, married Maximilian, Duke of Leuchtenberg in 1839. Leuchtenberg was the younger son of Eugene de Beauharnais, the stepson of Napoleon I. The Leuchtenbergs made their home in Russia and became intimates of the imperial family and finally cognates of it. Maria Nicolaievna was much interested in education and was also for a time president of the academy of arts.

Maria Pavlovna (1786–1859) was a daughter of Emperor Paul I and in 1804 she married Charles Frederick of Saxe-Weimar. She was a gifted woman and developed her propensities to drawing, music and reading by associating with the many talented men attracted to the court at Weimar. She became the patroness of numerous intellectuals and founded a museum devoted to the memory of Goethe,

Schiller, Wieland, etc. She first attracted Liszt to Weimar in 1842; Goethe referred to her as one of the outstanding women of her time. Her son, Charles Alexander (1818–1901), married her niece, Sophie of Orange (1824–97).

MARIANNE OF ORANGE (1810–83), the only daughter of King William I, was a charming but somewhat eccentric individual. She fell in love with Gustavus Vasa, the son of King Gustavus IV of Sweden, who had been deposed. Prince Gustavus was a prince without a kingdom. He was an Austrian army officer and as a youth had been a ward of Emperor Alexander I. Because of international complications the marriage arrangements were broken off and in 1830 – during the early stages of the Belgian revolution – she married her cousin Albert of Prussia (1809–72). She had three children, Charlotte (1831–55), Alexandrine (1842–1906) and Albert (1837–1906). The marriage was an unhappy one – the Prince was a philanderer and the Princess eccentric – and in 1845 the couple parted. She retired from Berlin, making her home first in the Netherlands and then in Italy. She formed a connection with Johannes Van Rossum, a member of her entourage, and by him had a son, Johan Willem von Reinhartshausen (1848–60). Kings William II and Frederick William IV were much scandalised by her activities. However, in 1849 a divorce was arranged since Prince Albert wished to marry Rosalie von Rauch. Marianne could not marry Van Rossum since he already had a wife but the princess and her lover continued to live together at Schloss Reinhartshausen until his death. She died in 1883 and was buried beside Van Rossum and her son. Marianne was not liked by Anna Pavlovna, who felt that she had disgraced the family. Queen Sophie was less critical and Marianne even stayed as her guest on several occasions. Marianne was not accepted by Queen Emma, and in fact from the time of her divorce in 1849 she really lived outside the royal circles completely.

MAURICE OF ORANGE (1843–50), the second son of King William III and Queen Sophie.

ALEXANDER SERGEEVICH MENSHIKOV (1787–1859), Russian officer, initially served in the army in the War of 1812. He was unable to get on with Arakcheev, the chief military adviser of Alexander, and Menshikov entered the navy. In 1827 he was appointed to command the navy – he had held the rank of general in the army. In 1853 he was sent as special envoy to Constantinople during the dispute over the Holy Places. Menshikov attempted to bully the Sultan, but the latter, supported by Stratford Canning, refused to give way; relations between Russia, Turkey, England and France declined and the Crimean War broke out. Menshikov was supreme naval and military commander at Alma, Balaclava and Inkerman. He retired in 1855.

MICHAEL NICOLAIEVICH (b. 1832), the fourth son of Emperor Nicholas I, served in the army, reaching the rank of Field-Marshal in 1878. From 1863 to 1881 he was Viceroy of the Caucasus and commander of the troops. In 1881 he became President of the State Council. He married Olga, the daughter of the Grand Duke Leopold of Baden; their children were Nicholas, Michael, George, Alexander, Serge, Alexis and Anastasia.

MICHAEL PAVLOVICH (1798–1849), the youngest son of Emperor Paul I and, with Anna Pavlovna and Nicholas, part of the Triopathy. Michael was always very intimate with Nicholas. Michael was a master of military drill and he was excessively interested in the army; he took no part in politics. He was not popular with his men because of his severity and pedantry. He was cheery, gay, and somewhat irresponsible in character and obviously much petted by the family – he was nicknamed 'cadet' by his older brothers and sisters. In 1824 he married Charlotte of Württemberg – on entering the Russian family she took the name of Helene – but the marriage was not very happy; she was too intellectual for his taste and he was too brusque and military for her. He was much attached to his brother Constantine, whom he visited very frequently and whom he emulated in dress and style. He died of a stroke after taking part in a cavalry drill in Warsaw in 1849; his death was a great blow to all of the family and especially to Nicholas. He had no sons, only five daughters, Maria (1825–46), Elizabeth (1826–45), Catherine (1827–76), Alexandra (1831–33) and Anna (1834–6).

NICHOLAS NICOLAIEVICH (1831–91), the third son of Emperor Nicholas I, he entered the army and fought at Inkerman in the Crimean War. He was active in the military reorganisation of the army after the Crimean War and was particularly influential in improving the engineers and the cavalry. During the Russo-Turkish War of 1877–8 he was the Commander-in-Chief of the army. In 1856 he married Alexandra Petrovna, the daughter of Prince Peter Georgevich of Oldenburg. The latter was the son of Catherine Pavlovna by her first marriage and hence Alexandra was Nicholas Nicolaievich's cousin once removed. There were two sons of this marriage, Nicholas and Peter.

NICHOLAS PAVLOVICH (1796–1855), third son of Emperor Paul I, was educated by his parents (unlike the elder sons, who were educated under the supervision of Empress Catherine II), his tutor being General Lamsdorff, a harsh disciplinarian. He early evinced his enthusiasm for military life but at the same time he showed considerable talents and enthusiasm for the arts and languages. He was a handsome youth – charming and affable. He was very affectionate and his fellow-members of the Triopathy were the recipients of his kindness throughout their lives. In 1817 he married Princess Charlotte of Prussia; she took the name Alexandra Feodorovna when she became a member of the Russian Orthodox Church. They had a large family, Alexander Nicolaievich, Constantine Nicolaievich, Nicholas Nicolaievich, Michael Nicolaievich, Maria Nicolaievna, Olga Nicolaievna and Alexandra Nicolaievna. During his brother's reign he served in the army and upon Alexander's death was surprised to learn that he was his successor – the decree of 1820 concerning Constantine Pavlovich's renunciation was not known. Immediately upon his accession he was confronted by the Decembrist Revolt (14 December 1825) and this event made a deep impression on him. He came to value loyalty and obedience as the virtues in all men; his motto became 'orthodoxy, autocracy and nationalism'. He suppressed the Polish revolution of 1830 and came to the aid of the Habsburgs in crushing the Hungarian revolt in 1848. He had the idea of partitioning Turkey, but this was opposed by the Powers and in the end the Crimean War resulted. The Russian failures in the Crimean War disheartened him and he died during the war. Nicholas had particularly strong ties with the House of Orange – King William II he regarded as one of his dearest friends and Queen Anna Pavlovna his confidante. She constantly turned to 'Nikki' for advice, consolation, affection and assistance and he never failed her. He was an autocrat but not a bad man, and has possibly been somewhat maligned by liberal historians.

OLGA NICOLAIEVNA (1822–92), daughter of Emperor Nicholas I, married King Charles I of Württemberg.

ALEXEI FEODOROVICH ORLOV (1787–1862), a member of the famous princely family long devoted to the imperial dynasty, was active in defeating the rebels in the Decembrist Revolt. He later became Head of the Third Department. He served as an imperial emissary on a number of occasions and while not particularly brilliant he was notable for executing orders with great precision and totally avoiding his own initiative. Prince Orlov was much favoured by Nicholas I and was accounted one of the Emperor's few personal friends.

VICTOR NIKITICH PANIN (1801–74), Russian noble, served in the diplomatic corps until 1832 when he transferred to the Department of

Justice. In 1842 he was appointed Minister of Justice and held the post for twenty years.

IVAN FEODOROVICH PASKEVICH (1782–1856) began his career as a page at the court of Catherine II, then he joined the famous Presbrazhenskoe Regiment. During the wars with Napoleon he served in Moldavia and Wallachia where his bravery and abilities brought him promotion. In 1817 he was attached to the suite of Michael Pavlovich and accompanied him on his European tour. He took command in the Caucasian Wars of 1827 and in three months subdued the two richest trans-Caucasian provinces. For this he was given the title of Count of Erivan. After the death of Diebitsch he took command of the armies sent to Poland and soon defeated the rebels. He was given the title of Prince of Warsaw and became Viceroy of Poland. He was ruthless in his administration and worked to Russify the Polish kingdom. He died in Warsaw, soon after Nicholas I, in January 1856.

PAUL PETROVICH (1754–1801), the only child of Emperor Peter III and his wife Catherine II, was educated by his great-aunt Empress Elizabeth I. He was always estranged from his parents and resented the fact that his mother, Empress Catherine II, had him kept from the throne after the *coup* of 1762. He was educated by Count Nikita Panin and he was an accomplished linguist, had some knowledge of the arts and was aware of the ideas of the Enlightenment. In 1773 he married Wilhelmina of Hesse but this marriage terminated when his wife died in childbirth in 1776. Some six months later he married Sophia Dorothea of Württemberg (1759–1828), who took the name of Maria Feodorovna when she joined the Orthodox Church. They had a large family – four sons and six daughters. During the reign of Catherine II Paul and his wife lived at Gatchina. He succeeded to the throne in 1796. His reign began well, but his policies became increasingly inconsistent and he began to show signs of incipient insanity. He began to make threats against his own family – he saw his sons as dangerous rivals and he threatened to confine his wife in a convent – and to behave with much severity towards the nobility. On 11 March (O.S.) 1801 a group of conspirators attacked the Emperor in his bedchamber and murdered him. Evidently the original plan had been to force him to abdicate, but either by accident or design he was killed instead. Emperor Paul is always portrayed as an homicidal maniac, but this is not correct. He had many redeeming qualities and it may well be that his apparent eccentricities covered a plan to organise Russia on the pattern of Prussia, a state which he much admired.

PETER FREDERICK GEORGE OF OLDENBURG (1784–1812), referred to as George, was a member of the Holstein-Gottorp line of Oldenburg which had come to Russia in the reign of Peter III. The Oldenburgs, like the Leuchtenbergs, married into the imperial family. Prince George married Catherine Pavlovna in 1809. He was Governor of Tver, Novgorod and Jaroslavsk until his death. His widow married King William of Württemberg in 1816.

PETER GEORGEVICH OF OLDENBURG (1812–81) was the son of George of Oldenburg (1784–1812) and his wife Catherine Pavlovna (1788–1819). He was educated in Oldenburg and then joined the Russian army aged eighteen. He married Theresa Wilhelmina of Nassau (1815–71) and their eldest daughter Alexandra Petrovna married the Grand Duke Nicholas Nicolaievich in 1856. Peter of Oldenburg was much interested in education on all levels and founded the Institute of Jurisprudence. He held many state offices and presided over numerous institutes of higher learning.

PHILARET, METROPOLITAN OF MOSCOW (1783–1867), born Vasili Mikhailovich Drazov, became Metropolitan of Moscow in 1821.

IVAN ALEKSEEVICH POTEMKIN (1780–1849), army officer who joined the diplomatic service and held a number of posts abroad, became the Minister at The Hague from 1832 to 1838. In 1835 he was made a Privy Councillor.

ALEXANDER PUSHKIN (1798–1837) came from an impoverished aristocratic family; he was educated at the *lycée* at Tsarskoe Selo and when he graduated in 1817 he joined the Ministry of Foreign Affairs. In 1820 he was expelled from St Petersburg, travelled in the Caucasus and lived in Odessa, Kishnev and Pskov until 1827, when he was allowed to return. He wrote a number of poems including *Ruslan and Ludmilla*, *The Bakhchisarai Fountain*, *Boris Godunov* and *Eugene Onegin*, and he may well be considered the father of Russian national literature. In 1831 he married Natalie Goncharova, but this was not a success; his wife had a liaison with d'Anthes and he was made the victim of scandalous gossip. He was killed in a duel with d'Anthes, whom he had challenged in order that his honour be restored. Pushkin's death was regretted by all in Russia, and d'Anthes and his patron, Heeckeren, were ostracised and in due course both left Russia.

DUC DE REICHSTADT (1811–1832), better known as the King of Rome, the only son of Emperor Napoleon I and his second wife Marie Louise of Austria. After the 100 Days his father abdicated in his favour but he never reigned and the Bourbons were restored anew by the Powers. Napoleon II was taken to Vienna where he was brought up under the care of his grandfather Emperor Francis II. In 1818 the young prince was made Duke of Reichstadt, a Bohemian duchy. His life was unhappy, he refused to think of himself as an Austrian and wished, naturally enough, to emulate his father, the Emperor Napoleon. He died of tuberculosis; his death was in many ways a great relief to European statesmen since it removed the possibility of a Bonapartist restoration and an upsetting of the decisions of Vienna. His memory is much treasured in France and he bears the sobriquet 'L'Aiglon'.

ALEXANDER RIBEAUPIERRE, a Swiss war chief, gentleman-in-waiting at the court of Nicholas I and a member of the State council. He was ennobled in 1856.

KARL JOHANN SCHULTZ (1793–1858) was born of Baltic parents in St Petersburg. He attended the university and became a doctor of philosophy. He worked as a colleague of Rumiantsev on various works of a literary and bibliographical nature. In due course he entered the service of Anna Pavlovna and became one of her secretaries.

JAN SKRZNECKI (1787–1860), a Polish army officer, joined the revolutionary forces in 1830 and commanded a division. After the battles of Dobro and Grokhovo he was chosen Commander-in-Chief of the Polish army. In spite of initial successes his leadership was questioned, and after the battle of Ostrolenko he was replaced by Dembinski. Following the fall of Warsaw he went into exile; later he served in the Belgian army.

SOPHIE OF ORANGE (1824–97), the youngest child and only daughter of King William II and Queen Anna Pavlovna, was the much petted baby of the family. She married her cousin Charles Alexander of Saxe-Weimar in 1842. There were four children born of this marriage, Sophie, Alexandrine, Elizabeth and Charles Augustus. Sophie continued the intellectual traditions of the Weimar court and it was a centre of the polite arts and learning. She restored Goethe's house and also opened a Goethe–Schiller archive. She was politically a liberal and there is a tradition that she inspired her father in 1848 to participate in the democratisation of the Netherlands. She often visited her homeland and is referred to by Dutch contemporaries as 'our princess Sophie'. For a brief time she was considered as heiress to Queen Wilhelmina and there were many who hoped that the latter might marry into the family of Saxe-Weimar. Sophie of Orange was the inheritor of Queen Anna Pavlovna's private papers and part of the collection now reposes in the archives in Weimar.

SOPHIE OF WÜRTTEMBERG (1818–77), the daughter of William I of Württemberg and his second wife Catherine Pavlovna. Sophie married William, Prince of Orange – later King William III – on Waterloo Day (18 June) 1839. She was not popular with Queen Anna Pavlovna since the latter had disliked Sophie's mother and saw in the daughter many similar traits of character. Sophie was an extremely intelligent woman and she surrounded herself with savants and corresponded with many intellectuals. Her married life was not particularly happy and she and her husband had few interests in common. They had three sons. Sophie was always gracious and charming and she had many friends all over Europe.

ALEXANDER GRIGOREVICH STROGANOV (1795–1891), Russian army officer, was a member of the Corps of Engineers. He entered the Ministry of Internal Affairs in 1834 and fifteen years later was appointed to the Council of State. In 1854 he was commandant of the St Petersburg garrison and then for the next nine years Governor-General of Novorossiisk and Bessarabia.

KARL FEDOROVICH TOLL (1777–1842), a Russian officer, served in the Italian campaign under Suvorov and later at Austerlitz. In the War of 1812 he was Quarter-Master-General of the Russian army. He later fought under Diebitsch in Turkey and in Poland.

VASILI SERGEEVICH TRUBETSKOI (1776–1841), a Russian prince, was Adjutant-General, senator and member of the Council of State. He was an aide-de-camp of Alexander I. In 1830 he was sent as special envoy to London to congratulate William IV upon his accession. In 1831 he was for a brief time governor of St Petersburg.

BARON VAN DOORN was a 'kammerherr' of King William II and he was one of the officials appointed to act to bring some order in the financial chaos of the royal family following the death of the King.

DON JUAN VAN HALEN, a Spaniard resident in Brussels, was appointed by Charles Rogier, the leader of the radicals, as commander of the forces in Brussels during the revolution of 1830.

LOUIS VAN HEECKEREN (b. 1791), rumoured to be possibly a natural son of King William I but this was most unlikely. He entered the Dutch diplomatic service and became his country's envoy to

Russia. He was well liked by Nicholas, who honoured him with his patronage and his approbation. As an individual he was very urbane and sophisticated and a bit 'smarmy'. He became the patron and later the father – by adoption – of d'Anthes, and the two of them played an unsavoury role in the Pushkin affair. Van Heeckeren was blamed by all and sundry and his usefulness at St Petersburg was at an end. He was recalled but his diplomatic career was continued, and he later went to Vienna where he was very successful and popular.

GRIGORI IVANOVICH VLAMOV (1771–1842), the secretary of Empress Maria Feodorovna, was placed in charge of her charitable works following her demise in 1828. Vlamov was the confidant of the Empress and was as close to her as any other person except her family.

JOHN PHILIP WESSENBERG (1773–1858) joined the Austrian Diplomatic service in 1801 and worked under Prince Metternich for many years. In 1848 he succeeded his chief as Foreign Minister and later in the year was briefly Minister President, but the revolution of 1848 became more violent and he retired in November.

WILHELMINA OF PRUSSIA (1751–1820) was the daughter of Prince August William and his wife Louise of Brunswick. She was the niece of Frederick the Great and sister of King Frederick William II. She married Prince William V of Orange in 1767 and accompanied him into exile. There were three children, Louise (1770–1819), William (1772–1843) and Frederick (1774–89). Her son William became King William I of the Netherlands. She was a rather formidable dowager and, like her daughter the Princess of Brunswick, was not greatly impressed by the grandeur and pretensions of Anna Pavlovna and the Romanovs. She was the aunt of her daughter-in-law, the wife of King William I, and the great-aunt of Charlotte, the wife of Emperor Nicholas I.

WILHELMINA OF PRUSSIA (1774–1837), the daughter of King Frederick William II of Prussia and his wife Frederica of Hesse-Darmstadt. She married William of Orange in 1791 and they had four children, William (1792–1849), Frederick (1797–1881), Pauline (1800–6) and Marianne (1810–83). She was a charming and agreeable woman and was much approved of by all. She constantly acted as peace-maker between King William I and his sons and daughters-in-law. In the correspondence she is referred to as 'the Queen'. When she died in 1837 she was much regretted.

WILLIAM I, KING OF THE NETHERLANDS (1772–1843), referred to in the text as 'the King', was the son of the Stathalter William V.

During the French Revolution and occupation of his country he lived in exile, chiefly in Prussia. He returned to the Netherlands in 1813 and was recognised as 'sovereign prince'. In 1814, after the Congress of Vienna decided to unite all of the Netherlands, he was made King. He was a traditionalist and a conservative and often found his son and daughter-in-law too advanced for him. He preferred his Dutch to his Belgian subjects and lived more in The Hague than in Brussels. After the Belgian revolution of 1830 his obstinacy prevented a settlement, and it was not until 1839 that the matter was finally resolved. He was twice married – his first wife was Wilhelmina (1774–1837) of Prussia, and his second wife was Henriette d'Oultremont. He abdicated in 1840, married Henriette in 1841 and retired to live in Berlin where he bore the title of Duke of Nassau.

WILLIAM II, KING OF THE NETHERLANDS (1792–1849), was the elder son of King William I. He served in the British army in the Peninsular Campaign and at Waterloo. He was semi-engaged to Princess Charlotte, the daughter of the Prince Regent, but the arrangements were terminated, and in 1816 he married Anna Pavlovna of Russia. He and his wife lived in Brussels where they were quite popular. He made many trips abroad and visited Russia several times. He was much attached to the Romanovs and very proud of his connection with them. In the Belgian crisis he played an active part – at one time he was considered as successor to his father, who had been formally deposed – and during the Ten Days' War he commanded the Dutch army. In the 1830s he and his father were often in conflict since the king was growing increasingly reactionary. He succeeded his father as king in 1840 and reigned for nine years. The climax of his reign came in 1848 when he accepted a liberal constitution for his country. He died at Tilburg on 17 March 1849. He was a charming, agreeable, affable, lively, easy and generous individual and generally extremely popular. He was much interested in the arts and made a great picture collection, much of which went to Russia after his death.

WILLIAM III, KING OF THE NETHERLANDS (1817–90), the eldest son of King William II, was born in Belgium. As a boy he was considered difficult and much less affable than his father. Later he became more popular. In 1834 he visited Russia, and two years later he went to England. He studied briefly at the University in Leiden, but the army was his chief interest. He fell in love with his cousin, Sophie of Württemberg, and married her in 1839 despite family opposition. The marriage was not very successful; however, there were three sons, William (1840–79), Maurice (1843–50) and

Alexander (1851–84). During his father's brief reign he remained very much in the background, but upon becoming king in 1849 he did very well. He was very pro-French in his outlook and he played a rather prominent role on the international scene. After his first wife's death in 1877 he married Emma of Waldeck-Pyrmont and they had one daughter, Wilhelmina. All of his sons by his first marriage predeceased him and he was succeeded by his daughter.

William, Prince of Orange (1840–79), the eldest son of King William III and his wife Queen Sophie, studied at Leiden and served in the army. He travelled widely and was a very popular prince. He never married, but for a time was very friendly with Countess Mattie Van Limburg Stirum, but for reasons of state was not permitted to marry her. He stayed in Paris a good deal where he was very much the *grand seigneur*. He died in June 1879 and was buried at Delft.

William I of Prussia (1797–1888) was the second son of King Frederick William III. In 1848 he opposed the concessions made by his brother and wished to use drastic measures to suppress the March revolution in Berlin. On account of his conservative views he had to leave Prussia for a time. In 1858 he became Regent and three years later succeeded as King of Prussia. He was not brilliant but had much common sense and was loyal and conscientious. In 1862 he appointed Otto von Bismarck (1815–98) as Minister President of Prussia and from then on King William had few difficulties. In 1871 he was proclaimed German Emperor. He married Augusta of Weimar. He was always very courteous, dignified and highly esteemed by his family and by his subjects.

William I of Württemberg (1781–1864) married Catherine Pavlovna in 1816. She died in 1819 leaving one daughter, Sophie, who married William III of the Netherlands. In 1819 he made Württemberg a model state by voluntarily giving the country a constitution. In 1846 his son and heir Charles married Olga Nicolaievna, the daughter of Emperor Nicholas I.

Peter Christianovich Wittgenstein (1768–1842), Russian noble and army officer, served in the French wars; in 1812 he commanded the cavalry. Briefly, he was Commander-in-Chief after the death of Kutuzov, but, following the battles of Lützen and Bautzen, he was replaced by Barclay de Tolly. In 1828 he commanded the Russian armies on the Turkish front and became a Field-Marshal. He retired after Varna was captured.

1815–25

THE decade following the Battle of Waterloo on 18 June 1815 found European politics largely dominated by the decisions made at Vienna. The new Kingdom of the Netherlands under King William I was established, the Kingdom of Poland, nominally a separate state, was really part of the Russian Empire since Tsar Alexander was its sovereign; Italy was still 'a geographical expression' and Germany was a mosaic of independent states loosely united in the Germanic Confederation. This was the age of the Holy Alliance, the Congress system and legitimacy.

The first signs of disruption came in 1820 with a revolt in Spain, followed by outbreaks in Naples and Portugal the same year. The eastern European sovereigns – Russia, Austria and Prussia – met initially at Troppau to deal with the crises, and after further discussions intervention resulted. Only England of all the great powers refused to participate in these decisions.

The state of affairs was made more complicated when the Greeks rebelled against the Sultan of Turkey in the spring of 1821. Traditional Russian interests in the Balkans and her concern with the Orthodox Christian community in the Ottoman Empire ran foul of the accepted policies of the great powers. Russia had long been anxious to enlarge its authority in the Balkans, and Tsar Alexander was torn between duty to the alliance and an historic mission.

The death of Tsar Alexander I on 1 December 1825 marked an end of an age. His brother Constantine, whose renunciation of the throne in 1820 had not been known, was proclaimed in St Petersburg, but after some delays the state of affairs was clarified and Nicholas became the next Tsar. However, his succession was marred by the Decembrist Revolt which occurred on 14 December 1825; the revolt was crushed but it convinced Nicholas that autocracy and orthodoxy were to be the basis of his power. Tsar Alexander had been a key figure in the Holy Alliance and he had been concerned with the congress system, his successor was to be much more a Russian nationalistic sovereign.

THE GRAND DUCHESS ANNA PAVLOVNA, THE PRINCESS OF ORANGE, TO THE EMPRESS MARIA FEODOROVNA:

Brussels,
30 November 1817

Dear good excellent Mama,

I am deeply sorry in advance for the sorrow that the contents of this letter are going to cause you, but the day has finally come in which it is my duty to speak the sad truth, such as it is.[1] You know, dear good Mama, with what prudence I have always written to you by post until my letter number 109,[2] when the gazettes forced me to speak to you about a subject which they themselves mentioned and, consequently, you would have been justified in finding that I lacked confidence in you, dear Mama, by keeping silent on an item which is public property. But the details were reserved for my letter by the military courier. You know, dear Mama, that William was entrusted by the King with making the inspection of the troops and fortifications in the southern provinces, and with making a report to him on the state of the army as he found it. The army is in the most deplorable condition and totally demoralised, and under the bad system adopted by the government it is becoming worse every year. I know that General Chernyshev[3] made his report to the Emperor along these lines last summer. William, who had not seen it since the Battle of Waterloo, found it in a worse state than it was then, with the exception of some battalions of infantry and some squadrons not as bad as the rest. He found it necessary to show his dissatisfaction to several generals and officers as well as to praise those who deserved his approval. He made a superhuman effort to raise the spirits of the soldiers and to encourage the officers and generals, and he had the good

[1] This letter was written when the Grand Duchess Anna Pavlovna was under considerable emotional strain; hence, it is not a polished epistle and at times is slightly incoherent.

[2] The Grand Duchess numbered her letters in case any were lost in transit and a duplicate could then be sent to keep a consecutive narrative. She generally wrote to her mother about once a week. The earlier letters to her mother were not in either of the collections in The Hague or in Weimar.

[3] Alexander Ivanovich Chernyshev (1785–1857) fought at Waterloo. He later became Minister of War.

fortune to earn the approbation of that part of the army that he had inspected, and to inspire in all the soldiers the desire to see him occupy the place of Minister of War. William bore the title of Minister of War, General in Chief of the Army and Inspector of all the Armies, although he was not in charge of the affairs of this department, the Chief of the War Office being Lieut.-Gen. Count Goltz.[1] William refrained from the work only because of the difference of opinion which existed between himself and the King on the subject of the army, and only out of delicacy towards his father so that he should not be in a position to oppose his father, unable to say yes when his conscience would have told him to say the opposite. However, as soon as the King gave him the task of making the inspection he obeyed immediately, but he had to speak as an honest man and reveal his opinion to his sovereign since it had been demanded of him. This is what William did in a detailed report which he presented to the King. William had hardly come back from his inspection when Goltz, seeing the good effect that it had gained for him in the army, wanted to deal him a severe blow, not only in the eyes of the soldiers but also in the estimation of the southern provinces. Therefore, all those Belgian officers who, according to their own request, had been recommended by William to Count Goltz so that they should be placed on the active list in the continental army, were put on half pay, deported to Batavia and put at the disposal of the Governor of Colonies. Among the number of officers recommended by William were the three Parisians, and Belgians who had just come from Russian service. Count Goltz, as you see, dear Mama, was lacking in obedience to his superior in putting into exile all the officers that William had particularly recommended to him. The King had signed this decree. If Goltz had not told the King that these officers had been recommended by William how was he not guilty? But if he told him and the King had wished it thus, what a King; and what a father!

As soon as William received this decree he wrote to the

[1] Friedrich Adrian von der Goltz (1770–1849), a German who entered the Dutch army in 1785. He was Commissioner-General of War; the Prince of Orange held the office of Minister of War but was subordinate to Goltz in the military hierarchy.

King immediately to tell him that these officers had been recommended by him to Goltz, and he begged the King to take into consideration the bad effect that this measure would produce in the country against the government, and he recalled to his mind that the three Parisian gentlemen had come from Russian service. He told him that he was personally wounded by this measure, and added that he was convinced that his father did not know that these officers had been recommended by him, and he bore even more of a grudge towards Goltz, feeling these proceedings should not be kept secret from the King. To Goltz he wrote a very strong letter in which he reproached him for his insubordination and treated him as he deserved to be treated. The same day he addressed a circular to the officers on half pay to assure them that he was not at fault in their misfortune and that he had recommended them to be placed, according to their wishes, in the continental army.

The King's reply to William was a tissue of lies and feeble excuses in order to excuse Goltz, but he said that he had not known that these officers had been recommended by William. He added that he found him very bold in accusing Goltz who was only fulfilling the duties of Commissioner of War out of kindness for William, who had wasted his time for three years and done nothing. Goltz, on his part, replied to William that an order from the King was not without appeal – that if it was without appeal it was in fact equivalent to an exile – and that he had been wounded by William's reproach, and if he did not give him *satisfaction* with the shortest possible delay he would demand his resignation from the King.

William replied to the reproaches that his father made him by quoting the facts in his defence. In respect to the kindness with which Goltz fulfilled the duties of Commissioner of War, he recalled to him that it was only out of obedience to his father that he had accepted the title of Minister of War and that he only held aloof from the work because he was afraid of finding himself of an opposing opinion to the King, that this would be very difficult for him and that, in order to do any good, he needed much more power as Minister of War than the King wished to grant him. But he had, nevertheless, executed with speed his father's orders in inspecting the troops and he had made his report. That during the three years that the King accused him of wasting his time and of having done nothing, the battles of Quatre Bras and Waterloo had taken place, that being General in Chief and Inspector of all the Armies he had the right to demand that a Lieutenant-General, his inferior in grade and in the Ministry of War, should not be guilty of insubordination by disobeying his intentions and sending officers recommended by him into exile. He told the King that Goltz in his reply had given him to understand that an order of the King is not without appeal and was thereby putting into his hands a power which did not belong to him, being knowingly the cause of the resignation of a minister when William had only asked him for reparation for his insubordination which, as his chief, he had a right to demand. But seeing that he could not attain the reparation he would like, he asked the King to accept his own resignation from the title of Minister of War so as not to find himself any longer in contact with Goltz, and he was sending to the King a copy of Goltz' letter. To Goltz, William replied that his insolence was overwhelming and that he was interpreting the orders of the King in an entirely blameful manner, and that as for his resignation, he should know himself what to do about it.

The King, instead of replying to the points contained in William's letter, wrote him a *sly* letter and finished by telling him to come and explain himself in person at The Hague. William, who would have been required to meet Goltz at The Hague, begged the King once more in writing to make Goltz apologise or else to accept from one or other the resignation that they both demanded, and he added that he would avoid all verbal explanations because he knew his devotion to his father too well not to be certain that, if he should see him, his feeling of honour would not give way to affection, and that in the circumstances he could not and should not give way; his honour and military discipline demanded that his inferior should give him satisfaction or make reparation by confessing himself wrong, and that as the affair was public it should be terminated publicly otherwise William would be completely compromised. He begged his father to do him justice and not to allow him to be publicly compromised. Several days went by without any news from The Hague. Finally, William received a letter from Goltz in the same tone as the first, in which he told him once

C2

more that he had asked for his resignation from the King. William did not reply to this letter and awaited the King's decision, counting on royal justice and on the justice of his cause. All at once one morning they came and told us that the King had arrived. As William was completely unable to see the King for the reason that I have noted above, dear good Mama, he left Brussels. Here I shall add that the King, in verbal remarks with his son, treats him with a violence and a harshness which makes any reply impossible for William who, in these moments, thinks only of containing himself in order not to reply in a disrespectful way. Think, dear Mama, that the King threatens his son and that he already told him some time ago that he would refuse to treat him as his son. So I was given the task by William of giving the King a letter from him and of telling him that he was making a tour of the country of unfixed duration, as was in fact the case. After having sent one of his aides-de-camp to ask me when William would return to which I replied that I did not know, the King came to see me himself. Mama, dear Mama, what dreadful details you are going to hear. Believe me, it is with regret that I feel obliged to tell you them. Here are my letters to William containing the moderate portion of the King's words. I had to hide from William the horror of some of the rest.

In the first conversation with me he tried to move me, to flatter me, and to frighten me. He told me William was an unnatural son, a rebel. He did not have any common sense, his misfortune had been to have commanded the English army here; 'but I shall take care in future that this hothead does not have any power, for if he wishes to have any he will have to go over my dead body. Either he or I will perish and naturally I shall not hesitate; it will be he. Or else I shall have him imprisoned.' I remained silent; after I had recovered from my emotion I told him that in threatening his son he would not frighten him but that he would pierce his heart. As for me, my personal interest would never have any bearing on the matter and I was ready to share the fate of my husband whatever it might be, but I begged him above all to remember that, according to the Constitution of the Kingdom, he did not have the power to imprison any member of the country, still less the Prince of Orange. I added that William was deeply devoted to him, that he had always spoken to me of him with the greatest devotion and respect. Here is my letter number 1 to William. Next day I received a reply from William to the King, in which he recapitulated to him the whole affair and asked him to accept either Goltz' resignation or his own since he knew from Goltz himself that he had asked for his resignation. The King was furious. 'My son has me with my back to the wall because he is not leaving me any choice between the Minister and himself; and I cannot *dismiss my Minister* who is the executive of my wishes. I mean by that that I am pleased with him. If William had done no other wrong than the report that he made on the army for me he would still deserve to be condemned.' 'What,' I said, 'the truth is a crime in the eyes of your Majesty?' 'Yes,' he replied, 'as William opposes my opinion, that alone condemns him.' I then asked innumerable questions on William's alleged wrongs, pretending to know nothing of the details of the affair, and I succeeded in drawing him out so well that he betrayed in all his remarks his jealousy towards his son and said to me, 'He is a bad soldier and a bad general.' Then I asked him how it came about that the Duke of Wellington had been pleased with him. And that William had beaten the French on the two days of the 16th and the 18th [of June 1815]. 'Yes,' he said, 'that's true, but he was lucky to have been wounded because otherwise he would have been beaten. I,' he said, 'beat the French also at Quatre Bras during the revolution and nobody said anything about it because we were unlucky. Why does he want his resignation?' I replied to him in the most formal manner; 'But,' I added, 'think, Sir, if your son is innocent, as I am convinced because I know him to be an honest man, what an injustice you will be committing.' 'But if William is right what am I then? I shall be the King of Diamonds.' That was the royal expression. 'What would you do, then,' I said, 'if war broke out?' 'If that were the case, William would be subservient to the wishes of my Council of War and there would be some Field-Marshal or other above him. He shall have his resignation; this boy deserves to be punished;' here is my letter number 2. He left me after that and sent Colonel Dukailar to see me. He said to him, 'I am afraid I said too much to my daughter-in-law. She asked me questions. I do not know why I replied to her, I misjudged.' Dukailar told me that he replied: 'Your Majesty may rest assured that the Grand Duchess is not only the Prince's wife but his best friend, and if she asked questions it was only with the best of intentions.'

The next day I received a reply from William for the King and here, dear Mama, is the conversation I had with the King; it is given almost in entirety in my letter number 3. He said to me further: 'I am afraid I said too much to you yesterday;' and he said, 'do you still remember the odious remarks that William made in front of you against marriage. He said that a bachelor was happier than a married man.' 'I remember,' I said, 'and I agree in fact that a man who is badly matched with his wife is most unfortunate; but I know also that William makes me perfectly happy.' 'I think I have noticed,' he said, 'that you believe that I do not love my son.' 'I thought that,' I replied. 'My opinion could only be founded on your own remarks, Sire, and on your behaviour towards him.' He got up and left me. He sent for Dukailar and told him the same things as he told me, and Dukailar made the same reply as I did, without our having discussed it. A few moments later I received the decree, what is called in Dutch *besluit*, of William's dismissal from everything, all his offices and military ranks, with a letter worthy of a Philip II. The next day the King came to see me and the first question he asked me was – how you would have acted, dear Mama, and I towards you? [under such circumstances]. I replied that you could not be used as a comparison with anyone since your *bounties* towards all your children, your good deeds on their behalf, the confidence with which you honoured them and the loving care with which you continually watched over their happiness spoke too eloquently in your favour and imbued too much respect for your sacred and cherished name for it not to be invoked with all the veneration that your virtues inspired. Dear good excellent Mama, I was happy to pay you this homage. God who heard me in this moment surely gave me the courage to say it with all the overflow of emotion that I experienced in thinking of you and saying it to the King, of whom it was a condemnation. You, dear Mama, in comparison with this modern Philip II! The very idea is dreadful. But I am coming to what I said in addition. 'I know,' I said, 'that my mother as Empress of Russia, (I thought I had to express myself in that way because it was necessary to make an impression on him) treats all her children equally well, but I have the right only to speak of what concerns me personally. For a long time, even before I reached my majority, she always condescended to speak to me with the greatest confidence on what concerned me,' and [I said] that you had always been good enough to tell me you would never decide anything concerning me to which I had not fully consented and of my own free will. That if it came to sacrificing a child, even to the interest of the state, you had told me, dear Mama, that nothing in the world would make you do it. And I believe, excellent Mama, I have more right to say this than anyone because I remember former times and my gratitude to you will only finish with my life. I said to him further that having reached my majority before my marriage you had been good enough to read to me my marriage contract and had authorised me to say what I would like to be changed in it. 'You have never been in opposition to your mother?' 'No,' I said, 'because Mama has always been just towards me. To show you how just,' I added, 'at the time I left Russia she gave up the desire she had to keep me with her for some time yet to the particular obligation I was under to leave. As for me, at that time my whole desire was to celebrate the 22 July with Mama; but she did not hold it against me for leaving.' Then he got up and, embracing me, said, 'I see that we have obligations to you.' 'Refer these obligations to Mama,' I said, 'and how just she is, because I do not want to praise myself in your eyes when I have my own conscience.' 'But,' he said, 'do you never discuss business in writing with your mother?' 'What else have I done for a year and a half since I have been separated from her,' I said. 'Moreover,' I said, 'a woman is never in a position to have public business to discuss with her mother, so the case is impossible; but all I can say is that my mother loves to make her children happy and that if we had done her wrong, from which God preserve us, we would receive pardon and indulgence from her and never condemnation. Mama is much too religious for that.' He said to me: 'His report alone would condemn him; but at the moment that is only a trifle.' 'Think,' I said, 'how much it must have cost William to relate such facts in it which have brought this blow upon him, according to your opinion.

But as an honest man the peace of his conscience must count above all.' Then he came to ask me if I would go to The Hague alone according to what I had said previously. Excuse me, dear Mama, for having forgotten this little detail in my long account. William had said to me that if he could not go he wanted me to go for the 18th of November, the Queen's birthday, in any event, except for some unusual circumstance concerning him. I replied to the King as in my letter number 4, here enclosed. He trembled all over and left me. He sent for Dukailar again and said to him: 'I found my daughter-in-law very firm and more decided than usual.' 'Put it down to your decree,' said Dukailar. The King repeated again that he was afraid he had said too much to me. Here is my letter to William, number 5, and you will see the outline of the denouement, dear Mama. Next day the King did not come near me all morning. At six o'clock in the evening I wrote to him that I had received a letter from William for him, included in my own, and that I was to give it to him. He came and, after having read William's letter, he turned towards me and said: 'Let him not think he shall ever dare to present himself in front of me in Russian uniform.' 'Sire,' I said, 'this personal caprice, which I feel very keenly, amounts to nothing, for having once granted him permission to wear it, according to Article 66 of the Constitution that William quotes in his letter, there is no Article in the Constitution which gives you the right or authorises you to forbid it to him.' He started to insult his son; I reminded him of his services; I showed him the splinters of his bones. Neither my emotion nor anything I could say could touch him. The only reply he made was to say, 'services and spilt blood do not put him above the correct form.' I replied to him, 'Your son has never failed in it, that is a slander.' At that moment William came in. They embraced. William was in dreadful despair and could only weep and embrace his father and me; and this was the moment the King chose to reproach him. Seeing that there was going to be a scene I said to the King: 'You see, Sire, in what a state your son is, how can you reproach him?' He turned to me trembling with rage. 'If I cannot speak to him in front of my daughter-in-law I shall speak to my son alone,' and he spoke to William who had been forbidden to come to him. Finally, he came and embraced me before leaving with the expression of a real false Judas. I was ill several times over and when I finally recovered I saw William at my side and he said that he had not left me, being afraid to see me in this state. He told me he had written to the King to tell him that he could not leave me. The King left the same night for The Hague. Since then the King and the two Dowagers[1] have held it against William for having stayed near me at that moment and have written to him reproachfully. I have not had a day of health since that day, dear Mama. My nerves are horribly upset with the excessive emotion that I felt. I did everything that I could, dear Mama, to prevent this happening, in everything that you see I said to the King. Since I have been in the country I have neglected nothing in order to maintain peace in the family; but since my confinement, and particularly since the departure of General Chernyshev, the King often says disagreeable things to me, above all against Russia. He hates this country [Russia] and I think I have noticed that he had a personal spite against the Emperor. He was angry because William put on Russian uniform on my brother's name day at a ball that we held, so much so that he even turned his back on him. He also made a coarse remark to me that day. He said to me one day at his table: 'All Russia and your brother himself were led and governed by Poles.' I replied that that was completely untrue.

There, dear Mama, is the state of affairs. I am heartbroken and I do not know where it will finish. I believe it is my duty to tell you everything. I have been silent up till now about these details, but at the moment I believe it necessary for them to be known because, in all honesty, with the King's character you never know what is going to happen. The English Ambassador, Clancarty,[2] is supreme here and leads the King; it is he who under the guise of conciliation kindles the fire of disunity. The King instructs him in all family details. Chernyshev has also informed the Emperor about all this. Since he returned to The Hague the King has written friendly letters to his son but the two dowagers, the Princess of Orange and the Duchess of Brunswick, who have been informed on the details of the affair

[1] The grandmother and aunt of the Prince of Orange.

[2] Richard le Poer Trench, second Earl of Clancarty (1767–1837), had accompanied King William I to The Hague in 1814 and later was appointed ambassador. He supported the union of Belgium and the Netherlands.

by the King only and through his false interpretation in which he slanders his son, write letters full of invective against William. The Princess of Orange is occupied solely with backbiting in the family and tries to interfere in everything. It has been reported in the English papers that I do not like The Hague; do not care to go there and that instead of wearing mourning for Princess Charlotte I had taken it off and appeared in public in colour. One is as untrue as the other. Here is the reply of the Countess Lieven to my letter after the death of the Princess which contains my justification for the way in which I reacted to this news. The same accusations have been made against William. They are both equally false. Here is a letter from the Queen to me which will show you, dear Mama, what an *angel she is*. I am also sending you, dear Mama, a letter from the King and a note from the Queen which will show you that I have given the King all the attentions that I could and that the failures of good manners were not mine nor William's. Here is a copy of a letter from William to me which I hope will please you in all respects. According to the Constitution of the Kingdom there is a statutory law that the King has no power over the Prince of Orange and heir to the throne. The law speaks only of the rights of the Prince of Orange, Articles 37 and 72. The King does not even have the right to supervise the education of the heir presumptive nor any other prince of his house. The Constitution does not give it to him and there is no family law here. Well, the King tries to exert rights over both of us which he does not have, and he claims to be the only one with the right to decide upon everything that concerns our little son. He even gets angry because we did not ask his permission to have him vaccinated, and he does not even want a maid to be appointed for him without his permission. He reproached William for having given a ball celebrating my churching. To seal the ignominy which he wishes to stamp on his son he had Goltz write the order of the day in which his resignation was announced to the Army; something that has never been done here until now. Dear excellent Mama, please show this letter to the Emperor. William is writing to him and says that my letter contains details that he wants him to know, for there are some that only I can give. William does not have the courage to describe them himself and there are some that I have had to hide from him. Mama, dear Mama, I implore your blessings for William and myself; he asks me to kiss your hands for him and begs you to retain your goodness towards him. He never stops telling me how happy I am to have you for a mother and it is what I feel myself most deeply. I embrace our dear Emperor, my good brother, and thank him again for having chosen William for a husband for me because I am happy with him and love him and respect him more and more each day. I only ask one single favour and that is for Mama to tell me if she is satisfied with me and if she finds that I have acted well. I beg my brother also to say if he is pleased with me. More than ever I need the affection of my family and their esteem. I kiss your dear hands a thousand thousand times, good dear excellent Mama. William does the same and we are, until the last hour of our lives, your devoted children. I am, with the unlimited devotion that I bear you from the bottom of my soul and with the deepest and most inviolable respect for my dear good excellent Mama,

Your wholly devoted and submissive daughter.

We are leaving tomorrow for Holland. I embrace our good Countess and I am sure that she will be interested in what concerns us.

EMPRESS MARIA FEODOROVNA TO THE GRAND DUCHESS ANNA PAVLOVNA, THE PRINCESS OF ORANGE:

[Moscow]
9/21 January 1818

I have just finished my letter for the Dutch courier and I am taking up this one again, dear Annette, which will be handed to you by one of our couriers, sending it to Count Vorontsov;[1] so, dear child, I shall write to you with the same complete frankness and confidence with which I spoke to you when we were together and with which I shall speak to you all my life but, dear Annette, I hope that you will know how to distinguish the language of truth and that you will strip it completely of

[1] Michael Semenovich Vorontsov (1782–1856), a Russian diplomat and soldier.

any thought of reproach. I can put myself in your place and feel that a young woman, who, so to speak, has just entered the world scene, separated from her mother's aegis, can only see and judge according to the way her husband sees and judges and that analysis is scarcely possible; but, my dear child, age, reflection, experience and above all a most perfect knowledge of duty leads to an analysis of actions that is more severe and more just. The Emperor has communicated to me William's letters as he requested. I have communicated to him your letters according to your wishes. We have read them and reread them with the greatest attention, and both – and this must certainly be so because our hearts which love William so tenderly find it so – agree, finding William in the wrong towards the King in this last affair. The Emperor himself has read to me some of William's letters to the King and has shown me clearly that, as to the military matter, William was wrong in the expressions he used to Monsieur Goltz and in authoritatively supporting a cause to the Minister which permitted, at the most, a respectful plea and the favour to turn to the King himself on behalf of these individuals. William should not have allowed himself to express himself as he did about Monsieur Goltz who, in fact, was not under his orders because William himself had asked him to bear only the title of Minister of War *ad honore* and had not wished to get involved with the business [of the army]. This was the first mistake and from it follow all the others. The style of William's letter to the King is not that of a submissive respectful son. Many expressions and many sentences must wound the King even more cruelly as father than as sovereign. William's departure on the arrival of the King is yet another great mistake which leaves the cruellest impression, not of the King as William would have it, but of William himself. It is to sound the alarm and to give the most unfortunate publicity to this quarrel, and that in a country which is a volcano where the slightest spark can cause a disastrous eruption. The King asks you about him, dear child, often with an expression of grief. William makes conditions and lays down the law to the King, demanding either the dismissal of the Minister or his own. The King, pushed to the limit, forgets himself, it is true, and allows himself to make harsh wounding suggestions when speaking to you; he was wrong to do it but, dear Annette, a King and father who sees in his son the first of his subjects, and sees him in direct opposition to himself; who sees him flee his presence and lay down the law to him – this King, I say, must be a model of goodness in order not to forget himself. I certainly do not excuse him his rages, but I see in them only the usual conduct of a man wounded to the quick by his child. Finally the King, who on this occasion could not without injuring justice according to the firm belief of the Emperor send away Monsieur Goltz who was not wrong, accedes to the wishes of William and gives him the demanded leave. William returns; they see each other in your presence and it could certainly be foreseen that the first interview would be unhappy. The King sees the effect it is producing on you and tells his son to come to him. The latter agrees but later, instead of going to the King, he writes to him that he cannot leave you and he will go to The Hague when your health permits. Dear, dear Annette, this was a great mistake. Caring for you while you were ill could delay his visit to the King for some hours but as soon as he saw you were better he should have flown to him in order to place himself at his command. You are a mother, dear Annette. Put yourself in the King's place; what would your heart feel if your son had acted like this? You will tell me, 'I would not have allowed it to happen.' I am not discussing past mistakes that the King may have committed; I am only speaking of this last instance where the wrong cannot be laid at his door. Those are my remarks for William. Here are my remarks for you, dear child. I find that you spoke too strongly to the King – one does not bring round a father in this way, even if he be wrong. The surest weapon for leading him back to the paths of conciliation and love is gentleness, dear Annette, and it is the only one which you must use. You must temper the animation, the rage of the father, by your gentle winning manners, by friendship and endearments; you must modify the son's liveliness and his excessive vulnerability towards his father by an unwavering gentleness which, however, must not be at odds with the calmest presentation of the duties that the sacred character of father and sovereign imposes on William; those of respect, submission, and the example and obedience to be given to all subjects. You must always look for the good side of things, and above all you must convince yourself and William that the King cannot have it in mind to harm you, as this would be to harm himself. He can only harm you when William errs in a way which invites general blame, as is the case in this unfortunate episode. Only those who love trouble can have flattered William on his behaviour in this affair, but all those who think nobly, who have the desire and the will for good, will have been unhappy about him. I know very well that William's motive in seeing and acting as he does is solely to prevent an action that he believes and tells himself is unjust. But it is not, and even if it were, his position as a son and a subject would point to another path to follow in order to prevent it. I beg you, dear Annette, return to the position, in all your relations with your new family, that you had until last summer; redouble your attention, your cares, your favours for all its members, and the service you will do William thereby will be immense. Be continually the conciliatory angel, and even if there are some clouds between father and son, lighten them by your care, your kindness. *There* is your true vocation. Never write in the post a word which can wound and can be badly interpreted. I am afraid that your last letters, had they been opened, would have made a bad impression. You must prevent the bitterness which is always the consequence of blame; let slip by those from whom one has the right to demand respect and indulgence. I am coming to a conclusion, dear child, and here it is: the King has just given publicly a great avowal of confidence, let us even say condescension, to William in reinvesting him with all the power pertaining to the position of Minister of War; and so not only public opinion in your country but everywhere in general exalts and praises the King's behaviour, and voices unite in pronouncing that William *will achieve* the impossible to deserve and claim his father's goodness. I use a positive word in saying that William *will achieve* the impossible because opinion about William's heart, about his fine and noble loyalty is certainly unanimously in his favour, so there is no room for doubt. I, however, my dear friend, while agreeing in all this profusion, know the circumstances. I know the rift between William and Monsieur Goltz; I know the personal offence – excuse me this expression – that he has done him in his letters to which, in all honesty, the Emperor and I find that Monsieur Goltz has replied with the nobility and dignity of a man who has a clear conscience and who does not feel himself in the wrong. I tell myself that it will cost William dear to work beside him and I am afraid that at the slightest contradiction or difference of opinion William will believe himself outraged and that fresh incidents may arise. But there is a sure means of preventing that happening and I find it in William's loyalty of heart. He has done an injustice to Monsieur Goltz by his suppositions; the most perfect being is capable of these mistakes and then one word of kindness, of regret spoken with frankness to the person, not only causes them to be forgotten and erases them from his memory but sows the seed of the most complete devotion. This is how it will be with Monsieur Goltz if William follows the impulsion of his own heart; then affairs will go well and William will be useful to his country, and with these difficulties smoothed out the King, seeing William's good and noble character in action, will be unable to upset him. A course of action, different from that which my love for William causes me to outline, will renew the quarrel and will have consequences all the more upsetting in that the King is protected from public opinion by the avowal of confidence that he has just given his son; the general discontent will fall on William and he will be in disfavour with the public. But may God preserve us from this misfortune! And my William, who has captured all my maternal love, will weigh in his conscience the counsels of his loving mother and will find them in conformity with the voice of duty and honour; for they are drawn from the rules laid down in our Holy Gospel, our only true guide. I beg you, dear Annette, to take every care to show the Dutch that you like being in their country which is, moreover, William's cradle. Try to give them the assurance that you enjoy being among them and, to convince them, use the same assiduity as you did in Brussels and in which you succeeded well. I know that the beginning of a pregnancy is always accompanied by suffering; but please surmount it as much as possible for after all that has happened, believe me, your retreat from the world and society will be attributed much more to temper than to the consequences of your condition. Be as serene as possible, affectionate to your family and courteous towards all. In short, dear Annette, be my old Annette and erase with Christian charity all past disagreements. Those are my wishes and my prayers. They are the ones that all those who love you will send you; our good Countess [Lieven] entreats you for it as I do. This is a long epistle, my child, but reading it can only give you renewed assurance of my love for you and my friendship, of my good opinion of you and of my heartfelt conviction that the language of truth will be forever dear to your heart. Good-bye, dear Annette. This letter is for you as [it is] for William if he can assure you that he will listen to the counsels and advice of a mother with the perfect conviction that they come from a heart which belongs wholly to him, and which is interested in his happiness as in that of my sons.

I embrace your dear little son, yourself, my good friend, and give you all my most tender blessings. The Emperor to whom I have just read my letter, dear child, wishes to tell you that it expresses his sentiments as it does my own, and he embraces you tenderly. I am sending to you the enclosed [a letter to William].

THE EMPRESS MARIA FEODOROVNA TO WILLIAM, PRINCE OF ORANGE:

Moscow
10/22 January 1818

I am making use of the courier who is leaving today to write to you, dear, good William, and thank you for your letter from Brussels of 30 November. You were in no doubt, dear son, I am sure, of how distressed I was by the contents of your letters and those of Annette and all the uneasiness that I experienced. It was due as much to the cause of the event as to the effect that it produced and, my dear good William, who shows confidence and friendship to his mother, will certainly wish her to reply to them with the greatest frankness and the language of truth which, in the mouth of a mother, is constantly coupled with the most loving sentiments for her son, and so will not wound but will go straight to the heart of this cherished son. I have replied at length to my Annette; read my letter, dear William, if you have any trust in me, and tell yourself that if I allow myself to find you wrong in this affair it is only after the most mature reflection, forcing myself to set aside maternal indulgence, consulting my conscience and analysing the facts and submitting them to human and divine laws. But, dearly beloved William, I know also that certainly you did not wish to make a mistake and that you have been drawn along by your loyal heart which thought to uphold the cause of justice. But it did not, dear William, and there followed all the consequences we have seen – finally, happily the affair is finished – and from now on it depends only on you, dear, good William, by following the direction of your generous heart, to turn away from all new vexation and to justify by your deeds the confidence the King has just shown in you. You will earn the approval of your father and reap the blessings of all those who think well of you and who see in the harmony of the family the happiness of the state and the guarantee of public peace. The duties of the heir to the throne, as son and subject, are perpetuated from reign to reign, and your son, dear William, one day finding himself in the same relation to you, will follow the good example that you will give him in this respect, as well as that which you have already shown him by your noble achievements in war. That is my expectation, the object of my wishes and my prayers. It is doubly painful for me to know that Annette is unwell and fears she will be unable to fulfil her duties towards her family and society as she should, particularly at this moment when I am convinced that my dear William will do what he knows so well how to do to capture the approval of the Dutch as he did that of the Flemish. My Annette must play her part, and play her part in it she certainly will as best she can provided that her health does not present an obstacle.

Our dear Alexandrine[1] is progressing happily in her pregnancy and she is bearing it marvellously since passing the half of her term. She sends you her friendly regards, dear William, as do Nicholas and Michael. The latter is about to begin his grand tour in seven or eight weeks and so he will certainly see you, dear William, and perhaps this happiness lies ahead also for — but hush. Let us not anticipate this moment of happiness. Good-bye, dear good William. Tell yourself that my friendship and my devotion to you will follow me to the grave and I am for life your good, faithful, loving mother and friend. Our dear

[1] The wife of the Grand Duke Nicholas, later Tsar Nicholas I.

Countess assures you of her continual remembrance and of her devotion.

THE GRAND DUCHESS ANNA PAVLOVNA, THE PRINCESS OF ORANGE, TO THE GRAND DUKE CONSTANTINE:

Soestdijk,
21 May 1818

Dear Brother,

I hasten to take pen in hand today to offer you my congratulations and the wishes I am making, and shall endlessly make, for your continuing happiness. You well know, dear Brother, that on your name-day[1] my first thoughts are all given to you, and it is very pleasant for me to express to you everything I feel for you. Michael spent a few days with us and left us on the 30th of this month to be in England before Parliament rises, at which he has been advised to be present. He will stop two days at Maubeuge to review Count Vorontsov's brigade,[2] and I think that on the 5th of June he will embark at Calais to be in London on 6 June. He spoke a great deal about you, dear Brother, with the feelings you know he bears for you. He cannot stop talking about the fine bearing of the Polish troops and seems delighted with his stay in Warsaw. We are lost in admiration at the Emperor's speech at the closing of the Diet, for, since we too live in a constitutional country, we are in a position to appreciate its value.[3] About us, I shall only be brief, dear Brother, to let you know that we have been settled for twelve days on the fine estate which the Dutch States gave to William and where we are very happy. The air is dry and very healthy here and the spot is delightful, the house just as much as the woods near by, and in general the entire holding is beautiful and pleasant. My health, which until my arrival here was bad, has entirely

[1] In Russia it was customary to celebrate the 'name-day', i.e. the day in the Church calendar commemorating the saint whose name one bore. The 'name-day' was more important an occasion than the official birthday.

[2] Part of the allied army of occupation in France following the defeat of Napoleon. This occupation force was withdrawn after the meeting at Aix-la-Chapelle in September 1818, when the French were assumed to have met all of the obligations imposed by the victors.

[3] Poland was technically a constitutional monarchy with Tsar Alexander I as the king.

recovered since I have been in a dry place, as humidity is very harmful for me.

Our little fellow, whom I recommend to your affection, dear Brother, is growing and developing a great deal. William is writing you too: I shall say nothing to you from him, but I myself embrace you most tenderly in thought and beg you to count upon my affection for always as I count on yours, dear Brother, being for life your very affectionate and devoted sister.

COPY OF A LETTER FROM THE GRAND DUCHESS ANNA PAVLOVNA TO CATHERINE, QUEEN OF WÜRTTEMBERG:

[Conference of Aix-la-Chapelle]
[September 1818]

Dear good Sister,

William and I are heartbroken that we cannot accept the pleasant and friendly invitation from your husband and yourself to come to Stuttgart and spend some time during our mother's stay there. It would need a very real impediment to prevent us from making use of this mark of your friendship and that of your husband which we appreciate keenly. Man proposes and God disposes; this is really the place to say it because William left me yesterday to spend a month at the camp at Soest which the King has put him in charge of, and he will not return here to the spa until the 15th or 16th of October, new style,[1] so he cannot undertake this charming journey that you propose to us, and he asks me to express his sincere regrets to you. You realise, dear Sister, that without him I should not be able to travel, even if my cure did not provide an obstacle in itself, because it will not be finished until the 8th of October, new style, seeing that my health, although good, needs to be looked after and husbanded in these first months in order to strengthen it completely and not to be as after my first confinement. My[2] mother herself has recommended me to look after myself well, and as

[1] The Russians were on the Julian Calendar, which was twelve days behind the Gregorian Calendar.

[2] In writing to her family Anna Pavlovna nearly always refers to her mother as 'my mother' even if her correspondent was a brother or sister. It rather emphasised family feelings.

she has written that she will be in Brussels on the 20th of October, old style, 1st of November, new style, I shall only just have the necessary time. The Emperor, who is shortly arriving at Aix-la-Chapelle, writes to me that the nearness of this spot will often give him the occasion to see me. So you can see for yourself, dear Sister, that if it is possible for me to take up your pleasant invitation, it would have been doubly agreeable for us to accept because we have twice already missed the pleasure of seeing you. I beg you, dear Sister, to be the intermediary for us both with your husband and tell him how sensible we are of his friendship and invitation, as well as of the sincere regret that we feel at being completely unable to accept it when it would have meant seeing you both in your home and seeing Mama that much sooner.

THE GRAND DUCHESS ANNA PAVLOVNA, THE PRINCESS OF ORANGE, TO THE GRAND DUKE CONSTANTINE:

Brussels,
14 April 1819

. . . I thank you, dear Brother, that you are keeping the promise you made me to write to me more often than in the past. I have found some crosses of the size you wish, exactly matching the design which was in your letter, and some ribbon of the same width as the sample. Here is a piece of it and two crosses. I do not know anything interesting to tell you about us, dear Brother, for our kind of life is as uniform as before and is varied only by the walks we make to take advantage of the magnificent spring we are enjoying. Everything is getting green and the countryside is well out.

I have recently become acquainted with the Duchess of Kent[1] – former Princess of Leiningen – who greatly praised your kindness to her some time ago. We have here the Prince of Löwenstein who, I believe, has the advantage of being known to you, dear Brother, and who is also among those who cherish the memory of having been honoured by you. He was in the Austrian army and it was then, I believe, that he met you. Our

[1] The mother of Queen Victoria and sister of Julia Henrietta of Saxe-Coburg, the wife of the Grand Duke Constantine.

children are growing and prospering; the eldest is a big boy who is chattering and is already becoming a companion for us. We are thinking of going to live in the country soon, and it will be the same place as two years ago, really only a small stopping-place until our own house is finished. I suppose this summer you will make a trip to Petersburg: perhaps Marie will do so too, for Mama really needs this company. Fortunately her health is good, but the poor Countess[1] – your beloved – has been very ill; she is better now but far from being recovered. I am afraid that the trip may have been too much for her.

THE GRAND DUCHESS ANNA PAVLOVNA, THE PRINCESS OF ORANGE, TO THE GRAND DUKE CONSTANTINE:

Brussels,
26 May 1819

Dear Brother,

As Count Batovsky has asked me for a letter for you, I hasten to seize this chance of writing to you. He can give you details about us and tell you about our children whom he often meets in the park where they usually are. Our house is magnificent, but as one is almost never happy here below, we are complaining of the too-fine weather and we want rain for the good of the soil. Next Saturday we are going to move to the country and during next week we shall run into Ghent and come back by way of Antwerp. According to all appearances and our plans, we shall be travelling often this summer, for we shall make another tour of Flanders at the end of the month of June to see Bruges, Ostend, Ypres, and Courtrai, and at the beginning of July we shall have the pleasure of meeting Marie[2] on the Rhine. *The* event here is the inauguration of the new theatre, which took place yesterday; I find it very beautiful to look at but it does not have the comfort and the pleasantness of the old one which, in spite of its old-fashioned air, will I think be generally regretted. You know, dear Brother, through experience, that

[1] Joanna Grudzinska (1781–1831), 'Jeannette', the second wife of the Grand Duke Constantine.

[2] The Grand Duchess Maria Pavlovna.

nothing is more disagreeable than to ruffle habits and comfort. Well, the public had been accustomed for ages to being in the theatre as if they were at home, and in this new theatre in the loges it is like being in public – you cannot chat without being heard. Moreover, the place frivolity holds in this world is great; the more one lives, the more one becomes convinced of it. . . .

THE GRAND DUKE CONSTANTINE TO THE GRAND DUCHESS ANNA PAVLOVNA, THE PRINCESS OF ORANGE:

Warsaw,
15/27 May 1820

Dear Anne,

It was with the greatest excitement, my friend and very dear Sister, that I have just received your kind and charming letter dated 27 April. I could not express my thanks to you as I lack the strength for it, and I just admit to you in all happiness that I wept like a child while reading it. Your good wishes went straight to my heart which is very grateful to you. I shall not go into the motives which made me wish to take action, but shall write here everything which has to do with the matter. Let me tell you purely and simply that I felt I should do it to bring about a permanent solution.[1] It becomes painful to remain separated from my wife and involved in an illegal union as I grow older; a youthful folly may be excused, but at the age of reflection, and especially after the age of forty, it is no longer good. Nor do I feel called to become a monk. Moreover, dear Sister, I am so sure of His Majesty the Emperor that the consequences [are advantageous] for me. May the good Lord grant health, prosperity and long life to the Emperor! Those are my most ardent and most constant wishes. Were I to remarry with a princess of my rank, able to have children, I would be putting them all directly in front of my brother Nicholas. This is repugnant to my conscience and my scruples, especially for him

[1] This letter refers to the decision, approved by Tsar Alexander I, that Constantine should be permitted to divorce his first wife Julia Henrietta of Saxe-Coburg, from whom he had long been separated, and marry the Countess Grudzinska. The latter was to be his morganatic wife. At the same time, although not publicly, Constantine renounced his rights to the throne in favour of his brother Nicholas.

who is married to a Princess of Prussia; that is to say, that the Prussians can never lose sight of the fact that they have a daughter of the house married to a younger son, while the older one would be married to a princess of a less illustrious family. To resolve everything and to give me some peace in a home, I felt it best to seek the hand of a private person who, according to the stipulations of the manifesto of last 20 March, would in no way hinder the established state of affairs. For all this I had the Emperor's authorisation, and since then, in writing, my mother's [blessing?] for the confirmation of the new union which I have just concluded by remarrying a lady of the court named Grudzinska, an astonishing person and kind, a lady of twenty-five or twenty-six years who pleased my mother exceptionally at the time of her visit here. I have sought her for almost six years, and thanks to the goodness of the Lord who has appeared to protect me, I married her on 12/24 May. I am convinced that she would have appealed to you; she is well-bred in all ways. I made my obeisance to the Emperor over this, and I have even asked Mama's forgiveness for the sake of her previous kindnesses towards me. I am happy, content, and I have my home established the way I wish it, with a wife who is not, thank God, a Grand Duchess and does not wish to be one. Time forces me to hurry. Keep kindly thoughts of me, dear, good Sister; you are happy with your family and I am beginning to be so. Protect my wife, whom I place at your feet, and who is made to be loved and known. Tell all this to your husband as well as the reasons which I set forth for you above. Kiss your children for me, and ever count upon the tender and unchanging friendship of your grateful, faithful brother and friend.

TSAR ALEXANDER I TO THE GRAND DUCHESS ANNA PAVLOVNA, THE PRINCESS OF ORANGE:

[Tsarskoe Selo]
9/21 July 1820

It is from the bottom of my heart, dear friend, that I offer you my congratulations on your fortunate delivery. I blessed Divine Providence a thousand times that everything happened so well and so quickly. You cannot doubt my wishes for your speedy and complete convalescence. But I beg you, be serious about sparing yourself and do not be imprudent. I would so much like to clasp you in my arms, and spend a few days with you as we did at Spa or Brussels. But, unfortunately, I cannot even foresee when and how that could be done. It seems to me that it has already been so long that we have been separated.

I am indeed going to undertake a three-month trip, but it is to the interior of the Empire, and, therefore, very far from you. Will you never come to see us? We would be so pleased to receive you and have you at home with us! In the meantime, keep your friendship for me, and count upon the truest and tenderest attachment on my side. Farewell, dear friend, I am yours with heart and soul lifelong. Kiss your children for me, and many kind regards to your Ladies.

THE GRAND DUKE NICHOLAS TO THE GRAND DUCHESS ANNA PAVLOVNA, THE PRINCESS OF ORANGE:

[Pavlosk?]
16/28 July 1820

Receive my sincere congratulations, dear and good Anna, on the occasion of your happy delivery; you know that I love you, so do believe in all the prayers I am making from the bottom of my heart for your happiness, and for that of the new-born babe. I have not been as fortunate as you. You already know from Mama about the cruel accident which happened to my wife which was followed by a miscarriage; the dangers from which she escaped at Peterhof made me less sensitive to the loss which I have had, which at another time would have been very painful for me. God be praised that everything has taken place favourably; she is in her eighth day and all goes well. I am convinced that you are still holding my silence against me, but what can I say to you? You are too sure, I hope, of my feelings, and I count on yours. Moreover, you have been told about everything I am doing by Mama; so what can I tell you which might interest you?

We are going to leave for foreign parts as soon as her

brother has recuperated; then I hope to see you for a few days in Brussels unless you yourself arrive with the Queen[1] in Berlin; pray Heaven that this may be! In any case, I beg you to inform me of your intentions here or in Berlin. I leave here with regret; there are so many things which hold me here, and now more than ever I would not like to leave my homeland. It is really the greatest sacrifice for me to take leave of my excellent wife to whom I owe this great pleasure; I shall be happy if a trip can compensate her for all the sacrifices she has borne for me. My children are really delightful; the little fellow is definitely a soldier; the little girl is becoming a delicious little creature, she has the neck and shoulders worthy of a fifteen-year-old! She turns my head. My boy shoots with a big army-issue rifle and rides horseback with me. What pleasure I shall have at seeing you with your three boys.

THE GRAND DUCHESS ANNA PAVLOVNA, THE PRINCESS OF ORANGE, TO THE GRAND DUKE CONSTANTINE:

Soestdijk,
11 August 1820

. . . Your interesting letter dated 15 May, which you had entrusted to Mr Verstolk to deliver to me, was sent by him as soon as he arrived in this country, and if I have not yet replied to it, attribute my silence only to the condition in which I was this summer, for I gave birth a good deal earlier even than I had expected, and you are not without knowledge of the unfortunate family event which preceded the birth of my little Frederick Henry, who came forth following the emotions which I felt about that [imbroglio]. I have hardly recovered from all that, and I have been upset again these recent days, which completely prevented me from taking pen in hand as I would have wished. Finally, I write today to offer you my wishes for your happiness; may they completely match your desires as well as those wishes which are made for you by people who are most attached to you. The portrait you draw me of Princess Grudzinska's qualities, her age, and her outward advantages

[1] Of the Netherlands.

make me hope that Heaven will bless your union, and as a true sister I can only repeat to you my most sincere good wishes, begging you, dear Brother, to tell the Princess of the interest I bear for her. William, who shares my feelings, desires me to assure you of his affection, and gives you heartfelt thanks for the frequent signs you give him of yours.

At this moment, you are lucky enough to have our dear Emperor in Warsaw and, although I plan to write him, I ask you to greet him tenderly for me, which is what I would like to do in person; but my health forces me to go to Spa as I greatly need to strengthen myself, and those waters and the air of the place always do me good after I have given birth. My children are growing and prospering a great deal; the youngest is still very small and is only a miniature compared to what his brothers were at the same stage. The older ones already have their guns on their shoulders and chatter like Dutch and French magpies.

Miss de Sybourg,[1] who is here, casts herself at your feet to thank you for your former kindnesses towards her. Many thanks, dear Brother, for the work you sent me concerning the Kingdom of Poland.

THE GRAND DUCHESS ANNA PAVLOVNA, THE PRINCESS OF ORANGE, TO TSAR ALEXANDER I:

Brussels,
9 November 1820

Dear kind Brother,

. . . I am very delighted with the hope, of which you give me a glimpse, of the possibility of bringing about our wish to make a trip to Petersburg. The arrangements to be made concerning the children are of chief concern, for you can imagine, dear Brother, that for personal enjoyment I would not be able, without reproaching myself, to leave my children at the risk of what might happen to them. As we would have the eldest with us, it seems to me that the difficulties would be partly diminished,

[1] Julie Toul de Sybourg, known to the family as 'Bourcis', had been the Grand Duchess Anna Pavlovna's governess and had accompanied her to the Netherlands at the time of her marriage to the Prince of Orange.

Queen Anna Pavlovna of the Netherlands in Russian dress, painted by J. C. Valois in 1845

Tsar Alexander I (1777–1825)

but we need your support, for without it the King would certainly put all possible obstacles in our path. I also, definitely, do not want to be in the situation of making this trip without William, for when they see me leaving alone I think that spite would work upon our household, and you can imagine, dear Brother, that from another point of view it would be completely wrong of me to leave William at a time when one has been given the dreadful certainty that ill-will is causing him trouble. At such moments, he has only his home to console him, where trust and certainty are a slight compensation for what he endures from all others. He has the deep feeling of being misunderstood, and often ill-appreciated, and finds in you alone, dear Brother, more kindness and support than in his family. You know that the King did not hesitate to speak to him about *shutting him away* before his trip to Warsaw; knowing that William is exposed to such things, it seems to me that I would be very much to blame at leaving him as I can never count on a similar circumstance not repeating itself. I am, moreover, very much convinced, dear Brother, that you would always prefer me to fulfil my duties to their full extent rather than see me make the slightest fault. So we must trust in Providence, in whom I place all my hope, as much for our happiness here as for the prospect of my trip to Russia. As I know all William's scrupulousness concerning this, you can imagine that it imposes on me the obligation of being more punctilious in my actions, and that I must submit my opinion to you in a most detailed way.

THE GRAND DUCHESS ANNA PAVLOVNA, THE PRINCESS OF ORANGE, TO THE GRAND DUKE CONSTANTINE:

Brussels,
12 February 1821

. . . As you were kind enough to speak to me with some interest about the *attodaphee* [*auto-da-fé*] with which we ended the year,[1] I must tell you that the gazettes have, as usual, very much embroidered upon the details, but that in truth we were in the greatest danger as we had only a few instants to save ourselves;

[1] The royal palace was totally destroyed by fire.

the fire had caught at night without anyone's suspecting it; we attribute it to the heating pipes in the greenhouse. When I escaped, it was burning beside and under me, and a few moments afterwards the corridor through which we had passed fell in. I lost almost everything I possessed, and in the space of a few hours I was reduced to what I had on my body. Brussels society showed us a great deal of hospitality in the crisis, and it is owing to the kindness of several people that we are indebted for a roof for our children and ourselves for three weeks. Now we are living in the house which you occupied with Michael. William bought it as being the most suitable under the present circumstances. For the time being it is sufficient for us and contains us, each of us having our little corner.

THE GRAND DUCHESS ANNA PAVLOVNA, THE PRINCESS OF ORANGE, TO THE GRAND DUKE CONSTANTINE:

Brussels,
28 May 1821

Dear kind Brother,

. . . . May you, dear Brother, enjoy all the happiness you would want for yourself, and I hope, especially, that Divine Goodness grants you some of that felicity which one enjoys in one's home and which is the dearest of all, and one which you well know how to appreciate. I beg you recall me, as well as William, to the mind of your wife. I can still give you the best news of our children who are greatly prospering; the third edition is beginning to walk and will be only a year old in a few days. We had the visit of cousin Naryshkin;[1] he is still the same, gay and kindly, and he is returning to Russia, even being conscience-stricken about getting back soon. The Countess de Lieven[2] has been among us for several days and will come to Spa this summer; her husband went by sea to Petersburg. Mama writes me that Michael will go to take the waters at

[1] Leo Alexandrovich Naryshkin, distantly connected to the imperial family. By custom he was referred to as 'cousin'.

[2] This probably refers to the famous Dorothy Lieven, the wife of the Russian Ambassador to the Court of St James'.

Carlsbad, and that his health is not good; he is in pain on one side, which is beginning to worry us. It appears, moreover, that it is the family illness, for I too have a severe pain in my side – that is pushing sympathy too far –

I cannot prevent myself from telling you of a whim of the *cousin*: he is travelling accompanied by a male and a female parrot for his wife, one of which says *I love you* and the other *faithful* – I really felt a *family* joy at seeing him again and laughing with him. How happy I would be to see you again, dear Brother, but I am afraid that this desire is limited to the wishes I make for it.

THE GRAND DUKE CONSTANTINE TO THE GRAND DUCHESS ANNA PAVLOVNA, THE PRINCESS OF ORANGE:

Warsaw,
31 May/12 June 1822

Accept, dear Sister, my most sincere congratulations for the occasion of your delivery. May the good Lord keep you all, father, mother and children. Your husband's letter reached me the day before I left Vilna where I had been to present my homage to our dear and excellent Queen. Before that, I immediately informed our young brother of it, as he was dining with me. You can imagine our mutual happiness, especially when we learned that everything took place in the most fortunate way possible. I came back here with Michael who is going to the races at Carlsbad. I am delighted to have him here; he is staying until 15 June. Our whole day is spent together and you can well imagine that sadness is banished, and that gaiety and the most intimate and hearty pranks reign all of the time. We are living under one roof and right within reach. Thanks to Heaven, my wife has hurried to my side and is embellishing our reunion with her loveliness, and is the charm of my life. If she had had the good fortune of being known to you, she would certainly have earned your approbation. She asks me to offer you her congratulations as well as all her good wishes. Accept, dear Sister, my thanks for your letter dated 11 May, as well as for everything you said about my name-day. . . .

THE GRAND DUCHESS ANNA PAVLOVNA, THE PRINCESS OF ORANGE, TO THE GRAND DUKE CONSTANTINE:

Brussels,
2 October 1822

Dear kind Brother,

I have been owing you thanks for a long time for your letter dated 24 August; I would have expressed them to you sooner except for the sad circumstances in which we find ourselves, as the youngest of our children has been in the most dangerous condition for nearly three months. We are living in the midst of continuous worries; the poor little one has water in its head, so you can imagine that there is scarcely any probability of preserving it, although everything is possible for divine Providence. I appreciate your kindness with heart and soul, dear Brother, and am very grateful for the trust with which you speak to me; I understand your reasons perfectly and put myself in your place as I feel the delicacy of your situation. I would, however, still be sorry not to have seen Michael, for it has already been four years now since we said good-bye to each other. We arrived here a week ago, and except for our poor little fellow we are all very well. Our two oldest are already big boys and are beginning to take lessons; William has been teaching them to read for a year and now they have been given over to the care of a tutor who comes to instruct them every day, and Papa teaches them geography. The third one is still only playing, but he developed so much when we were in the country that he cannot be recognised. All this makes me feel old, dear Brother, and as you have always known me as little Anna, you would be astonished to see me with such big children. Their tastes are completely military and their greatest pleasure is in shooting guns.

You ask me, dear Brother, from which of us two the lace shawl comes. It is from William who, after learning in Warsaw that your wife liked lace, gave himself the pleasure of offering her this product of this country's industry, and it would be very pleasing to him to know she liked it.

TSAR ALEXANDER I TO THE GRAND DUCHESS ANNA PAVLOVNA, THE PRINCESS OF ORANGE:

Verona,
16 November 1822

You have done justice to my feelings, dear good friend, when I learned of the cruel grief that has bowed you down.[1] My pain was very sincere and it is the same as yours. I know everything your heart must feel! But what touched me beyond any words is the resignation and submission with which you bear your grief as William informs me. That, dear friend, is what it is to fulfil your duties towards the All-Powerful Being from whom we possess everything, and consequently on whom it depends to remove from us everything He has given us. There is always attached to this a merciful purpose which most often we cannot perceive, but which is none the less real in spite of that. Continue, dear good friend, to fortify yourself more and more with these sentiments, bend humbly to the desires of divine Providence, for in doing so you will draw upon the only true consolations which benefit the soul. As for my prayers, they are addressed to God daily for you and for all you hold dear. I pray to Him especially to strengthen your soul at such a moment and to teach you to do His will.

I would so much have wanted to see you again but unfortunately our business here is not yet finished and, as the season is getting on, I am obliged not to prolong my stay outside of Russia as I urgently need to be back in Petersburg in January at least. So tell yourself, dear friend, that if I do not come to Brussels to see you it is through no lack of good will, for I wish to terribly, but solely because it is impossible to do so.

Farewell, dear, good friend. As I cannot hold you in my arms I do so at least in thought, loving you most tenderly. My heart and soul are completely yours for life.

[1] Little Prince Casimir, Anna Pavlovna's son, who had 'water' on the brain, had recently died.

THE GRAND DUCHESS ANNA PAVLOVNA, THE PRINCESS OF ORANGE, TO THE GRAND DUKE CONSTANTINE:

Brussels,
6 March 1823

Dear kind Brother,

. . . I am touched by the kindness you show me and by the trust which you show me by telling me of your domestic happiness and your way of life; I assure you that, although I have not had the pleasure of meeting my sister-in-law, I recognise in her the highest motivations; since by making you happy she has earned real claims to our affection. I thank you too, dear, kind Brother, for the wish you express of seeing us as we pass through Poland on the way to Russia; I am extremely anxious to bring about your plan and I am delighted with it. But it is not this spring but this coming autumn, in the month of October. Our route is not completely fixed yet, and if you permit me I shall tell you about it when it is, for I am clinging too much to the pleasure of seeing you again not to be eager about making the way clear for it. At the end of May or the beginning of June I must go to Ems, where the waters and baths are prescribed for me to recover my health which is not good. I hope that after this cure, from which I am promised marvels, I shall be in condition to undertake the Russian trip, and I shall write you about it immediately.

I do not know, dear Brother, if you remember a young Englishman named Northklif [Northcliffe?] who must have stayed some time in Warsaw. I am only writing to you of him to tell you that he has not stopped praising the kindness you showered on him and has spoken of it to everyone around here, like someone who is deeply grateful. He has returned to his fortunate isle completely delighted with you and Warsaw. Our weather is frightful and the storms do not let up. As for lively pleasures, Lent has interrupted them, but plays and evening parties continue as usual and are frequent. The children, whom you were good enough to remember, are well; they are growing a great deal and are as strong and husky as we could wish.

THE GRAND DUCHESS ANNA PAVLOVNA, THE PRINCESS OF ORANGE, TO THE GRAND DUKE CONSTANTINE:

Schlangenbad,
25 July 1823

Dear kind Brother,

. . . To know that you are happy and contented is perfect bliss for me and I thank you for telling me about it. I see too by the content of your letter that gaiety is the order of the day, and I shall not fail to present arms for you to my boys, with beating drums and sounding trumpets, as you express it, dear Brother. I confess I laughed heartily when I read that passage of your letter, as well as the one in which you speak of life at a watering-place and what a certain famous dead person said about it. But at the same time, to be truthful I must lower my flags before the baths and craters of Ems, which have done me infinite good. For from being feeble and thin as I was, I have become lively even to the point of mounting the donkeys; I do not know whether I dare make this confession to a cavalry general? – But what more do you want; one must, says the proverb, know how to run with the wolves and be content with donkeys for lack of anything faster. My sons were delighted with this kind of amusement, and they were as proud as Sambo on that fine mount. I am at Schlangenbad for what might be called my bleaching, for these waters have a special quality for the skin; but thanks be to Heaven, the day after tomorrow I shall be finished with this aquatic regime in order to return to my hearth full of inexpressible joy at being back after a two-month absence. I have found a compatriot here, Prince Golitsyn,[1] who has a great ambition to be given a post in one of your chancelleries, dear Brother, and asked me to recommend him very strongly to you. This is impossible for me to do as I only know him by sight. The only thing I can say is that he was attached to the Spanish legation which he left two years ago. He is married to a Countess [Koutaisov?], and he is travelling for the sake of his wife's health, all the while complaining, at least in words, about the nomadic life he is leading, and very

[1] Michael Alexandrovich Golitsyn (1804–60), later Russian envoy to Spain.

much wanting to go back into service; he is, into the bargain, a gentleman of the Chamber. That is all the panegyric I can make to you of him as I am not at all the sort to meddle in things which do not concern me. William is at home in the country; as soon as I have joined him I shall tell him all the friendly things your letter has for him, and I know ahead of time that he will be very touched by it.

THE GRAND DUCHESS ANNA PAVLOVNA, THE PRINCESS OF ORANGE, TO TSAR ALEXANDER I:

The Hague,
6 February 1824

Dear and excellent Brother,

William arrived yesterday in perfect health and as happy as possible with his stay in Petersburg; I assure you that you were present in thought at our reunion, for that was almost our first word; and I hasten to thank you for the affection you show me in your dear letter which touched me very much and gave me real pleasure. Many, many thanks too for the charming lithographs of Tsarskoe Selo; this is one of the things which gives me the most pleasure since these are the scenes of the place you are fondest of; hence they are on my table while I am writing to you and will never leave me. The children too were very pleased to see their father again and very happy too to put on the Cossack uniforms which Mama sent to them; how I would have liked to have shown them to you clothed like that! William has told me so many interesting things that I am completely preoccupied with them, and I am living on everything that concerns the family and Petersburg. I blessed God to have William back so well and so happy, and he does not stop talking about it. Excuse me if I put down my pen without finishing my letter. I do not dare to write for long at a time and I have too many things to tell you to finish it completely yet, so I am limiting myself to embracing you tenderly in thought.

10 February

Today, dear Brother, I take up my pen again; until now I

have had much difficulty in writing. The condition I am in[1] and the happy emotion at seeing William again made me incapable of doing anything at all reasonable. He is, thanks to God, completely recovered from the weariness of travelling and happy to find us all in good health. We chat a great deal of you, dear Brother, and of everything that concerns the family, and you can imagine how much that interests me and partly makes up for the deprivation I felt at not being on the spot this year. Everything he tells me about Helen delights me; it is so rare to find a person who combines so many qualities and outward advantages. She wrote me that she was very touched by the way in which the family had welcomed her. I must again thank you, dear Brother, for your kindness in giving up the Moscow visit because of us; you would not believe the pleasure that gives me, I could hardly believe it, not that something good and kind could astonish me coming from you, but because I find that it is a very great concession to put yourself out in such a way for a single individual. I figure that in seven months I shall be near you. What happiness it will be to embrace, to find one another again! I shall take care of myself more than ever this time in order to be more than ever at your disposal during this dear visit over which I am rejoicing with heart and soul. Thanks to everything William tells me, I feel so close to the changes made in the palaces at Petersburg and Tsarskoe Selo, and in the people of society, that it seems to me that I have never left. William told me that you were kind enough to find to your liking the lithographs of this country which I sent you two years ago; that is true indulgence on your part, dear Brother, for I found them so mediocre – especially those which have come out since – not only in the execution but in the small amount of care taken in choosing the scenes that I hardly no longer dared to continue to send them to you; moreover, there is neither a description nor scarcely an indication of the places and those to whom they belong. However, since you still want them I shall send them to you at the first chance which comes up. I am saying nothing to you of my kind of life, for there is no change except for William's presence, but then it is everything for me to be reunited with him and to see him so happy as a result of his visit to Petersburg. I scarcely dare leave my four walls and must

[1] She was expecting another child.

remain very quiet during the two months which remain before my delivery. I shall welcome with pleasure the moment when all that is finished, and I pray Heaven to grant us a healthy child. . . .

THE GRAND DUKE CONSTANTINE TO THE GRAND DUCHESS ANNA PAVLOVNA, THE PRINCESS OF ORANGE:

Warsaw,
28 February/11 March 1824

Do not go and accuse me of laziness or other things, dear Sister, if I have taken such a long time to send you all my wishes and my most sincere congratulations for the occasion of your name-day. But as I was travelling to Petersburg from the second day of this month – rushing night and day for five days to arrive by a very strange chance on the day before our good Michael's wedding, then stopping for fourteen days and travelling for four days to come back – it was completely impossible for me to write earlier. Moreover you know – and to use your own expression – what a fourteen-day visit to Petersburg is like when one is there as a bird of passage, and the pace of life such as they have you lead there. So I am taking advantage of the first moment I have to myself to fulfil a duty which I wanted to perform on the day itself, at the same time urgently requesting you not to hold it against me as I was unable to write this letter earlier. Indeed my brother will already have told you all the details concerning Michael's marriage and it is for that very reason that I have felt it unnecessary to inform you of them in this letter. I shall only tell you that I arrived at Petersburg almost as if it were on purpose on the day before the wedding-day. For certainly I did everything possible not to be present at it considering all the reasons which I fully explained to your husband when he passed through here. I had reckoned that my arrival would come either when the wedding was over or else well beforehand, it not being able to take place until after Easter. Instead of that I discovered that the proverb was right in saying that man proposes and God disposes. In short, I was at the wedding. The Emperor as well as my mother, all the [friends ?] and the entire city were in ecstacies over it, if I may say so, although it is very hard for me to understand it. They were kind enough to attribute to me the improvement which has taken place in Michael's attitude towards his wife, since I found that she was very likeable. It seems to me that it is wronging my brother to say that I influence him so hugely in these opinions. In short, as at Vilna, I was showered with praise and thanks which were hardly deserved as I did nothing, said nothing which might bring criticism down on me, and my only true merit consists merely in arriving by chance. As for our new Sister-in-Law, I found her very likeable in every way and especially in private. In public she has a very noble bearing and expresses herself wonderfully well; is to the point and [touching ?], added to which is a charm which suits her. In spite of this she is less capable of discretion than Nicholas's wife. As far as I was able to judge, she is very witty and feels things very keenly and intensely, with a great deal of sensitivity. In short she pleases me greatly in every respect. As for Michael, he is incomprehensible to me. In spite of the fact that he could love his wife, he maintains a unique coldness and unawareness towards her. Whether it is the newness of the situation, shyness or another reason, I was not able to make it out, and to every question which I asked him about it he always answered me in such a way as to make me think that he was pleased. Thus, I took my leave of them, carrying away with me the conviction that the married state is an accessory which he might have been able to do without. I hope that in time there will be a real change in this regard. The two things he cares about are giving service and sleeping. The rest hardly concerns him. You know, dear Sister, of the sincere affection and closeness I have for Michael and consequently do not doubt the good wishes I am making for his happiness. Both of them deserve to be so in every way. But the one thing about which I warned Michael is his wife's intelligence which, in my opinion, is much superior to what it is believed to be. She has many decisions to make on various matters. At the time of my visit in Petersburg I was overwhelmed by kindness, considerateness, obligingness and friendliness by everyone without exception, starting with the Emperor and my mother . . . , so my gratitude is fully offered to her. And I admit that I cannot get over it as I myself have absolutely no way of knowing what could have involved me in such a state of affairs. While on the road, I received your letter in reply to the one which I had written to you through your husband; please accept my thanks for it. Give my greetings to your excellent husband whom I love with all my heart and soul, and tell him that I was very touched by his behaviour toward my wife who is very sincerely fond of him. My hugs to the three nephews. I hope that shortly a fourth one will come to increase their number.

THE GRAND DUCHESS ANNA PAVLOVNA, THE PRINCESS OF ORANGE, TO TSAR ALEXANDER I:

The Hague,
2 March 1824

Dear good Brother,

Although I wrote you a little while ago, I could not know of your illness without telling you of all the concern we both felt and how happy I am to learn from Mama's letters that you are better; she is kind enough to keep me posted on the state of your health. God be praised, dear Brother, that you are recovered and that you spare yourself as you do; erysipelas is very disagreeable while it lasts, but I have seen cases where it has only been a guarantee of health for the future and I have hopes in Divine Goodness that this will be so; I assure you that our good wishes for you are most sincere and most constant. I wait for each of Mama's letters with the keenest impatience and I hope to receive one tomorrow in which I may be lucky to find the news that your health is entirely recovered. I am very touched, dear good Brother, at your remembrance; since Mama writes in every letter that you entrust her to send your affection, I thank you tenderly for it. The chapter on our acts and deeds is hardly of much interest, for uniformity is our motto; the pleasure of chatting with William is my chief pleasure and, thanks to the Lord, I am feeling much better now than during the rest of the winter, which makes me hope for the happiness of having a healthy child. Our big boys are in excellent health and I dare say for all things concerned; yesterday they had the pleasure of receiving the Russian Hussars' uniforms of the regiment you gave to William, which Mama sent them. They were extremely delighted to try them on and they suit the two eldest very well; Henry is still too small but he nevertheless put his on and thought himself very handsome. I think the eldest will have very much his father's figure, and as for Alexander, he has the face of a fine jolly fellow and still does not look like anyone, but he is a nice boy, as comic as possible. I am still wishing that there may be some congress in our neighbourhood purely for the pleasure of introducing to you this little battalion which I would be very happy to show you; for myself, I hope to be reunited with you in seven months, dear Brother, and I am very often carried away in thought to that happy time. Today we have had a sample of the Russian winter because of the snow which fell last night and which stayed for a few hours; such is the month of March with its usual charms, for we had already enjoyed some fine days and the trees were beginning to leaf. Here is a letter which has taken on a dimension which makes me afraid of taking advantage of your patience, dear Brother, so I finish it with a tender greeting for you.

THE GRAND DUKE NICHOLAS TO THE GRAND DUCHESS ANNA PAVLOVNA, THE PRINCESS OF ORANGE:

11/23 April 1824
at St Petersburg

Receive my congratulations, dear friend, for your new and felicitous motherhood;[1] I rejoice in it with all my heart for you; you are going to have a companion for your later years, and over there [in the Netherlands] that is really what is done, considering the ease with which young ladies are settled down in your country; an immense and invaluable advantage for those who have daughters. My little damsels are very sweet each in their own way; none of them resembles any one of the others although the youngest is like her brother. The latter has been developing a great deal for several months. You perhaps already know that your old acquaintance Julie Baranova is the governess

[1] The birth of Princess Sophie.

for my little girls, which suits me perfectly. I very much hope to be as fortunate for my boy who requires someone very sensible near him; he has an angelic but very absent-minded character, so one must combine kindness with firmness in order to be useful to him.

When are you planning to come here, and are you coming all alone or with some of the children? Marie has not yet set a date for her arrival and it would be delightful if you were to come at the same time. I have not yet seen my comrade [Hasp ?], but I am expecting him very shortly. [Later] I have seen him, he gave me the best news of you all, and I shall do what I can to make his stay less boring; he seems to be a very brave loyal soldier, very simple and open.

I say nothing to you about Michael's household, but Mama certainly must speak to you about it. He is working hard now to get children for them, but it appears that this is still unsuccessful. They do seem to be in perfect agreement which makes us all very happy. You know through William how things were in his time, so you can imagine all the joy this fortunate change has made us feel. God grant that it may continue to last; progeny especially would do them a lot of good.

I beg you to give a thousand kind regards to William, and I thank both of you for the title of godfather to your little girl. Please give my best to the Citizeness [Sybourg] and to all yours.

TSAR ALEXANDER I TO THE GRAND DUCHESS ANNA PAVLOVNA, THE PRINCESS OF ORANGE:

Tsarskoe Selo,
12/24 April 1824

Receive, dear Sister, my most tender congratulations upon such a fortunate delivery and the birth of your Maria Sophia. I felt extremely joyful about it and from the depths of my heart thank Divine Providence, asking only for your rapid and complete recovery and for the child to grow and prosper to your satisfaction.

All yours with heart and soul for life.

THE GRAND DUKE CONSTANTINE TO THE GRAND DUCHESS ANNA PAVLOVNA, THE PRINCESS OF ORANGE:

Warsaw,
3/15 July 1824

Accept, dear Sister, my very sincere thanks for your good kind letter dated 21 May, as well as for the good wishes which you so kindly make for me on the occasion of my name-day. I am certain that they will bring me good luck as they come to me from you, dear Sister. . . . You will be very astonished to learn, dear Sister, through this letter, of my wife's sudden appearance at the waters of Ems. Doctor [Griffé ?] of Berlin, who came to spend some time with us, made us decide upon the trip to settle the patient's jangled nerves. . . . I frankly admit that I am very sorry to see her go but nothing ventured, nothing gained. As for me, I shall leave the same day as my wife to make my tour of inspection in Lithuania and Valhynia. I wrote to the Emperor to obtain permission from him to pick up my wife once my duty is done and I hope and trust that I shall receive it. What makes me think I shall is that during the past twenty-nine years that I have been on active service I have not had a single leave of absence of any consequence, while others have had them. My wife's health is fairly good at the moment but her nerves must be strengthened. If she is lucky enough to meet you some time during her travels, please take her under your protection and give her your friendship as she already has that of your husband. My tender and sincere affection to your husband, dear Sister, and kiss your children for me. Do not forget me and always count on the sincere affection of your faithful brother and friend.

THE GRAND DUKE CONSTANTINE TO THE GRAND DUCHESS ANNA PAVLOVNA, THE PRINCESS OF ORANGE:

At the Bath at Ems,
2/14 August 1824

Accept all my thanks, dear Sister, for your kind good letter and for the interest which you so kindly take in my wife. If she is not replying to you herself it is because she is extremely weak and that all work is expressly forbidden to her. However, thank God, since she has been here her state has slightly improved. I cannot imagine where and how she was able to recover her health to such a point. Day follows day, and one is scarcely like another. For example, three days ago my wife was able to take the air, both on foot and on a donkey, [after ?] that she spent the other day entirely in bed. Yesterday the day was exciting and I do not yet know what today will be like. Your kind suggestion of coming to see us in Coblenz would have given us great happiness and if my wife's health does not put any obstacles in the way we shall go there without fail. In any case I shall go there, dear Sister, and I am already rejoicing [at the thought of] embracing you as well as your husband to whom I beg you to give my kindest greetings. In the meantime, will he be so good as to keep his affection for me. As for what concerns me, I have nothing very interesting to tell you. I am playing the role of nurse; the rest of the time I am so bored I could swallow my tongue. All the beautiful views and the valleys and mountains of the Lahn shores are not at all to my taste and especially not the *far-niente* life which is led in these regions, I shall bless the Heavens when I shall be able to get out of them and my wife completely recovered. I confess that the days are very long during the treatments and I cannot imagine how there are so very many people who find such a life pleasing. . . . Please give me four days previous notice before the day you intend to go to Coblenz so that I can be there for certain. . . .

THE GRAND DUCHESS ANNA PAVLOVNA, THE PRINCESS OF ORANGE, TO MLLE DE SYBOURG:

Soestdijk.
6 August 1824

My dear Bourcis,

Here I am, I have arrived in this dear spot and am reunited with my dearest darlings since last Saturday, 31 July. I found all my family in good health and my little girl has grown tall and fat in my absence. William came to meet me in the fog and my three boys received me on the steps holding bouquets from their gardens. These are trifles perhaps, but these trifles are dearer to me than anything in the world, and I neither know or can imagine true happiness other than like this in the middle of one's family and in all simplicity. The next day, which was the day before Alexander's birthday, we gave him our gifts in the evening and of them all, the one that gave him most pleasure was your billiard table; so you have attained your end and we were delighted by the pleasure that this great news would give you. The King and Queen were kind enough to come here for dinner on the birthday itself, and in the evening there were fireworks on the other side of the water opposite the house. Alexander was enchanted. Our little girl has beautiful eyes and a fine complexion, a great deal of vivacity and a healthy look, thank Heaven, which it gives one pleasure to see. We are planning a drive to the zoo at the end of this week. . . . The Prince asks me to send you his kind regards, dear Bourcis, and I embrace you tenderly.

THE GRAND DUCHESS ANNA PAVLOVNA, THE PRINCESS OF ORANGE, TO MLLE DE SYBOURG:

Pavlovski,
2/14 October 1824

My dear Bourcis,

Here then is the first letter that I have written to you since I had the happiness of being near Mama again and in my native country. In the first few days I did not have a moment to give you my news myself, so I asked Mlle Nicholls[1] to do so, begging her to inform you that we had arrived safely. Mama was kind enough to come to meet us two stations before Gatchina, and as we had done the journey from Kovno to here in five and a half days we were four days in advance of the date fixed for our arrival. You can imagine the happiness that I feel in finding myself again with Mama and seeing again so many people I

[1] A lady-in-waiting.

know. Mama, the Countess [Lieven],[1] and the ladies ask for your news and Mama asks me to send you her compliments. My sister-in-law Helen has a great deal of wit, she has a beautiful [blank in the original] and resembles the late Queen of Prussia in the shoulders. Nicholas' children are very sweet and Olga, the youngest, is a beauty. I found Mesdames Baranova and Faubert looking after the little girl. Our Countess is always the same, but still gentler and more obliging than in Brussels. She told me that *you were une fatale*! General Chernyshev is with William and so is Colonel Dournov, an aide-de-camp of the Emperor. My old Nuchka is still the same and is carrying out the same duties for me as before. The weather has hardly been clement since our arrival; snow has fallen and the air as in December at Brussels. All Gatchina is as it used to be and is in the same place; however, I am not in my old chambers but in the ones occupied long ago by my sister Alexandrine and the Archduke after their marriage,[2] which, as it has a door adjoining my mother's, is a very agreeable arrangement for us. The Countess is underneath where she used to be previously, and Madame de Wassenaer and her daughter-in-law occupy the apartment in which you used to be. As it is always necessary here for everything to be mingled with some sorrow, we experienced that at not seeing the Emperor who has not returned from his long tour in the interior of the country, but he is expected toward 22 October and the news of his health is excellent. I have still to speak to you of Mr de Stouts [?] who asks about you a great deal, and Mr Aledinsky [?] whose recollection of you will give you pleasure; Mr Oberkov [?] is here, still the same, and Mr de Vilamov, who also has grown old, is as amiable as when you knew him. They all showed such joy at seeing me again that it was indeed touching. I must not forget Mlles Divov [?] and Katcholov [?] who are as they were when you left. Good-bye, dear Bourcis; I hope that you will be satisfied by the length of my letter and the details in it. William sends you his friendly regards.

[1] 'The Countess' was Charlotte de Lieven (1743–1828), the former *gouvernante* of the elder daughters of Tsar Paul. She was the confidante of Empress Maria (Mama) and an intimate friend of all of the imperial family. She was the mother-in-law of the famous Princess de Lieven.

[2] Alexandra Pavlovna (1783–1801) married Archduke Joseph in 1799.

THE GRAND DUCHESS ANNA PAVLOVNA, THE PRINCESS OF ORANGE, TO THE GRAND DUKE CONSTANTINE:

Gatchina,
28 October/9 November 1824

My dear Brother,

. . . I had planned to take up my pen to give you news of the Emperor as soon as I saw him again. We had that happiness on 24 October, and I can say that it was a day of rejoicing mixed with much emotion as I have not seen the Emperor for six years. I find that he looks very well and his health is good although once again a small wound has formed recently on his leg; this is attributed to a lack of foot exercise on the last part of his tour, during which there were humid days which had prevented him from walking. The Emperor seems so delighted with his expedition that he takes pleasure in hearing it talked about, and the satisfaction he displays at seeing us again is truly touching.

THE GRAND DUCHESS ANNA PAVLOVNA, THE PRINCESS OF ORANGE, TO MLLE DE SYBOURG:

Petersburg
10/22 November 1824

My dear good Bourcis,

It is affection that puts pen in my hand and the wish to reassure you about us all after the terrible flood that has just spread desolation in Petersburg. I would not like you, dear friend, to hear news of this nature through the *Gazette*. We are all well and no one in the family has been exposed to the slightest danger. The catastrophe was caused by a violent sea wind which caused the Gulf of Finland to overflow, and the Neva River was driven back contrary to its natural direction. It overflowed all over the quays outside the canals so that in the space of one hour the square in front of the Winter Palace, the boulevard and the streets which lead to the Palace showed a terrible sight of a raging sea with waves and eddying water. The Winter Palace appeared to be an island battered by the waves. Towards evening the water disappeared reasonably quickly, but imagine the consequences and the disasters. I have not the time, dear friend, to tell you more, only know that we are well and that the Emperor is truly like a father in trying to help his children. All possible activity is directed to assisting the unfortunate.

THE GRAND DUCHESS ANNA PAVLOVNA, THE PRINCESS OF ORANGE, TO THE GRAND DUKE CONSTANTINE:

Petersburg,
30 January/11 February 1825

. . . These last few days I have frequently seen several of your old acquaintances and *brothers-in-arms*, among others, Generals Potapov and Tchitcherin, and you can well imagine that we speak of you and are sorry you are not with us. During carnival-time pleasures have been taken up again at their usual pace; there were several plays at Mama's and one at the Hermitage where we missed you: without my willing it, my eyes went to the place where you used to stand at the entrance of the theatre. There were also dances at Mama's, in the Service Hall; on Michael's birthday there was a magnificent one in the White Room which amazed everyone around us. Mama is planning to give two more balls, one of which will be a ball-let, as Michael has labelled the little balls. There will be a play for us in the big theatre and a masquerade at the Winter Palace. I hope that that will be enough for the admirers and those who are curious.

Without being in either one or the other category, I confess to you that I am delighted to see a masquerade again, as it is the most national of pleasures, and that I greatly enjoy seeing our fine beards again. You must know, dear Brother, that while I am in the midst of worldly pleasures here, as Michael says, my little girl is doing very well at home as are our three big boys; William, who often gives me news of them, is very pleased with them and I hope that in six or seven weeks we shall see him here again. As happy as one may feel in the midst of one's family and one's homeland, you can imagine that a husband and four children are strong ties of affection whom it is natural to want to see again. I dare not hope that you will make a trip to Petersburg this year, and yet I would be very sorry, dear Brother, to give up completely this prospect.

TSAR ALEXANDER I TO THE GRAND DUCHESS ANNA PAVLOVNA, THE PRINCESS OF ORANGE:

[*This letter is headed by a note in Anna Pavlovna's handwriting:* 'This letter contains the flattering opinion that Emperor Alexander had of the Prince of Orange, my husband.']
I am most appreciative, dear good friend, of your kind letter and all the friendly things for me in it. My heart repays you for it most sincerely. It is with profound grief that I read the description in William's letters of the disasters that have struck the Low Countries. Please express to him all the sympathy that I feel concerning them. I am delighted that the King authorised him to go to these places. That makes me certain that measures for assisting the unfortunate will be taken promptly and with sagacity, for I have great confidence in William's heart and head. I have written to him by your last courier. I enclose here two despatches that came to me after we had left each other and which give almost the same details. I assure you, dear friend, that it costs me a great deal not to see you these days. I must say that it is a true privation for me but duty demands it, and you have no idea of the business that I am getting through here. All yours for life with heart and soul.

Alexander
[Saskotella?]
17 February/1 March 1825

A thousand things to your ladies.

THE GRAND DUCHESS ANNA PAVLOVNA, THE PRINCESS OF ORANGE, TO THE GRAND DUKE CONSTANTINE:

St Petersburg,
27 April/9 May 1825

Dear kind Brother,

. . . According to the latest news from Warsaw, it appears that she [Jeannette] is well and I am sincerely delighted about that. You will be happy to have the Emperor with you for some time yet and to show him the fine troops you have trained, and, according to all those who see them, they are magnificent!

I hope that the weather is more favourable for you than for us here where it is still very cold; however, I think that we are going to move to Pavloski next week. Your birthday was celebrated with a big dinner-party which Mama gave at the Winter Palace where I had the pleasure of seeing your former aides-de-camp and service friends such as Tchitcherin, General Potapov and Orlof. – We remembered that formerly, *in the good old days*, that day used to be celebrated in the [Tauridan ?] way! and that at that time I remember you already held a protecting hand over your little sister, and that since then you have shown me an affection which is very dear to me, which I beg you to keep on giving me, dear Brother. The Winter Palace seems rather like a seraglio since the departure of our dear Emperor and William; my brothers are so busy and for us, at least, feminine society triumphs over all other company.

TSAR ALEXANDER I TO THE GRAND DUCHESS ANNA PAVLOVNA, THE PRINCESS OF ORANGE:

Warsaw,
23 May/4 June 1825

It was with infinite pleasure, dear friend, that I received your letter and that I found again in it the expression of an affection which does me so much good, and to which I believe I have some right in return for that which I bear for you so openly. I want to tell you too that being deprived of the pleasure of seeing you and spending a few moments every day with you is very trying for me; in a word, I miss you a great deal. So the last mail which brought me your letter gave me deep satisfaction.

William has arrived here with us, perfectly healthy and apparently very happy from his stay in Moscow. I am delighted that our former capital pleased him; it is worthy of exciting interest. You will easily understand all the joy I feel at being reunited with William; when one knows him one must love him, and it is what I am doing too with all my heart. He showed me your last letter, dear friend. With my usual frankness I want to tell you that it caused me some distress because of your impatience to leave us, not that I misunderstand the motives and the kind of feeling which causes this, but think how rare and far-spaced are our opportunities to be together again!

Here, thank Heaven, everything could not be better; the temper is excellent and the Diet operated as well as one could wish. In nine days I hope to set off to come back to you, and you can certainly imagine the impatience with which I await the moment when I shall find myself with you again. Farewell until then, dear friend, count upon the tenderest friendship from me. Kind regards to your Ladies.

THE GRAND DUCHESS ANNA PAVLOVNA, THE PRINCESS OF ORANGE, TO TSAR ALEXANDER I:

Naron [?]
26 July/7 August 1825

Dear and most excellent Brother and friend,

I feel it essential to tell you again, and in writing, of all my regret at leaving you. I cannot become accustomed to the idea that I shall not see you for a long time, and it still seems to me that we shall meet in a little while. May God watch over you and grant you the most precious blessings, may He return to you all the goodness you have given us and me with your advice which shall be dear to me to the last day of my life. I am filled with the desire to follow it, wanting nothing in my future but the preservation of all those who are dear to me and of everything as it is now, and that Providence grant me the means of contributing as best as I can to William's happiness, to *family union* and to the general good. Continue to send me your advice in writing and your opinions if anything unfavourable reaches your ears.

May our two brothers, Nicholas and Michael, take our place near you, this is what we both most desire, and as for Michael, I must say that I left him with a very heavy heart, because I wish he were happier in his domestic situation.

That will come with time, if God so pleases, and it will be the result of their mutual behaviour. I beg you, dear Brother, to embrace that good Michael for me. I am very touched by all the affection he displayed for me, as well as Nicholas, for whom I am at ease for he has everything to make him happy. Many many affectionate regards for the Empress and many good wishes for her, we await with sincere concern and with much interest what will be decided by the tour. We are going to start out again by carriage so I am finishing these very blotted lines.

TSAR ALEXANDER I TO THE GRAND DUCHESS ANNA PAVLOVNA, THE PRINCESS OF ORANGE:

Tsarskoe Selo,
29 July/10 August 1825

I pen these lines to you, dear good friend, to thank you for those which Chernyshev gave me from you, but especially for all the friendship which you displayed for me the whole time we spent together. I am also writing to William, but I need you to repeat to him again from me how deeply I was moved by the extremely kind offers he made me in your letter. I count upon him as upon a true friend, the two of you have in me one who cherishes you with all the facets of his soul. . . .

THE GRAND DUCHESS ANNA PAVLOVNA, THE PRINCESS OF ORANGE, TO TSAR ALEXANDER I:

Tervueren,
10 September 1825

Dear and very excellent Brother!

I write you with a feeling of happiness and joy which words can only weakly convey, at finding myself again with William and the dear children whom I find delightful. The children came to meet me with their father at Liége where I arrived last Monday, and Tuesday here where I disembarked at the home of my Sophia whom I find very pretty and sweet although rather small; after greeting her we went to see the Queen and the meeting took place in the street, and I can certainly say that I was welcomed like a *true* child returning to its family. The King too was so affectionate, so joyful and we were all so moved that one can feel it better than express it. I met Louise,[1] who made a very favourable impression on me, not because of her face, which even struck me with its ugliness, but because of her way of being calm and dignified; far from being cold towards me, I found her as demonstrative as I could wish, not *in any way* resembling the rest of her family, neither in face or bearing, for she is sedate and not at all sneering. I bless God for that! I am undertaking, dear excellent friend, to follow your advice, and as I feel more than ever the importance of daily behaviour and of my way of life here, I crossed our frontier praying Heaven to bless my resolutions and to inspire me in everything. I assure you that I found everything just as I could wish it; to begin with the most important, William is overwhelming me with affection and attention, my children are delightful, the family could not be better, and at all the stops, people seem to be pleased to see me again, each one shows me that in his own way, to the extent that I am astonished and very much touched. I find a cordiality which is precious to me. The King looks very well, but the Queen has become very thin and aged, Frederick too – who seems to enjoy perfect calm at home. Louise is very suitable in all ways and seems to be good and sensitive to

[1] Louise of Prussia (1808–70) married Prince Frederick of Orange in 1825.

behaviour. She paid me a visit; we were at their residence, and invited them to the theatre in our box; there I was completely surprised at the kind welcome of the public – you know that here that is the way they show if they are well-disposed or not. I found all my colony[1] going marvellously well, and my priest and Harry [?] grateful and moved to tears at everything you had the kindness to do for them. Madame de Nagel is very good in her situation and really she has taken infinite care of our little girl, who is a sweet child. Pauline is all right but weak, and cannot praise enough the care which the lieutenant [?] took over her trip; Countess Cornelia[2] is marvellously well, and both of them, as well as all those who are returning from Russia, big and small, cannot stop showing their satisfaction with the kindness of which they were the recipients.

THE GRAND DUCHESS ANNA PAVLOVNA, THE PRINCESS OF ORANGE, TO TSAR ALEXANDER I:

Soestdijk,
20 September 1825

I am reopening this letter, dear kind Brother, because of the delay undergone by the mail which has been directed by way of Warsaw, so I took my epistle out of Mama's letter in which I had included it and am sending it to you directly. Moreover, I know too well your affection for our dear William not to be convinced of the way in which you share the joy we feel at his recovery! He caused us the greatest concern for several days as he had been attacked by a strong fever and a chest cold which came close to being an inflammation. Thanks to God and the promptness of the remedies, he overcame the illness, but you can imagine our feelings. He recovered quickly, and nothing is left now but some weakness and a little nervous agitation. We must hope that the change of air and place will help him regain his strength, for our departure for Tervueren is set for tomorrow. My heart is heavy at leaving this spot of which I am so fond, to go where my heart does not lead me; and instead

[1] Her immediate entourage – specifically her Russian attendants.
[2] Daughter of Countess Sophie van Wassenaer and member of the Grand Duchess's household.

of the former *good Brussels winter* I now say the *painful* and *difficult winter* in a place where we *only have time-servers*; and for me to submit myself to a kind of life which goes against my tastes, which cannot become accustomed to a place where I find no stability of feeling! Farewell, dear good Brother, keep your remembrance and affection for me so that this feeling may be like a port in which I can always anchor my heart and thoughts.

THE GRAND DUCHESS ANNA PAVLOVNA, THE PRINCESS OF ORANGE, TO TSAR ALEXANDER I:

Tervueren,
Sunday, 21 September 1825

Dear Brother and friend,

I take up my pen again to congratulate you with heart and soul on your name-day; may Heaven bless and return to you all the goodness you do through both your kindness and your advice; and may the happiness which you establish for other people be imminent in everything so as to add it to your own. All that I can say to you is that my good wishes for you are made every moment and that they originate in a most sincere attachment and gratitude which will only end with my life. In what place will you spend the day? I do not think that it will be at Petersburg, for I suppose that you will be in a hurry to escape from the day's ceremonies, and as Mama writes me that you are going on ahead of the Empress, I do not know where to find you. I learned of this decision with emotion; God be willing that it is salutary for the Empress[1] to whom I send tender greetings; dear Brother, offer her all my good wishes; I would have liked to write to her but I lack the time, as soon as I have some leisure I shall take pen in hand to give them to her myself. These days are filled with social duties which scarcely allow one to draw breath. How distant are we going to be from each

[1] The journey to Taganrog was made in the hope that Tsar Alexander's wife would recover her health. The tour had special significance beyond this since the imperial couple had been on somewhat formal terms only with each other, and this journey indicated that the reconciliation, which had occurred a short time before, was real and complete.

other? It makes one heartsick, for with every pleasant thing which happens to us, every time we see something fine and happy, we think of you and exclaim that that would give joy to or would please our mutual friend. As I like you to know everything, I shall tell you that I am keeping *my moral order* in connection with my ladies, that I am doing what I can to make their lot pleasant, and that I am doing my best to choke back that dear impatience which is in my blood and is certainly my greatest enemy; pray for me, dear friend, so that Heaven may answer my efforts. One more word to tell you how much I have found Tervueren embellished, cared-for and completed; the colonnade has been adorned by William with screens of climbing plants like those at Petersburg; it was a surprise he was keeping for us. We lunch there, surrounded by our four children. The little girl is absolutely sweet, her eyes are a very dark blue with long black lashes which delight me, I must confess. Farewell, dear Brother, dear friend, come to see us, that would make us happy, you would at least find here cordiality and much simplicity; I hope this wish will come about some day. Keep your affection, trust and remembrance for me, and allow someone to send us regular news of the Empress's health, it would be a real service to us.

I am leaving for town immediately to attend mass, and the whole day will be filled up with receptions; there will be a dinner at Laeken and the theatre where Talma[1] will be playing, so that I shall be sleeping in town and shall not come back here until tomorrow morning.

THE GRAND DUCHESS ANNA PAVLOVNA, THE PRINCESS OF ORANGE, TO TSAR ALEXANDER I:

Tervueren,
9 October 1825

Dear and most excellent Brother,

It is in the utmost haste that I take up my pen to take advantage of the mail in order to tell you how happy and satisfied I am,

[1] Joseph François Talma (1763–1826), a French actor who was particularly celebrated for his performances in tragic roles. His special attributes were his fine appearance and above all his magnificent voice and diction.

and to assure you that the affection I bear you, and that with which you have showered me, acts as my guide in my desire to do what is good and to follow your advice. I resort, constantly, for everything and in everything to Divine Providence, and when I feel irritable and impatient I raise myself towards it, and I find that afterwards I feel a calmness and an ease in overcoming myself which could not come except from that. But I must tell you how pleased I am with the feelings I find in the family and in all those whom I have occasion to see; and I can say that I am surrounded only by every appearance of the most sincere good will. I am very touched by the behaviour of the King and Queen who seem to have taken it to heart to act in the same way towards the two sisters-in-law, and concerning this I was very moved during the King of Prussia's visit during which our King and Queen did not cease to show me a very great deal of affection. I came back to find them even more affectionate than I had left them. I am – if I dare make use of this expression – very pleased with my sister-in-law whom I have examined closely at home with us, at Tervueren and in general in different houses, and I must say that she is as suitable, quiet and dignified as I can wish, without appearing to sneer or mock, or disparage in any way at all; quite the contrary, she admires the country a great deal and praises everything that is praiseworthy. I confess to you that I am delighted that she in no way resembles the rest of her family. Far from being cold, she is very sensitive to behaviour and affection, and I tell to you in all confidence that she and Fritz have thanked me several times for my way of acting with Louise. I have taken it to heart, dear Brother, to follow your advice in this situation and it is the subject of my devout prayers. As dear William's happiness cannot consist of, or be stabilised on, anything but a union of goodness and security, I am trying my best to watch over every detail of my behaviour; my worst difficulties are with myself and more than anything I fear my impetuous character and susceptibility; so I have only one resource and a single hope to overcome this, which is to constantly implore Divine Providence. – That is our present situation. . . . Keep sending me, dear Brother, your affection, your remembrance and your advice; make note to me of what you hear about us and I beg you, tell me about Michael's marriage which is the subject of my most sincere concern; you, better than anyone, know how to discern the truth so I count on you to tell me how they are getting along together.

I add two words to tell you that I must in all fairness do justice to the Prussian princes who were very decent during their visit here, and I had no occasion to notice the disagreeable traits[1] which formed the subject of my conversations. In general, this business of the King's visit worked out well.

[A NOTATION IN THE PAPERS OF ANNA PAVLOVNA, THE PRINCESS OF ORANGE.]

19 November, Tuesday

At the dinner-hour there arrived the letter of 5 November of His Majesty the Emperor, which announces His return from Taganrog with a slight indisposition.

18 November, Wednesday, in the evening Grand Duchess Helen received a letter from Her Majesty the Empress Elizabeth, of the 9th, which begs her to inform Her August Mother that the Emperor is feeling better and that She is not writing to Her so as not to appear to give too much importance to this indisposition.

The 22nd Sunday during the morning there arrived the letter from Her Majesty the Empress Elizabeth, of the 12th, which speaks of a recurrence of His Majesty the Emperor's fever, which was preventing him from writing himself, but She adds that within a couple of days She hopes to be able to speak of other less important things.

The evening of the same day, Wylie's[2] bulletin from the 4th to the 12th gave rise to many anxieties: He says that the fever, which he characterises as a gastric bilious one, after being intermittent, had become continuous from the 11th to the 12th and was accompanied by some alarming symptoms.

Wednesday, the 25th: at eight o'clock in the evening the letter of 15 November was received in which Baron Diebitch[3] speaks of the progress of the fever, which he designates as

[1] As a family, the Hohenzollerns were thought to be pushing and somewhat arrogant, excessively proud and rather generally lacking in grace and tone. These views applied particularly to the male members of the family.

[2] The court physician.

[3] Ivan Ivanovich Diebitsch (1785–1831), chief military councillor to Tsar Alexander I. He accompanied the Tsar on all of his numerous travels.

bilious: he says that from being intermittent it had become continuous and increased on the 13th and 14th and that finally the Emperor's condition appeared so alarming that on the 15th those who were with him advised that the Holy Sacrament be administered; the Emperor took it with his usual piety and spiritual strength. Since then, remedies have been used which reduced the fever somewhat; the doctors were not losing all hope, but did not hide the fact that the noble patient's condition was very dangerous.

Thursday the 26th at noon: at the end of Mass the Courier arrived bearing the letter of Her Majesty the Empress Elizabeth, of the 17th, announcing that there is a decided improvement in the Emperor's condition, which was confirmed by a private letter from Prince Volkonsky,[1] who added that in the morning the Emperor recognised the people who were around him and spoke in a fairly strong voice to the Empress. Wylie says in his bulletin of the same date, the 17th, that through the use of extreme remedies, they managed to arouse the Emperor from the comatose condition into which he had lapsed, which increases hope.

The evening of that same day there arrived a letter and a bulletin from Wylie, of the 16th, showing that the Emperor was that day at the last extremity with very alarming symptoms, but as that bulletin was delayed, the improvement of the following day, the 17th, was already known.

Finally on the 27th, between 11 o'clock and noon, there arrived news of the greatest sorrow. His Majesty the Emperor died on 19 November [O.S.], Thursday, at 10.50 A.M.

THE GRAND DUCHESS ANNA PAVLOVNA, THE PRINCESS OF ORANGE, TO THE GRAND DUKE CONSTANTINE:

The Hague,
27 December 1825

Dear kind Brother,

You will imagine what emotion I feel as I form these words after the frightful blow which has just struck us all; and you, dear Brother, whom I have seen so happy, I pity you from the

[1] Peter Michaelovich Volkonsky (1776–1852), a personal friend of Tsar Alexander I.

bottom of my heart as I am convinced that as Providence guided you, you have acted according to a conviction of your duty and that that feeling will give you moral courage and serenity which can only be felt by fulfilling it. My good wishes and my prayers are with you, and I shall add the sincere affection I bear for you as a true sister, whatever the events may be. I hope that out of affection, dear Constantine, you will believe that my feelings for you are completely independent of the events and to count upon them if you become a sovereign;[1] because then deep affection can make up for cares, or whether you are what you were before in Warsaw, in a situation in which your domestic bliss and your way of life made you so happy that it brought us mutual joy. Do you remember what we were saying in the barouche going to Mainz, 'that our family union is an alliance which everything must help consolidate.' At the time I am writing you I have absolutely no knowledge of the decisions which have been made by you, and according to our latest news it was to you that everyone had paid fealty in Petersburg; if things stop there I am sure that you will often miss the Belvedere. If your decision had been different, I confess to you that I admire you from the bottom of my heart, because it is noble and would be unprecedented, I think, to constrain oneself to obey a younger brother. But knowing you, if you decide on that, there will be no more faithful executor of his word than you.

It will perhaps be a unique example to see two brothers fighting over who will *not* have the crown! It is true that one would have to be very presumptuous or very blind to want it! and as I know you both I know how well you appreciate things at their proper value. It is very fine for those who have nothing to decide in this question to have only to love and honour. It is with these feelings that I shall never cease to be your faithful sister and friend. I send tender greetings to dear Jeanette and you, dear kind Brother, as I am for life your very affectionate and devoted, sister.

[1] On reading this letter one cannot but fail to be struck by the doubt that the Grand Duchess Anna Pavlovna has concerning her brother's position. It is difficult to ascertain if she had some idea that perhaps Constantine had given up his rights of succession. Certainly, the whole tone is exceedingly ambivalent and it would appear that she was in considerable quandary. From the Grand Duke Constantine's reply dated 19/31 January 1826, it appears that she addressed the letter to him as Tsar.

Tsar Nicholas I (1796–1855)

The Grand Duke Constantine. An engraving by J. Lex after a painting by Kiel, 1832.

A sketch of Tsar Nicholas I after Landseer, published in 1855

1826–29

GREECE was of major concern to Tsar Nicholas I and for the first few years following his accession a number of attempts were made to settle the problem. The obduracy of the Turks and the foolishness of the Greeks combined with the jealousy of the powers prevented any real solution from being reached. The climax was reached on 20 October 1827, when the allied powers – France, England and Russia – destroyed a combined Turkish Egyptian fleet at Navarino.

Early in 1828, when it became clear that reason could not settle the problem, war broke out between Russia and Turkey. The former were generally successful in their attacks and the great fortress at Varna fell in October 1828. The diplomats had not been idle and on 22 March 1829 England, France and Russia negotiated the London Protocol which established that Greece would be an autonomous principality, but with a sovereign not chosen from the ruling families of Russia, France or England. The war between Russia and Turkey was ended by the Treaty of Adrianople 14 September 1829; a further meeting in London in November decided that Greece should become an independent state and Leopold of Saxe-Coburg was chosen as king. He declined to accept the offer and Count Capo d'Istria continued as *de facto* ruler. It was not until 1832 that the question was resolved with the accession of Otto of Bavaria.

While Greece was a major problem demanding Tsar Nicholas's attention, other questions demanded answers. Relations with Persia declined and war followed, concluding with a Russian triumph.

In Portugal a civil war broke out following a *coup* by Dom Miguel, the uncle of Queen Maria II, and while Russian sympathies lay with the conservatives, the kingdom of Portugal was too remote for any support to be given to Miguel. Moreover, this was also a British sphere of interest, and Anglo-Russian co-operation was essential for a solution to the Greek question.

The new kingdom of the Netherlands created by the powers, while satisfactory enough to the Dutch did not intensely please the Belgians. The Dutch dominated the new state in almost all spheres of the national life. In addition, economic and religious quarrels did not improve the state of affairs. Relations between King William and his Belgian subjects, both clericals and liberals, went into a complete decline following the signing of a concordat with Rome which allowed the

King the right of veto over the election of bishops – thus alienating the clericals. The liberals were distressed by new legislation against the Press and increased censorship. Everywhere in the southern provinces agitation for a free Press, freedom of worship and for ministerial responsibility began to be heard. This liberal agitation was accompanied by economic distress and unemployment as a result of a depression. However, the Dutch King made no attempt to alleviate the situation.

THE GRAND DUKE CONSTANTINE TO THE GRAND DUCHESS ANNA PAVLOVNA, THE PRINCESS OF ORANGE:

Warsaw,
7/19 January 1826

It is to offer you my most sincere good wishes, dear Sister, that I take pen in hand on the anniversary day of your birth – good wishes which have to do with your prosperity, good fortune and contentment especially. It was with a full heart that I learned that they were received by you, dear Sister, with kindness and goodwill. I have not seen you at any time, dear Sister, since the terrible blow which fell upon us all, as well as upon you. I can easily imagine the state into which it must have thrown you. The only thing I can say to you is that you are a wife and mother, and that your situation has dedicated you to your husband and children. I earnestly hope that the good Lord will have preserved your health as I understand that your husband went to Petersburg, because otherwise he would certainly not have left you. As for myself, I can tell you nothing about that sad event and those who went on to Petersburg and elsewhere. You know me too well, dear Sister, not to imagine the pain I must feel. My trust is in God, and I hope that He will deign to let us emerge from this crisis through His divine protection. . . . My wife, to whom you are gracious enough to address yourself, was very ill as a consequence of the loss of our dear dead Emperor whom she loved with all the warmth of her heart, and she came very close to a serious illness from which, thanks to Divine Grace, she has escaped. But she will need a great deal of time and care to recover. I hug your children with all my heart, dear Sister, and beg you to preserve for me your kindness and your affection as I am for life your faithful brother and friend.

The Grand Duke Constantine to the Grand Duchess Anna Pavlovna, the Princess of Orange:

Warsaw,
19/31 January 1826

It was via Petersburg that I received your dear kind letter, dear Sister, dated last December, 15/27, and for which I beg you to accept all my sincere good wishes. In spite of the fact that the address on it was done with a title which has never belonged to me I [unsealed] it nevertheless, as it came to me from you, as I did not know whether you were up-to-date on everything which has happened. I read, dear Sister, with tremendous satisfaction the excellent opinion which you are good enough to have of me, and I dare to hope and trust that you will not withdraw it from me. On the contrary, I hope that everything which has just taken place will prove to you even more the uprightness of my principles and my behaviour in the serious and difficult situation in which I most unexpectedly find myself. In short, I hope that you will continue to give me your esteem and affection which I hold extremely dear. Your letter informs me that in spite of the irretrievable loss which we have all just suffered – as much as we resemble the rest of the world – your health has not been impaired, for which I thank the good Lord from the bottom of my heart. I shall never forget our conversation in the barouche between Frankfurt-am-Main and Mainz, and I repeat that as long as the family is unified and [full of faith ?] it can win out over all events and face up to all dangers, and I completely share your opinion in this respect. You will not find me wanting in this regard, and Nicholas can count on me as well as upon my zealousness and devotion to serve him. What seems difficult to you in my position, to obey his orders, is not so for me as I have been accustomed to obey since my earliest youth and God knows whom I have not obeyed during my military service and my life. Moreover, I owe it to my own honour and our late master's wishes which will still give me the happiness of serving him after he is no more. My behaviour is set out and I hope that Nicholas will be happy with me. As for *him*, it is not up to me to teach him what *he* must do. My wife, whom you are kind enough to remember, requests me to thank you. She is pleased at the idea that you keep your affection for her. She was seriously ill after the news of the death of our dear adorable Angel whom she loved passionately and who honoured her with his full trust and friendship. Until the time she feels a great deal better, she is remaining under the doctor's care. As for me, I leave it to you to imagine for yourself what I must have felt as a result of all these events. . . . My greetings to your children, dear Sister, do not forget me and always count on the tender and sincere affection of your faithful brother and friend.

THE EMPRESS MARIA FEODOROVNA TO MLLE DE SYBOURG:

St Petersburg.
20 January/1 February 1826

Mlle de Sybourg,

I received your letter of 4 January, and I thank you most sincerely for the sympathy that you express for our misfortune. You have known he whom I shall mourn eternally, you know what he was to me beyond what he was for Russia and for Europe, and you have appreciated the grief that crushes me, I was annihilated by it, and it is only by particular assistance and Divine bounty that my health is able to resist such a terrible shock. Add to that the uneasiness that torments me about the effects that such crushing news must produce on my absent children, and then the deplorable happenings of 14 December.[1] It is good that God sustained me and I implore Him always to grant me the necessary resignation. You can imagine what I felt in seeing the Prince of Orange again; our tears flowed and mingled. This perfect harmony of sentiment makes his presence

[1] The Decembrist Revolt.

so precious to me and such a great consolation that I cannot thank my dear daughter enough for her sacrifice, this is what I beg you to tell her, and be assured of my sentiments of sincere good will.

I am most obliged, my dear Sybourg, for your interest, and I recognise in it your sincere attachment to me and my children.

THE GRAND DUCHESS ANNA PAVLOVNA, THE PRINCESS OF ORANGE, TO THE GRAND DUKE CONSTANTINE:

The Hague,
5 February 1826

Dear excellent Brother and friend,

. . . You may imagine how often I have thought of you these days, how much I have admired you, recognising in everything your noble character which inspires in me a respect sweet to possess. You, the *Bayard of the family*, who always recalls to me those words of the famous man which are so rightly applicable to you, about whom everyone can say, *'contemplate the august humility of Bayard'*! To know your worth and hold you dear become sacred duties and are joined to the feeling of affection which we bear for you, knowing you in the way circumstances have made you known to the world. In the midst of the greatest grief, Providence has deigned to grant us all the dearest consolations in the behaviour and character of our family by giving us brothers of whom we are proud. You have all given the world an example unique in history; may the true grandeur of it not be misunderstood! Just today I received from a Russian courier good news of my dear William who had arrived at Petersburg, which you must have known about for a long time. How much he loves and esteems you. I wish you could have made a third with us in order to hear him talk about you with the devoted attachment he has for you – you can guess that in these circumstances – and he is congratulating himself at knowing you and being able to cherish and reverence you. May God soon return this dear William to us and may He watch over him! You will probably see him – for he very much wanted to pass through Warsaw in order to see you. My children, news of whom you ask, are well; they are a consolation to me now. For you know from experience what I must have felt on receiving the news of the death of our beloved late Emperor, and every day this loss is felt more; add to that my separation from William and the sad news about the events in Petersburg and Kiev. Perhaps the latter are giving you a chance, dear good Brother, to give more services to the homeland, to add more lustre to the *titles* your services have already promised for you, and through them to strengthen the tranquillity of Russia.

Upon hearing the first news of the Emperor's death I wrote you through Prince Golitsyn, who was sent to Petersburg, hoping that that letter would reach you wherever you were. If it did not reach you I beg you to ask for it, for I am anxious that you see how much I am thinking about you and everything I feel.

THE GRAND DUKE CONSTANTINE TO THE GRAND DUCHESS ANNA PAVLOVNA, THE PRINCESS OF ORANGE:

Warsaw,
30 March/11 April 1826

I am taking advantage of your husband's departure, dear Sister, to write you and thank you for your kind and amusing letter dated last 20 March. I am very upset to read in it that your health is not of the best and that you are suffering from weakness and restlessness. That scarcely surprises me, dear Sister, knowing your heart and feelings after everything that happened at home. More or less the whole time that we have existed we have paid a tribute demanded by society to unfortunate occurrences. I hope, however, that the pleasure you feel in seeing your husband again will give you back and completely restore your natural state. Moreover, scientific knowledge, which is growing, and the nearness of Ems – that true source of health, to which in part I owe mine – can contribute to your recovery. Concerning what you tell me, that I am the only one in the whole family who puts nothing exalted in my letters and that you are happy not to see me dreaming in broad daylight, for this I thank you most sincerely as your support and good opinion mean a great deal to me. You know me well enough, moreover, to know that I am more earth-bound and understand nothing else but what concerns my duties and my affairs. I would be afraid to be found lacking if I busied myself with astronomy and lifted my nose high to look around, and as mine is naturally very short, if it so happened that I received a blow on it for having lifted it, it would be very painful for me, and in any case I want to keep it intact as I have nothing to lose by that. . . . Your husband spent three days with us and is leaving again this evening. I was very happy to see him again; he was the first person in the family whom I have seen since that very unfortunate month. No one could be more perfect or better towards my wife and myself than he is. It was very kind and good of him to have spent those three days with us. My wife is very touched by the way you remember her affectionately and for the kindness you show for her. Thanks be to God, her health, while not of the best, is bearing up in spite of troubles and worries. Hug your children for me and thank your excellent husband for spending those days with us through his kindness. All yours with heart and soul, dear Sister. . . .

THE GRAND DUKE CONSTANTINE TO THE GRAND DUCHESS ANNA PAVLOVNA, THE PRINCESS OF ORANGE:

Warsaw,
17/29 May 1826

I am taking advantage of Count [Batovsky's ?] departure, dear Sister, to thank you for your kind good letter which you sent to me for my birthday, as well as for the good wishes you are kind enough to make for me. I am certain that they must bring me good luck as it is you who send them, and I accept them with the most profound gratitude. All the flattering things you say to me, dear Sister, about my behaviour make me very happy. I hope that I shall never give you cause to change your opinion. The approbation which the Queen so graciously grants me touches me too much for me not to beg you most earnestly to be good enough to place at her feet for me the homage of my profound gratitude and warmest thanks. Her Majesty has always deigned to display towards me a very special kindness from the first moment I had the good fortune to be presented to her twenty years ago in Berlin. Forgive me, dear Sister, if I express myself in this way: that the support of good people has promoted my ambitions, and that of the Queen is all the more precious to me. It is truly one more certificate of good behaviour. I hope that by now you possess the letter, news of which you were asking me. I used a courier to [Weimar ?] to send it to you as you especially recommended that to me. I thought I was acting wisely and if I was wrong excuse me, and only see in it my wish and zealousness to serve you well and according to what I thought were your desires. So here we are plunged once again, dear Sister, into new mourning because of the death of the Empress Elizabeth, which happened while she was travelling, in a little town in the government of Tula called Belev on 4/16 May at 5 o'clock in the morning. This news reached me through General Toll who is major-general of the 1st Army. Up to now I have heard nothing about this from Petersburg or from Mama in Moscow. The Prussian Consul-General living here received yesterday morning a letter from the Prussian envoy at Petersburg of 9/21 of this month which informs him of the same news, and adding that the coronation had to be put off until the month of August. This very morning Nicholas sent the same news to Prince Charles of Prussia who was to go to Moscow [to see his sister ?] so that he could postpone his trip. I have not mentioned my opinion about this death and I limit myself to making the most sincere and fervent wishes for the repose of the soul of the dead Empress who finished her existence after giving all she could to her immortal husband. As for us here, up to the present we are quiet, thank God, as in the past, and one would not even imagine a change of reign or anything similar. For several days the heat has been very heavy and the summer magnificent and completely settled. My occupations go on and are still the same as during the life of our late adored master, and if He were to come back among us He would find no-one to criticise about anything. Thanks to God, my wife's health is passable and improved after her latest indisposition of Easter week, and she asks to be remembered to you. Give greetings to your husband for me and assure him of all my affection and my sincere and unchanging attachment. My kisses to your children. Do not forget me, dear Sister. Keep remembering me with affection and count always and in everything on the tender and true friendship of your faithful brother and friend.

The weather is so fine here today that if it depended on me, I would have been in Coblenz and Ems, regions of which I am extremely fond, especially from the top of Ehrenbreitstein.

THE GRAND DUKE CONSTANTINE TO THE GRAND DUCHESS ANNA PAVLOVNA, THE PRINCESS OF ORANGE:

Warsaw,
22 June/4 July 1826

Do not be annoyed with me, dear excellent Sister, if I have taken so long to answer you and thank you for your good kind letter date 21 May/2 June, for the occasion of my name-day as well as for the good wishes which you are kind enough to make for me. I accept them with the most profound gratitude and I am sure that they will come to pass as you send them to me. You know whether I value your affection and remembrance; preserve them for me and be convinced that I shall constantly try to prove to you again, my dear, that I am not unworthy of them. My wife joins me in thanking you for the remembrance and affection which you show for her. She is very touched by that. Thanks to God, her health, while not of the best, has become passable, but all the shocks of different kinds which she has undergone since our late immortal Angel's death have all worked badly upon her health and brought it low. I hope that time will restore everything to its place. . . . Our summer is magnificent and stifling hot. Since 1798 I do not remember one like it. Every day I go into the water in order to breathe a little. Our activities are still the same but begin two hours earlier than in preceding years to avoid the heat. I sleep very little – at the most five hours a day. In such heat Orange groves usually thrive, and I trust and hope that the dear and much loved Mama is doing the same. Please hug them for me. . . .

THE GRAND DUKE CONSTANTINE TO THE GRAND DUCHESS ANNA PAVLOVNA, THE PRINCESS OF ORANGE:

Warsaw,
16/28 September 1826

I promptly received at the proper time, dear Anne, your good kind letter dated 17/29 July for which I do not know how to thank you enough as everything you tell me is certainly more than I deserve. Your kindness, your affection, dear Sister, and your trust are my highest goals and I hope that the good Lord will help me during the rest of my life, as He has deigned to help me in the past, to act in such a way as not to be unworthy of them. About everything you are good enough to say to me, dear Sister, I have only one answer to give, which is that I acted in all situations which have occurred in the last year, and in those which have been provoked by them, only through pure honour alone without holding back effort or [. . . ?] and with no ulterior motives. I acted for the sake of action and to keep my honour intact and I hope that it is so. Speaking of actions, my arrival in Moscow was a notable result of this, since my object in the first place was not to go there because everyone has fussed so much *for*, *on account of*, *in order to*, etc., etc., etc., over my situation – I could not foresee whether new idiocies might not be brought about by my presence. But basically there was a completely different purpose involved which I abstain from putting in writing. So, out of respect for a mother, and having a moment of freedom for myself, I went to Moscow to throw myself at my mother's feet; she who has overwhelmed me with kindness, goodness, and if I dare say so, respect, what could I bring as tribute – nothing if not my honour and heart, pure and unsullied. God, that worshipful and consoling being who sees into the depths of hearts and thoughts, having granted me purity of feeling and guided all my actions and behaviour, obtained for me the most wonderful welcome from everyone, beginning with my mother and going right down to the dregs of the people. Up until then, all went well and my full and complete gratitude was offered to them in return. But once the enthusiasm, the acclamations, the praise, the flattery, the comparisons, the historical [. . . ?] and other such preposterous things began,

I found it too much for me and said to myself, 'well, you must be off,' and that as fast as possible to prove that all that racket does not please me and which, moreover, in my delicate situation might have given offence, since that state of affairs is often worse than sneering at the true state of things. So all things considered, I went away to show everyone the simplicity and purity of my behaviour. Moreover, it is up to the public to unravel what is not true for the simple reason that it is not. These, in short, are the facts. I see nothing praiseworthy or notable in that. If my behaviour deserves your approval it is more than I can discern in it. My wife asks me to thank you for so kindly remembering her, and begs you not to forget her. Her health is fairly good but requires care and [attention ?]. My most tender and sincere greetings to our dear William whom I love with heart and soul. *Idem* for my hugs to your children. And for you, dear and excellent Sister, accept my assurance of the tenderest and most sincere affection which your faithful brother and friend bears for you.

THE GRAND DUCHESS ANNA PAVLOVNA, THE PRINCESS OF ORANGE, TO THE GRAND DUKE CONSTANTINE:

Tervueren,
27 September 1826

Dear excellent Brother,

. . . I have not received a sign of life from you for four months. I am very upset about this; what have I done to deserve this long silence? I, who love you so tenderly, who only want to keep your friendship and who bear for you true reverence. So I am taking advantage of a Russian courier going through here to give him these lines which I put under Mama's protection to get them to you more quickly than by mail. I hope that our dear Jeannette's health is good, for I also know nothing about this subject which is so interesting for all of us. Will you give her tenderest greetings from me and ask her to please me by sometimes sending news of you. I have nothing but good news to give you from here where, thanks to God, we are all well and lead a kind of life which suits our tastes. The autumn is superb, but I must say that as of yesterday winter has begun with frost and the first snow. That did not prevent me from taking a long walk in weather which was not cold. I have finally managed, dear Brother, to find two oil paintings showing two Amsterdam scenes, which I think will satisfy your wishes. They are done with scrupulous exactness and you will see that the painter has left out neither bricks nor wigs. And I recommend to you the doorstep scene in which an old lady makes her deep curtsy to a gentleman, or *mijn heer*, according to the language of the country, who is bowing deeply to her. So, without having been in Holland you can have the illusion of knowing it. There is no way of rolling these pictures as you wished to have them sent to you, for it would risk spoiling them, so instruct me, dear Brother, about how I should send them to you. Would it not be better done next spring, by sea to Petersburg, whence I shall ask Mama to be good enough to send them to you when a courier leaves. This type of picture is so sought after in England that they are beginning to become very rare, and it is only by a lucky chance that I was able to obtain these for you; for they are all going off to adorn the mansions of the fortunate isle. Our young people have greatly thrived this year, the stay in the country makes them grow like plants. My sons are very strong and tall for their age; on the contrary, the little girl still retains dainty proportions, but she is developing a great deal nevertheless, and shows signs of intelligence.

What days these are for memories! One finds them at every moment and I am sure that we are all together in our thoughts and regrets, for they will only end with our existence.

THE GRAND DUKE CONSTANTINE TO THE GRAND DUCHESS ANNA PAVLOVNA, THE PRINCESS OF ORANGE:

Warsaw,
11/23 October 1826

It was Marianne who was kind enough to send me the letter you wrote me, dear Sister, dated last 15/27 September for which I beg you to accept my most sincere thanks. I am very sorry, dear Sister, to have unwittingly caused you pain and I hasten these lines to you to beg your pardon. Grant it to me, dear Sister, and be convinced that never did such an idea enter my head. You know the sincere affection and friendship which I have vowed to you; may they be my advocate with you to obtain pardon for a fault which certainly occurred without my being aware of it, and for which I would not even want to be considered the ally. Your letter, dear Sister, gave me the greatest possible pleasure as it once more shows me the affection you bear for me and which I guard jealously. I avow this frankly, I hope that you will be good enough to remain so for me. I have nothing very interesting to tell you from here. Everything, thanks to God, bathes in the most perfect tranquillity, and I hope and trust that the good Lord will deign to preserve this state of affairs for us. If ever there was a *status quo* and a *semper idem* on this earth, it is very much the case with our state of affairs here. Every day is alike, and you can tell ahead of time what will happen in it; as for me, I bless the good Lord for this with all my heart and soul and beg Him to continue and preserve us in the same way. My wife's health is still not of the best. She often suffers from very heavy colds and very violent migraine headaches. With that sort of limitation put to one side, she is well. But what I do not like is that these misfortunes return too often, which in the long run lessens physical strength. . . . Concerning your paintings, dear Sister, the ones which you are kind enough to send me; I shall begin by thanking you for them very sincerely as they show me that you remember me kindly. That without doubt is of the greatest value. When they arrive, as I see the lady and gentleman bowing to each other, I shall say to them *Goeden dank* ?] and they have only to [*Wij zijn* ?] me. . . . About the shipping of these pictures, if they cannot be sent overland, I think that the shortest way would be to ship them to Danzig to our consul-general [Marlavowicz ?] who will look after their transportation here and [will inform me when they will arrive]. In any case, the greatest value of these objects is that they are coming to me from you, so all my gratitude is offered to you most sincerely. Please, dear Sister, remember me to your dear William and assure him of all my affection. Please give my greetings to the little Orange-grove, and for yourself, accept the expression of the tenderest, most sincere and most unchanging affection which I have eternally vowed to you. . . .

THE GRAND DUKE CONSTANTINE TO THE GRAND DUCHESS ANNA PAVLOVNA, THE PRINCESS OF ORANGE:

Warsaw,
7/19 January 1827

Accept, dear Sister, my most sincere good wishes as well as my congratulations on the occasion of your birthday. May the good Lord deign to preserve you in health, happiness, prosperity and contentment with your husband and children. I hope and trust that you will be kind enough to accept my heart's feelings with goodness and indulgence, as they are offered to you from its depths and with full measure. Keep remembering me affectionately, dear Sister, and be sure that you have no other person in the world who is more devoted to you than I am. . . . I hope that the whole family is well and that the Brussels visit is completely satisfactory. As for us here at home, I can tell you nothing very interesting; my poor excellent wife is still ill and it seems to me that this happens more frequently to her than the others. God knows what causes it – the rheumatism, these nerves, these other things and so on – but, in short, she is still in the care of doctors who work on her and do not accomplish any positive results. However, I hope that things will improve. Some days she is completely indisposed and others she seems to be well. Moreover, our good town is full of sadness and the most dreary monotony during this carnival. The high society ladies have passed the word around not to dance and not to hold open house until the fate of the prisoners[1] involved in high treason and *lèse-majesté* is decided and this, because of their own interpretation of a feeling of patriotic vanity, is enough to make one

[1] A reference to those Polish officers who had been arrested following the Decembrist Revolt in the previous December. The Poles were members of an organisation known as the Patriotic Society. Tsar Nicholas had wanted to try them in St Petersburg, but his brother had objected and consequently the Poles faced their judges in Warsaw. The sentences were mild and Tsar Nicholas was much displeased, but he confirmed the judicial decision. Certain other Poles who were officially Russian subjects were tried by Russian courts and received stiff sentences.

shrug one's shoulders. But the most completely ridiculous thing is that most of these ladies visit Russian houses under the pretext of not being disrespectful but really to have a good time and dance away the evening. It is, as Molière said, that there can be no compromises with Heaven. As far as I am concerned, I lead a most retiring life as I only go out to perform my duties and the rest of the time I spend at home with my wife. The only pleasure consists of making long jaunts on horseback every day before dinner and after the morning's work, which is very long and very boring most of the time. Please tell your husband, dear Sister, that there has arrived with us a [*goeden dank mijn heer* ?] that is to say, L. C. van der Paul [?], whom I was very pleased to see again, having last seen him here four years ago. My affectionate greetings to our dear William and tell him that I love him with heart and soul. He will already know what that means as he knows the warmth which governs it. My greetings to the whole Orange grove and be sure, dear Sister, that you have no more sincere friend than your faithful old brother.

Tsar Nicholas I to the Grand Duchess Anna Pavlovna, the Princess of Orange:

St Petersburg,
8/20 January 1827

You will cry *Miracle* I think, dear Anne, when you see my writing again, and anyone would. I wanted to break my silence at a time of good omen and I have chosen your name-day to do so. Accept all my very sincere prayers for you and for the preservation of all those dear to you; if you enjoy all the happiness I wish for you, you will certainly lack for nothing. Believe in the sentiments of an old friend who counts on your affection in order not to be misunderstood or, particularly, misinterpreted; my feelings have never changed for you *in spite of my silence*. If you can, perhaps, recall the pace of life of our Angel and remember that his task has fallen on my shoulders – I, who am so little designed for this, who was so little prepared for it – you will really understand that I can barely do the absolutely indispensable things. Ask William about it all; he was a witness to the last agony and can and has certainly drawn you the picture of my inner state.

This time it is you whom I entrust to say many tender regards to our William; it is impossible for me to write him this time, but I shall the next. Hug your dear children, and my homage to the King and Queen.

THE GRAND DUCHESS ANNA PAVLOVNA, THE PRINCESS OF ORANGE, TO THE GRAND DUKE CONSTANTINE:

Brussels,
12 February 1827

Dear excellent Brother,

. . . I am positively touched by the way you constantly remember my birthday, in spite of the fact that it has been at least fifteen years since we have spent it together; well, I confess to you that I presume to count on your affection as upon a solid foundation. Everything you tell me about yourself and your way of life interests me enormously; I am delighted to learn that you regularly take exercise on horseback, for I am convinced that constitutions such as ours need to do a lot of this, and continuously. As for myself, it has been years since I have mounted, I walk in the park, as much as possible considering the season we are in. It has been freezing continually for a month now and an enormous amount of snow has fallen, to the degree that people do not remember having seen so much in this country. Those who love sleighing have taken advantage of it, but the paraphernalia has such unusual forms that it looks like a masquerade at high noon; mythological monsters and humble farm-yard animals are mixed up in it; and a dragon, a swan and a cock go walking by; my children were delighted and so was I, but it was at seeing the joy of the idlers.

Your dear excellent wife wrote me a long letter which is precious to me and gave me real pleasure with the details she gave me about your activities, and what she says of it according to her way of seeing things; I cannot but share it completely and I thank her for her trust. I wish that her health were better and that you were quit of this worrisome subject which is a very upsetting one. I understand that the life of high society does not tempt you; after the object of our constant regret, who among us can seek it? It is possible to be in the midst of it as we are, out of obligation, and to perform this sort of thing out of duty, but for the intrinsic pleasure of it our feelings do not agree with that, for the memory of the one for whom we still weep comes and stands beside everything, and then, how can one be gay! As for those people, dear Brother, of whom you speak and who, because of a kind of patriotic feeling do not entertain; as a general thesis I find nothing more stupid than badly understood patriotism, and that everywhere it occurs in false guise, one might believe that it comes from the homeland of Midas. At least this reflection has occurred to me sometimes during my life. So here is a long letter. . . .

THE GRAND DUKE CONSTANTINE TO THE GRAND DUCHESS ANNA PAVLOVNA, THE PRINCESS OF ORANGE:

Warsaw,
5/17 April 1827

Dear Sister,

I eagerly seize upon the occasion of the Easter celebrations to send you my congratulations as well as my most sincere good wishes for your constant happiness and contentment since I was unable to do so for your 3 February name-day – being then *en route* to Petersburg – I do so for this celebration like the whole of Christianity. I dare hope, dear Sister, that you do not doubt the feelings of affection and true closeness I have for you and the happiness I retain at repeating this to you on every occasion. On your name-day on 3 February I was between [Narva ?] and Petersburg, dashing down the road, stuck in snow, battling against cold, impatience, boredom and the weariness of a journey of five days and five nights to arrive as quickly as possible at my mother's side. I shall not tell you about my Petersburg visit, which lasted twelve days, and about the pace of life which I led during it, in which every moment was occupied to such an extent that I had absolutely none left for myself. My whole time was spent with Mama to whom I had dedicated my visit. She was not going out in society, and I did the same, and I admit that all the memories were still too burning for me to be able to do so. In short, as in Molière, everything is in the same place, everything is as it was in the past except for the two persons whom the good Lord saw fit to remove from our happy midst. It is a feeling which is difficult to describe; it was very upsetting for me, and especially as I had to keep watch over myself so that such a natural feeling would not be interpreted completely differently from what it is. Well, I found that I was completely comfortable. It was when I was near my Masters' tombs, and I confess that I saw them again with a kind of satisfaction which Petersburg no longer offers me. I returned here in five days and nights, and I am happy to be back and especially to be far away from places which were never to my liking and at the moment are even less so. You see, dear Sister, that the trip alone was the obstacle which prevented me from sending you my good wishes in time. Please accept them now with your usual kindness. Nothing new with us, thanks to God, everything is very quiet here; the spring has a very good start and all through these last days it has been very fine. During my last visit to Petersburg Mama deigned in her charitable way to speak to me of my son,[1] to show interest in him, to display kindly dispositions towards him, and even more, grant him her blessing. You can judge for yourself what must have taken place in me on that occasion. Therefore my whole gratitude is fully given to my mother as well as to God from the bottom of my heart and soul. . . .

My wife wishes to be remembered to you as well as your dear William, and Paul, who has just been very sick with burning fever, very humbly offers you both his homage.

[1] Paul Constantinovich Alexandrov (1808–57) was the child resulting from the liaison between the Grand Duke Constantine and Mlle Friedrichs, an actress. He lived with his father in Warsaw and entered the army. Within the family circle Paul Constantinovich was recognised as a relation.

The Grand Duchess Anna Pavlovna, the Princess of Orange, to the Grand Duke Constantine:

Brussels,
27 April 1827

Dear excellent Brother,

. . . We have not been together at this time [to celebrate his birthday] since the year 1811, so that makes sixteen years! You were always so good to your little sister and accepted with so much affection the humble offerings I gave you that, at the time, it was one of my pleasures. At this moment, there are two pictures which I place at your feet and they are on the seas or have perhaps already reached you. They were sent from Amsterdam to Danzig to the Russian Consul, whom I have asked to hold them for you; I hope that they will arrive safely and that the little bricks, the canals and the bewigged heads will meet with your approval. As your birthday is also that of my sister-in-law Marianne, we were together *en famille* to celebrate the day; at dinner, when the King learned that it was your birthday, he paid me the kind compliment of toasting your health as did the whole family, and I thought that when I wrote this to you it would prove to you the feelings you inspire, ones which are sweet for me to collect in order to pass them on to you. I received, with much pleasure, your dear letter dated 5 April which you were good enough to write to me at the time of the Easter holidays. I am very touched at how you have remembered my name-day. I could not expect a letter at that time as I knew you were travelling then but I assure you that I counted on your remembering, and that since then I was longing to have news of you. Everything you tell me about the impression Petersburg made on you moved me to tears; I would feel like you if I were there again, and certainly those who knew and valued our beloved brother and benefactor can only be profoundly affected by seeing the places which recall him at each step without every being able to find him there again. Never shall I be able to be consoled for his loss, but to the last day of my life I shall miss him and cherish his memory. I am sure that these are your feelings too, so, as we are together in feeling this way and we do so every day, you will not hold it against me, dear Brother, to have mentioned them in this letter.

I hope that Paul has completely recovered from his illness; I am sending him good wishes for his continued health and ask you to give him my kind regards.

THE GRAND DUKE CONSTANTINE TO THE GRAND DUCHESS ANNA PAVLOVNA, THE PRINCESS OF ORANGE:

Warsaw,
12/24 June 1827

All my tenderest and most sincere thanks are offered you, dear excellent Sister, for your kind letter and your remembrance at the time of my birthday, and for the good wishes you are kind enough to send me. I am certain they will bring me happiness, coming from your affection for me. I like to think you do not doubt the value I put on your remembrance and your affections; all my thoughts will be constantly bent on proving to you more and more that I am not and shall not be unworthy of them. Your letter [*via* St Petersburg], dear Sister, reached me fairly late, and I am answering it in the same way as I wanted to tell you of the arrival of the pictures you were kind enough to send me, but as I had no news until today I lost patience and began to scribble this letter to you, a weak interpreter of the gratitude I bear you for remembering me as well as for the gift you sent me. I hope, however, that one of these days it will reach me unless it has gone down to furnish the shark's gallery and the other watery inhabitants at whom I am very annoyed, as I think they are worse connoisseurs than I in matters of artistic works. All the instructions have already been sent through to Danzig for their quick forwarding here, and even the severe Minister of Finance, Prince Lubecki,[1] has deigned in his generosity to remove all obstacles. I come back to your affectionate letter, dear Sister, and am happy to read in it that you share my opinions about our melancholy Petersburg. I must say frankly that if my mother were not there I would be able to give a plausible reason for never again soiling my feet with it, and each time I reflect that respect must lead me back there at

[1] Ksawery Lubecki (1779–1846) was Minister of Finance 1821 to 1830.

certain seasons, I cannot do so without heartache. It seems to me that each time – and this with no exaggeration whatever – when I go through the granite arch I leave liberty behind me to enter prison. You will agree with me that it is in no way pleasant. When I was there I was given word of mouth invitations, which were repeated to me by all those who came from the court, to come and spend two months and the whole summer at Pavlovski[1] with my wife, where she would receive the best care and would enjoy every freedom, convenience and comfort. Thanks to the kindness of our dear late Emperor my duties and my occupations detain me far from that visit which you know about better than I, with its customs, arrangements and ways of behaving. You will remember perfectly that when I was still young I lived there only for a few hours every week and that I used to spend my time at Strelna. As I did not find it to my liking then, now, as I am over forty-eight years old, showing myself in the vicinity of the court – from which, thank Heaven, I have been distant for fifteen years – would be more than painful for me to become accustomed to again. However, my wife's delicate, if not feeble, health is against it and even with all the conveniences and care promised her, she would be a victim of a type of life completely different from that to which she is accustomed, and in spite of the so-called precautions would be on her feet from about 10 o'clock in the morning until midnight or 1 o'clock the next morning. You understand what I mean in any case, dear Sister, as you know the ground even better than I. My wife, moreover, is ailing and has given me very sharp cause to worry because of quite a strong cough exactly like the one you heard she had a Coblenz. Thank God, she got over it fairly quickly. It was only the result of a chill caught, Heaven knows how, during great heat and magnificent weather which we have been enjoying without let-up since this spring. After the cough there was an inflammation in her head and a toothache which made her suffer impossibly. For the time being she is better. As she knows that I am writing you, dear Sister, she begs me to tell you again of all the most tender feelings she has for you as well as for our dear William, to whom I beg you to give all my greatest affection. My hugs to your charming Oranges. My boy is slowly getting better from

[1] The residence of Empress Marie.

his arthritic pains which caused me very sharp anxiety for him. At nineteen years old he was truly gouty. However, there is a real improvement. Father and son are at your feet, dear Sister, and thank you for remembering us. . . .

THE GRAND DUKE CONSTANTINE TO THE GRAND DUCHESS ANNA PAVLOVNA, THE PRINCESS OF ORANGE:

Warsaw,
28 June/10 July 1827

All my thanks are sent you, dear excellent Sister, for your kind letter for my name-day as well as for the good wishes you are kind enough to make for me. I accept them with the most profound gratitude and like to tell myself that they will bring me happiness. If I have delayed so long at setting down on paper the expression of my gratitude, please do not blame it on anything but the time of year in my occupations which, so to speak, take up all my time. All the news you give me, dear Anne, about your household and your family gave me the greatest pleasure since I see that you are satisfied and content with your family life, without which there is no true happiness in this world below. I shall say exactly the same of mine, I am happy with it and content, but one thing which sometimes troubles me is the delicate health which my wife enjoys and which is really a [burden ?] for me. In spite of magnificent weather and heat worthy of St Dominic, she was [silly ?] enough to catch cold and to acquire such a violent cough again that I was reminded of our first trip to Ems. Thank God, she has just stopped coughing, not completely but almost. Then, headaches are, so to speak, her continuous lot and certainly, out of the week's seven days, cause her to be ill four and even five. Moreover, when you look at her, she looks badly and then sometimes one can see her becoming healthy again. The attacks are so sudden that they take hold of her from one moment to the next, and having seen her an hour before completely gay and in good humour, the next you find her in her bed. However, I dare hope from God's kindness that everything will be cured and brought back to the wished-for order. My boy also caused me keen anxiety because of attacks of gout or else arthritic pains, from which the poor young man suffered impossibly two whole months, one of which he spent in bed. This whole summer is concerned with family ills and with several attacks of fluctuating fever, in spite of care and drugs. He had his twentieth birthday and you must agree that it is a very sad way to make one's entry into society. My hope is in God and I trust that the whole business will only be a passing phase. As for myself, I feel extremely well, and for almost four years now I have not even felt a single time an attack of my accursed back-pain. Our heat has been, as I mentioned to you above, almost unbearable, and really one could breathe again only at 3 o'clock in the morning. We have had entire nights of 18 and 29 degrees of heat, and during the day there were no less than 28 in the shade. So you can imagine what it was like in the sun. I am counting on leaving here to make a tour in order to inspect the troops I have under my command in Lithuania and Vilna, and shall be away twelve or fourteen days. Our trial of the prisoners for state crimes has just started and is conducted as far as the prescribed formulae permit according to the constitutional jurisprudence of this country.[1] I like to think that everything will finish in good order and very quietly. Up to now we are enjoying complete tranquillity, and it seems to me that nothing will disturb it. Our military plans continue to proceed at their usual pace to my great and complete satisfaction. The progress is visible. I shall not speak to you about the public or political affairs of our countries considering the distance we are from one another here, as it seems that everyone's attention is focused on the south, and that in two places. May the Supreme Being lead us not to regret one day the [remedies ?] of the moment, and that he who boasted of having Æolus and all the [adventurers ?] of the universe at his command does not make us pay very dearly for the trust we have placed in him. So there, without meaning to, is some political chat in spite of myself. My most affectionate greetings, dear Sister, to our dear William and my hugs to your children. My very respectful homage to the Queen if she deigns to accept it, and be sure to tell her from me that I hold extremely dear the continuing of her gracious benevolence. My

[1] Cf. page 130, note.

wife asks me to remember her to you, especially as I am writing you. Do not forget me, dear Sister, and keep your affection and kindness for a brother who cherishes you with heart and soul and who is for life your faithful and sincere friend.

THE GRAND DUKE CONSTANTINE TO THE GRAND DUCHESS ANNA PAVLOVNA, THE PRINCESS OF ORANGE:

Warsaw,
25 July/7 August 1827

Dear Sister,

I am taking advantage of L. C. van der Paul's [?] departure to pen these lines to you, to thank you for the two charming paintings you were kind enough to send me and which came to me by way of Danzig at the very time that I was going to set out for my annual inspection tour of Lithuania and Vilna. When I returned, I was sick for fifty-four days with dysentery and haemorrhoidal colics which I acquired while travelling, and which made me impossibly ill and removed all strength to work from me. Once recovered I was immediately obliged to take a trip to [indecipherable] and when I returned we were enormously busy with things, both civil and military, which has prevented me, up until today, from sending you all my gratitude for this charming present. Immediately I went to look for the lady and gentleman of the [*goeden dag mijn heer* ?], and when I found them I offered them mine. These two pictures adorn my drawing-room and have been much admired by connoisseurs. My wife is sending your husband, dear Sister, a drawing of another sort and one which will have value for both of you who know so well what feelings we have for you and, what is more, what heartfelt sentiments are. Finally, our family has been increased in the masculine gender. It is very kind of the Emperor and Mama to have given my name in remembrance of me to the little fellow. It is that kind of thoughtfulness which goes right to the heart. Michael has also delivered his package and so there I am, godfather of these two children. May the good Lord have that new Constantine find the same protection and the same happiness with the new Alexander which the old one did with the older one who, alas, lives no more. Michael has been with me for three days and is planning to stay here about two weeks. You can well imagine, dear Sister, the happiness this makes me feel. So all our time is spent together and with my wife. He is still the same, the best of brothers and friends, and the best and gayest of companions. My affection to the little Orange-grove and keep remembering me affectionately, kindly and with goodness, dear Sister, and always count on the tender and sincere affection of your old brother and friend.

My wife asks me to remember her to you.

Tsar Nicholas I to the Grand Duchess Anna Pavlovna, the Princess of Orange:

St Petersburg,
9/21 September 1827

Your long friendship for me, dear good Anne, has been enhanced at the thought of the pleasure you will feel when you learn that the good Lord has deigned to grant me a second son, Constantine.

You can imagine our happiness! Everything went very well and fairly quickly. I am happier than I would have dared to believe, and I give thanks to God from the depth of my soul. Now, permit me to remark to the William household that it might be said that they have been keeping us waiting for a long time for the same procedure; that the holidays have been fairly long; and that I cannot let them off without a half-dozen.

I suppose that William has not come back to you yet, and on this matter may I remark judiciously that I have had occasion to notice that returns after absences are unusually productive and propitious for this purpose. So I hope that soon we shall be able to exchange congratulations. My homage to their Majesties, especially to our dear Mama; kind regards too to the Fritzes.

The Grand Duke Constantine to the Grand Duchess Anna Pavlovna, the Princess of Orange:

Warsaw,
7/19 January 1828

All my good wishes and all my congratulations are offered you from a full heart, dear Sister, on the occasion of your birthday. May the good Lord deign to preserve you in perfect health and prosperity, dear Sister, along with everything in the world which you may hold dear, and may His special blessing rest upon you, your husband and your children. I dare think and hope that you will be kind enough to accept my good wishes with goodness and indulgence, as they are offered to you with the feelings of affection and sincere attachment I bear for you as well as your husband. It has been a very long time since I have received news of you, dear Sister, and the details I have had I obtained from our dear William who informs me that you are well. I presume that you are spending this year in Holland according to your established routine. As for us, we are still in our usual *semper idem* and up to now nothing has yet disturbed it. I shall not talk to you of the day's events, you know them as well as I do. Moreover, both Russians and Poles are preparing themselves for any outcome, and all risks which might come along. All our sights are set towards our neighbours,[1] especially those to the south and those who seem to support them. Our geographical position in relation to those countries demands the greatest surveillance, surrounded as we are on three sides by them. Our way of life here is still the same, that is to say, very withdrawn and very monotonous. I presume that near the end of the month, if nothing prevents it, I shall undertake my usual yearly jaunt to Petersburg to present my respectful homage to Mama, which will not take any longer than usual. I confess that if I did not have this reason, nothing would drag me there at this season, and especially this winter which is extraordinarily fickle as we move from 23 degrees of cold to 2 or 3 of heat in the space of twenty-four hours, and vice versa. Moreover, I am so unaccustomed to society, to the court, to the constraint, that

[1] Persia and Turkey in particular; the former had been at war with Russia since 1826, the latter was to go to war with the Tsar in the spring of 1828.

the very thought of it makes me apprehensive. I am comfortable only at home, near my wife, with my quiet habits, withdrawn into the centre of my own family who are good enough to wish me well and show me so each time I absent myself from them, and any travelling is very upsetting for me, especially when it is a question of going back to see places where everything recalls to me a time which, alas, is no more and which will never return, the principle figure of which has been snatched from us and who gave it true charm for me. Moreover, I have absolutely nothing but praise for the goodness and thoughtfulness of our new masters, they shower me with kindness on every occasion, but ever considering all that, one cannot prevent one's thoughts from reverting to the past. Please, dear Sister, if the occasion occurs, place me most humbly at the feet of Her Majesty the Queen and convey to her my respectful homage. My sincere and tender greetings to our dear William; as soon as possible I am counting on answering his two letters. All my tenderness is sent to your children, dear Sister. At the end of this letter, accept, dear Sister, my good wishes for the year which has just begun as well as the thoughts of affection, equal to all tests, and the sincere attachment which I have devoted to you for so long.

THE GRAND DUCHESS ANNA PAVLOVNA, THE PRINCESS OF ORANGE, TO THE GRAND DUKE CONSTANTINE:

The Hague,
30 January 1828

Dear and excellent Brother,

. . . I thank you tenderly, dear kind Brother, for the letter which you had entrusted to Colonel van der Paul [?], it reached me the day before the second anniversary of the cruel loss which fell upon us all. With the greatest emotion I saw the portrait of our late beloved sitting at his work-table in his study in Warsaw; the total ambience recalls him in a striking way. My thoughts cannot get used to other times nor other states of affairs, and I can imagine better than anyone how much it must cost you to take yourself to places which had no charm except through him, and where all the appearances have changed! But at least by going there you are sure to give pleasure to the whole family and to make Mama happy with your presence; that is the word for it, the letters in which she speaks to me of you are really touching; in her we all have a treasury of love and maternal interest. May God be willing that all the preparations of which you speak to me are only precautions, and that there will be no need to use them. Those are, however, the consequences of that Navarino[1] skirmish, which, as glorious as it may have been for the respective fleets, is none the less a real incendiary brand tossed much farther than it is possible to calculate. That is my own little opinion; and no one will be more charmed than I if it can be proved that I am wrong in that.

I hope that our dear Jeannette's health is good, and as you do not speak to me about it I assume it is so; I embrace her tenderly. We are having the mildest winter I can remember; after a few days of frost and snow, we have gone on to spring; the trees are leafing, the lawn is covered with daisies, never have I seen anything like it in January! It is very pleasant, provided we shall not have to regret it later on. My children are all wonderfully well and my little girl is my delight; she is developing a great deal and promises to be extremely intelligent. As for our pastimes, the winter is going by very quietly; now and then we have a ball at court, at home or in town, and the rest of the evenings are given over to hand-work or reading. It is very agreeable.

TSAR NICHOLAS I TO THE GRAND DUCHESS ANNA PAVLOVNA, THE PRINCESS OF ORANGE:

St Petersburg,
16 February 1828

Two of your name-days have gone by, dear Anne, without my being able to send you my wishes except *through the air*; and this will prove to you that I am taking advantage of a moment of leisure to send them to you directly. Moreover, according to the way I feel, paper is a silly thing, and friendship does not need ink or paper in order to be kept alive; this is my opinion, for it is based on experience with you as with many other people

[1] A naval engagement on 20 October 1827, between the combined fleets of Britain, France and Russia versus Egypt. The latter was totally annihilated. The Turks, allies of the Egyptians, were furious. It was all part of the background to the Russo-Turkish War of 1828.

whom I love a great deal, even though I cannot write to them.

Again, with the two of you, it is to William that I most often have occasion to write, and I hope that he does not forget to remind you of me.

According to the King's kind note, which touched me a great deal, I hope to embrace our dear William soon; will you accompany him on the trip? Mama hopes so, and the members of the [family ?] who are here hope so too. I do not yet know where our meeting will take place; I suppose that it will be in Warsaw, although there is nothing settled yet.

I am told that your little girl is delightful and that your young gentlemen are handsome, good, and noisy. Those are three excellent qualities for boys in my view; as for my own, here in two words is the family portrait: my eldest, growing a lot, has an *angelic soul* and is a perfect good devil, he is learning well and resembles our late Angel a great deal; *Mary* is in the giraffe stage, is pale and thin, but has charming characteristics and will be a delightful individual; *Olly* has kept her kind of face but is getting thin and is growing a lot. *Adine* is very small and very mischievous, but I do not think she is pretty in spite of others' opinions. Master Constantine is a big fat handsome fellow, so quick and heavy that I cannot hold him; he seems really to belong to the family as the only thing he hears with pleasure is the drum. I am always so pleased to look at the portrait of your three boys copied from William's.

Kind regards to the Fritzes and tell them that I have been very pleased with them since I discovered that Louise [a drawing here to indicate that she is pregnant]. It is your turn now please.

THE GRAND DUKE CONSTANTINE TO THE GRAND DUCHESS ANNA PAVLOVNA, THE PRINCESS OF ORANGE:

Warsaw,
26 February/9 March 1828

Dear Sister,

My trip to Petersburg – the visit I had there during the last days of the carnival which were completely given over to celebrations, balls, theatrical representations, etc., the life full of tumult which is led there, all the hours of which are filled and turned up-side-down, in short, the time which is lost since in the end you do not know how to account for it – and then the return to Warsaw – the affairs which involved me again, the back-log of work brought on by my absence, and new military occupations caused by the events of the moment – have prevented me until today from sending you my good wishes and congratulations at the time of your name-day, which, although they are late, are none the less sincere and true. Please accept them, dear Sister, with your longstanding affection and believe that they come from a heart which is devoted to you and cherishes you with all its might. My twelve day stay at Petersburg was a fresh proof to me of the touching benevolence with which Mama is kind enough to honour me, and that of our whole family which, thanks to God, I found in perfect health, except for my sister-in-law Helen who is still ill from her last child-bed, and this can give rise to real anxiety. However, as long as her strength supports her she appears in society, but when she over-does this, it takes her back to bed where I left her on my departure. Peterburg has greatly changed since the death of our late immortal Emperor; for the time being there is nothing but celebrations, balls and pleasures. I have really had my fill of it and in the twelve days I spent there I went to three plays and six dances, having begged off one, and then there was a play and ball cancelled at Mama's home because of the sickness of our respectable old Princess Lieven which was causing great anxiety for her life. Moreover, in that dear Petersburg the day's twenty-four hours are not enough, at least seventy-five would be needed to make people feel comfortable. I never went to bed before one or two o'clock in the morning. There you are always, so to speak, on the *qui-vive*, the morning passes in work, visits and conversations; then comes the parade hour, set according to a new plan between noon and one o'clock, and rarely finished before quarter past two, to which one must add the distances between the Winter Palace, the exercise building of Michael Palace, the Michael Palace itself, and the Marble Palace, and you will have a slight idea of the continual dragging about one finds oneself doing; sometimes on top of that you have to add the Anichkov Palace. I leave you to guess from this description the difference there is between my daily habits here and my type of life in Petersburg, and I really assure you that I would not trade those two existences for all the gold in the world. I came home back to my wife with a feeling of real happiness and not at all dazzled by the temptations and brilliance of the big city. On the contrary, it made me have serious and rather painful thoughts. My age is too advanced, I have lived too long, looked at the world too closely for too long for my opinion to waver or change. Very far from me is the idea of being a hermit, on the contrary I like people to amuse themselves as I like to myself, but there is a time for everything as well as a limit to everything. So you can imagine how I must feel when I know that everything is sacrificed to it; to this impression add that of seeing people whom I formerly saw affecting to be horrified by pleasure, taking delight in prayers and religious practices, to have changed and taken kindly to only the pleasurable side, to the very point of having to be carried half-dead from the ball-room and needing to be bled three times to be brought back to existence. That was so with the wife of P. [rince] Trubetskoi, whom you saw in Brussels in my day. Just imagine what a man of honour must feel on seeing such things. That was the most striking example. I could quote many others from many conversations and gossip which I heard. Poor humanity, how you make yourself seem immortal to yourself by acting that way! As far as what concerns me in relation to the public, I can only be very grateful to it for the respect it is kind enough to show me on all occasions and in all the classes, high and low. In short, it deigns to express regard for me, kindness and a sort of respect – if I dare use that term in speaking of myself – which is very noticeable and which it seems to like showing everythwere. I confess that it embarrassed me a good deal and that I was very happy to get away from that state of affairs by coming back here. I shall not speak to you of my trip which, as usual, was most fortunate and most rapid; each of the stages took me four days and eight hours. As for the political situation in which we find ourselves facing the world in general, it needs another pen than mine to give you a brief résumé of it and I summarise by saying that I pray the good Lord from the depths of my heart to make us avoid all the evil I foresee arising from the eastern question once we are really physically in it, since I see with the greatest anxiety the thoughtlessness we have shown in going into it morally with our protocol treaties of 7 April 1826 and 6 July

1827.[1] We saw the results in the regrettable day of Navarino which, although very glorious for our navy, is none the less a monstrosity in regard to the rights of people. I presume that our dear allies, and especially the islanders, have done everything in the world to [muddle ?] us up in the east in order to turn our eyes away from the west, considering our influence with the disturbers of public peace in all nations which was supported by the physical strength of our means which, divided between the east and west, diminish its effect. Figaro in his wisdom claims that it is not necessary to know things to reason about them and that is true of me. You see that I am being just with myself but while being so I allow myself to add, to justify myself, that as justice has been [undivided ?] since the world began, we must not permit and [bear ?] evils by allowing on our neighbour's property anything whatsoever which one would not tolerate at home, unless one wishes to be charged with a lack of logic, admitting and supporting an emancipation for one's neighbour and authorising, as is reasonable, a similar thing in one's own country which I know is contrary to good sense. In all wars there is a goal and an end which one has in view. Ordinarily the capitals are the goals but arriving at Constantinople the cause is not finished and has only begun, and many different interests will play a part in it. If, however, things proceed as well as possible, will we be left alone there? Would it be to vilify Mohammed by teaching him to reign a little more and civilise them? What would we gain if, on the contrary, once having arrived at Constantinople we were to find a second Moscow?[2] The lesson which we gave over that would only make the Turks begin, and that was resolved at Fontainebleau and Waterloo.[3] So there, without my intending to, I have scribbled about politics, and I correct myself by stopping....

[1] April 1826 – St Petersburg Protocol – Anglo-Russian agreement to mediate between Turks and Greeks to gain for the latter complete autonomy.

July 1827 – London Protocol – France, Russia and England agreed to use force if necessary to ensure an armistice in the Graeco-Turkish war.

[2] An allusion to the destruction of Moscow in 1812. The French, on reaching the city, found it put to the torch by the inhabitants.

[3] The Emperor Napoleon abdicated at Fontainebleau in 1814, and was decisively and finally defeated at Waterloo. Constantine is implying that the Russians might learn to their cost that an invasion of Turkey could be as much of a disaster for them as the invasion of Russia was for Napoleon.

The Grand Duchess Anna Pavlovna, the Princess of Orange, to the Grand Duke Constantine:

The Hague,
2 April 1828

Dear and excellent Brother,

. . I understand perfectly, dear Brother, the impression that. your stay in St Petersburg must have made on you. When one arrives somewhere with one's heart full of indelible memories of those whom one has loved and lost, and one finds oneself in the midst of a tumult of pleasure instead of being able to give oneself up to one's overriding feeling, the soul must be affected, and I realise better than anyone how worn out one can be, not having time to breathe in twenty-four hours; I find, as you say, that the hours are too short for everything that one tries to force into their frame. The periods of waiting and the conversations occupy such a large number of *so-called moments* that together they add up to hours which generally slip away doing every thing except what one would like to do. But at least you have the sweet satisfaction of thinking of the happiness that you gave Mama by your presence; her letters about you are touching. You are now the only *contemporary* whom she retains among her children. You are the *only one* who has witnessed the old times and with whom she can talk about many things which interest her and that none of us nor those around her now have seen. Princess Lieven took with her to the grave a thousand precious memories, and Mama misses her acutely; she leaves an irreparable gap, and for my part I confess that I cannot imagine Mama's circle nor the Winter Palace without her. Was it not her exclusive privilege to scold the family, for this is granted neither by decree nor by hereditary title. As one divides history into periods, this one is a life which finishes with death.

As for the people you mention, I admit that the change in them does not surprise me. I should have been more astonished to see them persevering in their devoutness than to know they have abandoned themselves to pleasure, for with these people piety was only one more instance of coquetterie, and as for instability and resolutions which depend on which way the wind is blowing, I am of the belief that this frame of mind is cosmopolitan, with the sole difference that it is according to the country whether it is the wind from above or the wind from below which makes its influence felt. Poor mankind is so adept at compromising itself that every day I tell myself to keep a watch on myself because I am among them. There must be a true sympathy between us, dear Brother, because I share your opinion in every respect about the big interests of the day and the night, this is what I call the dark part of the subject. No one knows better than I how to apply Figaro's opinion, that it is not necessary to know something to argue about it. On these grounds I cannot prevent myself thinking about and judging the facts that come to my knowledge. About the *cause of causes*, the only difference that I can see is that there are turbans on one side and red caps on the other. But I have another personal reason for being interested in the maintenance of the Ottoman Empire. I am very sensitive to cold and as it is the only empire in which everyone has the privilege of wearing a fur-lined coat in all seasons, I can only wish for its preservation in the hope that this good example will one day be extended. Tell me if the troops march to the air of Goconde, 'A crusade has been sworn upon, we are going to fight the infidels'. One could add this theme to the collection of marches.

We ourselves, dear Brother, live here in perfect calm. Only my children vary the daily monotony by their games and their noise. The older ones are growing up a great deal; and the little girl is becoming very gay, she is bright and lively and has, I believe, the sort of face to find favour in your eyes because of its mischievousness; she is still at the happy age when she has not even reached ABC yet. Our spring is very cold and there is even snow today! It was milder in January.

THE GRAND DUCHESS ANNA PAVLOVNA, THE PRINCESS OF ORANGE, TO THE GRAND DUKE CONSTANTINE:

The Hague,
9 May 1828

Dear excellent Brother!

. . . I trust these lines will find you at Warsaw, at least I must suppose so, since sister-in-law Helen is taking her route by there, and William writes me that when he leaves Petersburg he will go to Warsaw. I frankly envy them both the happiness of seeing you again which I have wanted to do for so long. It seems that at Petersburg everything is being prepared for some unknown reason? Reports from the family of successive departures of guards regiments, and there Mama is, left all alone, isolated, and once again having nothing to do but worry without being able to find anyone from the family near her who could be of aid to her! I admit this distresses and worries me; if it were only possible for me to do something! I wish I could find something interesting to tell you about from here but really I can only speak to you about my children; as for the fair in the midst of which we find ourselves, it is offering many fine goods, games, trained dogs and even *cats* and puppets. You will admit that at the very most this is only enough to make you smile but not to converse about with you. The weather is very changeable, the spring is late after an extremely mild winter. We have only had a few pleasant days to enjoy the first greenery and the delightful scene which The Hague and the surrounding countryside offer at this time of year. Everything is like a huge garden; on all sides you see charming country houses built of bricks and worthy of winning your favour; everything is so well cared-for that it is a true delight for the eye. I made an excursion to Haarlem in honour of the tulips and hyacinths; I saw a few wigs and distributed more than one *Goeden dag mijn heer*. I am convinced that, knowing your tastes, dear Brother, this country would please you, even outside of a painting.

The Grand Duke Constantine to the Grand Duchess Anna Pavlovna, the Princess of Orange:

Warsaw,
18/30 May 1828

I received your three letters consecutively, dear Sister, and take true pleasure in sending you all my thanks for them as well as for the affection you show for me in them. Please be convinced, dear Sister, that I think of you with infinite tenderness and am very attached to the good opinion you are good enough to have of my person. Also, dear Sister, accept all my grateful words for your good wishes and your congratulations for my birthday. Your good wishes can only bring me happiness and I hope that they will be answered. Your letters addressed to the Emperor and our dear William were immediately sent on to them, and I presume that at the present time they have already arrived at their destinations. Your husband informs me that Mama keeps him in order to spend my day of celebration with her and that immediately on the following day he will set out to return to you by way of here. So I am counting on being fortunate enough to see him again around 26 or 27 May, our style. I do not hope to keep him more than three days from what he tells me, and in order to take greater advantage of this I shall have him lodged in the [Lafinski ?] Palace right beside me. All eyes are turned toward the east and our world offers nothing of interest. One must agree that our *semper idem* is of unequalled monotony. It is only the stopping-off of important people who are going from foreign parts to the army in Turkey,[1] and the coming and going of couriers which sometimes interrupt our solitude. Our position or situation is a real autumn, and ordinarily man prefers to found his hopes on the spring, so we see people rushing in from all sides. All hopes are on the roads to Odessa, [Ismail ?], Bucharest, the Danube and even Constantinople, and, to use an oriental expression, we back here are like the seraglio where the worn-out mistresses are sent. Who knows, perhaps the future holds in store for us the happiness of being useful. Often old arsenals where weapons have been stored have been made use of to supply armies which were known to be deprived of necessities. I confess on the other hand that it is very difficult, if not impossible, to maintain order among those subordinates who, seeing only the impressions of the moment, worry very little about the morrow as they think only of the present. Then ordinarily, newness is pleasing, all good luck, all hopes are attached to it. That is the fate of humanity in all countries and under all governments. With us everything is quiet, our neighbours seem to have changed their minds and want to be on our side, at least they are not for the moment

[1] Russia declared war on Turkey on 26 April 1828. England disapproved, but France supported the Tsar, and Austria accepted the situation but somewhat unhappily.

openly opposed to what we shall do. May Providence grant us its care, otherwise I am certain that these same neighbours will find many pretexts to do the opposite of what they are doing. My last news of the Emperor was from Odessa and [Ismail ?], Michael is giving siege to Brailov and our troops have already occupied Bucharest. Since I last wrote you, dear Sister, I had the happiness of having with me my sister, Marie, her husband and her daughter, who were good enough to spend ten days with me. You can well imagine how happy I felt at seeing them again. So, those days went by like lightning spent in the warmth of friendship. My sister-in-law Helen was also staying with us on her way to take the waters in foreign parts. Her health is in a very wretched condition, but I hope that she is not altogether lost; however, it is very close to that. In her, everything has been affected, both physical and moral qualities, and the latter enormously influences the former. So, one must agree that this young and charming woman was very gratuitously and very uselessly sacrificed. Her position is frightful . . . and what is worse, no one wants to put themselves in her place to understand it. My wife and I did our very best to bring up her morale which was at a completely low ebb, and we trust that hope has returned to her soul. Faced with this, how do you imagine that people for whom everything has succeeded since they have been in the world, who are not competent to conceive of a reverse of fortune, can assess the situation of a person who has had only unhappiness as her lot and who in her nature is a very superior being to those who take delight in passing judgement on her and can understand nothing about it at all. As I spoke out the living and definite truth to my brother in Brest in 1823, I now see all my predictions coming about. I said the same thing to [Mama ?] and to Marie. The latter cannot or will not look at it from the point of view of feeling and only sees the exterior and the evident, completely denying what goes on inside. I do not know whether my home-truths should be charged against me or badly attributed to me but, all things considered, the truth still remains the truth and all family considerations and any others cannot stand up against it. My sincere greetings to your children and I notice, dear Sister, that your daughter takes the place of a doll for you at the moment. So that is how it is for you young mothers? You are all cut from the same cloth. My wife asks me to send you her tender affections, dear Sister. My big son throws himself very humbly at your feet and is more than grateful for the gracious way in which you deign to remember him. I add all mine to his and assure you of the tender and sincere affection which I ever bear for you and with which I shall never cease to be your completely devoted brother and friend.

TSAR NICHOLAS I TO THE GRAND DUCHESS ANNA PAVLOVNA, THE PRINCESS OF ORANGE:

Ismail,
22 May/4 June 1828

I must thank you, dear good Sister, for your two letters, one by courier that I received some days before leaving Petersburg, the other yesterday *via* Warsaw. I can assure you that both gave me the most deeply felt pleasure, for I have reread them as indubitable proof of your friendship, and you know the Triopathy[1] still holds. I am sincerely obliged to you for your wishes for the success of our campaign and for us both personally. I have placed my confidence in God and hope that all His mercy will lead everything to a happy conclusion. It is in Him that I have placed my hope and my confidence; the rest depends upon His inscrutable will. Michael is in charge of the siege of Brailov and I hope will reduce them shortly to surrender and will take it by storm. We are shortly going to force our way across the Danube; this enterprise has been delayed as high waters have made it absolutely impossible to try it. As for your personal commissions for the Sultan, I frankly confess that I should be amply pleased not to be in a position to fulfil them, and in any case I promise you nothing as I do not like to share out the bear's hide before I have it. But if you would like some Turkish bullets as a souvenir, it will be much easier for me to give you them *manu propria*. . . .

Please excuse me in that our correspondence cannot be very continuous, it is not within the bounds of possibility. I beg you

[1] A family club consisting of Anna Pavlovna and her brothers, Nicholas and Michael. Their mother, the Empress Marie, was an honorary member.

to give my regards to their Majesties and above all to [Mama?]. A thousand dear regards to Fritz and his wife and to Bourcis. Good-bye, dear Anne, think sometimes of your Trans-Danubian friends, and wish for their prompt return to their Penates. For life from heart and soul,

Your faithful brother and friend.

THE GRAND DUKE CONSTANTINE TO THE GRAND DUCHESS ANNA PAVLOVNA, THE PRINCESS OF ORANGE:

Warsaw,
31 May/12 June 1828

am taking advantage of our dear William's departure, dear Sister, to write you these lines in order to give you my regards and assure you of all my affection and tenderness. I hope, dear Sister, that you do not have any doubts about them and that you will always keep yours for me. Our dear William was extremely kind to give up four days to us which flashed by with lightning-stroke rapidity, like all good and happy things. We are seeing him go with the greatest regret, my wife and I, and are making the most ardent wishes that he may have a fortunate journey and that he returns to you in perfect health. The four days which we spent together were given over to the most absolute affection and trust, and there was not a subject upon which we did not discuss and completely plumb. It would be impossible to give you the particulars of all this and I leave it to him himself to give you the details in person. It has been a long time since I have spent more pleasant moments, and I truly assure you that the memory of them will not be blotted from my mind. It is so good here in this world to find someone with whom one cannot only exchange words but thoughts, and who is capable of understanding you, that one seizes avidly upon such chances which occur so seldom. It is unfortunately very much my case. I have nothing of great interest to tell you about from here. Everything is quiet. Our weather is horrible, and cold as if it were October, and very sad and grey along with it. All attention is turned toward the east, which is very natural. On our part, we are well aware for whom we are destined and I presume that our *semper idem* will remain so without being disturbed. Please, dear Sister, pass on all my gratitude to your husband for the extreme kindness he was good enough to have to stay with us those four days, and tell him that they will most assuredly be, and remain, graven upon my memory. My affection to your children, dear Sister. William was perfect towards my wife and boy and that is one more reason for my gratitude. Remember affectionately a brother who cherishes you with his heart and soul.

THE GRAND DUCHESS ANNA PAVLOVNA, THE PRINCESS OF ORANGE, TO THE GRAND DUKE CONSTANTINE:

The Hague,
2 June 1828

Dear excellent Brother,

. . . Our spring is quite fine, at least fine enough not to have one's walks interfered with. This year I am half a city-dweller; that is to say, as The Hague is a city and as I am here, I am as much of a city-dweller as one can be when everything in it makes one think of the country. I am reduced to telling you about the vegetation which is magnificent here; there is so much shade that there are dozens of walks to choose from. It is in this fine shade that I follow my brothers in their adventurous careers. You will see that in a little while all the fashionable colours will be named – Russian cannon-smoke, Constantinople mud, Sultan's beard and other pleasantries like that. You also see that my politics are enclosed within the limits of my sex; that kind of neutrality completely suits my sluggish mind, but activity recurs in the worries which are so easy to feel for our two brothers. May God preserve and bless them!

THE GRAND DUCHESS ANNA PAVLOVNA, THE PRINCESS OF ORANGE, TO THE GRAND DUKE CONSTANTINE:

Soestdijk,
17 July 1828

Dear and excellent Brother,

. . . Your two dear previous letters keenly interested me, especially the first one in which you tell me about Helen. Now, without our having told one another our opinion about her position, it is remarkable that my view about her agrees completely with yours, dear Brother, in that I too feel that she is a very noble person – completely sacrificed – who, in my opinion, only indulges in the small defects for which she is blamed because she has been provoked or soured by an uninterrupted succession of difficulties about which she is still both too young and too lively to become resigned. However, this decision seems to me to be the only one she can make, and perhaps if Michael could consider her calmly, he would have more respect for her. I pity both of them, they have so many noble qualities which seem designed to bring happiness, but their characters are not suited to one another. If Helen had met a man who would have loved her and known how to give a *pleasant* direction to her spiritual advantages, she would have been a charming woman; and if Michael had married someone who suited him, he would have been an excellent husband. Helen really has nothing left to do but accept the situation, to *soften* her feelings and, with that, her character, and for Michael to *think out* his behaviour towards her. That is my entire opinion, and at the risk of being accused, as Bridoison said, I think, 'my own opinion is that I do not understand anything about it, for it is sometimes a puzzle.' We have one of a new kind in the family here because of the marriage planned for my sister-in-law Marianne with Prince Gustav,[1] who is assuming the title of Prince of Sweden. To my mind it would be a sad position to have my sister-in-law married in that way; she would have an establishment in this country and one in Vienna, without having a settled position anywhere, and what a source of discord, worry and apprehension in European politics. It is deplorable! I beg you, dear Brother, *inform me* in a sure way what you know about this Prince Gustav, his personality? his behaviour? and his conduct at Vienna? upon which Marianne's fate will so entirely depend. He seemed to me to be very awkward physically, his face is pleasant enough when he is chatting, and what he says is fine, but he has with him a certain Count Polier-Vernaud, his former tutor, who now

[1] Prince Gustavus Vasa (1798–1877) the son of King Gustavus Adolphus IV of Sweden. The latter had been deposed and all of his family excluded from the throne. Prince Gustavus had no real position in the complicated royal circles in Europe and hence was not a very eligible *parti*. The Bernadotte dynasty, then reigning in Sweden, objected to his use of the title Prince of Sweden.

pushes him ahead in everything and is himself in Metternich's pocket. Do you know anything about them or not? Forgive me all these impertinent questions but your affection and trust have made me accustomed to acting in this way. Except for this complication, I am content and happy in my home and lead a kind of life which is completely pleasant for me, in a countryside of which I am fond above all others. Inform me, I beg you, of what you are doing and if the troops are going to camp this year.

I ask you to remember my children affectionately. Please give my kind regards to Paul. I hope, dear friend, that you will not conclude from what I say about Michael that my affection for him is not as true as it has always been, and I shall say of him '*In spite of your faults I love you passionately.*'

THE GRAND DUKE CONSTANTINE TO THE GRAND DUCHESS ANNA PAVLOVNA, THE PRINCESS OF ORANGE:

Warsaw,
15/27 July 1828

I begin my letter by throwing myself at your feet, dear Sister, not to offer you my gratitude for those which you were good enough to write me but to beg pardon for having delayed so long in replying to them. I have no excuse to produce for this and if I had it would be very maladroit of me to have recourse to it. In short, I am guilty and I beg full and entire pardon which I hope to obtain through your constant and long-standing kindness of which you never cease to show me proof. Your letters are evidence to me of it and put me in the wrong. I beg you grant forgiveness to me. If in spite of what I confirm here I might be permitted to state whatever might stand in my favour, I would allow myself to say that the season in which we now are, the events of the day which, so to speak, keep us on the alert in spite of the fact that we are not called upon to share the dangers, the hazards and the glory of the war considering our remoteness, our occupations of all kinds; in short, this state of tension and continual anxiety in which we are held by events made me fall short of my duty of replying to your dear good letters. Having once made this statement, permit me, dear excellent Sister, to offer you all my gratitude for your letters to the number of three, as well as for the good wishes you were kind enough to make for me for my name-day and that you expressed to me in such a kind way. Please believe, dear Sister, that I am extremely touched by that and grateful in spite of my long silence, and that I am counting on them to bring me happiness. Of your three letters, two reached me by the post and the last through the *Feldjäger* who accompanied our dear William and whom he sent on to the Emperor. All your news interested me keenly and I am happy to learn from you yourself that you are well and greeted your husband again with the greatest pleasure on his return from Petersburg. I am absolutely of your opinion concerning Helen and I hope that time will make both her and Michael see what there is to be done in order to come to an understanding. I think that the whole business arises from misunderstanding and relatively false positions, and I dare say so now, and even repeat it to anyone who wishes to listen, that if my advice had been followed right from the outset and beginning, many sorrows and disappointments would have been spared. I was alone in my opinion at the time, as I had to struggle up hill and down dale, but I did not give them up, and the facts proved that I was right then and now. Moreover, what is done is done and there is no way to do it over again. It seems that since the separation, things are going better and from the letters which go through my hands I notice that the correspondence is fairly active. Helen must be very proud of the glory Michael has acquired, although it was bought at a very high price and cost us many good men, in my humble opinion sacrificed almost for nothing and very uselessly. It is a lesson taught by Providence which ought to throw some light on the future. Concerning what you ask me about a future relative of yours, I shall say that I am not in any way acquainted with him as I have never met him. All the opinions I have heard about him are very varied indeed and I could not make a proper judgement about him. As for my own experience, I can tell you that I have had nothing but politeness and kind attention from him. At the death of our late immortal Emperor, when I was least expecting it, he was polite enough to write me from [Milan ?] a most kind letter to express his sympathies to me, which I answered and he replied to me most kindly.[1] That is all the two of us have in common. Once in Vienna he tried to enter the regiment which has the honour of forever bearing the name of our late Emperor; I do not know the reason why, because of earlier occurrences, he cannot bear a special affection for Him. On the other hand, public gossip says that he is selfish and discreditable and in short supply of fortune; I do not know whether it is true or not, I am only repeating here what I have heard. About the person who accompanies him and who, according to what you say, does with him whatever he wishes and leads him to such an extent that he says and does nothing without him – without his guidance and directions in the slightest little things – they say he is an intriguer and a swindler and was once his teacher or else his tutor, at the same time he was according to some the lover, according to others the secret husband, of his late mother, and at the present time he must be an agent of P. [rince] Metternich and his general man of all work. Very recently he was created count in Vienna which, for one of Swiss nationality as he is, is rather strange. However, one can surmise that he is from the aristocratic cantons. In Petersburg I saw his brother who is married to the widow of Count Schuvaloff, *née* Princess Tchaikowsky, and who, if one credits backstairs gossip, was her lover while her husband was still alive, as the man was at that time lieutenant in a regiment. He is a Swiss who has gone over to the service of France – he had himself naturalised as a Russian citizen – and is decorated with the free slap – the so-called Legion of Honour. I met him at Count Kochubey's home making up a game with old Lady Fugretski [?]. He is a handsome man and built by nature to be a good lover for the ladies who want one; the words of the proverb, so they say, can be applied to him: no money, no Swisses. In general, the two brothers are thought to be very self-seeking. In spite of the fact that my letter reaches you by post and can be read, it matters little, I am only reporting in it some gossip and am confirming nothing. You really made me laugh, dear Sister, with what you tell me in your letter of 21 May by teaching me the fashionable colours such as Warsaw smoke, Sultan's beard, etc. I am very much afraid that there could be added to them

[1] The Grand Duke seems to have forgotten that Prince Gustavus Vasa was the nephew of the Empress Elizabeth, and Tsar Alexander was his guardian.

that of Russian blood, Army's sweat and Eastern loss. We 'westerners' are on the sidelines and are waiting for a decision to be made about us, busy as in the past at doing our duty in silence. The military outing of Constantinople is being accomplished, so it seems to me, more slowly and with more difficulties than had been imagined, and perhaps to end [it], the year 1829 should be used, which would mean that we westerners would have to take part in it. I said so to our dear William. May the good Lord bring this unfortunate war to as quick an end as possible since, if it drags on, the results could be completely different from those expected and imagined. All the liberal public papers had been pushing us for three years into this unfortunate war, and since it started they seem to be saying: 'Now that Russia is caught up in the struggle, the larger part of its forces are in it, we have free rein and we can look after ourselves in the west, the Colossus can only put up against us half or the smaller part of its forces.' I am writing to you, dear Sister, as if I were speaking to you. In my isolation here I could be wrong. In any case, I shall stand by my opinion until events prove the contrary to me. My sister Marie with her daughter Augusta passed through here on her return from Petersburg, and I was fortunate enough to have them for five days counting those of arrival and departure. You can imagine my happiness at being reunited with some of my own family; that has happened to me so seldom during the almost sixteen years that the superior powers have assigned to me a post separated from them. Have your husband tell you what the Chateau of [Lafinski ?] is like, where my sister stayed; he also stayed there the last time he stopped off and saw it in all its finery at the time of the last Diet in the days of the late Emperor. It is a delightful place. Fine weather blessed my sister's visit. My wife asks me to pass on to you her gratitude for so kindly and affectionately remembering her. . . . My tender and sincere affection to our dear William. Tell him that in a few days I shall answer his long letter which came through the *Feldjäger*, as I do not have time to do so today. My affection and compliments to your children and homage to Miss Orange. Continue sending affections, kindness and goodness to your old brother, dear Sister. . . .

THE GRAND DUKE CONSTANTINE TO THE GRAND DUCHESS ANNA PAVLOVNA, THE PRINCESS OF ORANGE:

Warsaw,
28 August/9 September 1828

Dear Sister,

How can I tell you of the cruel and painful loss we have just experienced, in such an unexpected way. Mama, alas, no longer lives; the good Lord has deigned to recall her to Him after a ten-day illness. One must have more than resignation to the decrees of Providence to be able to bear such blows. It is only in religion that strength can be acquired. Mama will receive in eternity the reward for her great virtues which so eminently characterised her, and I am certain that the good Lord will have her enjoy them fully. Eight days before her death she deigned to write my wife and I, telling us that she was doing so in order not to give us cause to worry about her condition. This letter reached us on the day after that on which she had died in Petersburg. You yourself can imagine the cruel sorrow and pain I feel over this. A new era is beginning for us who are now orphans in this world below. My wife is most worthy of belonging to the family because of the sorrows and pain she feels, and I admit to you that I am not resting easily about the results. My hope is in the Lord and in His pity and clemency. As for you, dear Sister, permit me to recall to you that we well know the *true* distress which this cruel occurrence must necessarily make you feel, but you must remember that you are a mother and that your own obligations are to your children. Remember too our dear and excellent William for whom your preservation is precious. Keep holding for me, dear Sister, your long-standing kindnesses and goodness and always count on the tender and sincere affections of your faithful brother and friend.

THE GRAND DUCHESS ANNA PAVLOVNA, THE PRINCESS OF ORANGE, TO THE GRAND DUKE CONSTANTINE:

Soestdijk,
20 September 1828

Dear excellent Brother,

. . . I read with the keenest interest the details you were kind enough to give me about Prince Gustav and his hangers-on. I would even say that that long interesting letter seemed to have reached me at Ems to give me the impression of hearing you speak and have you join the family reunion, during which you were very frequently the subject of our conversation, dear good Brother. Helen was very moved by the affection you showed for her during the visit she made in Warsaw; the interest which you displayed had made her feel better, and I have had occasion to observe that such is the effect which affection produces in her. A very kind letter which she had just received from Michael at that time had made her happy. I found that she had grown prettier and it seemed to me that her way of looking at things had improved. No one would cavil at her wit; I am sometimes afraid that she displays too much of it to have one understand her fully, and the inconvenience which results from trying to find her meaning may be one of the chief causes of her disagreeable position. At least I can affirm that those presently with her are very delighted with her, they speak highly of her behaviour; and if I wish for something for Helen, it would be for that amenity and patience which form the basis of our dear Jeannette's charming personality, and I think that if anyone in the world could have a good influence on Helen it would be your wife, dear friend, for Helen would see that wit is compatible with sweetness and patience; but I am afraid that she is not enough convinced of this truth; for her wit is better than her personality, and in the long run this does not make for ease. Let us hope for good results from absence and isolation; moreover, pushed aside as she has been by her own family,[1] by the King of Württemberg[2] and by her grandmother,[3] what is left for her? if it be only to try and gain for herself a tolerable life by reflecting upon the true and only means of reaching it by valuing what is good in her situation in Russia; nevertheless, I quite believe that in this world difficulties are reserved for noble personalities. On the one hand, may it please Heaven that the anxieties and dangers of the Turkish war may make Michael value his home-life; he is a dear but unique combination

[1] Her father was Prince Paul of Württemberg and her mother was Princess Catherine. They had promoted the marriage.

[2] King William I; he married the Grand Duchess Catherine Pavlovna and was not much liked by Anna Pavlovna.

[3] Augusta of Brunswick, wife of King Frederick I.

whom one must love with all one's heart because no one is better than he for spiritual qualities. So there once again, dear Brother, is my little opinion about them which I express to you with all my usual frankness.

All the details you have communicated to me about Prince Gustav were known to me, partly from his visit here and partly since; among other things the *liaison* or *secret marriage* which seems to have existed between the late Queen,[1] his mother, and his tutor Polier-Vernaud, a fact that, whichever it may have been, seems to me to be extremely base on the part of a mother regarding her son's tutor; when one thinks that she was no longer young, that she had gone through griefs which seemingly ought to have made her retreat from this world's weaknesses, and that after all, the King her husband, although deprived of his reason, still lived and was none the less the father of Prince Gustav, whose tutor had become either his step-father while the father was still alive, or a criminal individual. How can one put a child in such a false position, or, to put it another way, between duty and scorn! These are doubly deplorable examples because they rock more than one foundation which supposedly should be immovable, and such ideas should not be admissible in the social order. This century would make Diogenes run away with his lantern in his hand. In any case, I would not be astonished if, to the number of fashionable colours for next winter one could add to those I listed for you the colours of Diplomats' worries and Swedish snow. For it seems that the latter are already beginning to pile up, in so much as the title of 'Prince of Sweden' is opposed for Prince Gustav and it is embarrassing to know what title to give him when naming him officially. Austria, or to put it correctly, Metternich, has not thrown out a brand of discord for nothing, to try and shuffle the cards for fear that the game was going too well and to try to make themselves influential or necessary in the midst of the difficulties which may take shape. It seems that the first good

[1] Frederica of Baden, sister of the Empress Elizabeth of Russia. King Gustavus Adolphus and his wife separated after the king was deposed. He became increasingly eccentric. He refused to accept any form of financial assistance and lived in total retirement, calling himself Colonel Gustafson. Whether Polier-Verraud was the Queen's lover is an open question. Certainly he was a very intimate member of the royal circle, but in exile there were few loyal servants; moreover, all such attendants are the victims of gossip.

impression which had overcome L.L.M.M. [*leurs Majestés*] here is little by little beginning to evaporate, only to leave behind a hint of all kinds of embarrassment which the proposed union would bring with it. In all this I am sorry for my sister-in-law Marianne, who is a charming, interesting person, because I could not foresee a chance of happiness in her future. Her position will be false and the Prince is not personally distinguished enough to make up for this disadvantage. In a short while we are planning to leave this place, of which I am particularly fond, to move to Tervueren for the rest of the autumn and then spend the winter in Brussels. God grant that it be a quiet one, and that the subject mentioned above does not bring about unpleasantness which could disturb our home-life and thus cut into the only true happiness in the world in my eyes, that of a quiet daily routine.

TSAR NICHOLAS I TO THE GRAND DUCHESS ANNA PAVLOVNA, THE PRINCESS OF ORANGE:

St Petersburg,
18/30 November 1828

I have been waiting for [Wickolosky ?] to go to write you, dear Anne, as all this sad period has not made it possible for me to do so; moreover, what I can tell you from here is not likely to interest you. This frightful time has been somewhat lightened for us by the presence of Constantine who came at once to join us after the sad painful news; I cannot begin to tell you how good and excellent he has been towards us and of what help he has been – particularly to me; his friendship has always been precious; now it has become an indispensable necessity for us all, for it is in him that all our affection meets, as being the eldest of our family – something which he understands perfectly. Our existence is more monotonous than ever; mine is shared between the duties of my service, my children, and that is a consolation which the good Lord in his mercy has granted me and which is invaluable; since I have been deprived of them for six months, I am enjoying them fully. Apart from ours, we shall have Michael's, who has given them to us with confidence and whom we appreciate.

Orders have been given that you will no longer be importuned by the presence of any of our people whatsoever in your chapel,[1] unless they are expressingly called there; that is all I can do in regard to your wishes; as far as going back to the past or giving instructions of the type you wish, I believe I would offend you in so doing, for I do not think it worthy of your dignity to indulge in conduct which is perhaps imprudent but in which no intention of the guilty parties could include you. More, I would say that if I were called upon by you to criticise them, I cannot do it without naming you, and consequently meting out *punishment* – for if the circumstance has deserved such a complaint from you it becomes too serious to be terminated in any other way. But that is enough about that tedious chapter.

Please hug your children for me; farewell dear good Anne, keep some remembrance and friendship for your old brother and friend.

THE GRAND DUCHESS ANNA PAVLOVNA, THE PRINCESS OF ORANGE, TO THE GRAND DUKE CONSTANTINE:

Brussels,
22 November 1828

Dear and excellent Brother,

What can we say to each other in the frightful grief which has struck us all, except to pay homage to her memory by doubling our affection for one another if possible. How touched I was that you remembered me in this calamity; once again, I found that kind tender brother who is always the same for me. *What a loss!* what an abyss for us all; you are very right to say that a new era is beginning for us, and for me, dear Brother and friend, more I think than for all the others; Mama was my refuge, my support, I could open my heart to her and she deigned to

[1] Apparently visiting Russians had taken advantage of the attendance of the Grand Duchess Anna Pavlovna at the Orthodox chapel and they had used these occasions to ask her for special favours. Their behaviour finally became so bad – the Grand Duchess often found it hard to refuse requests made in church – that she complained to the Tsar. He put a stop to the whole business. It all grew out of the ancient tradition of petitioning the prince for favours after divine service.

encourage me with her advice! All of that is finished, so I feel so alone in the universe that nothing equals my desolation; I must pray Heaven ceaselessly to support me and to help me fulfil the duties it has imposed on me and which are surely dear to me provided I succeed, for I am aware of all the difficulties. Dear good William is very afflicted, but is as well in health as possible, considering the past, the present and so many many things which have shaken his health. Dear Brother and friend, let me tell you how desolate my heart is and beg you to keep being affectionate to me and remember me trustingly. Let me write you regularly, *once every week*, I ask you for this as a proof of kindness which I need if only to cover up the void I am left with at no longer being able to correspond with her whom we have lost. May God support you when you are near her dear mortal remains and give you the moral strength to bear this whole harrowing time. May God grant that Jeannette's health does not suffer from this new shock and that you may always be for each other what you are now. I embrace her in thought like a tender sister towards whom my heart ceaselessly inclines me. As I suppose you will see Michael at Petersburg, give him many affectionate regards from me; he knows how much I love him but I cannot write him this time. I shall do so at the first opportunity by mail. I have yet another real favour to ask of you, which is to send me regular news of my dear ones with you and of what is happening in Russia, for I am completely isolated from everything by this event.

TSAR NICHOLAS I TO THE GRAND DUCHESS ANNA PAVLOVNA, THE PRINCESS OF ORANGE:

St Petersburg,
29 November/11 December 1828

. . . How unfortunate it is that the frightful news reached you at the very moment you had just moved into your superb new lodging;[1] what a painful impression this circumstance must have given you and our poor William who was celebrating and

[1] They moved in on 15 November 1828. It replaced the old one destroyed by fire in 1820.

rejoicing at knowing you settled, agreeably and willingly, in that new house to which he had devoted all his care for that purpose! I suppose, too, that it was that circumstance on top of everything that brought out your black mood more than usual and which impelled you to ask me to do you a favour, the kindness of which I appreciate but which, according to the natural order of things, I hope will fall to someone else; I am speaking of your last will and testament and all it involves, for, truthfully, it is not likely that I shall survive you. But for the moment let us chase away these sad thoughts and let us trust, for that as for everything, in Providence which will arrange everything for the best. I have transmitted your orders to Williamov and he will conform to them.

Not before Monday can we break the seal on Mama's papers; and as it was said that she named testamentary executors, it will only be to know her wishes concerning this. You will read this Will, and the most painful emotion awaits you in this reading, but also how many reasons it gives us for feeling consoled. Since Michael is one of the executors, it is to him that you will be able to address yourself in order to get back what you wish; before restoring to you your [letters] which Mama bequests to me, I want to know if you persist in your intention of having them back; in that case I shall separate myself from them, but with a double feeling of grief I confess to you; if you leave them with me, I shall hold it as a real sign of friendship on your part.

I am deeply grieved by William's condition, I am doing what I can for him by begging him to follow the doctors' advice and not to hurt you unnecessarily.

All this makes me fear that we shall not be able to see one another again for a long time. To give up the prospect completely would be cruel, I admit; and I still hope that when the good Lord grants us quiet times, you will want to come and see your old friends! Forgive me for this confession. I informed Michael of your wish, but it was not easy to foresee his reply. The 21st – A courier for London is leaving this evening and I am sending you this letter as I do not want to delay any longer in replying to you. I had hoped that this courier would be able to bring you the copy of the Will but Michael has just told me that they have not been able to finish the copies yet, but you will have it as soon as possible. As for the objects which are to come back to you, I shall get them to you through the excellent Grimm, my mother's footman, whom you will perhaps find it pleasant to see again.

The Grand Duke Constantine to the Grand Duchess Anna Pavlovna, the Princess of Orange:

Warsaw,
7/19 January 1829

Receive, dear and most dear Sister, my tenderest congratulations for your birthday as well as my most heartfelt good wishes for your happiness, contentment and perfect prosperity. In my thoughts I do not separate you from our dear William and your children and my good wishes are sent to you all together, reasoning the way I would for myself as I cannot separate my well-being from that of my wife. According to what I am saying to you, dear Sister, I trust and hope that you will have no doubts about the sincerity of the good wishes I offer you from the depths and fullness of my heart. If they are to be granted, certainly nothing will be lacking for your happiness on this earth. I have complete trust in God's clemency about this. I received your two letters, dear excellent Sister, one in answer to mine in which I informed you of our irretrievable cruel loss, and the other, very recently, which you addressed to me knowing that I had returned from my Petersburg trip. Please accept my very sincere thanks for them and be sure that the sweet interest you have for me is more than precious to me, and accept my assurance that I shall constantly do my best to deserve it in every possible way. I cannot tell you anything about Petersburg except that the scene is the same but that it is no longer like what we knew it to be in the past. Since the death of our late immortal Emperor it was no longer the same in my eyes, but Mama still prevailed there and to her they were accustomed to paying gifts of respect, homage and adoration, which she knew so well how to inspire; in short, she was the keystone. With her loss the charm is destroyed and a new era has just begun. Certainly it is not up to anyone at all, and even less to me than anyone else, to set myself up as judge or investigator of what is being done or what is happening there, but I think I am allowed, without harming anyone, to feel nostalgic for what is no more and to return in thought to times to which my affections call me back more and more for many many reasons. Our old Winter Palace is no longer the same in my eyes, only the outside has not changed, the rest shows signs of today's vicissitudes. I shall not dwell upon the hollow spectacle of Mama's funeral. Those sorts of ceremonies are all more or less the same, it is only the emotions which are different, and in this respect it was heartrending. After arriving at Petersburg I became so ill that my doctor, who has known me for thirty-eight years, was very worried for forty-eight hours, but thanks to his care, God's goodness and the general interest which they were kind enough to display for me in all classes, I had recovered at the end of a week. The Emperor, the Empress and our dear Michael showered kindness and attention on me and showed for me a most heartfelt and eager attentiveness. As soon as the burial was over – passing forty-eight hours with the family to show them how keenly grateful I was – I left Petersburg, and, after spending twenty-four hours at my dear Strelna, I came back here after one of the most painful and longest trips I have made. Everything was against me, rain and rivers overflowing, an infernal road – as I was forced to camp for fourteen hours in cold reaching 10 degrees [. . . ?] having been caught in the ice on the [Vilna ?] down from Kovno – in short, the keenest of travellers would have found enough to be disgusted with in any travelling. I arrived here in fairly good health, but I suffered slightly from [colic ?] which soon went away. I do not know exactly to what I should attribute my illness but I suppose it is the result of last summer's worries after the fine things of the last campaign, sorrow at the loss of my mother and other small incidents, each one more unpleasant than the next. Once again with my wife I no longer think of them and I am happy to be near her and my son. Thanks to God, everything is quiet with us and I send up my most ardent prayers that the good Lord will deign to preserve us in this state of affairs and that completely unnecessary incidents will not stir it up, as last year's experience seems to have done no good for the future. Moreover, I would have had many things to say about that but

a word to the wise is sufficient, as the proverb says. . . .
At the renewal of the year, my most sincere good wishes for your happiness, dear Sister, and that of your whole family.

The Grand Duchess Anna Pavlovna, the Princess of Orange, to the Grand Duke Constantine:

Brussels,
10 February 1829

. . . It had been a long time since I had had any news of you from you yourself, and what I have learned about you reached me through our sister and the newspapers. I knew that you had been ill and I was worried, so I was going to take pen in hand to ask for news of you when your dear letter arrived to reassure me for the moment, but also confirming that your health had been strongly affected at the time of our mournful loss, and that a painful time was a consequence of this. May God grant that your health entirely recover and that time may have the effect of softening a grief which each of us cannot but feel deeply and for the whole of our existence. In spite of all the harrowing qualities your last visit to Petersburg must have had for you, dear Brother, you presence was a consolation for Nicholas, and his wife and our good Michael. You cannot ever imagine how touched Nicholas was at your affection; his first letter afterwards is full of it. He wrote me that you had helped him bear moments which would have been too dreadful without the consolation of brotherly love. I recognise you in all that, and I see in it a consolation for our mutual unhappiness for which once more the event served to prove the whole sincerity of family feelings which form our bond. I understand perfectly the painful appearance and awful change which your heart must have found in that Winter Palace, once inhabited by so many dear people. There is nothing more natural than the sorrow which you display for the past; for that, I think no one could share your feelings more than Nicholas himself who feels all the isolation of his position. I hope that when this letter reaches you, you will be completely well, dear Brother, and that domestic happiness will have softened the impact of much sadness;

there is nothing dearer than being understood. As you tell me nothing about Jeannette's health, I suppose that it is good this winter and I beg you to give my tender affection to my sister-in-law. It will not be long before you see dear Michael arriving; according to the news which I have just received from Petersburg, he must be about to leave; it is because of that, dear Brother, that I am enclosing the letter which I address to him in yours, asking you to be kind enough to give it to him.

We have a winter worthy of the north, and snow one could boast about in Russia for sleighing. For the twelve years that I have been living in this country I have seen nothing like it, and from time to time there are fogs bad enough to make one appreciate the invention of candles – without which one would have to be like the Scriptural light which burns in darkness – in order to see. That is what it is like outside; as for our inner life, it is quiet around our family hearths, the affection which is enjoyed within the household and the very dear interest which is attached to the children softens life, and surrounded as I am in such a pleasant way, this winter is going by for me with agreeable monotony, that is all I could expect after a loss the memory of which mingles with everything.

THE GRAND DUKE CONSTANTINE TO THE GRAND DUCHESS ANNA PAVLOVNA, THE PRINCESS OF ORANGE:

Warsaw,
28 February/12 March 1829

Dear Sister,

I cannot let Grimm, our late Mama's valet, pass through here without giving him these few words for you. He is bringing you, and also to Marie, the bequest She was good enough to make to us all. As I recently wrote you at length I have nothing new to tell you from here. Everything is quiet, thank God, as in the past, and let us hope that it will remain so. The only interesting news is that we are informed for certain of the Emperor's arrival for the end of our April. William will easily understand my present position in comparison with the past, and especially in considering it in relation to four years ago.

He was a witness and actor at it. May God give me strength! Diebitsch has replaced Wittgenstein, Toll, Kisseliev. So much for the army. I can see your husband's face when he learns this news. Before conquering Turkey, Diebitsch must win over the confidence of his own army which he managed to upset to the point of hating him during the last campaign. I no longer have a moment to myself and I must finish up with my affectionate compliments to our dear William and my love to your children. . . .

THE GRAND DUCHESS ANNA PAVLOVNA, THE PRINCESS OF ORANGE, TO TSAR NICHOLAS I:

Brussels,
5 March 1829

'It is about the fourth page of my mother's Will.' [*Note in Anna Pavlovna's handwriting.*]

Dear good Brother,

Your two letters of 21 January and 5 February put me under obligation towards you, dear friend, for here I am late, I who have almost nothing to do while you have an empire to rule. But health is something, and even a great deal when it interferes by keeping one in bed causing cramp, a stitch in one's side, and obliges one to have leeches applied twice, after that fever, and you will have an idea of the pleasant way in which I have spent two weeks which have prevented me writing and delayed the wish that I had, dear Brother, to thank you tenderly. I was deeply moved and edified to read the first of the letters accompanying Mama's Will. I seem to hear her speaking for a last time and I confess I was stirred to the depths of my soul. Let me thank you for the wishes you expressed on my birthday, and all the affectionate things that you say to me retain for me your friendship, and let us always be united by our feelings as at the time of the Triopathy. May God keep for us both all the objects of our love, it is the prime possession of this world. You are truly a good and loving friend to enter into the details about my own Will. I am anxious that it should be in your hands and the half-torn letter should have been destroyed years ago. I burnt it. As to the other, it should be in your hands, and with the Will, you will see why. I should be happy to see you again and to merge in the feeling of sincere friendship all those emotions that stir in my heart in those places where so many regrets await me. Tell me only when and at what time you would like to see me. I believe that this journey would always be easier to make in summer than in winter. You must understand, dear friend, what sort of winter I have passed. I started to see people again as soon as I was able to and we had some parties, one of which was large and entertained by music and scenes from separate tragedies. On our eldest son's birthday the King insisted on giving a great ball. I was able to be present. At least I saw the first debut of my Alexander in the big world. I leave you to think what I felt, and I also claim that it was this ball that gave me the *coup de grâce* as I have not had a day of health since. The next day Mama's Will arrived, so it was emotion upon emotion, and it is not surprising that I should have felt the effects. Aside from that, I may truly say that as regards domestic happiness I have many compensations that are dear to me. William is most friendly and my children so affectionate and confiding that I am happy in my home. Add to that, cordiality and ease of our relations with those surrounding us, and in my view you have there the most essential components for happiness. Now that the first impression of the fatal event, the news of which we heard almost as we entered our house, is starting to fade with the habits that I am gradually forming in the new locale, I find myself agreeably situated. Everything here is beautiful and in good taste, and I know no reason why I should not try and like it as best I can. The large apartment is really beautiful and does honour to William's taste. I shall refrain entirely from discussing with you the public circumstances that have disturbed this winter. I have seen too few people since and avoided too much all the sensitive cords to be able to talk knowledgeably on opinions that I may have heard, and to inform you of what I hear in private would only be to repeat to you what you perhaps already know from the same source. In a word, I do not wish to take the risk of giving you false insights into what is not, thank Heaven, within my province and only touches me in so far as everyone is interested in what is happening in the country. I may even confess that I have been very glad that being less fit than ever to associate with society, to keep calm and to try and soften William's daily life is my only true vocation, more than ever in difficult times, as these appear to be.

About my mother's Will, I take up these lines again today, 19 March, having felt tired yesterday by writing. I went for a walk yesterday for the first time for a long time and I returned as a person drunk. I feel well, but weak, and for that time is necessary. I return today to the subject of Mama's Will. It is very edifying and touching in all respects and in all details in which her solicitude is for the good and the counsels that she gives us. For you, dear friend, this manuscript is a sort of true consolation for the satisfaction that Mama shows for you in it, and you may say, with truth, that you have sweetened her last moments. One can draw from this testament the most encouraging feeling when one sees to what high degree of virtue, perseverance and religious sentiment can help one to attain. And if anything in the world could have attached me more firmly to my duties, this script would have produced the effect on me. I was charmed to see that Mama favoured Marie as was right and proper, and that she should have thought to assure Michael's fortune on a solid base and forbidden him to touch the capital that she deigned to give him, for I have learned the most distressing details on the subject of his fortune, and one must admire the wisdom and the tender solicitude of this excellent mother for having wished, by the arrangements that she made, to guarantee forever Michael's welfare and that of his children. The item about Constantine's sword touched me greatly; this will be for the family as the Sword of Seed [?], will it not, do you think? What heart could feel it better than ours, and may the wishes with which Mama finishes her last desires be realised, dear friend, and the blessing of Heaven grant them to you and the state. After such grave matters, may I speak to you of my modest writings bequeathed to you, if only to tell you how much the friendly things that you say touch me and how pleased I am to know they are in your hands. It is only the copy of the Murillo[1] bequeathed to Constantine

[1] A Spanish artist of the seventeenth century. Most of his paintings were religious in nature and presumably this one under discussion was a religious subject. Could this be the Murillo *Assumption* which hung in the chamber of Empress Alexandra Feodorovna, wife of Nicholas I?

that I persist in claiming and I shall write to him about it because it was placed in the study where Mama spent most time. I am sending you my letter about my Will out of consideration for William whom I wished to favour, so that they will see one day that it is not he who has influenced me in this respect but that it is my own move. I must add several items to the Will that I propose to send you by agreement on his return; this I imagine will not delay its arrival. Your friendship, dear Brother, leads me to write to you a very long letter having at bottom nothing interesting to tell you. I am replying to what you yourself commented on to me. My own existence is very limited; however, in doing my best this gives me an occupation and my little girl, who is growing older, is going to give me more and more duties. Meanwhile one can always work for peace and that influences the whole house. I must at last finish this letter, dear friend, and in putting down my pen I beg you to retain your friendship for me and your remembrance of me. May we always keep mutual relations of confidence and always be as at the time of the Triopathy. I embrace you tenderly.

The Grand Duchess Anna Pavlovna, the Princess of Orange, to Mlle de Sybourg:

Belvedere [Weimar],
8 July 1829

In keeping with my promise, dear excellent friend, I shall give you some news of my sister and my family as soon as I am able to, and I will start by telling you that she asked me for your news with the most sincere interest as well as that of the Grand Duke and Mlle M [indecipherable]. All were delighted to learn that you are as well as when I left you and as I hope to find you again. You may imagine, dear Bourcis, what we felt at seeing each other again and what harrowing memories were attached to the happiness at seeing each other together. My sister is very well regarding her health, her friendship and her kindness are unequalled and leave me to thank Heaven for having given me the pleasure of seeing her again, but she has yellow spots or patches on her face which, they say, come from the liver and from circulating bile which cannot but make me uneasy as signs of the beginning of an illness which may develop. It is because of this tendency that the doctor has advised her to take the Waters at Carlsbad. I had the pleasantest journey in the world and never was a trip better organised. We have not had the least difficulty or the slightest hitch. The weather was favourable up until the last few days when there have been torrents of pouring rain, and there was even hail. The nature of the country that I passed through is so beautiful that my downcast heart looked for distraction in it by admiring the gifts of the Creator adorned and cultivated by the hand of man. It is truly the vast garden of nature. It needed the thought of seeing my sister again to sustain me, for I confess that my heart was broken at having left the dearest object of my affection. My nephew[1] reminds me of my Alexander, he is a charming child but above all it is primarily in his features that he recalls him for he is much quieter, also he has a lively mind. Belvedere is a most agreeable spot, comfortable, elegant and combining everything that makes the charm of the countryside. Marie has housed me in the apartment of her daughters and assures me that I have attained my avowed aim of filling the void that she dreaded experiencing on her return. I feel I am useful to her and provide her with distraction while she strengthens my soul and upholds my sentiments in the same way as you, dear Bourcis. With that she has kept her almost childlike bouts of gaiety which produce such an attractive contrast in her character which is so eminently rational. Give my love to my dear children, to my wonderful little kitten, our good little Sophie; my compliments to Mlle Chapuis, to Mr Rigot and to the professors of dead and living languages. I know that you are a punctilious agent and so do not forget anyone, for I set great store – as much at a distance as near by – that each one should know that I do not think less of the trouble they are taking. I embrace you tenderly; do not poison my husband with bad tea! How are you spending your evenings? I am anxious about that on William's account; how is he? May God bless you and keep you for our affection.

[1] Charles Alexander (1818–1901); he later married Princess Sophie, daughter of the Princess of Orange.

THE GRAND DUCHESS ANNA PAVLOVNA, THE PRINCESS OF ORANGE, TO THE GRAND DUKE CONSTANTINE:

Ems,
July 1829

Dear excellent Brother and friend,

. . . According to what Marie had told me and the rumours which are going about here, I had almost come to the conclusion that my stay at Ems would not pass by without having the joy of seeing you here, and you can imagine how happy I would have been! I am sorry to have to give this up, but I do not lose hope that we shall see one another again if you travel abroad. I was delighted to find that the General who is carrying these lines is an old acquaintance dating from fifteen years ago or more; I put aside all pretentions to admit this as well as the pleasure I found in seeing him again; he recalled to me the days of my gay youth; Madam, his wife, seems to me to be pretty and kind, and if I were not leaving Ems immediately I would be sorry that they are going away. What can I find to tell you from here, if only to say that I am very satisfied with the effect of the waters, but that I think happily of going to find my own family again from whom I have been separated for six weeks. Among the news from home, I can convey to you the union planned for my sister-in-law Marianne with Prince Albert of Prussia[1] as something more certain than the plans, fortunately now fanciful, of last year. The only thing which could be said is that they are too close to the same age as there is a difference of only six months. I am full of admiration for the way the Prussian family is busy getting itself married off, soon it will be the ancestor of the human race. There is nothing new at Ems, except for a spring discovered on the other side of the river with a heat of 50 degrees Réaumur. While the scientists are discussing the phenomenon and the university faculty deliberate upon the ills to be cured by means of this vapour-bath, they are bathing the donkeys in it and the beasts are doing very well, probably because one gets well on common sense.

[1] Prince Albert of Prussia (1809–72) was the youngest son of King Frederick William III; he was the brother of the wife of Tsar Nicholas I. He and Princess Marianne were married in 1830.

THE GRAND DUKE CONSTANTINE TO THE GRAND DUCHESS ANNA PAVLOVNA, THE PRINCESS OF ORANGE:

Ems,
14/26 July 1829

It is at your feet, dear excellent Sister, that I come to beg pardon for my long silence and for not having answered your letters. I am aware of all my guilt and am truly ashamed of what has just happened to me. I call upon your generosity as well as your long-standing kindness for me and your affection to obtain my forgiveness. But beside the rightful and very just accusations you have every right to make to me, may I be allowed to set down on these pages a few words of justification. Most of your letters reached me at the time of a visit the Emperor and I had with one another in Warsaw, and during which my whole life was so taken up with our different occupations that really I thought that I would become totally confused or very near it. Added to that state of affairs was an unbearable heat-wave in spite of which, willing or not, we had nevertheless to move about. Since then I have had to make two inspection tours amongst my commands, and literally I was reduced to a moral state in which I could scarcely manage to rub two ideas together. Add to that state of affairs the fact that my whole being, both physical and moral, was very strongly shaken up and I obtained permission to come and repair or recuperate at Ems. My wife's health was also very much prostrated by the visit of the Emperor and King to Warsaw; during this she was unfortunate enough to catch a certain fever which turned into a nervous state which had to be got rid of to put her into condition to be gay at all the ceremonies, celebrations, balls, etc., etc., which this visit called forth. This whole summer has been spent in trying to fortify ourselves as well as we can and necessitated the trip to Ems. We were not able to leave earlier because of my duties, as I did not believe it decent to leave them before the events of the war definitely declared themselves in our favour. So we have spent three weeks going here and there, and have been here for four days where each of us has begun our cure. Please, dear excellent Sister, accept all my most sincere thanks for all your letters and for the affection and trust you show in them for me. Be sure that I am keenly aware of your sentiments and that I shall constantly make efforts to try to prove to you that I am not unworthy of them. I shall not now go into the details of the Emperor and King's stay with us as they must be known to you through public reports, but I allow myself to add that in spite of the hundred thousand stupidities that were retailed concerning it, everything took place following a truly remarkable order – poise and decency without the smallest or slightest accident – to the great disappointment of those who seek only for scandal and gossip. It was because of that too that I [needed to persuade him] of their calumnies and persecution. The more these trashy people – excuse me the expression – torture me with idiocies, the more that proves to me that I am following the true road of honour and duty which have constantly been my only guides during a consecutive administration of thirty-four and a half years. However, I admit that at a certain moment I had decided to leave it in order to retire completely from the tumult of the world and that I am still hesitating about doing so, but the kindness of the Emperor and King for myself, my wife, and my household holds me at my post in spite of the fact that for many reasons it is very difficult, at my age, to become accustomed to a new state of affairs. In addition, there are many matters and many persons with whom it is very difficult for me to do a new apprenticeship. So it only remains for me to continue as long as things remain as they are and my strength, especially mental as much as physical, will kindly permit me to do so. Lack of rectitude was never my strong point, and I have always held it in horror so, on the other hand, I do not like to admit to it with regard to myself. Unfortunately I have made some mistakes in regard to this which give me some black marks. I hope that Ems with its health-giving waters will chase my bile away and that I shall return to my post fresh and ready to begin again better than ever and a great disappointment to those who would like to see me removed from it. It seems to me that, concerning this matter, the Warsaw visit of the Emperor and King was most helpful and that he deigned to unseal the eyes of those who would consider it meritorious, and even dutiful, to calumniate faithful and devoted servants in order to further their own interests to take advantage of his lack of experience and

King William II of the Netherlands (1792–1849). Painting by J. B. van der Hulst, 1848.

King William II with Queen Anna Pavlovna and their family. Painting by J. B. van der Hulst.

take a course of action, suitable to themselves, in order to lead things on to the subversive goal towards which they aim, and having once arrived at it would let fall their masks, but too late to bring about any remedy. I frankly admit that during last winter many things and many cabals were pointed out to me, and if it had not been for the extreme indulgence and goodness of the Emperor and King I could have been the victim of all that trash which is only, I dare say, held back by the most active watchfulness in every possible way. Thank God! I emerged victorious from this fight which proves once more that He will always deign to be on the side of him who follows a straight path and overwhelms intriguers. Our friend [Anstitz ?] communicated to me the letter you wrote him about me and I hasten to thank you, dear excellent Sister, as well as for everything you say in it and for the affection you show for me in it. My wife asks me to remember her to you and thanks you from the bottom of her heart for honouring her with your thoughts of which she is truly very worthy because of the sincere and respectful affection she has vowed to you. My son is at your feet, and father and son offer you their respectful thanks for all your kindnesses. He is a big lad now and a person in his own right as on the coronation day at Warsaw he became *Flügel-adjutant* to the Emperor and King. In spite of that, he is staying with his regiment to carry on with his duties there; a great kindness of the Emperor and King which I was very far from expecting, especially considering the delicacy and the way in which he deigned to nominate him. As soon as possible I shall write to our dear William, but I cannot do it this time since the [salts ?] are having a strong effect. Please greet him very cordially for me and tell him that my affection for him will only finish with my life. My loving hugs to your children, and for you, dear Anne, always tell yourself that you have no more sincere and devoted friend in the world, who can appreciate you most and serve you, than is your faithful brother and friend.

THE GRAND DUKE CONSTANTINE TO THE GRAND DUCHESS ANNA PAVLOVNA, THE PRINCESS OF ORANGE:

Brussels,
27 July/11 August 1829

I cannot leave Brussels and the hospitable roof you have granted me, dear Sister, for a few days without offering you my thanks for all the affection and trust you have shown me. Be sure that I appreciate all the value of them and that they will never be erased from my memory. If my coming and my advice may have been useful to you, I shall have reached the peak of my desires. At least it was all done with a devoted heart which only wishes for your happiness. May the good Lord preserve you, dear Sister, and restore you to health and tranquillity. I ask it of Him from the depth of my soul. Here is a letter which I have just received from my wife, the reading of which will show you once more what her heart is made of and that our thoughts coincide perfectly about the advice we allow ourselves to give you. Remember me to your husband; I trust and hope that he will not hold against me everything I said to him as it certainly was only for his own good. My loving hugs to the four little ones who have won over my heart. Do not forget a brother who cherishes you with heart and soul.

THE GRAND DUKE CONSTANTINE TO THE GRAND DUCHESS ANNA PAVLOVNA, THE PRINCESS OF ORANGE:

Frankfurt-am-Main,
30 August/11 September 1829

Dear Sister,

Accept my sincere thanks for your letter which Lamsdorff punctually delivered to me a short while ago, and for the trouble you went to to write me yourself in spite of your extreme weakness. I was greatly delighted to learn through the public Press that you were recovered enough and in shape to start out for The Hague. If my visit to Brussels was pleasant for you, dear excellent Sister, and if I proved useful to you in any way whatsoever I am more than happy about it, and I can guarantee you that it will always be the same with me when it is a question of doing you a favour, and you can make use of me with alacrity. I shall forever cherish the memory of my visit to Brussels with you, dear Sister, nor shall I forget the thought and care you put yourself to, to make it pleasant for me in spite of your feeble condition. When I went back to Ems, which we wished to leave within a week, I found my wife well and truly sick–to the point that a diagnosis of chest infection was made to us, which, thanks to God and the doctor's precautions, was immediately cut short, leaving, nevertheless, extreme weakness and her strength returning very slowly. Once it was possible to leave, we arrived here, where we have been obliged to stop to wait for certain small feminine episodes to go by. At last, today, my wife started her journey, and I am counting on doing as much tomorrow, to go directly to Warsaw, pausing forty-eight hours only at Weimar and then a few days at Dresden to consult Doctor Ludvig there. I feel in the best of health and am very sorry to leave this dear delightful Frankfurt of which I am very sincerely fond. I hope and pray that your health is completely recovered, dear Sister, and that time and experience will do the rest. All my good wishes go with you, my loving affection to all your children and hundreds of the kindest regards to Miss Orange, and I beg her to deliver a message of profound respect to her dolls for me. . . . My respects to your ladies and thank them for their kindnesses towards me. Mesdames des Sybourg and Chapuis receive my particular notice. Remember me also to your guests and say, in the French manner, that my purchases for my wife completely fulfilled her needs. My wife asks me especially, dear Sister, to thank you for the beautiful neckerchief which you were kind enough to have sent to her. Everything gave her the greatest pleasure. . . .

THE GRAND DUKE CONSTANTINE TO THE GRAND DUCHESS ANNA PAVLOVNA, THE PRINCESS OF ORANGE:

Leipzig,
6/18 September 1829

When I arrived at Weimar our dear excellent Marie gave me your letter, dear Sister, for which I offer you my most heartfelt thanks both for having written it and for having included in it the expressions of your affection and trust. I would have replied to it immediately, but on learning that in two day's time they were expecting Prince Charles of Prussia on his return from The Hague, and then the three days I spent there were so taken up by the social occupations of my visit that I had to put off doing so until I was at full liberty. So I am devoting the morning to it which I am spending here, where I am waiting for my wife for dinner to read her the letter from you which dear Marie was given by Prince Charles, and which she was very kind enough to communicate. . . . I shall not go into my visit to Weimar as it is limited to blessing the good Lord for having given me the happiness of stopping over the three days I spent there in the midst of affection and the ample trust of dear excellent Marie who showered me, as well as my wife, with kindness and attention of all sorts. Thanks to God, the latter is fairly well and is continuing her trip very well although a little slowly. I admit that I am waiting impatiently for the moment of settling in back home after having gone through three months from inn to inn and up hill and down dale. I am very well; our winter is announcing itself because for the last few days we have had 7 to 10 degrees of cold – one would think oneself in Russia and here we are in Germany. We are counting on stopping for forty-eight hours in Dresden, and, God willing, we shall be back in Warsaw by the end of this month, new style. My loving affection to our dear William and sincere thanks for the hospitality in Brussels. If the King, the Queen, Prince Frederick are good enough to remember me, please present my respectful homage to them. My hugs to your delightful children and many kind regards to Sophia, news of whom I asked of Prince Charles who is madly fond of her. My compliments to M. Chapuis and Mesdames Rigaut and Grovestin. Tell the former that I am deeply touched by her kind remembrance. If your ladies-in-waiting still remember me, please remember me to them. M. Everard will allow me to compliment him on your prompt recovery to which I know he efficiently contributed as much by his spiritual advice as by his physical techniques. Keep remembering affectionately, dear Sister, your true friend who sends you greetings from his heart and soul, and who is for always your faithful brother and friend.

My wife and son are greatly touched that you remember them and ask me to thank you for it, and recommend themselves to you for the future.

TSAR NICHOLAS I TO THE GRAND DUCHESS ANNA PAVLOVNA, THE PRINCESS OF ORANGE:

Tsarskoe Selo,
19 September/1 October 1829

I am writing to inform you of the signing of a good and glorious peace treaty, dear kind Anne, as well as to thank you for your pleasant letter for my name-day. The good Lord has blessed us in a very striking way by giving to our army a success which has gone far beyond my wildest hopes and by crowning this with the triumph of victory which is glorious and worthy in every way of our noble and beautiful homeland. Your kind letter gave me real pleasure; I found in it again your old friendship for me to which I cling more than you know. The picture of your domestic happiness – I see you happy with your children and that is certainly the greatest blessedness here below, and I assure you that for me a quarter-hour of such pure bliss as I enjoy with my good wife and children is dearer to me than any possible conquest.

Our poor William is furiously involved in tasks and worries; but he bears this as I like to see him do, with resignation and devotion to his King; it is difficult but in spite of that gives him strength for action, which perhaps he does not appreciate or feel enough yet for the moment. I know something about it. You must encourage him. I must stop here for I scarcely have the time to pen you these few words. Believe in the remembrance of your faithful brother and friend.

THE GRAND DUCHESS ANNA PAVLOVNA, THE PRINCESS OF ORANGE, TO THE GRAND DUKE CONSTANTINE:

The Hague,
20 December 1829

Dear and excellent Brother and friend,

. . . I think that you will be pleased with the royal approval given to the second chamber of the States-General, as well as with the law to repress abuses of the Press. William is the moving force behind two measures which are finding general support amongst the Dutch and among the reasonable people in the south. We are involved in a very interesting situation and William has given all his heart and zeal to affairs with an impartiality which really does him honour. After sketching these serious concerns, may I now come back to my home-life to speak to you about Sophia, of my small occupations with her, and of the intelligence she puts into reacting to them. She often remembers Uncle Constantine, and begs me to send him her regards as well as those of her dolls; then when it is raining or snowing she remembers Mr Grigouille who slips between the rain-drops. On Sunday she has dress-up teas in her apartments with her brothers, who are growing, and are applying themselves fairly well to their different studies. Now they are having fun skating. They often ask me for news of you, dear Brother, and M. Rigaut as well as Mlle Chapuis are very grateful for the souvenirs with which you honoured them and wish me to give you their respectful homage. My good Mlle de Sybourg most humbly wishes to be remembered to you, and my ladies also want me to thank you for your kind remembrances. Please, dear Brother and friend, accept with affection a chain of my hair *with two gold clasping hands*; I had it made as a souvenir of the time you spent with us and of the kindliness of which you have given me so much proof. Wear it on your watch, I beg you, and *do not take it off*. I hope that you will grant this liberty on my part. I embrace dear Jeannette and send many many good wishes for her health; I plan to write her at the first opportunity; I hope that you are both well returned to Warsaw and that you will spend happy days there. Keep your remembrance and affection for me, dear Brother.

The King and Queen often ask me for news of you with the most sincere interest. Many kind regards from me to Paul.

1830–39

The year 1830 saw a major attack on the system established by Metternich and his colleagues at Vienna. King Charles X of France, who had succeeded his brother King Louis XVIII in 1824, had become increasingly conservative. His appointment of Prince de Polignac in 1829 was followed by a reactionary policy culminating in the Ordinances of 26 July 1830. Two days later, after the Ordinances were announced, barricades were up in Paris, Charles X abdicated and by the end of the month Louis-Philippe, Duke of Orléans, was proclaimed King of the French.

The July revolution in France was followed by an uprising in Poland and Belgium. The former revolt was briefly successful, the Grand Duke Constantine withdrew with the Russian garrison to Russian soil, the moderates in Warsaw soon lost control, and the more radical elements took power. Tsar Nicholas sent in his army commanded by General Diebitsch, the hero of the Turkish war, but he succumbed to cholera, as had the Grand Duke Constantine, and Paskevich took over. The revolt was suppressed, the constitution was abrogated and Polish autonomy virtually vanished. Tsar Nicholas began a policy of Russification of the country.

Concomitantly with the Polish crisis, a revolt broke out in Brussels. Initially, the case was for autonomy with Prince William, Anna Pavlovna's husband, as Viceroy, but this situation soon changed. Independence was proclaimed and the Powers, under English leadership, suggested a conference in London. Meanwhile in Brussels an assembly formally deposed the House of Orange. Lord Palmerston and Louis-Philippe took charge since Russia was involved with the Polish question and neither Prussia nor Austria could act without her. In late December 1830, the Kingdom of the Netherlands was dissolved. Belgium became an independent state; the national assembly elected a son of Louis-Philippe as king, but this was opposed by the English, and in June 1831 Leopold of Saxe-Coburg was chosen instead. The Powers approved of this decision and attempted to mediate between King William and his former subjects, but without success. The Dutch invaded and a brief war ensued with the Dutch everywhere victorious. A French army then crossed the Belgian frontier and the Dutch withdrew; an armistice followed, but it was not until 1839 that King William recognised Belgium. While Tsar Nicholas was very sympathetic to his sister and her husband and would probably have come to their help had he been able to do so in 1830, in time he grew very irritated with King William and his obstinacy.

The decade following the revolutions of 1830 was uneasy. Louis-Philippe was forced to suppress radical outbreaks in Lyons and Paris in 1834. The King of the French became virtually as authoritarian as his predecessor. The Spanish monarchy was threatened by the actions of the pretender, Don Carlos, and for five years the country was plunged into civil war. England and France were much concerned by this attack on the constitutional monarchy. The situation in Portugal was somewhat similar, but here the English took a very active role. Dom Miguel, the pretender, was defeated, and in 1834 Maria II's authority was completely restored. Two years later she married Ferdinand of Saxe-Coburg, and the Kingdom of Portugal settled down to relative quiet.

The Italians, under the influence of Mazzini and 'Young Italy', had rebelled in the Duchies of Parma and Modena and in the Papal States, but these were soon put down by the Austrians. The Italians were no further forward in their attempts at liberal government or unification. Germany, too, was kept under tight control after some brief flurries in Brunswick, Saxony and Hesse-Cassel whose rulers had been forced to abdicate. The Diet accepted Metternich's proposals in June 1832, where the old order was reaffirmed. Metternich's own powers in Austria were somewhat diminished after the death of Emperor Francis I, when his son Emperor Ferdinand allowed court officials to play a larger role in the government, but even so Metternich's domination of the foreign office continued for over a decade.

It may be said that only England, under the Whig governments of Lords Grey and Melbourne, was truly enlightened. Everywhere else it appeared that reactionary forces had generally triumphed.

TSAR NICHOLAS I TO THE GRAND DUCHESS ANNA PAVLOVNA, THE PRINCESS OF ORANGE:

Alexandria nr Peterhof,
8/20 January 1830

See how much time has gone by since I was able to write you, dear kind Anne; and it has cost me that much more not to have done so sooner because I felt a real need to tell you how much all your latest letters have touched me, with all the affection they give me from you; the sending of your hair and the letter which accompanied it moved me to tears; but I would have liked to make you give up such black thoughts!

How grateful I am to you too for your excellent portrait which my wife gave me from you. The resemblance is perfect, and lacking the original I am the more delighted to see the copy.

Since I am not on the spot, it is difficult for me to judge correctly and to pronounce upon things which I can only hope to be false and invented! To blame my William is so painful for me, so hateful, that I can not bring myself to do it; but I shall certainly tell him everything I am told about him, for kindness demands that without question. As for you, if you manage to persevere in your resolutions – as everything leads me to hope – you will have an enormous advantage over him and he cannot be insensitive to that and be ungrateful to you; show spirit as well as gentleness. . . .

Do me the kindness to thank the King and Queen very sincerely for all the interest they have been good enough to show for me during my illness; I was very happy and generally very surprised at the affection displayed for me from all sides during that time. I had no right to expect it, so my surprise was that much greater and I admit to you that few things have given me so much pleasure in my life, and it is so good to know that one has friends; and it is so rare!

22 January – Finally a courier is leaving for London and I can have you get my letter in a sure way. Everything I have learned since I began this letter about the state of things with you pleases me greatly, all the more so because I think I recognise my William's share in it. The wisdom and firmness of the measures adopted by the King recently have the best effect,[1] and I put myself in the ranks of all those who want order and peace. May God support him!

[1] King William I had signed a concordat with Pope Leo XII in 1827, which gave the King the right of veto over all nominees to episcopal sees, thus ensuring a 'conservative' episcopate. A new Press law was also enacted which established stricter censorship. These were policies to be highly commended according to Tsar Nicholas.

We are up to the neck in dances, fourteen since New Year's Day! It certainly is the mad year, but I like people to have fun, for it keeps them busy and eliminates the time to say silly things. Poor Helen is in bed, apparently about to have a miscarriage; I hope for her sake that she will pull out of it as quickly as possible.

I am sending you some very badly done daubings which represent our favourite little corner of earth; excuse the humbleness of the offering, perhaps it will amuse you to see the very exact representation of a place where there lies a me with his wife and five children; it is *something* in this world below; and it is a *great deal* for your old brother who likes to withdraw to it as much as he can. So be it! But come and see us there when and as soon as you can.

A big kiss to each of the masculine Oranges and a kiss on the little hand of Miss Orange; kind regards to Bourcis.

TSAR NICHOLAS I TO THE GRAND DUCHESS ANNA PAVLOVNA, THE PRINCESS OF ORANGE:

St Petersburg,
13/25 February 1830

I must beg your pardon, dear Anne, for not having written you on the occasion of your name-day to offer you my wishes for the day; but it was impossible for me to do so; they were none the less offered to you in thought and with good heart. We celebrated the day with a ball at Heekeren's residence, which in spite of the smallness of the setting was really delightful. Here, there is no lack of balls and celebrations this winter, and this evening I am taking part in the twelfth ball since New Year's; and since they do not begin until 10 o'clock and only finish at about 4 in the morning, it cannot help but be a little tiring; I admire our ladies for being able to stand up to it so well. We have never had so much fun. My friends the Turks have been among us for some time; they attempt to be European, the poor people, but it [the Europeanisation of Turkey] only limps along. Halil,[1] however, has an agreeable

[1] The Turkish ambassador to Russia. He was particularly charged by the Sultan with reducing the indemnity to Russia and shortening the period of the Russian occupation in the Balkans.

presence and seems to be witty; you can imagine that our gapers have had enough to amuse themselves for two weeks; and I believe that in principle it is so much the better.

Helen is finally free of her miscarriage or something similar, but she must still look after herself for some time to come. My strumpet is all right for the time being and I hope to keep her so for a long time.

THE GRAND DUCHESS ANNA PAVLOVNA, THE PRINCESS OF ORANGE, TO TSAR NICHOLAS I:

The Hague,
2 April 1830

Dear good Brother,

. . . I bear you a very real gratitude, dear Brother and friend, for your kindness in granting my good Harry [?] the request that he ventured to make and in doing so with a generosity which fills him with happiness and gratitude. He wrote to me about it in a most touching way, and as for me, dear friend, I am infinitely grateful to you for it. Although our winter cannot rival the brilliant season in Petersburg, it has, however, been very animated. We have had several fine balls at court and some more modest ones given by us, some charming ones given by Fritz and his wife, and in addition I was present at two balls in the Casino, and this week at a charming [?] *dansant* given by the Danish Minister. There have been a great number of similar occasions with private individuals. In a word, carnival has invaded Lent, for here the time of 'retreat' is only in the first fortnight following the New Year and also during Holy Week which is religiously observed. I hope, dear friend, my presence at these balls in Lent will only be counted in the number of my venial sins and that you as head of our church will, indeed, limit yourself to giving me only a slight admonition on the subject, starting from the principle that nothing as much as indulgence brings back those who only sin by following [the example of others].

From this profane subject I pass to the satisfaction that I feel in knowing that, according to the most recent news that I have from Williamov, you are completely recovered from your illness and that it had not done you any harm, also that you had visited the military colonies. May you everywhere find only happy subjects! Perhaps you went to our ancient capital, and what joy there will have been among these great inhabitants to see you there again. The cold this winter has been long and harsh in this country. March made amends somewhat by a series of fine days, but the first of April came to deceive our expectations by bringing snow. Yesterday, also, we closed our little pleasure by an evening of conversation at the residence of the Minister of Finance without speaking a word of arithmetic or even of subtraction. Our good children in whom you are interested, dear friend, are all very well. They all survived the harsh winter perfectly. I am pleased with them. Their hearts are such as I could wish for, they are very affectionate towards their mama. As for our good little girl, she is already company; I spend a great deal of time with her and I am happy to see her responding to my cares in a most interesting way.

Now, dear Nicholas, I wish to broach a subject for which I claim in advance your indulgent friendship. It is a question of the reduction of interest from 5 to 4 per cent. I supposed that it was to concern the capital which each of us possesses, and it is in this respect that I decided, after mature reflection, to address myself to your fairness, and I speak to you as to a good father to understand the motives which have decided me on the course of action that I am now taking with you. I intend the capital that I possess in Lombard,[1] independently of my dowry, to form, one day, my children's fortunes and particularly those of my young children. The oldest is the only one favoured by the state, and it is my duty to compensate the younger ones as much as is in my power. The theft of the most considerable part of my jewels removed the principle fortune or resources of my children. Add to that Mama's heritage which has disappeared completely. It has been painful for me to think that besides these losses the capital would no longer obtain for my children the value on which I was counting and had calculated to assure them one day an agreeable amount of independent means. You know,

[1] The Grand Duchess Anna Pavlovna had her money in the care of English bankers in Lombard Street, London. She always referred to her bankers as Lombard.

dear friend, the public cricumstances, and you will agree that it is as just as it is natural that a mother should wish to shelter her children from needing to make pecuniary demands on those who never seem eager to grant them. All these reasons combined, dear Brother and friend, have caused me to explain myself frankly to you and without delay, if possible before you should have made any resolutions in this respect. I wish that the remaining part of my fortune should be considered on the same footing as that of people who have suffered considerable injury without it being their fault, and so I want you to allow either that Lombard should continue to pay 5 per cent interest on capital or else to appeal to your generosity, and if the interest can be only 4 per cent that you should be good enough to make up the capital in such way that, receiving only 4 per cent, the total interest will produce the same sum as up till today. If it were a question of me alone, dear Brother, the idea would never have come to me. Moreover, I only withdraw interest from the principal in order to pay the annuities that I owe and the rest only in urgent cases when my annual revenue is not enough for the annual expenditure. But for that I do not even need it. It is entirely for the sake of my children that I turn to you in this case, given the circumstances described, and I do not wish to overlook anything that can contribute to their future wellbeing. Whatever your decision may be, dear Brother, I shall believe it dictated by justice to me, and my spirit is at rest having done what I should. Only excuse me for writing at such length and for everything that may displease you by putting yourself an instant in my place. Frankness can sometimes cost dear, and this is now my case for it is painful for me to act in this way which, however, I believe I must so as not to neglect anything. Your friendship will understand what is taking place in my soul, and I should believe myself to have misunderstood your feelings if I noticed on this occasion restrictions which could have grave consequences for the fortune to come to my children, who might come to think that personal repugnance alone prevented me from seeing to their interests. This is a very long epistle for which I claim your indulgence, dear friend. I beg you to retain for me your good and old triopathic feelings.

I embrace your dear children most tenderly. Good Mlle Sybourg is very touched by your remembrance and wishes me to send her humble respects. She has been dangerously ill and unfortunately is aging a great deal.

THE GRAND DUKE CONSTANTINE TO THE GRAND DUCHESS ANNA PAVLOVNA, THE PRINCESS OF ORANGE:

Warsaw,
9/21 August 1830

[*The following note is in another hand, probably that of Anna Pavlovna:* 'Letter from Grand Duke Constantine containing his opinion of the Revolution in France of the month of July 1830 and his suspicions about the influence of the directors' committee. I bequeath this letter to my sons, it could be of use to them as Constantine's opinion was interesting to know, being that of a man of sense and experience.']

Dear excellent Sister,

I am beginning my letter by begging for a pardon which I cannot imagine obtaining otherwise than through your magnanimity and generosity. I am not at fault but I am in your debt and [only] that friendship which has bound us for so long and which has been cemented not only by blood-ties but by our mutual feelings [will remove the obligation]. I have nothing to put forward to excuse my long and unforgivable silence except that I beg your pardon for it. . . . All your dear excellent letters reached me promptly in the past; accept my thanks also for your good wishes for my anniversary celebrations and the kindness you show for me. I should have replied to it some time ago but it was such an active time for me, considering the Emperor's visit, the sittings of the Diet and my military preoccupations, that really it was impossible for me to do so. Since then, I have been travelling to fulfil my duties and my unforgivable wrong begins there. I repeat to you; I am wrong, very much wrong and I shall claim from your mercy a very ill-deserved pardon, I know [this] only too well.

I had obtained from the Emperor permission to go with my wife to Ems, I was on the point of starting out – I was hoping to push right through to Brussels to beg forgiveness for myself and in person – when the events in France came along to set up a most definite obstacle to that. In such serious circumstances, and ones which could lead to results which human foresight cannot conceive, it is extremely urgent that each man remain at his post to be in a position to act immediately, according to the supreme commands and instructions on which he depends; you know only too well, dear Sister, the truth of my statements. I confess frankly that in spite of all my fore-sight and my imaginings in the past almost six years, I was far from thinking that events might become as important and as decisive. That God may resolve everything for the best is my keenest wish. But how can one expect results of stability when one sees what is happening in France. Mirabeau said at the beginning of the revolution that the people had been unmuzzled, let us see who will know how to and can re-muzzle them. I expect no one. Everything is criminal in France; the Polignac Ministry[1] first of all, then the revolution of 27, 28 and 29 July; and then the consequences of the King's[2] election. Everyone wanted to carry out and has carried out *coups d'état*. That charter, which they say was violated and for which the blood of a misdirected populace has been spilled, had no other goal than to violate that same charter by a *coup d'état*. Everyone wanted to have one, the strongest as well as the weakest. Everyone granted themselves rights which they did not have, and God knows where that will stop. In my humble and [simple ?] opinion the French nation has covered itself in every way with shame and an ineffaceable smear. . . . Shame on the army for defecting a third time[3] in the space of sixteen years. Now, with one's hand on one's conscience, how can one not believe in the existence of a directing committee which prepared everything to the point that everyone at the time of the insurrection knew his post and his role. How anxious you must be, dear Sister, being so close to the events! I would have been happy to be near you in these serious circumstances for a few days in order to convince myself with my own eyes about what point you are at. I would have

[1] Jules, Prince de Polignac (1780–1847) was appointed by Charles X of France to head a government of 'Ultras'. The policies of this ministry led to the July Revolution.

[2] Louis-Philippe, Duc d'Orléans, elected King of the French in August 1830.

[3] Once against Napoleon in 1814, and a second time in 1815 against Louis XVIII; this third occasion is against Charles X. In each case the army had given its oath to the sovereign.

liked to exchange my thoughts with yours. But nothing can be helped as it is impossible. Please, dear Sister, keep me up to date about what concerns you as well as your family. For some time a rumour has been going about here concerning plans for a trip for you to Italy or Russia; there are such different versions that I cannot trust them. . . .In good faith and conscience, how can one accept as a principle that since one party does not keep its word, the other is authorised by the facts themselves not to keep its own. In my opinion it is an absurdity and monstrosity in logic. However, in these days this principle is so much accepted that I am almost certain that the Polignac party was pushed by the opposing party, and also advised to give itself up to *coups d'état* in order to be able to do as much all the more easily for its part once it had the upper hand. What is William doing in all this? Tell him from me, dear Sister, that my good wishes go with him, that my thoughts follow him and that I am raising the most fervent prayers to the good Lord to bring back peace and tranquillity around you. Please greet him for me as well as your children. Also give my compliments to Mesdames Rigaut and Grovestin. My respects to Mme Chapuis and your ladies. Loving hugs to our delightful Sophia. If the King and Queen deign to remember me, please pay them my homage and offer them my most sincere and glowing good wishes. Sometimes I have a notion to start out to go to you but I am held back by reflection. I would give anything in the world to be able to see you for a few seconds and chat with you in an open-hearted way about things. It infuriates me to be prevented from doing so. Here, everything up to the present is quiet, thank God! and I must allow full and complete justice to public opinion for showing itself to be on the right side according to all reports from every direction. There are, of course, the incorrigible ones who find their happiness only in plots and [*coups* ?] but they are in such a tiny proportion that it is as if they did not exist. The events in France fill all minds and, quite rightly, the majority does not approve of them. It would be otherwise perhaps if it were a question of the D. [uc] de Reichstadt.[1] May

[1] The son of Napoleon and his second wife, Marie Louise of Austria. The Grand Duke Constantine implied here that France *might* very well have supported a *coup* to favour the restoration of the heir to the Bonapartes, but not the elevation of the Duc d'Orléans to power.

the good Lord keep us in peace and tranquillity and prove by that that the goodness of our late immortal Emperor did not lay up ingratitude and creatures ready at any opportunity to rebel. In addition, I ask the good Lord to save me from the shame of having spent sixteen years of anxiety and toil to organise a country which would show itself to be unworthy at the first given moment. On the contrary, I trust in His mercy that this good people will show itself to be grateful if danger arises and will be worthy of itself by being orderly and submissive. My wife asks me to remember her to you; thanks to God her health is fairly good for the moment. I am well, but am very worn by my duties and events. I am finishing my letter by begging you once more to grant me my forgiveness and assuring you of the tender sincere devotion which forever is held for you by your faithful old brother and friend.

TSAR NICHOLAS I TO THE GRAND DUCHESS ANNA PAVLOVNA, THE PRINCESS OF ORANGE:

Tsarskoe Selo,
15/27 August 1830

. . . I am happy to see that you have given up your travelling plans; what has just happened in France proves to you, I hope, that now or never is the time to be firm and united between ourselves in order to exorcise the storm. What infamies, what meanness and deceits on the one side and what atrocities on the other; what a frightful result for fifteen years of quiet, and what are we yet destined to see and hear! It is certain that the Bourbons gave themselves the last killing blow through their cowardly conduct in this affair; they inspire only pity; as for regret, it is impossible to give them any. I hope that the King, helped by William, will take wise firm steps to prevent any accident in your country, and I place hope in God that he will inspire the Duke of Orleans not to attack his *neighbours*; if that were to happen they will find their friends in arms ready to fly to their aid without even being asked. But as I was saying, I reject with all my hopes such an outcome. I find the behaviour of the Duke of Orleans so infamous that I cannot find words to express it strongly enough. I cannot understand how my colleagues, outside of the English, could ever recognise him as King; as for me, I want at least to be the last tô do so, because even if I do so, I will yield only to the advice of others without changing my own convictions. What sacredness, what inviolability is there in this world if there is no principle of legitimacy! And it is with that principle that they would like to compromise. A thousand kind regards from me to their Majesties if they were thinking of me, and affectionate greetings to the Fritzes; hug your dear children and believe in the affection of the one who is for life with heart and soul, your faithful brother and friend.

Embrace Mlle Sybourg for me.

THE GRAND DUCHESS ANNA PAVLOVNA, THE PRINCESS OF ORANGE, TO TSAR NICHOLAS I:

The Hague,
1 September 1830

Dear good Nicholas,

. . . Prince Golitsyn will inform you of the events,[1] dear Brother, which it would be too terrible for me to relate to you and it would not perhaps be with all the precision with which you should be informed. My dear William and Fritz, touching in their fraternal sentiments as well as their feelings for things, have left to fulfil a sad and imperious duty, that of trying to restore order. What will be the means to re-establish it – that is one of those questions of Providence the answer to which we await with anxiety. May God watch over him! this dear being – for I love William and not the Prince Royal – so, whatever reverse in the situation may strike us, may He only let his dear existence be preserved! We are in such a position that even the affection and enthusiasm of the Dutch are frightening for fear that these feelings, so happily in existence, should not take on the character of a national war. William, in leaving, recommended calm and peace to me, so it is the command word of our

[1] The Belgian revolution; it had broken out on 25 August 1830.

house and in keeping with the feelings of my heart. It is not the moment to speak of the past, but it is certain that there was a conflict of large and small circumstances which seemed to compete to provoke the present evil, but it is a moment for redoubling our prayers and putting our confidence in God alone, may He guide and inspire.

THE GRAND DUCHESS ANNA PAVLOVNA, THE PRINCESS OF ORANGE, TO TSAR NICHOLAS I:

The Hague,
24 September 1830

Dear good Brother,

It seems that I am destined to write to you on the days that are most decisive for this country and for our family, for our dear Fritz is in Brussels with the troops, bombarding the rebels, and it is in these circumstances that I am writing these lines to you! May God bless this worthy brother and spare as many of the innocent as possible. This is what the wishes of a woman must be confined to, whose role must not or cannot be other than that of conciliation, without, however, blinding oneself to the circumstances. But I am a wife and mother and I must try to reconcile general affection with those dear to me, to whom I am attached, and try in this way to prepare a favourable future for my son.

I recount to myself all the examples of magnanimity in my own family in order to bind myself to what is good; to subdue myself is the victory that I strive for and I repeat to myself: *He who deceives with words will be ashamed.* I gave Prince Golitsyn more than one commission for you, dear Nicholas, as I was unable to write because of my extreme weakness at that time, resulting from the emotions that I had experienced. What a day it was when our William entered Brussels! In my opinion it was the finest day of his life. He has conquered all honest hearts and the esteem of good people, and Fritz rids us of the evil populace, following the noble desire of his heart by acting in this way in order to deflect all the odium of an absolutely necessary action from the heir to the throne. It is in my eyes disinterested heroism. I hope that my Nikki will indeed have wished to hang the diamond medallion with an orange ribbon on the picture of the Virgin of Kazan after having had a Te Deum sung in her presence, in memory of this memorable 1st of September. The Queen gave me her portrait to wear with an orange ribbon on the shoulder, and allowed me to hang it on the Cross of Quatre Bras in memory of the day when William risked his life for his father. Send me, Nikki, I beg you, a garnet clasp with some of your hair and Alexandrine's, with your names and the date of the 1st of September. I should like to wear this souvenir which would unite with the initial letter of William's name in stone the dearest thing I can have from you both, who love us and feel all that it is to do one's duty. God knows what the consequences may yet be, but if Providence were to place William in the [princely ?] rank I wish always to retain my title of Grand Duchess; and let the rest be only added to this title. I ask that as an honour which I prefer to all others and I give you notice of it in advance. I am deeply touched by the affection the family shows me and very touched by the devotion that the Dutch show to the whole family. There is something which reminds me of the year 1812 in Petersburg. I am recovering gradually but I felt so weak that it made me think that if I were to experience several violent moral shocks in succession, they would drive me to the grave.

You wished, dear Nikki, to give me some things that belonged to Mama. I only ask you for one; it is the ring, similar to mine, that she wore for the Triopathy. I put mine, as a reward, on William's finger and I beg you to send me the one that Mama wore and that I had made for her at the time. If you wish to remind me of her heritage which I lost a year ago but for two days, have made for me a beautiful diamond clasp with a beautiful turquoise – it was her legacy to me – and have it arranged so that an opal may be placed in it if desired, which I beg Alexandrine to choose; for it was the setting that I had inherited. This, in one single thing, will recall to me what I shall never forget, and I count on the friendship of you both to send me this object. A thousand thanks for your good letter which gave me a great deal of pleasure. The events in France were deplorable, those here are deplorable and the instigators of the disturbances are despicable. But imperishable honour attaches to the King's behaviour and to the noble characters of William and Fritz, and honour goes equally to the Dutch and to the brave army in which Belgians fight valiantly. But I am not a political woman, I only wish to be a good wife, a good mother and a good sister, and it is with all the sincerity of these sentiments, dear Brother and friend, that I embrace you heart and soul, being for life your devoted sister and friend.

TSAR NICHOLAS I TO THE GRAND DUCHESS ANNA PAVLOVNA, THE PRINCESS OF ORANGE:

St Petersburg,
28 September/10 October 1830

Dear kind Anne,

I can send you only two words with a courier who is leaving immediately. We have just received the news of the King's decision to advance the army against the rebels; and I blessed God that he had resolved to do so. All our prayers go with this decisive enterprise, not only for all of you but for every one of us. How I pity you, dear friend, and how anguished I imagine you are; but, full confidence in Divine Mercy and *let come what will*. We are told that you are still ill and I can understand that, but in the name of God do not lose courage.

The times are serious, but all the more reason to keep oneself above the events and continue as you are doing; God will not abandon you. Yours for life with heart and soul, your faithful brother and friend.

THE GRAND DUCHESS ANNA PAVLOVNA, THE PRINCESS OF ORANGE, TO TSAR NICHOLAS I:

The Hague,
30 September 1830

Dear good Brother,

Once again under very sad auspices I take up my pen. As the attack on Brussels has not given the expected result, our dear worthy Fritz found it necessary to retire with the army, and it seems that he wishes to concentrate his forces on Malines. To stay at Brussels and [imprison himself ?] by defending the palace would only have been to expose the army to certain death. The course that he took does honour to his reason and his moral courage, for the moral effect of this retreat is distressing throughout the country. There are only a small number of sensible people who approve of it, and in their eyes Fritz must be more worthy of respect than ever, but also very much to be pitied, and it causes me great pain, knowing, as I do, his noble sentiments and the motives behind his actions. Our good Louise shows an imperturbable calm and an angelic sweetness. I love her and respect her more each day. At last has come the time for Marianne's departure, a terrible moment for the King, for our dear Queen and similarly for us all. Let Divine Providence help me to be for them what my William was for Mama at the cruel time when you left her to join the army; let me give them proof of the gratitude which their good deeds have spread throughout my heart. I attach an infinite price to sharing the misfortunes of the family and I assure you, dear Nikki, that William was never dearer to me than now. I experience a true joy in showing him how much I love him at a time when the party that had unworthily slandered our household has now thrown the country into revolution. The best denial that I can give to the whole world is to cling to his adversity and to that of his family. I have told him as well as the King, that as I owe the free enjoyment of my personal fortune to William's delicacy of feeling at the time of our marriage, I should make it his in the event that the country were lost or that Belgium alone were lost. William is losing almost everything he has and probably the revenue he is drawing from the state will be decreased. I feel so happy at giving him compensation that it is only now I feel the happiness of being rich. Those, dear Nikki, are my reprisals for the years of unhappiness. Alas, the public opinion of those same Belgians, that was so sought after by William, had used his conduct towards me as an arm against him, as well as my calmness and the loyalty of my behaviour. Qualities that I may have and my conduct at the time of the theft were blown up to the skies in order to harm him. The interest that they showed me then has always been repugnant to me and, thank Heaven, I did not encourage it, but I asked you at that time to show him that my happiness was dear to you. I asked you for his own sake in asking that. I wrote to you then frankly on William's affairs; now I have offered him my gilt plate, which happily was saved from Brussels, so that if there is any debt which may compromise his name, my possessions may be used to prevent this misfortune. My silver service has likewise been saved. But almost everything that William owns is in this unfortunate house in Brussels in which are, as well, all the rest of the things in my trousseau and a great deal of furniture with which I had decorated my rooms, fortunately at my own expense and not at the state's. I am writing to you, dear friend and Brother, just as we are learning of the defection of almost the whole of Belgium. Yesterday the States General pronounced the separation and revision of the statue law, so the gauntlet has been thrown down. Think what this means for me as a wife and as a mother! For me who for years have been very definitely uneasy about the Belgians' frame of mind, and seeing Count Guriev with no other political corner in this country than his connections and his relations with the Unionist Belgian nobility, living only at Brussels and coming to The Hague for only short periods, he has alienated the Dutch who despise him and distrust him. He has only sown in a mined field, moreover having a good time and spending his days gambling at the Brussels Club. At the time of the theft and last winter also he often talked to me of the interest and esteem that the Brussels public had for me; I replied to him that first of all I only bothered about the esteem of estimable people and that there was a kind of interest that a woman could not accept; that in a word, I should never accept any reputation at the expense of my husband. Having begun by showing me some interest, Count Guriev was as halfhearted as possible in making the necessary inquiries, and this winter, even, he was present at social functions at the house of the Princess de Chimay. He could only give you false facts about Belgium and the Belgians because he was surrounded by the revolutionary party, making at Brussels a strange diplomatic triumvirate with the ministers of Austria and Spain, both generally in disrepute here. On the other hand, the ambassador and his family reside here at the seat of government, as also does the Prussian minister and his;

that of Denmark and even that of Sweden. I do not know if it is that, or the esteem that they merit personally, or both things combined that gives them the regard which they enjoy, but I only see a result favourable to them in every way. Prince Golitsyn also appears to be very well looked upon. I personally have every praise for him and I am pleased to say so here. This is not the case with Count Guriev who, instead of making a point of showing me, at all times, the regard which he owes me as your sister, dear friend, has only striven to court the Prince's favour and to treat me as nothing, instead of contributing to the respect that was due to me in my own home by behaving with noble courtesy towards me. If he had taken this attitude he would have avoided years of unpleasantness with me but he believed that, supported by the Prince and leaning on the Belgian party, he was very strong and could balance the political influence of the English ambassador. Providence has thwarted his calculations and I told him so the other day, choosing to do so at a time when the state is moving towards its ruin, to prove to him how well he has done in this country and how honourably he has served his sovereign. Dear Nikki, if only you had listened to me two years ago when I insisted so strongly on his recall or on a sharp lesson given by you so that he should hold himself in check! Now, it is in the name of our disaster and to show you how much I count on your friendship that I ask you for his recall. Honour our misfortunes by sending us an honourable name and if you can do it without considering other problems, send us your general aide-de-camp, Prince Trubetskoi. My joy at seeing him again was great; he is a good man of good years, a good name and a veteran; what is more, he has the honourable distinction that you gave to the general aides-de-camp of our much-loved Alexander of wearing his number on his epaulettes, which is a very dear sight for me. Imagine that Guriev placed all his wife's diamonds in the bank at Brussels! and this poor lady will probably lose them all. Be good to her and her children but as for the father, rid us of him as soon as possible I beg you. I am very much afraid that the Austrian minister, that of Spain who is known to be a rogue, and the Apostolic nuncio had some part in the troubles of this country. You know that Don [Juan van Halem ?] is in command of the rebel troops in Brussels. That is the same Spaniard who served in Russia in the army under General Ermolov against the Circassians. He published memoirs about his service. I read them two years ago on the recommendation of Count Michael Vorontsov who commended them to me as giving a very exact description of the locality. At that time I was far from suspecting the role that he would play in these sad countries. I cannot account at all clearly for what has happened, we are seeing terrifying results but the true causes are still unknown. But I allow myself to believe that the French have made skilful use of the discontent that existed in Belgium to seize it, and in order to avoid the appearance of military aggression in the eyes of Europe they are making war in clauses instead of doing it in uniforms. We have four Belgians in the household of which two are ladies. One Countess d'Oultremont was as one in a frenzy at the time when the rising broke out everywhere and when the troops momentarily had the worst of it. The other lady is sad but quiet, and the Counts of Crocquembourg and Du Monceau are most worthy and seemly. As for the rest, just think that the most virulent unionist nobles are precisely those whom William saw most and who received most favours from him. It is heartrending at the very least. As for me, whatever my sentiments are towards this nation, I shall try to put the greatest spirit of conciliation into my conduct whatever it may cost me. I am a mother and I must try to prepare my son's future. May God bless our William! He has had very noble moments and I respect him from the bottom of my soul for I feel that he is suffering, and there is now no other past for me than the memory of good times. My health is recovering but there are days when I am very weak. I am greatly obliged to Dr Everard whom you saw in Russia; the poor man has all his possessions in Brussels and yet is staying with us, serving us faithfully at the risk of losing everything he owns. Give me this pleasure, send him a diamond ring to show him you are grateful to him for tending me with such zeal. Please grant to Madame Chernyshev, who has all her fortune at our house in Brussels, an annual gratuity in money as a reward for serving me so faithfully. Believe me, dear friend, in whatever class loyalty is encountered, sovereigns must reward it in these times. My heart bleeds in finishing this letter. Tell yourself, dear Nicholas, that my whole desire is to show myself your worthy sister as it means a great deal to be one of the Triopathy, and I pray to the Almighty to help me. Pray for me, embrace Alexandrine in my name as well as your children. Great God! under what auspices shall I write to you next time? But I take *firmness and hope* for my motto and, trusting to my Nikki, I embrace him tenderly.

THE GRAND DUCHESS ANNA PAVLOVNA, THE PRINCESS OF ORANGE, TO TSAR NICHOLAS I:

The Hague,
12 October 1830

Dear good Brother,

We have reached the decisive moment of our own and our political existence; all who still wish for a dynasty in Belgium only want William! And they announce this resolution to a devoted son. I leave you to think what we feel. Heekeren will give you these lines, dear Brother and friend, and will tell you by word of mouth much more than I can write, for my soul is so deeply affected that I can only see to pray, and in praying I implore Divine Providence to grant me the ability to fulfil my duties. To console, to alleviate and to reconcile in everything that depends on me is my sole occupation. But it is perhaps one of the gravest moments that has ever existed in centuries of history! You will, dear friend, be as surprised as pained to learn that in this vital moment when it is urgent to act with prudence and propriety, Count Guriev took it into his head to send Prince Golitsyn clandestinely to Antwerp without warning the government and forbidding Prince Golitsyn to ask me for a letter for William or even to see me to give him news verbally. I owe it to the faithfulness of the good Prince that he informed me of it secretly. How great was my astonishment to learn that Golitsyn dined publicly with William in Antwerp! Fritz warned the King that the secret was kept from me; the King knew nothing of the mission, and as for Verstolk, he only learned of it from me who informed him by telling him that the secret had been kept from me by Guriev. Verstolk thanked me, telling me that he had reason to be all the more astonished as Guriev had dined with him the day before without saying anything to him about it. It is annoying because William himself wanted Golitsyn beside him as he wants representatives from all countries as witnesses of what he is doing, for he would like, he says, to be under a bell-glass so that everyone and the whole of Europe can witness his conduct. Prince Kozlovsky had conferences and interviews with the provisional government in Brussels. I am simply noting the facts for you, dear Brother, for as sovereign you are the best judge of the conduct of your subjects. My good and dear William writes me so often that I have every reason to be most touched. He is in a terrible position, and towards him and the family I am taking the ancestral motto from the [indecipherable] years struggle 'Faithful until beggary'.[1] I have been showered with kindness by the Queen; the King was good enough to show me great friendship and Louise is a tender sister and friend. I recommend my children to your friendship. My oldest son has traced a little note-case for his cousin Alexander, on one side there is a knight in armour, on the other a hussar. It is an appeal from knight to knight for the age when they will be able to take up arms for each other. Dear Nicholas, you were godfather of our oldest son and you were present at his baptism in Brussels. My lion cubs are well with the exception of the little sea-lion who has whooping cough, the little lioness is also beginning to cough. I have a strong desire to cut her claws and to tame her early so that one day she will not scratch anyone and will be good. A thousand thousand wishes, dear friend and Brother, to your charming children whom I embrace tenderly.

THE GRAND DUCHESS ANNA PAVLOVNA, THE PRINCESS OF ORANGE, TO TSAR NICHOLAS I:

The Hague,
14 October 1830

Dear good Brother,

Half an hour ago I had the pleasure of receiving your letter dated 21 September, for which I thank you tenderly, for you

[1] The motto adopted by the Prince of Orange in the war for independence against Spain in the sixteenth century.

can guess what it is to have a few friendly lines from one's family at a time like the present, dear Nicholas. As for courage, my friend, it is perhaps because I do not count on myself that I have it, for my hope is in God. Good Prince Trubetskoi, whom I have had the consolation of seeing here for a few days and who will give you these lines, will tell you how he found me. To write everything is impossible so, dear friend, I limit myself to indicating the points on which I would like you to question him. I spoke to him with an open heart about all my conduct among the family and in public; about the way in which I have always looked upon my position in these countries. He knows my views on the question of religion. It is in William's favour that belonging to the Greek church I am in fact neutral in matters of religion. As he and my children are Protestants the Liberals see in that an advantage, and the Catholics, who have always been well treated by William and me, must now attach themselves to us for their preservation, for revolutions do not like Catholicism. I am very touched by the feeling that they show me here; I am asking Trubetskoi to speak to you of my plan for my burial and the reasons for it. He will give you something for the fortress from me. In general, he has my full authority to speak to you of my poor self. I am enclosing in this a note on the two people who seem to me the most outstanding in the revolution and I shall send to you, as soon as I have it, the speech of [Lusac ?] which I read today with Trubetskoi. It is true and just. Our family relations are, thank Heaven, good and we are facing the situation with no disagreement up till now. May God grant that it lasts like this. Retain for me your courageous friendship, dear friend and Brother, that which alone must unite us.

The Hague,
19 October 1830

Dear good Brother,

Not to let an occasion pass to recall myself to your memory, I am sending a few lines to you through the Russian courier which the legation is sending off. It would be as painful as superfluous for me to enter into details that I am partly ignorant of. May it suffice for you to know that eight days ago the King wrote to William that he was renouncing Belgium in his favour, granting to him and his dynasty the sovereignty of these provinces, moreover giving him his blessing.[1] I only know of this from the Queen and from one word of William's. It is then on the strength of this that he is acting, and it must be supposed that it is the urgency of the times that made him take the resolution to publish the proclamation which at the moment is plunging Holland into despair because of regret at the fear of losing William. The distressing thing is that the King has not made public the determination that he expressed to his son in giving him his blessing. In this as in everything I pray to Heaven always to grant me the favour of being a respectful daughter. I personally am heaped with friendship by the whole family but above all by the Queen. We have the alternative of either losing everything or of mounting a throne *of mud*. For my part, dear friend, I am doing everything I decently can to retain for William the patrimony of his ancestors and to maintain family unity by my actions. Convinced in all sorts of ways of William's devotion to his father and his king, of which his letters give further proof, I yesterday went to the Queen to assure her that if I could, by my personal conduct, give clear proof of it, I would place myself voluntarily as a hostage in the King's hands. She replied to me tenderly, assuring me that she, the King and all the family as well as honest people would never doubt William's feelings, and she added something personal for me which is too dear and too flattering to me for me to repeat. I expressed a desire to spend the day near her and she was good enough to invite me to dinner. I took my two eldest sons there and I returned in the evening on my own for tea and supper. Pray for us, for I confess that only Divine Providence can rescue us from these cruel circumstances.

William had Grovestin tell me that he was convinced that there was nothing else he could do. I must resign myself therefore. At this moment Count Stirum arrived and gave me a letter from my dear William in which he told me that the Count sees everything in black colours and I must not allow myself to believe everything that he would tell me with the conviction of truth. Those are the very expressions he uses in his letter.

[1] For a brief time it seemed possible that the Prince of Orange might become the sovereign of an independent Belgium, but on 10 November 1830 the Belgian assembly voted the formal deposition of the Orange family.

Stirum himself assures me there is nothing to fear for William's life. It must be hoped that Divine Providence will deign to take pity on us in all respects. My health is recovering, thanks to the sea bathes that I am taking regularly every morning *in camera*. Dear Nikki, think of us and pray for us. I embrace Alexandrine and your children.

Please let Constantine see this letter for if I do not have the time to write to him I do not think of him with any less affection and gratitude. I embrace him as well as dear Jeannette.

THE GRAND DUCHESS ANNA PAVLOVNA, THE PRINCESS OF ORANGE, TO TSAR NICHOLAS I:

The Village of Willemsdorp
nr Moerdijk,
29 October 1830

Dear and excellent Brother,

The date from the place in which I am writing to you will show you that I have flown to the arms of my William at his first call. William's position at Antwerp ceased from the moment when the rebels, deaf to his conciliatory voice, endeavoured to enter the town with an armed force. The King's idea, and William's also, was that he should go to England,[1] and it appears that only the wish to see me again as well as his children has induced him to land here. He called me and I came with our eldest son – the younger children have whooping cough. You may imagine, dear friend, what our meeting was like after all that has happened, and the cruel, disquieting, harrowing moments I went through at The Hague. To add to our misfortunes we had an alert one night when musket shots were heard in the palace garden. They say it was only a band of robbers – I like to hope that it was, but as no one was caught it is difficult to know exactly what to attribute the thing to.

[1] The English had been one of the most ardent proponents of the creation of the union of the Netherlands and Belgium in 1815. Therefore, their attitude at this juncture was crucial. The whole story, including a discussion of the use of Anna Pavlovna's fortune, is told in Harold Temperley, *The Unpublished Diary and Political Sketches of Princess Lieven* (London 1925) pp. 174–80.

The Hague,
2 November 1830

Dear Nicholas,

Compare these dates and tell yourself that, since I started this letter we have returned to The Hague; William, who followed me on the King's orders, has spent two days here and left this morning to embark at Rotterdam for England. I have already received some lines from him since he departed, of which here is a copy. May paternal blessings be the pledge of heavenly blessings, as I hope for this infinite bounty which never abandons those who place their hope in it. You see that everything is moving with giant steps. One hardly has time to take one's bearings and if one were not attached more firmly than ever to the only true guiding principles which are found in Divine precepts, one would surely be dragged from good ways. I had to sustain a harsh attack from the King who was totally against William coming to The Hague because, he said, that would *precipitate the fall of the throne*. I took the liberty of saying to him that what would precipitate it much more quickly would be the appearance of a quarrel between the King and the Prince Royal, as princes and as father and son. He wept a great deal; I asked to be allowed to bring him here for twenty-four hours to see his father, his mother and his two sick children. '*No, no,*' he said to me, 'for if he comes for twenty-four hours, I shall no longer be sure of being able to separate from him.' He told me, amongst other things, that he would like to be in exile already because then he would have his son close to him and he would be happy. All that will show you that he is a good and tender father, but that they incite the King, and may God confound those who are doing it. At last, after many negotiations, the English ambassador having heartily jolted Verstolk, the King felt the necessity of sending for William; I crossed with the aide-de-camp who was looking for him after I had left William at Willemsdorp, resigned to going to Soestdijk where I was to join him two days later with our children. Everything is better as things are now, and the essential thing is to see father and son on the best of terms together and the good people of The Hague happy to have seen William again, a sentiment that is shared to a high degree by honest people of the educated classes.

As for the others, I shall reply that there are wicked people everywhere. In the step taken by the ambassador I recognise the implementation of the view that I expressed to Guriev that now or never was the occasion for the Diplomatic Corps to speak out strongly, with dignity and in a body, in order to make an impression by its European preponderance on the pusillanimity and bad faith of this minister who is going straight towards ruining the state. I was very satisfied with Guriev on this occasion where he acted well. It seems that he opened his eyes and reflected over the past and that he felt that the opinion in my favour, which is growing more and more pronounced among the Dutch, left him no other alternative than to be on the same side and above board in his conduct. In that I found fault with him in the past and dislike his natural ways, I feel all the more obliged to do him justice in this instance.

Here I am again, dear friend, alone at The Hague with my dear children and the family, having to do my best to cultivate good relations in the family which spring entirely from the heart, and do everything which is necessary and fitting to retain the affection of the Dutch who deserve it for the sake of all the components that make a nation estimable and worthy of respect. I have a heartfelt attachment to them and they bear me touching feelings of which I see proofs in all classes and of which I received touching demonstrations *worthy of Russia* during the journey that I made to Willemsdorp, both going there and on my return. From what the King had told me I should have expected to be abused, but I was received by acclamations and heaped with eager attentions. The details would take too long but I feel them in my soul, for they spoke to me of my William and they gave us their blessing. What a moment it was when I embraced *William the magnanimous* and *the misunderstood*! But posterity will do him justice and the moment of awakening will be a day of triumph for him! My heart is content, and when I say that, Nikki may feel calm. Our Nagel distinguished himself in these circumstances by his zeal for William and for me and by his devotion to you. He it was who accomplished the impossible, together with me, by preventing that in the reply of the States General to the King's speech, there was any question of William. It was a matter of nothing less than speaking of his *dethronement*. We stopped that. Also, dear Nikki, I would like

The Royal Palace of Soestdijk, painted by Tekening in 1845

The three sons of King William II and Queen Anna Pavlovna, painted by Pasquier in 1825. Left to right: *William, Henry and Alexander.*

to ask you for the Great Ribbon of Saint Anne for Nagel, and the little Cross of Saint Catharine for his wife who looked after me in my illness like a sister. Give me this pleasure on both counts. Dear Alexandrine will surely not refuse me?

Here is a striking work in Dutch by Monsieur Collot d'Escury de Heinenvord, one of those most hostile to William but whom I won over simply by courtesy; and as he calmed down and even offered his country seat to William, thinking that it would be better than in the village of Willemsdorp, I strongly urged him to send you his famous work so as to ask you to allow it to be translated into Russian. It is most interesting and will enrich our literature. In this way I have sought to bring about, completely naturally, a kind reward from you, dear Brother, which I recommend to you as most essential in the present circumstances. You will be able to judge the merit of the man from his work. Please enrich the library of the Hermitage with it, that will flatter him greatly. William said that he is pleased with me and asked me to continue in the same vein. I shall try, with God's help, quietly to do my best.

I must draw your attention, dear Brother, to something concerning Austria. Monsieur de Wessenberg, who is known as a true gentleman, has just been named most unexpectedly to replace the Count de Mier. This has struck us all, since Count Mier is staying here for the winter – it is said because his wife likes The Hague – whilst last year when the Court was here and their duty would have called them here, they stayed at Brussels. You know that Mier went over the barricades to tell William what state the town was in and that royal troops could not enter it. Compare all these facts, adding to them that he is supposed to be Metternich's tool, and see if it does not seem likely to you that he is only staying here in order to be his true agent, while Wessenberg is only an honest decoration to decoy the government. I think there is something of Reichstadt[1] in all that. Someone who could well be accurately informed told me yesterday that [Don Juan van Halen ?] is strongly suspected

[1] It may be that Anna Pavlovna really thought that the Austrians were plotting to get Belgium for the Duc de Reichstadt, but there is no real evidence that Metternich had any such idea. Indeed, the Austrians had always played down any thought of political sovereignty for Napoleon's son because this might undo the decisions of the Congress of Vienna.

of being the thief of my diamonds. It seems to me most probable, comparing this accusation with the expression on the face of the Spanish minister, Andouaga, the day of the robbery at the great Court dinner, and his confusion when I met him in the park a few days afterwards. This Andouaga stole, as you no doubt know, from the English Government, so it is quite possible that the habit has stayed with him. Who knows if my diamonds were not kept in his house which, like that of all diplomatic envoys, is inviolable? This idea has often come to me, and do not forget that the doorkeeper of my apartments in Brussels was a Spaniard! However, I do not want to accuse the latter but it is surely a matter for speculation.

I am leaving this sad subject to speak to you of my children who form my happiness. They are progressing very favourably but none more than the eldest whose soul is developing in the most interesting way. This dear child came in tears to hand me the little note-case that he has traced for your Alexander. He has written to him and worked this little object under my eyes and with real pleasure. The King spoke to me praising your good intentions, dear Brother, with respect to your wish to send us troops for help. He holds it against Prussia for having prevented you from doing so and I confess that I regret it, for your armed intervention with the good reputation that Russian troops enjoy in these countries would have been of incalculable advantage. The national spirit in Holland reminds one of that in Russia during 1812. Young men from the most prominent families are going to serve as ordinary soldiers to defend their native country. The costume of the officers is exactly like that of the *apalchenie* [i.e., the Russian militia]. I beg you, dear friend, to show this letter to Michael and General Benckendorff. Then please send it to Constantine. My hand is trembling so much that I cannot write to Alexandrine as I had intended, but here is a ring with my hair, and garnets which signify William. Put it on your finger, you who love and know what it is to suffer!

3 November

Happily for me, Golitsyn is not leaving until tomorrow, which gives me a chance to finish this letter at my ease, which in view of my present position here is a dispatch. I would like to see our good Golitsyn here again as soon as possible. I like his character, he is noble and affectionate. May he one day deserve the word 'faithful' in his coat-of-arms. I leave it to you, dear and excellent Brother, who know how to reward with the sense of honour. I spent the evening yesterday with the Queen; I saw the King there and he was very kind and spoke to me of William with love. What happiness! Golitsyn will tell you that William was very well received in Rotterdam, a place that was depicted as so dangerous. I sent to the Russian Legation[1] in England the portfolio with the certificates of ownership of my personal fortune. It must be near the dear person of William of Orange but in the hands of the Russian Legation, out of delicacy for him. *William does not know about it.* I have just received a most touching letter from Alexandrine! How can I ever acknowledge so much friendship and interest? But at least let me assure you that your affection gives the dearest consolation to my heart. May the heavens repay you as you deserve. How touched I was by what Alexandrine wrote to me, that you had had the kindness, dear Nikki, to have arranged secretly to give me an ornament in turquoise. No, it is too good and too kind to give me with affection the stone of friendship, and one for which I was formerly indebted to Mama's kindness. I am most touched by it, but do not do too much for me and do not spoil me. I must finish this long letter. Here is a pin that I had on me when I saw William at Willemsdorp. Wear it, dear Nikki, out of friendship for us. And here is the other that I had on my belt. I give it to Mikki, embracing him tenderly. Let us always love each other as in the cherished time of the Triopathy; retain for me your affection and count forever on the sentiment of your most affectionate and devoted sister and friend.

TSAR NICHOLAS I TO THE GRAND DUCHESS ANNA PAVLOVNA, THE PRINCESS OF ORANGE:

St Petersburg,
16/28 November 1830

Dear good Anne,

I cannot tell you all the pleasure your three kind letters gave me with their contents full of affection, but also because of the

[1] Princess de Lieven reports in her journal that she received the portfolio. The latter the Princess sent to the embassy, but she kept the key.

sentiments with which I see you are filled in these times which are so cruel and so important for the country that has adopted you, as well as for your family and especially for our poor William. Such noble behaviour as his filled me with happiness, and you must see in this your reward through the results it has had of leading the King back to the duties towards a son whom he had so cruelly and uselessly compromised. William's mistakes are much slighter and more excusable in the eyes of those who, like me, are acquainted with everything which, because of the King, caused him to be placed in the most false and difficult position.

But let us drop that, and let us thank God for the inspiration which led you to insist to the King that he see his son again and thus remove the hatefulness of a family quarrel, especially at a time when everything must be bound together.

I want very much for the sojourn in London not to last too long, once the first moments are over. I think that too long a stay in England without any additional reason seems to me to be like a fall from favour and would be completely out of place.

Everything that has happened in your country makes one shudder, and truly I do not know what one should be more astonished at, the very calamitous the steps adopted by the government or the folly and audacity of the insurgents! How will it all end? In any case, I hope to see you standing by the principles that you have been following since all these disasters. The most perfect calm, the greatest respect for the King, and the most perfect union with the rest of the family; and the same tenderness and faithfulness against all odds for your husband; and for what remains, put your trust in the good Lord who often removes us from the most hopeless positions when we throw ourselves on his mercy with complete faith. *I know whereof I speak.* Along with this my wife sends you the objects you wished for; I do not know whether you will be satisfied with them – turquoises are very difficult to find, and the object is not yet finished. Many many thanks for the pin; this will be a dear remembrance for me of an extremely important time for you both in which you showed yourself as you should, and Heaven will bless you for it.

THE GRAND DUCHESS ANNA PAVLOVNA, THE PRINCESS OF ORANGE, TO TSAR NICHOLAS I:

The Hague,
30 November 1830

Dear excellent Brother,

It is in my first moment of gratitude that I seize my pen to express to you with an overflowing heart the sweet and consoling sentiments with which you fill my soul. It was only a moment ago that I learned with what generosity you deigned to heed my intercession in favour of my faithful Lady of the Bedchamber, Natalie Chernyshev, whose possessions were all in our house at Brussels and who was in the power of the Revolutionary Party; thirteen years of irreproachable service and praiseworthy zeal at the time which followed the theft; when, by drawing herself sketches of the objects and by describing others, she did in two days what might enable me at some time to retrieve the jewels that were taken from me. Think how I suffered at seeing fate strike her down and how I appreciate the sentiments of justice as much as generosity which caused you to agree to my wish in regard to her. My friend, it means that you are doing more for me than you could do for me directly, because nothing can be dearer to me than to see you reward those who serve me honourably. May God repay you, dear Nicholas, you who have caused *the first tears of joy to fall among our disasters*. This poor person came to throw herself on my hand, bringing me the Order of the Imperial Cabinet, telling me it was more than she had ever deserved, and she dissolved into tears.

4 December

I would have liked to have been able to finish and send off my letter the other day, but that was not possible because of all the obstacles in the way, so it is, only now, today that I have managed to continue it. While waiting, you will have received all those that contain the proofs of the trust that I owe you, dear Brother and friend, above all in our present grave circumstances. I am on the eve of finding myself more isolated than ever by the departure of the Queen, who is going to Berlin with Louise for about six weeks. You will easily understand what it is for me to remain alone like this with my children, deprived of the presence of my husband and of my mother-in-law, whose friendship is so precious to me. As the only remaining woman in the family, public attention will naturally be drawn to me all the more, and as I have never sought after it, neither would I wish for my position to make me the object of it. However, the thing is inevitable.

As events are becoming more and more interesting, and as I can foresee that conversations on matters of high concern will probably take place between the King and myself, it is necessary for me to be in a position to know *exactly* the nature of your principal decisions, such as those which concern this country and our affairs, so that my silence should not be badly interpreted and my words should conform with your intentions. It is this, dear Brother, that has obliged me to ask you to authorise your accredited minister to this Court to inform me of your future resolutions with regard to this country. In 1825, when the events of 14 December were taking place, Count Guriev informed me himself of the dispatch which contained the details of it; he did the same at the Peace of Adrianople, and so I thought I was authorised to ask him for the content of your recognition of the King of the French, since it was most important to me to know how much it agreed with the opinion you expressed to me about it in your letter this summer; likewise, I asked the Count recently for the circular concerning the measures taken with respect to the events in our country and the movement of troops, because the King had trusted me by speaking to me about it and asked me questions to which I could not reply, not being informed on what had been decided, and as he graciously added details of which I did not know the true source, it seemed to me I could do no better than to address myself to you completely openly, placing before you the case which makes my position more and more delicate, and asking you to inform me of what you think it necessary for me to know so that, as I have already said, my silence and my words may not be open to false interpretation. I have seen Prince Lieven again since my last letter; I was very touched by everything he said about your friendship for me, dear friend, and your opinion of my line of conduct in these difficult times. The inquiries that you asked him to make about Count Guriev show how good you are to pay attention to the opinion I expressed to you about him. I am not in the least surprised that these inquiries did not yield anything in the direction in which I spoke to you about him, because he will have been on his guard against inquiries and will have taken care that nothing official and written should be uncovered from these years of his true opinions or his conduct. But the attitude of Prince Lieven and his way of looking at the affairs of the country show me more than ever how much – if I may say so – you have been led into error on many important points which seemed as though [not correct ?] I was struck by how little informed Prince Lieven[1] was on the state of Holland, on its outlook, its interests, in short, how he seemed to consider it negligible. It is exactly the same tone as Count Guriev's, but it is a tone and a mode of behaviour that have a very bad effect here. He allows himself to speak, not only coldly, but even with disdain about the devotion and enthusiasm that the Dutch nation shows in the defence of its home. Perhaps that can be explained by the relationship that existed last year between Count Guriev and de Celles. They were both staying beneath the same roof and saw each other frequently. Perhaps these relations still exist for I assure you that some time ago he spoke to me about Belgium's affairs in such a way as to make me suppose that he had been informed, fifteen days in advance, that the dethronement of the family would be announced. Once linked with the Belgian Unionists, it is of little account to him to serve a government worthily and to inform it on the real state of Holland, provided that he remain faithful to the end to those with whom he is solely linked. I was frightened for our future and that of our children to see Prince Lieven consider Holland as counting for so little in the balance and Belgium as so excusable and so necessary. While all our moral strength is here and the rest is rotten to the core, the fine exceptions that this unfortunate country offers stand out like well-preserved fragments beside a ruined building. I shall be guilty towards you, dear friend, if I hid similar truths from you. They are hard, perhaps, and spoken without embellishment

[1] Prince Christopher Andrievich Lieven (1777–1838) was the Russian ambassador to the Court of St James's.

but all the more useful to know. As for me, I am glad to have seen cut short a question which falls back completely on the great powers; they will, perhaps, do us the service of deciding it in a tolerable way. My personal desire is never again to set foot in Brussels where the character of William was so grossly abused. I still do not know when we will be able to see him again here–according to my information not until the thirtieth. His presence here is much desired. I embrace you tenderly, dear good Brother, asking you to give my friendly regards to dear Alexandrine and to your charming children. Mine are all my consolation in these sad time. Retain your friendship for me and reply at least once to the frequent letters that I write to you from my heart and soul, dear good Brother. Your very devoted, faithful and tender sister and friend.

Please send us Golitsyn as soon as possible again. He is an honest man and the Legation here is singularly composed when he is absent. I would like Linievsky to be sent off with some disptaches to get him away from here.

TSAR NICHOLAS I TO THE GRAND DUCHESS ANNA PAVLOVNA, THE PRINCESS OF ORANGE:

St Petersburg,
4/16 December 1830

A courier is leaving in a few hours, dear Anne, and I want at least to tell you that I have received your two letters from Trubetskoi and by courier; I cannot thank you enough or tell you how much I appreciate the kindness you show for me.

So the revolution and everything that goes along with it has reached us too, as I foresaw; you already know everything that is happening in Poland;[1] it will be a week tomorrow since I have heard anything about Constantine; they say that he left with the Russian troops to come back to the Empire. You can imagine the task I have on my shoulders; but I rely confidently on the will of God, who has pulled me from positions more difficult than this one. I hope that He will protect us and help me perform my painful duties with his inspiration; without this

[1] The revolt broke out on 17/29 November 1830.

all-powerful help I could do nothing, but with it I face danger coolly. Our troops are marching; in a few weeks I ought to join them; the rest is written up above! And I submit myself ahead of time. My principles are unshakable, and I would rather perish than compromise with revolution. You can imagine that in such moments one can only be brief, and you will not hold it against me.

Many many thanks for all the wishes you make for me at the time of my name-day and for the charming seal. If William is near you, embrace him as well as your children for me. Farewell, think of us, and may God preserve you and yours. Yours for life.

Your devoted brother and friend.

THE GRAND DUCHESS ANNA PAVLOVNA, THE PRINCESS OF ORANGE, TO TSAR NICHOLAS I:

The Hague,
12 December 1830

Dear excellent Brother and friend,

Receive my most loving and sincere thanks for your dear letter of 16 November in reply to mine; all the affectionate things which you say to me touch me deeply and all the more because just when your friendship is spreading happiness and consolation in my soul you may be attacked by fresh strokes of fate. Dear Nikki, what will you have felt in hearing the news from Poland? These new misfortunes absorb me completely and are a diversion to those that we are experiencing here. It seems to me that we are not the most to be pitied. I can only think of you all and pray to God for you and place my hope in His mercy. How William will be affected by the news and the new trouble that it is going to give you! I must thank you again, dear friend, very tenderly, for having destined a present for me which expresses so much affection – the stone of friendship mounted in pansies [Fr. *pensées*] and in forget-me-nots. How precious this object is to me, both by its intention and by the moment in which you give it to me. I hope to introduce it on your birthday and if the heaven deigns to grant us a happier time I shall deck myself in it often.

13 December

My thoughts are constantly fixed upon you. If there is anything to be judged by the arrogant bearing and the exchange of remarks with La Rochefoucauld, the French Chargé d'Affaires who was presented to me yesterday, this country is greatly involved in the events of the north, and perhaps I may conclude from it that even in Russia something grave is about to happen. May Heaven watch over you all! I must return for the moment to the subject of your letter, dear friend. You will not credit how touched I was by the interest that you show in me, as well as the approval that you give me. It seemed to me that in my present bizarre, complicated and delicate circumstances I could only follow the feeling of conscience which alone guided me. Heaven deigned to inspire me and bless my intentions as much as my actions. Be in no doubt that I am too well aware of the difficulty of doing good for such precious approval to give me a presumptuous confidence in myself. It is, perhaps, dear friend, because I feel everything that I lack and that I have still to acquire that I shall try to be circumspect, calm and moderate, but firm in that and when I have to act. For we are living in times in which firmness is indispensable for any good to result. I look to my swarm and to my house, seeing that those who have to carry out the details entrusted to them acquit themselves well. I continue to be respectful to the King who is very kind to me during these times and takes a great interest in the affairs of Poland. My relations with the family are such as I could desire, but our dear Queen has left with Louise to return home in mid-January, I trust. This leaves me very isolated and with no possible hope of seeing William here so soon; so I am entirely reduced to myself and thereby my position fixes public attention. I continue to see some people at dinner in order not to isolate myself from society while living in the midst of it; it is a question of following things through without doing anything out of the ordinary but for which they might say that I have only spasms of benevolence whilst – and this sentiment is inscribed in my heart – I must be consistent in appearances. It is only gradually and over a long period that one is convincing – not through fine phrases – for effect. We are no longer in the age of tinsel and here one is only paid with sense, well-founded sentiments and esteem. Dear Nikki, do you know that if you could witness the estimable qualities that this country of two million is developing you would think, I am sure, that I should bless God because, since I had to leave my native country, it was to live in the midst of them. It is pleasant to be adopted by such a worthy nation. One may say without exaggeration that it should serve as a model for the rest of Europe which is prey to all sorts of disturbances, while Holland remains faithful and shows a touching enthusiasm in defending its sovereign and its homes. Imagine, taxes which under the present circumstances are doubled, are paid promptly; beyond that, voluntary gifts abound, and the annual collections for the poor throughout the country have brought in more this year than usual, since all the towns support at their expense the families of volunteers: finally, I shall never finish if I describe to you all the marks of devotion that come to my knowledge. I am entirely of your opinion, dear Brother, with regard to William's stay in England, that it is *preferable not to see it prolonged.* In many respects I should like to see him here. Opinion is beginning to swing round about him, they seem to attribute what was painful to unknown causes but they exonerate his intentions and they regret being deprived of his presence and his qualities. His past renown is not forgotten, and to me they show interest when discussing William with me. I have succeeded in persuading them that they can not be agreeable to me without speaking to me about him. My whole wish in these difficult times has been to conserve the patrimony of his ancestors for him, and I believe I have succeeded; my sole wish is to present to my William the fruits of my labours. The day on which I shall see him enjoy them and see him appreciate it will perhaps be the happiest of my life. Beside him my path is simply that of representation and I reveal things to him frankly as I see them. I would like to see him uniquely and openly Dutch, for the honour of the family, of honest people and his future good. Believe that there is no happiness nor *honour for us in placing our hope anywhere except here.* Belgium, in my eyes, is irrevocably lost and it is not by appearing to go towards it and by *wishing for it that one will obtain it* even were it desirable.

I am sending you the copy of a leaflet of which the original was entrusted to me by dear Fritz. It is necessary for you to read it to give you an idea of the political and moral perversity of the inhabitants, or the plotters, of this unhappy country. I am revolted by it to the bottom of my soul, and you should also know of the insulting way in which they criticise Russia's policy. It is dreadful that no magnanimity can make the rascals be quiet! But what can I say of these countries since the events in Poland; they surpass *everything*!

15 December

I cannot terminate these lines without returning again to our dear unhappy William! You would not credit how I dread the impulsiveness of his character and even the nature of his qualities at the present time. It is only too clear that they sought to destroy him through his qualities as much as through the weak sides of his character. His facility in communicating and his particular chivalry in placing his trust in another's loyalty are as good as disastrous qualities at the present time. Moreover, it is not necessary to see people who misreport your words and make a game of imposing them on your intentions; one finishes by being a victim of blame that one has never deserved, and that has often been the case with William, who really cannot resist his qualities, while there is the greatest necessity to restrict them in order not to open up the way for incalculable harm. You know of the defection of Goblet; it frightened me because of papers he was in a position to know about and information that had come to his knowledge about the Russian and Polish army. William, to whom I expressed my fears, replied that there was nothing to fear and he had taken the path that he had been seen to follow in order to be useful to us. In this I cannot share the opinion of my William; I would not like this way of seeing things to be known for it could damage him here. I can only see in Goblet a man whose wounded vanity has driven him to join the opposite party. He was only a captain and now he is a general and Minister of War. Our former Chamberlain, d'Emo de Bovay [?], voted for our dethronement! Would you have believed it? He is the only one who made me laugh. He is a fool who never was and never will be anything else. Would you let him remain a Chevalier of St Anne? William has done a thousand things for him and for three-quarters of those who have voted for the dethronement.

Perfidy, ingratitude, and credulity are the characteristic features of this unhappy nation. The true ill and disaffection date back two years from the time when William, in an outburst of righteousness, set about telling the truth to the Catholics. He conducted himself nobly in the eyes of honest people, but to believe that he would be pardoned for it is not to know this religion well, and one need take nothing further into account beyond that of being avenged for it. Almost the whole of the nobility is French in spirit, and I cannot see how one can prevent union with France, with the exception of the Flemish who have a character of their own. There was certainly something calamitous in the wretchedness of the government, but there was in everything. The ill was too grave to find an effective remedy, but I am happy that you gave a fair opinion of our dear William's conduct – he has, as you state very well, been as cruelly as uselessly compromised. It is a position from which it was almost impossible to withdraw in a satisfactory way, also I shall never forget how I trembled when he was sent to Antwerp. I bless God that the Congress pronounced the dethronement of the whole family! for what a dreadful position we would be in if in rejecting the King it had elected William. I hope that Heaven in its mercy will preserve me from ever returning to Belgium, at least to Brussels!

I am infinitely obliged to you, dear Brother, for having had the goodness to decorate dear Doctor Everard with the Cross of Saint Vladimir. He is very grateful for it; and you have shown a mark of goodwill to someone who has conducted himself worthily in these sad times. I am sending you the translation of a brochure about William that you will surely read with interest. There are some in Dutch by a certain Lipmann which it is very important for you to see, for they will give you an idea of the spirit of Holland and you have just had new proof that national sentiments cannot be forced. It is tiresome but inevitable. Yesterday, dear friend, the King spoke to me about you again with gratitude and interest, accepting with a great deal of friendship [the proposal] to celebrate your birthday by a dinner with me and to drink to your health. Receive my sincere and ardent wishes for your happiness and your preservation, dear good Brother, may Heaven watch over you and keep you for our affection.

TSAR NICHOLAS I TO THE GRAND DUCHESS ANNA PAVLOVNA, THE PRINCESS OF ORANGE:

St Petersburg,
7/19 January 1831

Dear kind Anne,

Receive all my sincere congratulations and all my wishes for your birthday; may the good Lord bless you and yours and grant you a calmer and happier year in every respect than the one which has just ended. Thank you very much for your letter, which I received with the mail from London. The King had the kindness to inform me that William was to come back today; that is certainly the best present for your celebration.

I cannot say anything important from here; the Poles are being as silly as your Belgians who can be satisfied with the King [of their choice].

After having exhausted every gentle means which I could use without betraying myself or the duties of my position, I am going to use force; and with God's help we hope to be able to re-establish tranquillity in that country in which, as elsewhere, the good people are weak and the bad ones triumphant. Constantine and Jeannette are both near Grodno; I do not yet know what he will want to do.

Hug William for me; I cannot tell him anything more this time. Hug your children and present my homage to the King. Farewell, dear good Anne, may God cover us all with his shield; keep a little affection for him who is for life.

Your completely devoted brother and friend.

THE GRAND DUKE CONSTANTINE TO THE GRAND DUCHESS ANNA PAVLOVNA, THE PRINCESS OF ORANGE:

Gov. de Grodno Brzestowicz [?]
7/18 [19 ?] January 1831

Accept, dear excellent Sister, my congratulations and my most sincere good wishes for your birthday. . . . Old Constantine offers them to you from the fullness of his heart and soul. At the same time accept all my most heart-felt thanks for your letter date 1 December which M. [d'Anstett ?] had delivered to me, as well as for the tender interest you have displayed in the outcome of the plot which was set up against me. Thanks to Divine goodness I escaped from it initially because of the conspiracy being discovered in time, but subsequent events were even more serious still, and the rebellion of 17/29 November in Warsaw and then [Mazowse ?] and the whole of [Potogur ?] just missed putting me a hair's-breadth from my destruction, and unfortunately the victims of that deplorable, infamous event suffered so. As for my personal staff, Lieutenant-General Gurdier [was] killed on the spot, the Vice-President of the city very seriously wounded and also three of my servants – one of whom died as a result of his wounds. God deigned to save me from that infamous trap which was accompanied by treachery, cowardice, and the blackest ingratitude. One would have to have seen it from as close a position as I to be able to credit to what lengths perfidy and infamy can bear men. The remainder of the details are too long to include in a letter and one would need a pen better trained than mine to give a brief account of it. In short, as a prize for the sixteen years of anxieties and continuous work against all odds I have seen myself forced by circumstances to leave a country to which I had given my every care, see its duties and oaths betrayed by my army, which owes to me its existence and well-being, under the vain pretext of nationalism and patriotism which no-one was thinking of removing or snatching from it. I returned over our borders with the Russian troops I had with me unharmed, having done twelve highly tiring marches in very rigorous weather, but having kept our honour spotless and flags, standards and cannon as well. Moreover, in spite of the uproar in which the pass-word of the rebellion was that the Russians are assassinating the Poles, I did not fire a single shot, and I proved to the entire world and to posterity that all the aggression and hostility began on the Polish side which, in spite of all good faith, is still keeping as prisoners up to this moment a large number of our generals, officers and employees who were peacefully in garrison in different parts of the kingdom and who considered themselves subject to the same master by doing their duties together. If that be patriotism, it is viewed in a strange way, and one very characteristic of the Poles. An even stranger thing yet was that during our march we saw that the majority of the inhabitants were sorry to see us go, and deplored the happenings, cursing and swearing against them, but in spite of that unwillingly joined the rebels to swell their number in order to prevent the deserved punishment. As for the subsequent events, they are of such a nature as to tear the heart and soul of every right-thinking and upright person who values good faith above all. In these terrible events, my poor wife has shown calmness, presence of mind and rare energy. She acted as secretary to me in spite of her illness and her sickly condition which has twice brought her to death's door. Thanks to God! she is still alive to be my consolation and I bless God for this from the depths of my heart. . . . My son was on duty at Aradrene [?] the day of the revolution and made a very good showing, as he was at the head from the first moment on, being the only officer present and having passed through a firing-line of rebellious Polish non-commissioned officers from the barracks who were to get to me. . . . Do not forget me, dear Sister; my loving hugs to all your children and greetings to your ladies and gentlemen. Completely yours with heart and soul. . . .

TSAR NICHOLAS I TO THE GRAND DUCHESS ANNA PAVLOVNA, THE PRINCESS OF ORANGE:

St Petersburg,
19/31 January 1831

I am taking advantage of the departure of a courier for London to offer you in advance, dear Anne, my congratulations for your name-day; my wishes for your happiness and your perfect contentment certainly do not need such an occasion to be more fervent or sincere. At the same time accept all my thanks for your kind letter of the 1st, which I have just received, and for everything you say to me in it concerning our Warsaw infamies. It seems that the language of reason and honour has had some effect, for Chlopitski[1] had the courage to resign from his

[1] Joseph Chlopitski (1771–1854), a Polish general, had been appointed on 3 December (N.S.) by the revolutionary government to act as commander of the Polish army.

functions, declaring that it was no longer compatible with the oaths of fidelity to the Emperor for him to continue his role; the rabble's miscalculation has been great, and the consequence will be terrible; we are calmly waiting for the results of this, and all our military measures are prepared so that with God's help the affair may be *short but good*. . . .

You are complaining that I write you little and that I do not reply to all the contents of your letters; on the contrary, I thought I was accurate enough to deserve a *spasibo* [Russian for 'thank you'] seeing that I scarcely have the time to do as much as I do. So I beg your pardon once and for all; but I cannot be more lengthy.

TSAR NICHOLAS I TO THE GRAND DUCHESS ANNA PAVLOVNA, THE PRINCESS OF ORANGE:

St Petersburg,
3/15 February 1831

. . . Alas, it is difficult yet to predict the end of our shared trials, for it seems that the passion for disorder and confusion only grows and blossoms.

We are waiting for the military decisions of our operations, the beginnings of which have been more than satisfying, considering the conviction that the populace is outside of the so-called national revolution, and that we were received with open arms as liberators. I am expecting from one moment to the next the news of some engagements; may the good Lord grant that blood flow as little as possible and that in the end reason may return to the madmen, who with light hearts destroy the happiness of a population which is peaceful, excellent, and fortunate in the institutions the value of which it appreciated.

Constantine marched at the head of the reserves, the excellent and agreeable Jeannette remained at Byalostok; how she is to be pitied!

I want reason to come back too to your Brussels madmen; I limit myself to that, and for a good reason. William wrote me by a London packet and still tells me nothing about his return.

My wife has *la grippe*, which has seized hold of almost the whole town and the suburbs, and almost all my children still have it or are over it. Other than that, nothing else to tell you; Michael is leaving us to rejoin his corps, and as for myself, Heaven will decide.

TSAR NICHOLAS I TO THE GRAND DUCHESS ANNA PAVLOVNA, THE PRINCESS OF ORANGE:

St Petersburg,
21 March/2 April 1831

. . . Just *this* day was it that I was informed *via* Guriev that William was expected in a Dutch steamer, and you can easily imagine how pleased I was to learn of his imminent return to his family; tell him so if he is indeed near you. Everything you wrote me about Lieven's transaction with money which belongs to you is a complete puzzle to me, I do not understand what has been done or where it can be. I shall ask Lieven for information, but knowing him, and having seen him in most difficult moments, I can confirm to you that he is incapable of doing anything at all dishonourable; he is honour and honesty personified. I admire him and especially esteem him; he deserves it.

The Vistula makes it impossible for us to follow up our advantage, and, in spite of what the newspapers say, that is the only thing which has momentarily saved the Poles, and we are very angry about it.

Insolence, lunacy, and lies; there, in three words is the act of faith of this *faithful* nation; completely worthy to march with their Brussels models. In the end the good Lord will decide the matter, and, in the meanwhile, trust in His mercy, constancy, prudence, and perseverance; here I am nailed to my chair, instead of sharing the dangers of my soul-brothers, which increases not a little the bad humour of the new Attila (a new title which has been bestowed upon me); it is handsome, energetic, characteristic, economic, etc., and I adopt it as such, grateful to those who have graced me with it. What do you think about it? – This poor Attila can think only of staying quietly at home, happy in being with his five-month pregnant wife and his children; his taste are all domestic; in short, he is the least hostile and the most peace-loving person on earth; – what a strange fate!

Tsar Nicholas I to the Grand Duchess Anna Pavlovna, the Princess of Orange:

Alexandria,
19 June/1 July 1831

You will be cruelly overcome, dear kind Anne, by the news which is painfully necessary for me to announce to you. You no longer have anyone left but Michael and me; our poor Constantine has been snatched from our affection by the terrible cholera, all within a few hours![1] You can guess at my state by your own, and add to that my fears for my family, for three days ago this evil appeared in Petersburg and you can but have a slight idea of it. But, may the will of God be done! in this as in all things. I bow myself to it without murmuring. Poor unhappy Jeannette, could one find a more unfortunate position than hers – do not hold it against me that I am writing you so briefly, but [I am overwhelmed with] despair and I lack the actual time.

Farewell, dear Anne, believe in the affection of him who is for life your faithful brother and friend.

Tsar Nicholas I to the Grand Duchess Anna Pavlovna, the Princess of Orange:

Tsarskoe Selo,
27 July/8 August 1831

. . . I only came back a few hours beforehand from the colonies of [Novgorod ?], where cholera had created a serious disaster; I had gone there to convince myself that everything had been put in order again, and I returned at midnight. At four the

[1] He died on 15 June 1831 (N.S.).

labour began. May this happy event foreshadow others! Tell friend William that I embrace him, but it is still impossible for me to reply to his kind letter which I received the very evening I had just written to him. *I admire*!!! everything that is happening about the *traitors* [?] in Brussels; and above all your King's patience; when will the scandal end! May the Heavens take pity on you. Hug your darlings and remember their Uncle to them.

The Grand Duchess Anna Pavlovna, the Princess of Orange, to Tsar Nicholas I:

Scheveningen,
4 August 1831

Dear good Nikki,

We are all in such extreme straits that I can only write a few lines, dear friend, convinced that you will understand what I am experiencing. I myself wished to give you the first good news; William's initial step has been a happy one and he opened his campaign by pushing back the enemy's outposts. He wrote to me that he went to bed content with the success of the first day. I am asking the Legation to send you William's Order of the Day, of which I guarantee the authenticity. And I beg you only to publish in the Petersburg journal the one that I send and not the French translation published by the newspaper of The Hague, which is full of inaccuracies and gives an odd turn to the sense of some sentences which it seems to me necessary to avoid. We are following the unique path of honour; I hope that God will deign to bless our arms and watch over our William, taking him under His guardian aegis. I gave him one of the sabres that you saw, after having had it blessed in my chapel; yesterday I had a Te Deum sung to bless this courageous enterprise which is so decisive for our political existence.

Nikki, pray for us. I embrace your wife and your children. '*Firmness and hope*' – William carries it on his finger in the ring of the Triopathy, and he told me that his sabre would not leave him. He had it by his side when he left. What I feel as a wife and mother cannot be expressed and I appeal to the heart of your wife to understand what is taking place in mine! I embrace you tenderly, dear Brother and friend; perhaps Holland will give her hand honourably to Russia to fight enemies of the public good. God grant it may be thus. It is an admirable nation, worthy of your esteem. Good-bye, my good Brother and friend. Forever your faithful and devoted sister.

Your last letter announced that we had just suffered the cruel loss of our Constantine. I could not reply sooner, precisely because I felt this blow so deeply. What a loss for us, what a friend has been taken from us. Everything is in mourning in these times, and your terrible cholera does not leave us in peace for a moment. Oh, my friend! May God preserve you.

THE GRAND DUCHESS ANNA PAVLOVNA, THE PRINCESS OF ORANGE, TO TSAR NICHOLAS I:

Scheveningen,
8 August [1831 ?]

Dear good Brother,

As I am convinced that you will wish to receive detailed news of our William's military operations and the whole of the movements, I thought you would like it if they were described to you by a military man, and with this in mind I have looked to a worthy officer of genius who is concerned with the education of my sons. He knows both Dutch and French, so he can give exact translations of the interesting pieces that appear, as well as those of the bulletins. Here, dear Brother, is my first dispatch; not having had favourable news to give you until this moment.

The letter of [C de G ?] that I received this morning from our dear William was most satisfactory. He said everything went much better than expected – those are his expressions; may this good continue, he said, 'and God bless our arms.' All the encounters have gone well for us so far. The Leiden students distinguished themselves by their bravery the first time they were under fire. Dear friend, join your prayers to ours; Heaven graciously sustains me; I implore its mercy for what is to follow. I am sending this news to you by Monsieur van den Hoop; I chose it as the most prompt and sure way, for these lines will reach you directly without going through diplomatic channels.

11 August

Good and happy news, dear Nicholas, our William is a conqueror; here is a copy of the letter that he wrote to me; I have had attached to it the principal facts of his report on the picture of military operations. At the same time, the London Conference[1] has us threatened by France on land and by England at sea; and Lieven signs this Act! Oh, my friend, it is not you, it is not possible. Rather send us Admiral Heyden with ships to defend us against this iniquitous, invading England; and I count on your help, dear Nikki; do not let us be crushed unjustly. I confess to you, my friend, that happy as is everyone here at William's success, I had a Te Deum sung in my chapel for the occasion to give thanks to the Almighty for having watched over our William's life. I invited the Legation to it, as was reasonable, and would you believe that Guriev did not even ask for news of William. He appeared to be ignorant of the object of the Te Deum, and he used the expression, 'What did *he* do then?' looking so annoyed that it struck my sister-in-law as well as myself and all those present. I learnt that before the Te Deum he had made offensive remarks and repeated the abuse the Duke of Orleans had expressed against our King when haranguing the French troops. Indeed, he was heard to say that what happened to Denmark might well happen to this country. Is that your wish, dear friend and Brother? Do you permit your minister here to make such remarks under my roof? They are such that it is no longer possible for me to receive him, but I shall soon see [Danaviof ?] and I shall single him out as much as possible. You see me heartbroken by all that, dear friend, and I appeal to your sense of fairness not to have me insulted any longer in this way. May you, dear good Brother, believe for once your most sincere friends and open your eyes to your diplomatic agents who give you colours that

[1] The so-called Eighteen Articles which regularised the separation and gave terms favourable to Belgium. Leopold of Saxe-Coburg, who had been elected King earlier in the month, approved the document but King William I of the Netherlands did not. The upshot was further fighting, a French invasion and a Dutch withdrawal.

you do not and cannot have. Everyone who expresses an opinion about it agrees saying, 'The Emperor Nicholas is noble and generous, but his Diplomatic Corps profit from the distance to deceive him.' They use your difficulties to force your decisions. *Alexander was the liberator of Holland*; do not give it a mortal blow. If such is your wish I shall bend beneath the hand of God and I shall follow my William in all extremities in which he may find himself, with the four children for whom Holland is the last patrimony. Blessing God for having granted William another day of glory at the head of a worthy and valiant nation, *but heart-broken* by all the rest. May the day of Justice arrive!

In this extremity I embrace you tenderly, dear good Brother, with your wife and children, wishing you well and recommending myself to your friendship, and being forever your faithful and very affectionate sister and loving friend.

It is my little William who lets you have his map with pleasure so that Uncle can see what Papa is doing.

Copy of enclosure (*letter from William, Prince of Orange, to the Grand Duchess Anna Pavlovna, the Princess of Orange*) sent to Tsar Nicholas I:

[Tirlemont ?]
14 August 1831

Dear Anninka,

You will have been at our church today to pray to God for us, and you will at the same time have thanked Him for my second victory, that over Leopold in person, of which the news will have been brought to The Hague this morning by Omphal, and which completes in entirety and crowns this short campaign, for without the French I should have been outside Brussels on the evening of 12 August. Yesterday General Belliard came to me as well as General Lavoestein, sent by Marshal Gérard, to speak to me of the arrangements made between the King and France, according to which I had to retire as soon as the French Army was in contact with mine; and now we are, for they are only two leagues from my outpost. I started to withdraw today and I shall go slowly and comfortably without fatiguing my people. I gave another Order of the Day again yesterday at Louvain which I ask you to read. Here is the first draft. Now there is no more war, it is a simple friendly evacuation demanded by France. My official report to the King, of yesterday, also has interesting information. I embrace and bless our dear children, and I am for life your affectionate and devoted old friend,

William

I must confess that God has protected us because, after all our successes, our losses have been almost imperceptible.

The Grand Duchess Anna Pavlovna, the Princess of Orange, to Tsar Nicholas I:

The Hague,
15 August 1831

Dear excellent Brother,

Congratulate us on our William. He has beaten Leopold at Louvain and has forced him to flee before him. What happiness! Let us bless Heaven for it a thousand thousand times. Here are the copies of William's letters, and the translation of reports and the military account will follow, but one may say that the events overtake the translations. We received this happy news yesterday at half past seven in the morning on the day fixed for public prayers for the blessing of our arms, so we were happily able to include thanksgiving as well. Going in and out of the Dutch church people threw themselves on my hands to kiss them as belonging to the wife of their defender. What a moment for my heart! How touching this nation is, how it reminds me in many ways of our own. Alas, these wretched English diplomats and the French army had to come and stop our magnanimous conqueror. The Almighty obviously deigned to take William under His aegis for he saw his horse killed beneath him when a cannonball removed two of its legs. Dear Nikki, what a supreme moment! Pray for us; for I count on your joy in William's glory as assured. I ask for a mark of friendship, dear Brother, and that is to give the name Vladimir to your future child if it is a son, for it is the name corresponding to William, and that of Sophie if it is a daughter. *I attach a great price to it*. William may well say, *'I serve my Creator with my soul and my country with my sword'*. Dear friend, I embrace you tenderly with your wife and children, and I am, as you know, for ever your very devoted faithful and affectionate sister and friend.

Albert and Marianne are with us; what a happiness for their poor parents and for us all. Albert came to my Te Deum with Louise this morning while my sons were firing their cannon.

Copy of enclosure (*letter from William, Prince of Orange, to the Grand Duchess Anna Pavlovna, the Princess of Orange*) sent to Tsar Nicholas I:

Curange,
9 August 1831

Dear Anninka,

Congratulate me: yesterday I gained the object of my first operations by taking Hasselt after having forced [Daine ?] to retreat, and I succeeded in arriving with my people on his flanks and his rear. Between Hasselt and Tongres we harassed his rearguard and we took five mortar cannons, many ammunition wagons, a large number of both cavalry and draught horses and many carts of military equipment; read my official report and it will give you all the news.

I am sending the boys three swords and three sabres which were taken yesterday. I think that they will be pleased with them, and for you I include here a piece of a shako with the Belgian cockade. Omphal has arrived; what pleasure it gave me to read your letter and to receive your portrait with the inscription on it.[1] I was deeply touched by it and thank you with all my heart. I embrace and bless the children. For ever your affectionate old friend,

William

Yesterday was one of the most important days from the military point of view.

[1] The inscription on the portrait is 'Sooner a cottage with my William than to subscribe to dishonour'. This is an allusion to unacceptable conditions of peace.

THE GRAND DUCHESS ANNA PAVLOVNA, THE PRINCESS OF ORANGE, TO TSAR NICHOLAS I:

Scheveningen,
17 August 1831

A few more lines, dear good Brother, sending you the copy of a letter from our dear William, which is very interesting, as well as a continuation of the narrative of military events. I include with it the copy of a letter from Stirum, the devoted Count, named thus by me because of his attachment through all trials to our William. Nothing can better depict for you what happened at Louvain than the tale contained in this letter. I am convinced that you will not be able to read it in cold blood. The enthusiasm for my William is so great here that on Sunday, on entering and leaving the Dutch church, people threw themselves on my hands to kiss them. Belgium has indeed what she deserves, and the Conference too. The affair of Louvain is like a good game of chess played in the presence of England and France, in which the result is a stalemate.

In the gratitude of my soul I made my devotions and took communion this morning. I prayed for you, my dear friends, and for the happy delivery of Alexandrine. Were you only able to come by steamer and make an appearance here, dear Nikki, what a happiness it would be.

Copy of enclosure (*letter from William, Prince of Orange, to the Grand Duchess Anna Pavlovna, the Princess of Orange*) sent to Tsar Nicholas I:

[Tirlemont ?]
12 August 1831

Dear Anninka,

Pray for your William; today he is going to attempt to take Louvain and to attack Leopold who is there. If the good God is with us, as he was during the affair at Hasselt, I shall have struck a great blow and there will be nothing between me and Brussels. Ever your affectionate and devoted old friend William.

I embrace and bless our children.

Copy of enclosure (*letter from William, Prince of Orange, to the Grand Duchess Anna Pavlovna, the Princess of Orange*) sent to Tsar Nicholas I:

Tirlemont,
12 August 1831

Dear Anninka,

Only two words to tell you that I have just come from a heated battle which was, however, completely in our favour. Today I beat Leopold and Tiecken in front of Louvain. They had to ask mercy of me and make an armistice from today until tomorrow midday, when they must hand over the town to my troops. Leopold is in flight towards Malines, for the Duke of Weimar has cut off his direct retreat to Brussels. Thousands of wishes to the children whom I bless. Omphal, who is bringing you these lines, can give you details on the battle. I shall only send my official report tomorrow, but I wished to deliver you all from the state of fear in which you must be while awaiting a battle. I am more pleased with the army than I dared hope for. Fortunately we lost only very few men, but we lost some distinguished officers – poor Colonel Gallieres of the cuirassiers lost a leg as did his son, and that from the same cannonball – Fritz and general headquarters had none killed. Grovestin was under fire for the first time and did very well. For life your affectionate and devoted old friend,

William

I must confess that the good Providence protects us singularly well. In ten days I have marched as far as Louvain and beaten two enemy armies.

Copy of enclosure (*letter from William, Prince of Orange, to the Grand Duchess Anna Pavlovna, Princess of Orange*) sent to Tsar Nicholas I:

Tirlemont,
13 August 1831

Dear Anninka,

A thousand thanks for your letter written since the arrival of De Vistre and the news of Daine's setback. I was sure of your joy. The affair yesterday within sight of the English diplomatists and under the nose of the French army greatly surpasses in glory the first. Now our operations are finished, for Cera, whom I sent to see where the French were, found them at Brussels. General Lavoestein is waiting for me at my outposts, sent by Marshal Gérard. Now we must see how to come to a friendly arrangement with them.

For life, your affectionate and devoted old friend,

William

I embrace and bless our dear children. I am using this opportunity to send my official account to the King.

TSAR NICHOLAS I TO THE GRAND DUCHESS ANNA PAVLOVNA, THE PRINCESS OF ORANGE:

Tsarskoe Selo,
17/29 August 1831

I must thank you, dear and good Anne, for two letters of 4 and 8 August. You can imagine how very interested I was awaiting the result of William's transactions, which fortunately have proved in the face of the world and the nation that he was still the same William, and that makes his old friend's heart swell. The rest depended neither on him *nor on me*; I was afraid of it as soon as I learned of the King's decision, noble as it is; but none of us were informed of his intentions, and that is much to be regretted. You know that I am too far away to be of any help except by the words which I can write and which are hardly listened to as long as it is known that I must cope with the Polish affair. The threats to burn Amsterdam were only silly expressions of wounded pride, they could never have been carried out. What, in another way, is very important and also extremely sad, is the occupation by the French of the whole of Belgium with its strongholds. I am convinced that no one will get them out of there unless the English finally become angry, but for that, common sense is necessary, and where can it be found in that poor English ministry.[1] So that, then, is the true danger, and at the pace with which these honourable affairs are

[1] The Whig government of Lord Grey. Lord Palmerston was Foreign Secretary. The Whigs were thought to be very radical indeed! and very weak too.

moving I do not know how things will turn out. As far as I am concerned, my principles are still the same; I would support my allies even though I had only a single grenadier free, and I am not at that point yet. At any moment I am expecting news from Paskevich from within Warsaw. But it must be decisive. May Heaven help us! This morning we paid our last respects to poor Constantine; you can imagine what I felt with the fourth such reunion in that setting within six years! Poor Jeannette has scarcely a breath left, and only the strength of her soul buoys up her frail body. She is coming to live with us tomorrow. My wife is well and requests me to embrace you tenderly. Hug your sweet ones, and my homage to their Majesties and to Louise. Farewell, dear kind Anne, may God enfold you all and give us at last some happier days. Yours for life.

THE GRAND DUCHESS ANNA PAVLOVNA, THE PRINCESS OF ORANGE, TO TSAR NICHOLAS I:

The Hague,
26 August 1831

Dear good Nikki,
Receive my most sincere and loving congratulations on the occasion of the birth of your little Nicholas. This happy news reached me on 20 August, the eve of the happy day when I saw my William again. I had wished, dear friend, to write to you from Tilburg but I did not have the leisure for it. However, we have never stopped thinking of you and of your happiness after so many misfortunes, and the part that you took in the events to which Divine Providence graciously accorded its blessings. The two days at Tilburg were the happiest of my life, and the one on which William returned to The Hague was everything that Heaven in its infinite mercy can grant of what is most dear and touching to a human being. That day is one of eternal memory, for the whole nation united in a show of gratitude. From Breda to here one saw the same outbrusts. At Rotterdam they had adorned the front mast of the principal ship with the Russian flag and there were many cries around me of 'Long live Russia'. Everywhere the town regiments and the military authorities asked me for your news, dear friend, expressing

good wishes for you and joy on the birth of your son; they would say naïvely. 'One more, so much the better.' Dear Nikki, I realised the dearest of my wishes since our William is the object of this worthy nation's enthusiasm. May God continue to grant us his blessing and to preserve Holland and those whom we cherish. Do you know, dear Brother, that your Nicholas was born on the day of the battle of Hasselt? It was William who discovered that, seeing the date of your letter. Oh, your dear good letter; how I thank you for it, and for the friendship that you show me, and for the way in which you speak with regard to us. Yes, dear Brother, lend us friendship and assistance and do not abandon us to the mercy of a conference which seems to believe it has the right to oppress the weakest; and what is even more sad is that your minister here acts and talks completely according to the line of the English minister. I beg you, dear Brother, at last take heed of the wish I have expressed for so long, to recall him and to send us here an honest man who will not put you in a false light. He has insulted me in my house by his remarks and his coarse manners, so that I can never see him except with pain, whatever reparation he may have made, for it is impossible to trust him. At Tilburg I saw a French officer on the General Staff of Marshal Gérard. He was most charmingly polite to William and particularly so to me. Imagine! he spoke to me of the feelings and the veneration the Belgians have for me, adding details on my dear little person. I replied that, although it was always preferable to leave a favourable impression of oneself rather than the contrary, I could only find that they had greatly exaggerated what had been said about me. He appeared very surprised by my reply. He asked me if I did not regret our house in Brussels; I replied 'No, not at all.' His astonishment was great. 'But it is very pretty,' he said to me. 'Yes," I replied, 'But not everything is material, and the impression that the death of my mother made on me during the first step that I took there cannot be wiped out. Moreover,' I added, 'in this place they do not appreciate what I hold most dear.' He seemed struck by these last words and as if moved.

I am amazed at William, whom it does one good to see in the midst of our brave men. He is so worthy, so courteous and so much a father to the soldiers that it is touching. How I would like to be able to come to you were it not for ten days in a steamer, to tell you about all that. I embrace dear Alexandrine and I propose to write to her on my return from the reviews where I am going tomorrow with my son, but I congratulate her tenderly in these lines, thanking her for her last good friendly letter.

THE GRAND DUCHESS ANNA PAVLOVNA, THE PRINCESS OF ORANGE, TO TSAR NICHOLAS I:

Amsterdam,
21 September 1831

Dear excellent Brother,

Receive my most loving and sincere thanks for the marks of affection, esteem and approbation that you give to my William. I was so happy at it, so touched, that I can only express it feebly to you in comparison with what I feel. May God repay you for it. Our Vladimir is very worthy of the motto of the order that you are sending him. I also thank you very very tenderly for your letter of 17 August that I received the day before my departure for Amsterdam. How touched I was by the friendship you showed me in writing to me the very evening of the burial of our dear Constantine. Oh God! what a strange and unhappy amalgam of misfortunes, calamities and unhoped-for happiness. Everything is great in these times, even happiness. Also my soul can only repeat, '*Oh God, work wonders!*' How I congratulate you from the bottom of my heart, dear Nicholas, on the peace of Warsaw and the intrepidity of your brave troops. – '*Great be the dominion of the nursery of the brave.*' – And for having preserved our Mikki and, finally, for having stopped by this decisive stroke the flowing of blood as precious as that of our compatriots. For you, my friend, other difficulties will arise and a rest for you exists only in your conscience, which alone can sustain you in the midst of storms, with the aid of this God who gives us strength in proportion to our trials. I bless Heaven for the recovery of Alexandrine and embrace her tenderly with little Hasselt Nicolaievich. Everything here breathes enthusiasm, the population is touching. They feel deeply, in all classes, everything that they owe to William. I likewise receive a touching reception, and certainly it fills my heart with the most just gratitude. Our fasces of seven arrows is indeed to be respected, union forms its strength. I am going this morning to prostrate myself in the chapel founded by Peter the First, where my tomb will be. Tomorrow I shall offer, God willing, a lunch in my cottage[1] to the King and Queen at Zaandam to celebrate William's successes. One more favour. The recall of Guriev. Nikki, watch this man. You do not know, dear friend, what affiliations he has with the demagogic party. His conduct is so two-faced that you could regret one day having trusted him. Send good Prince Trubetskoi or else Golitsyn; we are small now, so why should he not make his debut as a minister with us? Now it is time for the Parade of *Schutterij*.[2] Our William will appear in it with the Order of St Vladimir, and Madame, the Marshal's wife, on the balcony, imitating the graces of Alëna Ivanovna in her days of benevolence. This evening at the Dutch Theatre I shall appear with your delightful turquoise brooch. Here are some toys in the uniforms of different troops of our army which I am sending to your Constantine. I embrace your wife and children and the good excellent Jeannette.

[Later] I have just come back from the Parade of *Schutterij* and the dear good Queen told me that if I still had a little room in my letter I should add her thanks for your letter to William, and for everything which you said to him for which she says she is grateful. Louise and Marianne also ask me to send a thousand greetings to you. The expressions of your letter heaped joy upon the whole family. Dear Nikki, say indeed that happiness is not turning my head and that I shall always remain humble at heart as the wife of a Christian hero should.

[1] This is an allusion to the tiny house at Zaandam built by Peter the Great while he was living in the Netherlands. The little cottage was given to Anna Pavlovna by King William I. Later in the century, King William III, who inherited it from his mother, presented it to his cousin the Tsar. The Russians built a brick structure to cover the little building to preserve it. (The brick edifice looks not unlike a railway station in some provincial town.) The Russian government maintained the upkeep until 1917, after that time its preservation was re-assumed by the Dutch. Tsar Peter's house at Zaandam is still much visited and particularly by tourists from the Soviet Union.

[2] Literally the 'Marksman's or sharpshooter's queue'.

Tsar Nicholas I to the Grand Duchess Anna Pavlovna, the Princess of Orange:

St Petersburg,
3/15 December 1831

. . . What has happened in London all this time concerning us hurts me very badly; unfortunately, all I can do for you in the business is to say *no*; it remains to be seen if that will have a good result.

I am still hoping that what is happening at [Lyons ?],[1] which I regard as the precursor to many other similar events in France, may not result in some unexpectedly favourable movement for you in Belgium; but God alone knows. Our Nalagon business is finished, after many griefs, sacrifices, and spilled blood, and for us, the loss of two dear souls in whom all our affections were united; poor Jeannette has ended her sufferings which were truly supernatural. The day before yesterday I had the good fortune to see Michael again after a separation of nine months which were a period of glory and happiness for him, but also ones of cruel upsets. His health is fairly good, but nevertheless shows signs of all the weariness of the campaign. When shall we see each other again? That is what I often wonder without being able to foresee when! It is still possible to think that there will be time for it.

Tsar Nicholas I to the Grand Duchess Anna Pavlovna, the Princess of Orange:

Alexandria,
24 April/6 May 1832

. . . I begin by giving you sincere thanks for the friendy welcome you gave to Orlov. I would have been satisfied if he had been able to succeed in a mission conceived in all kindness and with the conviction that if the proposals which he was making had been accepted, it would have been the only way to get out of an intolerable position in a manner both honourable

[1] A series of riots by workers; these riots were put down by the authorities but only after considerable difficulty.

and useful to the country, going through the most unworthy indignity of the many which have taken place since the *glorious days* of July. The King thought otherwise, but that concerns him alone; it is up to him to know what suits him, but we too have our duties; I have a clear conscience at having behaved with openness and loyalty since the beginning of the affair; may the others be able to say as much. I am no longer becoming mixed up in the affair.

As for the example which the Dutch nation is giving, it is sublime and rare in our century and may you worthily appreciate it and may such devotion have the country's happiness and prosperity as a reward; such is, I assure you, my most sincere wish. I have nothing interesting to tell you from here. Everything is quiet, resting from the weariness of war. A deputation of the twenty most noteworthy Poles came to see us to beg pardon for their infamies and to give thanks for their newly organised government.[1] To the great annoyance of the rogues, all the great names of Poland shine among them, such as Radziwill, Walewski, Nemoyevski, Dembinski, Lubetski, etc., that is to say, all the notable names of the revolution; a superb new chapter for the turn-coats.

But I am in a good enough frame of mind to be willing to take all that literally, all the while having a fortress built under their noses in Warsaw.

THE GRAND DUCHESS ANNA PAVLOVNA, THE PRINCESS OF ORANGE, TO TSAR NICHOLAS I:

Soestdijk,
7 July 1832

Dear Brother,

. . . As it is not given to me to understand you in the present state of affairs, I pass over in silence everything you tell me concerning inevitable circumstances. As I am attached by feelings and by duty to the cause of the country to which

[1] The Organic Statute of 14 February (O.S.), which virtually abrogated the constitution of 1815 and declared Poland to be part of Russia. While Poland theoretically received a number of special privileges, in fact it was just another province of the empire.

Heaven has joined my fate, I respect the King as my sovereign and in so doing only share the feelings of the nation which aligns itself with him; the sacrifices which it bears are dear, and there is not one of us who would not give his life for this upright country. Our hope is also in that God of Mercy whose justice is above human counsel.

A year ago there was cholera in Russia, now it is with us, dear Brother, it has just broken out. Ten days ago it appeared in the village of Scheveningen; you gave us a great and noble example of courage in the midst of this scourge – that memory must serve as proof to us that Providence guards well and preserves from the greatest griefs those which it holds in its grace. On the 19th of last month I came here with my little girl to breathe the country air while William and my sons are at camp; up to now, the cholera has not appeared in this neighbourhood, but if it shows iself I shall do as you did, and in the meantime I am taking all the necessary precautions to bring prompt help.

THE GRAND DUCHESS ANNA PAVLOVNA, THE PRINCESS OF ORANGE, TO TSAR NICHOLAS I:

The Hague,
21 October 1832

Dear good Brother,

I wanted to wait to know that you had returned to Petersburg to thank you for your good affectionate letter of [?] in which you announce to me the appointment and departure of the priest which you had the kindness to allow Frederick to choose. I met him on my return from the country and, as far as it is possible to judge someone at first sight, it seems to me that he will answer to my plans which were to aid my former chaplain in duties which he has worthily fulfilled for sixteen years until the infirmities of age no longer permitted him to do so with the same strictness. I want, dear friend, to find out from you yourself, as the head of our rite, if you would approve of me taking this new priest as my confessor since the intellectual faculties of the old one are weakened. You can imagine that I hold dearly to the duty of scrupulously fulfilling the obligations connected with our religion and that I need to carry out that of confession and to do so with someone who is capable of answering this need. – I am very moved, dear friend, by the concern you have had over this question; William, my excellent William, has been my advocate with the King, who has given his support to this choice and to the earnestness and favour which he always shows for our rite; my chapel is even adorned with several objects which he has given me because of this, such as silver lamps and *holy vessels.* As for William, he says that I must always remain a *good Greek* and that he will watch over that as if it were a holy trust.

I had the joy of seeing our dear William in perfect health again for the opening of the States-General; happy to see him the centre of love and trust of his nation, and I myself surrounded by affection, trust and esteem within the family and in the country. I also had the very essential happiness of seeing my children thriving. I brought them all back in good health from the country to The Hague, even though the cholera was right under our *roof at Soestdijk*, but, thanks to kindly care, the afflicted person was brought out of danger by the skill of Everard, who gave him doses of spirits of camphor on crushed sugar and put mustard plasters on his stomach and feet. All my little institutions were exempt from the plague, even my hospital, named to honour William, where I found my wounded in good condition; although the house was surrounded by the sickness which carried off many people in the near-by streets. The nation bears up under this scourge with the calmness and religious resignation which characterises it. I am again very moved, dear Brother, by a kindness of yours, when I noticed in a despatch of Prince Peter Volkonsky addressed to Mr Schultz, that you wanted to know my opinion about a surveillance precaution you had taken concerning the lower clergy even if they are attached to a chaplain in a foreign country. Feeling that I must give trust for trust I replied according to what my heart felt and found that I had the pleasant obligation of giving praise and not lodging complaints. For sixteen years I have been trying to watch over this little colony like a mother and presume sometimes *to be severe* to avoid a greater evil. That is why, as I am satisfied with the footing upon which things have stood up to now, you find it natural that I wish to see this continue. All I can say to you is that Precentor [Frofilabtef ?], who had to leave me this spring to return at the wish of his mother, begged me to take him back into my service if he did not find a place in Russia. He has a *widowed mother* and brothers and sisters. I have since learned that they were good enough to place him in the court chapel; his behaviour here was exemplary.

I add these few words to tell you that the person suspected of stealing my daimonds was brought to this country and given over to our authorities. He wrote to William from New York to beg *his* pardon for all the worries and unpleasantness he caused *us*, adding that he feels tormented with remorse and unworthy of obtaining his mercy – as if it were possible for a noble sentiment to be foreign to the heart of the Prince of Orange.

TSAR NICHOLAS I TO THE GRAND DUCHESS ANNA PAVLOVNA, THE PRINCESS OF ORANGE:

St Petersburg,
3/15 January 1833

The unexpected departure of a courier for The Hague hardly leaves me any time to send you two words, dear Anne. Nevertheless, I want to take advantage of this to offer you all my sincere wishes for your name-day. May this year be happier than the one just ended, which, glorious as it is in the annals of your new homeland, was none the less painful for wives and mothers. Do I need to tell you with what interest and emotions we followed everything that was concerned with the glorious siege of the fortress at Antwerp, or to be more correct, I should say *with its defence*. There is not a Russian officer who would not have been honoured to be part of that brave garrison, and the portrait of the redoubtable Charles is in all our cadet corps.

THE GRAND DUCHESS ANNA PAVLOVNA, THE PRINCESS OF ORANGE, TO MME FOREL:

['Draft of a letter that I wrote to Madame Forel on the subject of Mlle de Sybourg in 1834.' *Note in Anna Pavlovna's handwriting.*]

I have received with the most sincere interest the letter that you addressed to me about your good and worthy aunt. As it seemed to me preferable to await the return of the Prince before replying to it, I wish at least to inform you that it has arrived, and, believing that it would be more agreeable for you to learn it through a compatriot of your acquaintance, I begged Mr Rigot to be good enough to express to you how appreciative I was of its content. You will easily understand, Madame, that the return of Mlle de Sybourg to her family is a very delicate matter for us who are tenderly devoted to her. The Prince bears her the most affectionate sentiments and continues to wish for her presence among us. It seems to us both so natural to try to give her the care that her age requires that we should believe ourselves failing in a duty by neglecting her. Our only fear is [that we should] not always succeed as we would like to. You will be touched to see how the devotion that your good aunt bears us survives her other faculties and how she differs in that from persons of her age among whom, in general, sentiments disappear. She appears to fear any change in her situation and clings to her habits in our home so much that as soon as Anne speaks to her of a plan that could take her away from it she expresses great repugnance to leaving us. I have often tried to broach the subject to her but I have always found her equally reluctant to listen to me. Already she is sometimes even afraid to going out in a carriage because of the idea that someone could take her away without her knowledge, and you will agree, Madame, that it would be infinitely repellent to us to use similar means while she is not sufficiently lacking in her faculties for it to take place without her expecting it. One would be afraid then that a very bitter feeling would fill her soul and shorten her days. As for the people in her service, they seem to me extremely tactful and full of attention towards her, and you may rest assured about her lot. As to the cares that her health requires, our doctor, who is always in her vicinity, merits your confidence in all respects because of his skill. After having entered into all these details, Madame, to reply to the confidence with which you wrote to me, I can at least find it completely natural to understand the reasons that make you and your family wish to see your good aunt among you again. This feeling is natural and all the stronger because it is difficult from a distance to get a true idea of her situation, and you will perhaps be grieved to accept the reasons that I have just stated, but I am certain that if you could be here you would not be long in convincing yourself of their reality. Please be convinced, Madame, that it is pleasant for me to receive proofs of the devotion that you bear your aunt and that each time you wish to discuss her with me I shall be charmed if I can help to reassure. The feelings that I have for Mlle de Sybourg make me take the most sincere interest in her family, and I have the pleasure, Madame, of assuring you of the distinguished respect that I bear you.

Tsar Nicholas I to the Grand Duchess Anna Pavlovna, the Princess of Orange:

Alexandria,
9/21 June 1834

Finally, dear good Anne, I embraced our dear little Henricatty, who reached us safely this morning; for several days we had been expecting him momentarily, and I assure you that worries at last invaded me; when the gun woke us at six this morning I went immediately to Cronstadt to receive him, and we hugged joyfully; I brought him back to dinner here with the family; and male and female cousins having been introduced, the dinner went off gaily. I acquitted myself as best I could of the duties of monitor for the food, and he seemed to me to be so good that I had nothing to say. He is perfectly well, in spite of the cold which he had on the way; he looks excellent and I find his resemblance to his father striking, especially his figure. I have already given him your two letters, which seemed to please him greatly. After dinner we took him over to move into his apartment, which is the same one you occupied the last time and which is drier than the others. I was greatly pleased to meet Captain Arriens, who seems to me to be an extremely distinguished man; we chatted with him about everything which concerns the little fellow, with whom he is extremely pleased; we have also arranged his whole timetable here, to have him see what concerns his trade and the most significant sights.

So, my dear friend, that is all I can tell you for the moment. Be sure that we are happy with the trust you put in us and we shall do everything possible to make the little one's stay with us useful and pleasant.

TSAR NICHOLAS I TO THE GRAND DUCHESS ANNA PAVLOVNA, THE PRINCESS OF ORANGE:

St Petersburg,
7/19 January 1835

. . . I was very pleased to meet *your* Alexander, who is really a very handsome boy, with such a perfectly proper appearance. I feel that he is more fortunate than his brothers in his looks. I would have been very happy to introduce to you my own, who is almost as tall as I; I am very satisfied with him and I am placing my trust in Divine Goodness that he will become a subject useful to the state until he replaces me.

We are very happy to be at home peacefully enjoying the good fortune of being with our children; my eldest daughter has become a *grown-up*, which makes me feel old, for here she is ready to make us *grandparents*. She is small for her age but may develop well in time. Olga is tall and really beautiful. Adine is a little *moppet* but sweet. Costy is small and ugly, but very unusual; the two little ones are very agreeable and are the apples of my eye. This, then, is a correct report to Madam Aunt on the state of affairs in our family.

Our winter has only just begun; yesterday a small masked ball was held to celebrate Twelfth Night; everybody appeared at it in the exact costumes of my father's time; very funny and very different, almost unbelievable, although we appear to remember it.

THE GRAND DUCHESS ANNA PAVLOVNA, THE PRINCESS OF ORANGE, TO TSAR NICHOLAS I:

The Hague,
25 February 1835

Dear kind Brother,

. . . The weather is not fair now; the storms do not let up and I can tell you that William goes out with great moderation and when exposed to the air. This weather also works against me very much and forces me to stay in my room – although I have been present at court dinners several times – I no longer leave my home because of the perpetual wind here. I cannot get rid of the pain in my chest nor the stubborn cough which I have had for months. I still do not know what I shall do for my health in the course of the summer, whether it will be decided that I should take a trip or not? and if it takes place? in what season I should undertake it? Many affectionate regards from me to Alexandrine whom I tenderly thank for her letter of 6 February which I received, as well as one of yours, on the day of my eldest son's birthday, who has come into his eighteenth year, *without for all that being declared* of age, as the papers said. All those who have at heart *his true welfare* and *that of this country* should want him to remain for a few years yet under paternal guidance. He has *great need* of advice given with intelligent affection. You see, dear Brother, that I am speaking to you like a friend.

TSAR NICHOLAS I TO THE GRAND DUCHESS ANNA PAVLOVNA, THE PRINCESS OF ORANGE:

St Petersburg,
3/15 March 1835

. . . I am delighted to know that you are planning to take a trip in [indecipherable]; that change of air, added to the enjoyment of seeing such a beautiful and interesting country cannot help but do you the greatest good. But I doubt if it will be the same for Switzerland, which is more than sick from a moral point of view, and where, without any doubt, some serious crisis is in preparation;[1] if I dare give you my advice, I think you would do well to avoid passing through there.

[1] The Swiss cantons had divided into two groups – the liberals, who on 17 March 1832 had banded together to form the Siebener Concordat, and the conservatives, who had formed the League of Sarnew on 17 July 1832 – and in the struggle for supremacy, politically a religious quarrel had also ensued. The liberal cantons had adopted the Articles of Baden on 20 January 1834. This document, and it is to its consequence that Tsar Nicholas refers, required a completely lay society. The Roman Catholic conservatives were much alarmed and the whole situation in Switzerland became very uneasy.

I congratulate you for your eldest's coming of age; may that young man acquire all the qualities that are indispensable for as thorny a position as the one for which Providence destines him; he has a model right in front of him in his father; and I completely share your opinion that it is preferable that he should not become too emancipated; which is also what I am keeping to for my son.

Embrace our William and your three boys for me.

THE GRAND DUCHESS ANNA PAVLOVNA, THE PRINCESS OF ORANGE, TO TSAR NICHOLAS I:

The Hague,
31 March 1835

Dear good Brother,

. . . I am very touched by that which you show for me personally in that last letter, dear Brother, and by the interest you take in my health which is still more or less in the same condition. The cough and the chest pain do not stop; as soon as I am in a situation where I must talk a lot and see people, I am shaken by violent bouts of coughing and sharp pains; as I see more and more, thus, I am obliged to do something serious to fight this illness. Everard wants me to take the waters and thinks that for the chest the waters of Baden in Switzerland, in the canton of Argovie, not far from Zurich, would be just the ones I need. But your letter leaves me in no doubt about the wish you have that I avoid that country, and certainly I would never be indelicate enough to put myself above your opinion for which I thank you for writing me so openly. If, however, these waters were necessary to me, would you be entirely opposed to seeing me go there? Please, I beg you, answer me with *equal frankness concerning this.* If it is a case of you persisting in advising me against it, I would have to limit myself to the Baden-Baden waters which are not as effectual for the chest according to Everard, who insists on a cure. For the time being I have given up the idea of a trip to Italy which would not accomplish a goal as direct as a cure, and which would take me away from my family for a long time which appears to bother William. So there is only one more resource which I am reserving in case the remedies do not bring about favourable results. How much we both thank you for the honour you have just granted Dr Everard by decorating him with the order of Ste Anne, second class. He feels very honoured at this mark of your kindness, and that has created so much pleasure here that people are even writing to him from the back-country to congratulate him on it. He cared for both of us very well and with a feeling of attachment which is rare in our time. As Potemkin had shown a continuing interest for me while I was ill, to the point of coming in person to inquire about me, I thought that you had been kept up to date about what concerned me, dear Brother, hence my astonishment. You will be pleased to know that William's health is perfectly good since he returned to Tilburg where he was welcomed with the most touching display of joy, and from all sides people were pouring in to see him and congratulate him on his recovery. You, dear friend, will also appreciate such feelings, held by all in this country, while in general they do not characterise the time in which we live. – I must have expressed myself very badly in my last letter if you understood that our eldest son was declared of age; the papers said so but it is not so; quite the contrary, he will not be of age until he is twenty-one. It is good fortune for him, so I accept your good wishes but not your congratulations. I am expecting William on 6 April with Alexander who went with him.

TSAR NICHOLAS I TO THE GRAND DUCHESS ANNA PAVLOVNA, THE PRINCESS OF ORANGE:

St Petersburg,
4/16 April 1835

I am hastening to reply, dear Anne, to your kind letter of the 31st which reached me these last days, and to thank you for the trust you bestow upon me; I shall reply with the same frankness. From the time the doctors decided that the waters of Baden in Switzerland were necessary for your health, there should not be an instant's hesitation and all other considerations must yield.

By warning you of the precarious state of affairs of Switzerland and of our very uncertain relations with it, I thought it a duty to fore-arm you against the possibility of unpleasantness in a trip through a country which is, in general, very badly disposed, especially against everything Russian; I do not even know if our missions can stay there. To keep you in ignorance of such circumstances at a time when I knew that you were planning to go there would have been completely unsuitable. But I repeat, as soon as it appears that this trip must be one for a cure and treatment for your health, there must be no hesitation in undertaking it.

Michael must have written to tell you that he is going to take the waters in Bohemia with his wife and children; he hopes *perhaps* to see you in Weimar. As for me, in September I must go to Prague to see the new Emperor[1] of Austria; I would have been so happy if near that time we might be able to see each other, to be with you for a few moments somewhere in the neighbourhood. *After ten years!* Truly, I must be allowed to wish that – and you will pardon me, won't you? I am delighted to know that our William is completely cured.

THE GRAND DUCHESS ANNA PAVLOVNA, THE PRINCESS OF ORANGE, TO TSAR NICHOLAS I:

The Hague,
3 May 1835

Dear good Brother,

. . . The interest you take in my health and the ease with which you have consented to my stay in Switzerland, in case that might be salutary for me, touch me deeply; but at the same time I am delighted to be able to tell you that there is no longer a question of going there. Information collected concerning the Baden-Baden waters were of such a kind to conclude that they would suit me. So it is there that I shall go and I have already made reservations. I assure you that it would moreover be too upsetting for me to think that they might want to insult Russia through me. I love our mutual homeland too much for that, and

[1] Emperor Ferdinand I (1793–1875).

the moral evil – if that were to happen – would be in my eyes worse than the physical ills. So I shall go quietly to Baden-Baden where I hope to recover peacefully, for it is time for me to try and get rid of this cough which is so stubborn that it starts up for no reason. In Amsterdam I limited myself to attending the necessary formal dinners and receptions and forewent plays, nevertheless the chest pain increased from these activities. William was received with joy in Amsterdam where people greatly desired to see him again after his illness; very kind feelings were shown to us both.

How moved I am, dear friend, by the wish you show me to see me again, and to take advantage of the time of your interview with the Emperor of Austria to try to meet me, somewhere. May God grant that that may come about! I feel a very keen desire to see you again and if *your climate* were not so harsh and my health better, it would be at home that I would be happy to see you again. I did indeed receive a letter from Michael in which he speaks to me of his plans and suggests to me a meeting at Weimar. I answered him immediately to inform him that I could not go as far as that, and suggested to him to come and find me at Baden-Baden, and please, dear Nicholas, tell him that my apartments *are spacious enough to be able to lodge him there, which would give me enormous pleasure;* we could see one another at all hours of the day. *I like to think that he will accept my suggestion.* William is very touched that you remembered him and tells me to send you many affectionate regards, dear Brother. He is going to take a jaunt to Helder with Henry to see the ship on which the young one is going to Surinam; Arriens will command it which makes him very happy. As for me, while I want our dear Henry to follow his career honourably and be useful to the country, my tears flow at night while I pray God to watch over him in the dangers to which one is exposed on that terrible element. It is his third trip already, and another four months' separation!

Alexander will go to Tilburg; my son William is staying here to continue taking courses at Leiden and will only go back to the army at the time of the university holidays.

The Grand Duchess Anna Pavlovna, the Princess of Orange, to Tsar Nicholas I:

The Hague,
15 June 1835

Dear good Brother,

Just prior to leaving for Baden-Baden I write you these lines, dear friend, the letter will be given to you by the wife of our worthy and faithful Schultz. She is going to Russia to take her two sons whom the father wishes to have brought up there as Russian subjects according to your *ukaz* concerning this. You will find it quite natural that I am taking care of the expenses which their education may call for as a way of recognising the zealous service of the oldest of my servants. Schultz wants to place the older boy *who is nine years old in your engineering school and the second aged seven in the artillery one.* I wrote to Michael some time ago to ask him to give me some details about the age of admission but as he has not answered me at all, and time is pressing, considering the limited period the mother will spend in Petersburg during which she wishes to see her children placed, it is to you, dear Brother, that I am addressing myself as you are the master of all things back there. Be so kind as to give me the necessary information about the admission of the young people whom I put under your protection as my children, *including the expenses which I shall allow no one else to assume,* for it is a great pleasure for me to oblige the parents. Madame Schultz is the daughter of the English consul at Cronstadt, where she is going to spend a few months with her father and will come back here during the course of the autumn. The good woman will be very happy to introduce her children to you and to give you this letter herself.

Tomorrow I am setting out, my heart heavy at leaving my family, and I console myself with the idea that perhaps I shall have the happiness of seeing you during my stay in Germany; may I ask you ahead of time, dear friend – if such is still your intention – that it may not be in a noisy place, *nor at a court,* but in some quiet surroundings where *we can see each other in comfort.* I am sorry not to have been able to meet Michael at Weimar but that was impossible for me, both because of the time and because of the fatigue which I can no longer bear. Moreover, you cannot imagine what the Weimar region is like during the summer heat, it is enough to make one fall ill; I experienced it last year.

TSAR NICHOLAS I TO THE GRAND DUCHESS ANNA PAVLOVNA, THE PRINCESS OF ORANGE:

Alexandria nr Peterhof,
30 June/12 July 1835

It was only yesterday, dear kind Anne, that I received your letter from the hands of Madame Schultz and I am hastening to reply to it; before I have a chance to write you, I always seem to have two or three of your letters to reply to; but truly, I live in the midst of such a whirlwind of occupations of all sorts that often I scarcely have the time to sleep; Michael's absence and, on the contrary, our children's presence even increase my difficulties. So pardon me if I only reply to you in the most hasty way. It would be a real pleasure for me to be of use to Madame Schultz's children, and I have already asked for her plans; it so happens that one of the children is three years under and the other is exactly the age necessary to undergo an initial entrance examination for the two institutions you mention to me, since these establishments are special upper schools and not preparatory ones. So it is a question of the mother's choosing meanwhile whatever other establishment she wishes in which to have the children prepared until they reach the required age. The second point, and one which interests me directly, is the possibility I can glimpse of having the joy of seeing you again *after ten years*. I think that I must bring you up to date, *as much as I know myself*, on what I know about what is going to happen towards the end of the summer and the beginning of the autumn. We are leaving here, God willing, in August for Danzig; from there I am going to Kalisch to join the King of Prussia towards the 14th at Liegnitz; on 29 August the King is arriving with us at Kalisch and will stay there until the 5th.

About 15 September I must be at Töplitz where I plan to

stay until 25 September. So that is the only time I could go to whatever place you wish in *Bohemia*, when we can stay twenty-four hours alone and without fanfare. Eger would seem to me to be the most appropriate place for this plan. To go outside of Bohemia is impossible for me for more than one reason. Now, dear Anne, decide and make known your wishes to me. I have done all your errands and everyone, myself included, embraces you.

THE GRAND DUCHESS ANNA PAVLOVNA, THE PRINCESS OF ORANGE, TO TSAR NICHOLAS I:

Baden-Baden,
20 July/[8 July O.S.] 1835

Dear good Brother,

When you receive these lines so short a time after those I wrote you for your name-day, you will say, 'another letter from my sister who usually writes so little!' And I admit that it is a very selfish reason that makes me take pen in hand, for it is for no other reason than *to ask an interview with you*. The burning desire I feel to see you again, dear Brother, will serve as an excuse for me with you if my request seems bold, and especially by adding to this the suggestion that we meet at Hofstettin *at the edge of Bavaria* and very close to the borders of Bohemia and Saxony. It is a remote place and at a distance which would be possible for me to cross from here without discomfort, because I must avoid becoming tired and everything which might overheat me after the cure I am taking so as not to destroy its good effect. I prefer to explain myself frankly concerning this, dear friend, before you set out, with the hope that if you have not already *completely* decided upon your plans, the wish which I disclose to you could lead you to grant my request, which is the desire of a sister who has not been seen for ten years and who had many things to tell you, for which we must see one another alone, for they are of such a kind that they can be confided only to a brother, and preferably to you, dear Nicholas. The plan would call for me to be at Hof on 26 August – if we were able to spend two or three days there together how happy

I would be! I shall also confess to you, dear friend, that I prefer you not to urge me to come either to Silesia or Bohemia because I could not accept it and yet it would be hard for me to refuse. Excuse my openness, but truly, it is better to explain oneself clearly than to fall back on empty phrases or evasions which lead to nothing but mutual recriminations. But please, dear friend, let me know your answer quickly and send it to me here at Baden where I shall stay until the middle of August, new style. God grant that this plan may meet with your approbation, dear Brother, and that you recognise the sincere feelings which dictated it to me. I have every reason to congratulate myself for coming here, the cure is doing me a great deal of good, the cough has almost stopped and my breathing is freer. But I am kept on a very severe diet and I must avoid all fatigue for as soon as I expose myself to it I become feverish. I cannot say enough in praise of the welcome I receive here, I find so much deference and politeness that I am touched by it. The Grand Duke showers me with kind attentions and he is, as it seems to me, an excellent man, well loved in his country. The Grand Duchess is a very distinguished person, full of wit and tact; their family happiness is good to see.

TSAR NICHOLAS I TO THE GRAND DUCHESS ANNA PAVLOVNA, THE PRINCESS OF ORANGE:

St Petersburg,
22 July/3 August 1835

When I received your dear letter of 8 July yesterday, my first sensation was the keenest joy when I came upon the word 'interview', but that joy was cut short when I read the date on which you wished to set it, for that makes the whole thing completely unfeasible for me; for, dear Anne, that is just the moment of our meeting in Silesia; it is 14 August that we must meet in Liegnitz as a prelude to Kalisch, and it is only 8 September that I shall be free to go where you wish. So I see that unfortunately I must lose all hope of seeing you again after *ten years of separation*. It is hard, I must confess to you. It would have been a real celebration for me to go and find you at [?], to spend one or two days there alone, in which we could easily have *hidden away*. Apparently I must have been mistaken in announcing the dates to you; for otherwise I cannot understand how the one you suggest to me for our meeting should fall precisely on the day for the one in Silesia. I dare not permit myself to suggest to you that you need not be back in time for the family celebrations, and I can well understand that Töplitz cannot suit you because of the tumult which will probably accompany that stay – a taste which I completely share with you. Under these circumstances, such moments are not pleasant for a reunion. So let us hope that God will not refuse us the happiness of meeting again another time; but when? – It is still He *alone* who can know; my life is so dependent on my duty that it is truly impossible for me to specify anything in advance. I have given your messages to the Fritzes and my wife; all want me to thank you for your kind remembrance. I am very happy to know that you are satisfied with your cure and with the welcome you received at Baden; as far as the other people with whom you are concerned, I would like to observe that they have only done their *duty* and I esteem them enough to hope that they will never fail in it except by chance, very much against their will.

THE GRAND DUCHESS ANNA PAVLOVNA, THE PRINCESS OF ORANGE, TO TSAR NICHOLAS I:

Baden-Baden,
18 August 1835

Dear and excellent Brother,

All hope of our seeing one another again is not lost, dear friend; yesterday evening I received your kind and affectionate letter of August, and I answer it this morning to put myself *entirely at your disposal both as to the time as well as the place at which you wish to see me*. I can now speak in this way with every assurance as I have obtained through the King's and William's kindness an extension of leave which, thanks to God, will put me in a position to join you *anywhere you please*. My joy, my happiness, my emotion at the very *idea of seeing you again*, cannot be translated into words. Dear Brother, dear friend, so we are going to see one another again, clasp each other in our arms after ten *long years* separation! So give me your orders, and please send your answer and your *instructions here* to Baden where *I shall await* them as I plan to stay here until *1 September*. The rest of my *manœuvres* will depend on you, for my single and unique purpose is to arrive on time at the place you will inform me of, *even at Töplitz*, if I could not see you elsewhere. As for the strains I might expect there, I shall beg your indulgence if my strength is not sufficient and I know that your affection is an inexhaustible fountainhead. William and the King were very kind to consent to the extension of *leave* which I requested of them in order to see you, and they are delighted for my sake about the happiness which was awaiting me. I wanted to reconcile my obligations towards them with the very great and very natural desire I felt to see you again in order to enjoy all the better the moments I would spend with you.

TSAR NICHOLAS I TO THE GRAND DUCHESS ANNA PAVLOVNA, THE PRINCESS OF ORANGE:

Kalisch,
11/23 August 1835

It was this very morning, dear good Anne, that I received your letter of 18 August, and I receive with true joy the certainty you give me that we shall finally be able to see one another again. Let us hope that the good Lord will put no obstacles in our way. I shall act in such a way as to be in Eger on 24 September, the only place where we can see each other again without *constraint* and *alone*; I would be able to spend 25 September with you and would not leave again for Warsaw until the night of the 25th to 26th. We could gain a half day if it were possible for you to go on to Carlsbad, which would be a very straightforward journey for me. Let us bless the Lord that we are able to see one another again even though our reunion will be so short. At Töplitz it would be an illusion to think that we could see one another comfortably, for outside of the inevitable weariness for you, the influx of Highnesses disguised as

Panurge's sheep[1] will be such that we shall be lost in the crowd. Michael and my wife are not here, but I shall do your errands for them on their behalf.

How happy I am, too, at the thought of seeing little Sophia for the first time; I certainly hope that she will come with you; so until our next meeting, dear Anne, and accept again all my thanks for the kindness you took to ease my way of seeing you again.

THE GRAND DUCHESS ANNA PAVLOVNA, THE PRINCESS OF ORANGE, TO TSAR NICHOLAS I:

Baden-Baden,
29 August 1835

Dear good Brother,

. . . There is a passage in your letter which is not completely clear to me; when you say to me '*that we could gain half a day if it were possible for me to go on as far as Carlsbad, which would be a straightforward journey for you*'. Please tell me, dear friend, if you want me to wait for you at Eger to spend the day with you which you are willing to devote to me and then that I accompany you to Carlsbad? or if you prefer me to go directly to Carlsbad to await you there and thus gain a half day by sparing you the Eger trip? I shall do so with the greatest pleasure *to prolong the precious moments which I can spend with you;* so please just tell me briefly what your *decision* is and send me your answer to Ratisbon about 17 September, as I count on passing through that place on my way to Bohemia. You cannot possibly know how much I would prize the good fortune of seeing you *alone* and in *a very comfortable atmosphere;* I *laughed* when I read how the Töplitz visit impresses you. Marie also expresses the desire to come and see me at Eger, but I shall ask that it *not be at the same time* as you, dear friend, for I think that after ten years, *I am permitted to want it to be without sharing*. As I shall be there ahead of the date you note to me,

[1] A reference to *Gargantua and Pantagruel* by Rabelais. Panurge's sheep were all silly enough to jump into the sea following their leader, and thus got drowned. Evidently it seemed that whenever there was a meeting of sovereigns, all of the nobility thought they should follow suit in a sheep-like fashion.

could Michael not make a little excursion there? As for our dear Alexandrine, I do not know whether I dare express so natural a wish as the one I feel about seeing her again! Finally your two dear travelling children? All that would make me so happy and perhaps you will find me very forward to mention it. I would have been very happy to bring you my Sophia of whom you were kind enough to speak, if she had been with me, but none of my children accompanied me on my travels. I am no less touched by the wish you have shown to see her and I would have enjoyed introducing to you the only one of my children whom you do not know. That good fortune is perhaps reserved for me for another time. Au revoir, dear and excellent Brother, I embrace you once again in thought before doing so very tenderly in reality; may Heaven watch over you and reunite me soon with my old friend and brother Nikki.

TSAR NICHOLAS I TO THE GRAND DUCHESS ANNA PAVLOVNA, THE PRINCESS OF ORANGE:

Töplitz,
14 September 1835

Dear kind Anne,

I arrived here this morning and it is only now that I can finally reply to your good letter which I received from the hands of [P. de MacKay ?]. You can imagine my joy at knowing myself to be so close to you. I now know for certain about the days and the schedule and I hasten to inform you that it will be 21 September that I will go to meet you and, if you can come to Carlsbad, I would also be able to spend the whole day of the 22nd with you, and on that day I will ask your permission to bring my wife and daughter to you. I have found a huge crowd here, princes and princesses are raining down from every direction; and I was right to call them Panurge's sheep – oh! what faces! But I cannot tell you anything more about it as I am being interrupted. My wife kisses you and I do too while we are waiting happily to do so in person.

TSAR NICHOLAS I TO THE GRAND DUCHESS ANNA PAVLOVNA, THE PRINCESS OF ORANGE:

Töplitz,
16 September 1835

You will say upon receiving this letter, dear friend, what an inconsistent fellow that Nicholas is! But he cannot do anything about it; this is what it is about. The Emperor having learned of your coming arrival, begs you to come and settle very near here in the magnificent castle of *Dux* belonging to the Count von Wallenstein. You will be near enough to have all the advantages of a stay here, without feeling all the disadvantages, such as visits and other similar calamities. If you accept, as we hope, inform me about it as soon as possible. The plan suits us for we shall gain more time to see one another. Answer me as quickly as possible. Michael has arrived and is delighted at the thought of greeting you, so we shall be – for once at least – all reunited. Hoping to see you soon then.

THE GRAND DUCHESS MARIA PAVLOVNA, THE GRAND DUCHESS OF SAXE-WEIMAR, TO THE GRAND DUCHESS ANNA PAVLOVNA, THE PRINCESS OF ORANGE:

Töplitz,
Monday afternoon
16 September 1835

Well, dear Sister, we are hoping to receive you in these parts, and concerning this my wishes of finding some establishment in the neighbourhood have been realised. Nicholas is sending you this by courier to tell you that the Emperor of Austria proposed to him to have you come and settle at the château of *Dux* belonging to the Count von Wallenstein; it is a short hour from here, and we all went there to see it this morning after the church parade which took place in the open air with a big review. You will be near here but less subject, however, than we to receive a call of politeness which must be returned, and therefore less likely to tire yourself; we hope to see you this coming Friday, and I write to tell you that we are delighted. Michael has been with us since this morning. This is my *third* letter; excuse the briefness, but I did not want to let the courier leave without sending you a few lines; as Nicholas has told you the rest, I limit myself to embracing you warmly.

Your faithful sister

THE GRAND DUCHESS ANNA PAVLOVNA, THE PRINCESS OF ORANGE, TO TSAR NICHOLAS I:

Franzenbrunn,
28 September 1835

. . . I prefer our *reunion* [not] to be numbered among *Panurge's sheep*, an environment to which I confess I am not in any way drawn; forgive me this nonsense with which your expressions have infected me – meanwhile, dear friend, I am delighted to know that you as well as Alexandrine arrived safely at Töplitz after all the strains you went through at Kalisch. I hope that your present visit will at least give you the pleasure of seeing Marie more or less comfortably so that you can relax and laugh with her at the odd moving picture you have under your nose. In the midst of the temporary solitude of Franzenbrunn I have twice received good news from William and our dear little sailor who had gone back on board to leave Surinam and continue his trip. His letter was dated 6 July, new style, and although he is in another hemisphere, he was nonetheless thinking of your birthday, dear friend, on which he congratulates me; you see that he remembers the kindnesses of his *dear* Uncle Nicholas as he always calls you. So 3 and 4 October will be my lucky days! I thank Heaven for granting them to me.

Excuse me if I do not welcome you with my ribbon [decorations] on my shoulder; as I left for Baden ill I had only taken with me what a sick person can wear. So I call upon your indulgence, for to borrow such things seems worse to me than to confess the truth to you.

THE GRAND DUCHESS ANNA PAVLOVNA, THE PRINCESS OF ORANGE, TO TSAR NICHOLAS I:

Franzenbrunn,
29 September 1835

Dear and excellent Brother!

. . . I shall set out tomorrow morning and will sleep at Saatz, so it will be the day after tomorrow, *Thursday, 1 October*, which will be the thousand times blessed day I shall see you again. I feel so strongly about it that words cannot translate the emotion! I bless God for this, and feel that there are moments in life in which one can credit one's happiness only to God, and thank him for His goodness and pray to Him from the depths of the soul to continue to give His blessings to us. So the *five of us* shall be reunited after ten years of separation! I think it is possible to call that a kindness of Heaven!

TSAR NICHOLAS I TO THE GRAND DUCHESS ANNA PAVLOVNA, THE PRINCESS OF ORANGE:

Tsarskoe Selo,
1/13 November 1835

Back two days ago from my long trip, I do not want to delay thanking you, dear kind Anne, for your good letter by return post; but especially for the good moments you gave us; it was true happiness for me to see you again, to hear you, and to find myself face to face with you as if those ten years had never existed. May you have kept as sweet a memory of this as remains to me. I finished my trip well; and although since Prague I have been nowhere more than two days, it was only the day before yesterday that I came back home. But what was that journey compared with the one your little Henry has completed so well. God be blessed that everything happened in a good way; and I imagine the happiness you will both have at being reunited. I found mine [the children] in very good health. Mary is still a little bit taller than her sister. Alexander has grown a moustache, Alexandrine has grown, and the two little ones are delightful. At last '*Thanks be to God*' I am a happy *man*. As you can well imagine, no one desires more than I that you may be able to say the same thing to me. I have heard nothing about Michael since leaving Prague. They claim that he is coming back to us shortly. We are in full winter and are thinking of going back to town in January for seven months, a resolve I am putting off as long as I can as I do not like my urban life.

THE GRAND DUCHESS ANNA PAVLOVNA, THE PRINCESS OF ORANGE, TO TSAR NICHOLAS I:

The Hague,
21 November 1835

Dear good Brother!

. . . It was six weeks ago that we said farewell to each other! and since then what immense distances separate us! You have taken a long trip while I spent my time very quietly in the country and only came back to The Hague a week ago with my three children, among whom is the dear little sailor; my eldest son was at The Hague and William had preceded me by twenty-four hours. I had the pleasure of finding them in good health and of finally seeing all my children together again; a very real enjoyment which I appreciate from the depths of my soul. Henry grew a lot and became very strong during that trip which was so fortunate that we cannot bless Heaven enough for having so visibly watched over him. The good Arriens is very happy to have brought him back safe and sound. As for me, dear friend, I think of you a great deal, of the affection you showed me, *of everything* you *were for me* during the happy hours spent with you which were all too short. This memory will be ever dear to me and our affection is like a port in which I know I can take refuge. I am also very moved by the love Alexandrine showed for me in the kindest way, with that perfect goodness which characterises her and which I feel deeply; tell her so, I beg you, and embrace her tenderly in the name of her sister Anne. I shall write her at the first opportunity as soon as I have some free time; since I arrived here I have scarcely had a moment to myself – visits to make and receive, dinners, evening parties, and the Queen's name-day celebrations have taken up all my time. Now that Marianne and Albert have left us, we are leading a more sedentary kind of life and I shall profit from it by having more time to give to my *absent friends*. Yes, do remind yourselves, all of you, how dear the memories of Dux and Töplitz are for me. I have yet to thank dear Olinka for having sent me, by Louise, a velvet *ribbon* to wear on my head which I often put on, thinking of her completely *charming person* which pleased me so much; I shall also write her to thank her for this souvenir.

After having quite severe frosts while I was in the country – seeing the ponds frozen over and *snow* for a week – it is as mild as spring for our start in our winter quarters, and I am hoping that the winter may be mild – you know that [is the kind of] temperature that suits me – and so I am feeling marvellous up to now. As for the rest, dear friend, I am still waiting before telling you anything that is personal or anything about the main subject of your recommendations. I am observing, and shall observe for a long time, before speaking to you of this, for you need something real and positive and not vague notions, with which I would only waste your time. The day of the Queen's celebrations I gave myself the pleasure of putting on a part of the fine Russian costume you had the kindness to send me two years ago – the train and the sleeveless dress and the head-dress – and it has been much admired already. My tenderest love to our dear Michael whom I thank for his good letter, I am also counting on writing him. I hope that he and Helen have arrived safely at Tilburg. May you all remember me kindly and may you, dear Brother and friend, hold to that very *true* and *very precious* feeling you showed for me at the time of our interview.

TSAR NICHOLAS I TO THE GRAND DUCHESS ANNA PAVLOVNA, THE PRINCESS OF ORANGE:

St Petersburg,
9/21 December 1835

I must thank you, dear Anne, for two of your kind letters, the second of which reached me the day before yesterday; accept, dear friend, all my sincere thanks for the kindness you show for me in them and of which you gave me so much proof during our short reunion in Töplitz. I also thank you for the wishes you send me for my name-day and which do me good, coming from you. I am very happy to know that you are pleased with your children; that is certainly the greatest happiness at our age, to see them prosper and succeed; and you are right to combine indulgence with justice. One must always keep before one the thought that these children have to be brought up to live in *their* homeland; and make them appreciate the good sides without hiding the weak, but at the same time make them prefer national customs to what may seem to be preferable elsewhere but would in no way fit in with the national character. I am delighted to learn that William is finally leaving his eternal Tilburg and coming to spend some time at The Hague; I am glad to see him take up this good habit again. We are in our Winter Palace but very quiet up to now; today the grand ball in the White Chamber takes place. Moreover, my wife is still more or less ill, and we are beginning to think of it as the start of pregnancy. She is very grateful for your kind remembrance, as is Miss Olly, who is still growing and is beginning to outstrip her sister. Kind regards to your children and to our good William.

THE GRAND DUCHESS ANNA PAVLOVNA, THE PRINCESS OF ORANGE, TO TSAR NICHOLAS I:

The Hague,
30 December 1835

Dear and excellent Brother!

. . . I hope that these lines will reach you on the day of the Russian New Year so that when you begin it you may receive the sincere wishes of an old friend who desires for you everything that can add to your happiness. I like to think that Alexandrine will have completely recovered by then, as I was very sorry to learn from my faithful correspondent Williamov that she was indisposed enough to have to stay in bed. Perhaps the winter should be blamed for this and the variable weather which you are having, according to what people write us; moreover, it is the same here, where we have *surges* of cold and snow followed by a complete thaw accompanied by brief storms. Up to now, I am still bearing up fairly well. I gave myself the pleasure of celebrating your name-day, dear Nikki, by giving a dinner for the Russian legation and the few compatriots I was able to gather together, to whose number I added the people most recently showered with your kindnesses and who know how to appreciate this. Louise and the good Fritz had come to congratulate me, the latter in Russian uniform which suits him marvellously well; that was a kind compliment which is like him. I have in him a very loving and sincere friend, and both of them are perfect towards me. Luckily the season did not put any obstacle in the path of William's return, he was able to come back on the day he had set – the thaw had arrived just in time to prevent the ice from hardening. On the whole, I am pleased with my children.

There is some improvement *in the direction we wished*, although there is still much to be done. I attribute this betterment to a very distinguished officer who has been near our lad since last spring and who has managed to make himself liked, and he fortunately takes advantage of this to apply him to a course of readings. The courses taken at Leiden are also doing some good by taking up essential subjects. What else is there to tell you, dear friend! Alas, it is better to be silent about it! But the things of which we spoke at Dux have come to such a pass that I am expecting the most unfortunate consequences from one day to the next. Do you remember what I told you of the inferior tastes and a certain licentiousness? All that has reached a most painful peak and really the time has come when true affection must make itself felt and heard to avoid still greater ills. – If you knew what I am sometimes exposed to, I am sure that your heart would be wrung – These are not secrets, everyone can see it and I have no doubts as to the opinions formed about this. It is time, high time, to remedy it.

TSAR NICHOLAS I TO THE GRAND DUCHESS ANNA PAVLOVNA, THE PRINCESS OF ORANGE:

St Petersburg,
7/19 January 1836

. . . Since the first of the year we have been more lively; my wife is a little less ill with her pregnancy and can take part. The usual masked ball was very sparkling, and we had twenty-six to twenty-seven thousand people[1] as guests; yesterday, to celebrate Twelfth Night and the crowning of the *Bean* King, [there was] a very funny small ball; everybody was in the costume of Peter the Great's time, and the military men looked as droll as possible with the grotesqueness and strangeness of their dress and turn-out. The cold pursues us, and during the blessing of the waters we had 18 degrees of frost which was too much of a good thing for us obligatory spectators. . . .

TSAR NICHOLAS I TO THE GRAND DUCHESS ANNA PAVLOVNA, THE PRINCESS OF ORANGE:

Tsarskoe Selo,
25 October/6 November 1836

I must give you a thousand thanks dear good Anne, for your kind letter of 6 October and for all the interest you show for me at the time of my unlucky accident.[2] I have recovered, thanks to the good Lord, and outside of a little weakness in my arm I hardly suffer from it any more. What delayed my cure was that, besides my shoulder, I had a broken rib which they were not able to see because of the swelling which covered everything. I rejoiced for you at your happiness at having friend Michael with you; at a time of cruel separation his presence was of double value, and I am sure he will have done everything to soften the bitterness of that cruel moment. I send my most sincere wishes for your dear little Henry; I am very touched by what you tell me about his remembrance of me. So you have a year of worry before you; may God help you to bear it! We do not know what to think of Michael's trip or where to find him, for, can you imagine, at the moment you were writing me that he was leaving for London, I receive news of his return to Frankfurt; from London, they do not say anything to us about

[1] This may seem somewhat incredible, but such a number of people was by no means unique. Regularly, on 1 January, 40,000 people attended a levee and were received and fed; similarly, on 1 July, an annual ball took place at Peterhof and here as many as 100,000 people were present.

[2] He was thrown from his horse.

him. He himself does not write, so that for a week we have been completely in the dark. I cannot imagine why he suddenly gave up his tour which was promising so much pleasure for him. I am still afraid that he will lose patience and that, instead of following the doctor's advice, he will come back here and so destroy all the profit of this journey – which was designed for his health – without having procured the result which it was supposed to bring about, thus risking having to begin all over again with less chance of success. I have nothing new to tell you of us at home; our children are well, Mary is better since her treatment but is only growing a little, while Olly is almost the same size as my wife; Sasha is approaching my height; the sailor is growing slightly but the way a true sailor does, and the two little ones and Miss Alexandrine are growing a lot. . . .

TSAR NICHOLAS I TO THE GRAND DUCHESS ANNA PAVLOVNA, THE PRINCESS OF ORANGE:

St Petersburg,
3/15 February 1837

. . . It was with much pleasure that I read the details of our friend Henry's stay in Rio de Janeiro, about which my mission informed me. I was delighted with the good little fellow, and he too seems to have been much pleased with the welcome which was given him. I suppose that at this moment he must be near his destination. God grant that the rest of his trip may be as fortunate as the first part. I am reassured from The Hague that you are taking this winter well; it is not the same with us as *la grippe* is working on more or less everybody, and my poor wife, ill for nearly two months, is only beginning to become better and still needs much care. Her brother Charles's stay is spoiling us a great deal; but we cannot entertain him as we would have wished. I myself cannot get rid of my cough. On the other hand, in town everyone is still whirling and dancing and it is an extremely gay winter.

Tell William, please, that I embrace him and am going to write him in the next few days as I have a lot to tell him about a certain tragic event which ended the career of the too-famous poet Pushkin;[1] but that is not be entrusted to the curiosity of the post.

TSAR NICHOLAS I TO THE GRAND DUCHESS ANNA PAVLOVNA, THE PRINCESS OF ORANGE:

St Petersburg,
30 March/11 April 1837

. . . I think that the arrangement you want to make regarding your priest's children is perfectly possible and cannot but be useful to your people, if that suits you. In any case, it was not in any way desired that the children come back for their education, as this measure concerns only those who stay in foreign countries for their own pleasure and not at all those who are there for duty's sake. My brother-in-law Charles is leaving us this evening and will leave behind with us a great empty space; he is a very excellent young man who has matured in character very well. We have news of Michael, but only from Florence; however, the children tell us of his arrival in Rome; he was fairly well but was complaining about the bad weather; we must hope that when his cure is really finished he will return to us gay, healthy, and cheerful.

TSAR NICHOLAS I TO THE GRAND DUCHESS ANNA PAVLOVNA, THE PRINCESS OF ORANGE:

Tsarskoe Selo,
31 May/12 June 1837

If I have delayed in replying to you earlier, dear kind Anne, it was with the desire to be able to reply that much better and to be more sure of satisfying your rightful wishes. I do not need to tell you how much I regret that the few Russians present in The Hague have been at the head of such a scandal,[2] the

[1] The events concerning the death of Pushkin are well known; suffice it to say that the part played in the fatal duel by d'Anthes, the adopted son of Heeckeven, the Dutch minister, is explained in full in 'Dramatis Personae' of this volume.

[2] It is not clear what the Russian community had been doing to incur imperial displeasure. Apparently, from the context, it was another crisis involving the private chapel of the Grand Duchess Anna Pavlovna.

seriousness of which is increased because of the place, the day, and the presence of their direct leader. Unfortunately it is not possible for us to answer for the behaviour of individuals brought up in such a way as to live peacefully among their own [people] within the customs of their clan, yet when they are thrown into another world and see and hear things completely different from what, from childhood, they were used to considering as *life*, they are thrown off the track, knocked over, and end up losing all memory of their principles and giving themselves over to every disorder. That is the way it was at Weimar, and unfortunately, here you are, witness of a similar scandal.

You did everything to bring them back to order, and patience cannot be pushed further. So the law must act against the guilty ones. Your priest behaved like a fool, and you are right not to want anything more to do with him. But it is not easy to make a choice which would bring together all the conditions which *I want to see for them.* To all the reasons I have noted above, I add another which is that since the law commands them to be married, they are usually burdened with a family and fear to leave their homeland, giving up their customs and even their dress. However, by luck I myself know an excellent court priest who is attached to the chapel here; I did everything to urge him to devote himself to your service, and after many conferences he has agreed to do so; he has no children and from that point of view, too, offers a rare advantage. His name is [Joanes Tavisrov ?]. I am taking all steps to have him leave as soon as possible.

I hope in this way to have carried out your commands. It is not the same for the deacons, and I beg you to be patient for you cannot have any idea of the trouble it is to find any who might combine the necessary qualities. . . .

TSAR NICHOLAS I TO THE GRAND DUCHESS ANNA PAVLOVNA, THE PRINCESS OF ORANGE:

Alexandria nr Peterhof,
28 July/9 August 1837

. . . Duke Bernhard[1] arrived and Schultz left in the midst of all the tumult of our grand manœuvres, which terminated three

[1] Duke Bernhard of Saxe-Weimar was a general in the Dutch army.

days ago, and the day after tomorrow we are going to set out by way of Moscow; I myself through Kovno and Kiev, and we shall meet again at Voznesensk; then from there to the Crimea, and finally, please God, I shall go to Georgia. Upon our return we are planning to spend a month in Moscow, which means that we shall return here early in December. It is with great regret that I am leaving our good peaceful cottage – a spot particularly full of affection and where one leads an extremely easy life – to begin my nomadic wandering again for almost five months!

Think of your poor brother far away from all that is dear to him, at the foot of Mount Ararat, for that is the most distant spot of my trip. Michael came back to us all jovial – and almost completely well. I only hope that his zeal does not run away with him so that he uselessly does over again the things that do harm to him; I am taking every care to prevent him from doing so. My boy is waiting for his mother in Moscow and will rejoin us at Voznesensk. I hope that you continue to have good news of Henry, but I long to know that he is back near you after such a long absence. I keenly miss our poor good old Sybourg; this is the way our old acquaintances are beginning to disappear! I say farewell to you, dear kind Anne, and probably for some time for I do not know when I shall be able to write to you *en route*; think of me sometimes, keep on loving me, and trust in the unchanging and sincere devotion of your old brother and friend.

The Grand Duchess Anna Pavlovna, the Princess of Orange, to Mlle de Sybourg, Sister of 'Dear Bourcis':

General Headquarters at Tilburg,
31 July 1837

Mademoiselle,

I was most touched to receive a letter from you on the occasion of the death of your excellent sister, our dear good Mlle de Sybourg, whom we cherished as a faithful and loving friend, and to whom I venture to say the Prince of Orange and myself bore a filial affection. I recognise something of the goodness that characterised her in the sentiment that has persuaded you to write to me. Believe that I appreciate it greatly, and that you have even foreseen the wish that I have expressed to Madame Fagel to receive from time to time news of the family of our dear, worthy deceased. The respects that were paid to her mortal remains were only a duty but they came truly from the heart, and the Prince set as great a price on it as I did myself. Her grave will be honoured like that of a mother and the ground that received these precious remains has become my property. I mourn in her an entire past which was dear to me, and an affection that even survived all her other faculties. Her condition was most distressing in the last years although softened by the assiduous cares of our excellent Rosette Dutoit, who with constant solicitude tried to soothe her mistress whom she loved sincerely and whom she regrets as a daughter who mourns for her mother. This person made herself very loved in the eyes of those who saw her care for Mlle de Sybourg, and I cannot recommend her enough to your favourable interest. I shall keep, Mademoiselle, the letter that a hand eighty-four years old took the trouble to write to me, it is precious to me, and I would like you to be convinced of all the interest that I have sworn to you as well as to your family. Gratitude is indeed from my heart, and I hope that you will always believe me when I assure you of the esteem and distinguished sentiments with which I am your affectionate

Anna

How can I not be aware of your goodness when, in the first moments of your grief, you should be thinking of the intentions pronounced by your dear deceased – which were also known to me – about the things that she intended for me; but believe me, Mademoiselle, I consider such things too precious to her family to deprive them of them, reserving for myself the choice among these objects of a souvenir, some little thing that will have an infinite price in my eyes because it belonged to a dear and faithful friend.

THE GRAND DUCHESS ANNA PAVLOVNA, THE PRINCESS OF ORANGE, TO TSAR NICHOLAS I:

The Hague,
6 February 1839

Dear good Brother,

I am very appreciative of the wishes that you express for me on my birthday, and for the affectionate recollections that you have for a date which always recalls so vividly the past for us and the happy times of our childhood. This year the day passed agreeably for me, above all because of the signs of affection and good feelings that I received. First of all, there was the happiness of being reunited with William, who had come back expressly from headquarters, and with my Henry, who had not been among us on this day for several years past. Then the kindness of the King, on this occasion, who came to see me so affectionately in the morning. Finally, many other proofs of kindness which seemed to show that I had not wasted my twenty-two years' existence in this country. Monsieur de Maltik celebrated my birthday with a charming ball which gave great pleasure to the young people. I see that your winter was not very lively and the Empress's health required consideration; I think it is very necessary and I send her my sincerest wishes as well as everything that can contribute to your happiness, dear friend. A letter from your Sasha, dated the 6 January, from Rome, told me that he was intending to come here towards Holy Week [the Russian Orthodox one] in order to make his devotions in my chapel. You can imagine how I am looking forward to seeing him and having him among us. But it is not the most favourable time for offering him the pleasures and distractions of his age, and I hope that you will permit him, dear friend, to spend Easter Week with us so that we shall be able to entertain him at least a little. Our season is not very lively, which must be attributed to the uncertainty of our present circumstances. You will have been edified by the admission of General Skrzynecki to Belgian service, that alone characterises them enough. William left again this morning for Tilburg where he is busy getting our frontier in a good condition to defend it against any aggression. I hope to see William back here next Monday. As the thaw has set in, difficulties in crossing rivers should have stopped. The death of Princess Marie will have struck you that our little cousin is beginning to reap the fruits of his honourable conduct![1] One sees that ingratitude does not bring happiness.

I learnt recently, dear friend, with what generosity you graciously fixed the salary of the priest attached to my chapel. I recognise in it a very great proof of your kindness, for which I am glad for him who is the object of it, because he seems to me to be a good man. But, as you know, in this world a favour granted to one makes others prick up their ears, and so I have resolved to put the case before you plainly. Here it is. When you graciously promoted Monsieur Schultz, my secretary, the salary that he receives from the Minister of Foreign Affairs was not increased. The priest who has just entered my service enjoys a higher salary. Schultz has been serving me for twenty-two years – I cannot prevent comparisons being made – and I would add that the latter has a wife and seven children to support and bring up, while the priest has only one. I would gladly add from my own pocket to the salary I give to Schultz if it were possible for me to do so. But it is already quite considerable. He receives 4500 florins, which makes nearly 9000 roubles. I have many other obligations in this country and they have increased considerably since the death of the Queen because the maternal societies of the country, which formerly depended on her, have been added to everything that I was trying to do before. I cannot, then, increase the salaries of my servants which are, I may add, on a very reasonable level. On the other hand, the necessities of life and housing are so expensive here that I think one would have difficulty in making do with what would be sufficient everywhere else. Here, dear Brother, are my reasons for calling on your kindness to grant Monsieur Schultz an increase in salary which would give him a pecuniary advantage over the priest, because of the twenty-two years he has been in service. He is a faithful, zealous man, adept at business, and I should regret losing him very much; excuse me, then, dear friend, for turning to you in this case which is a very important one to me as he administers all my fortune with irreproachable integrity. Look at our circumstances and what we can expect. I would like to retain a man who is useful to me

[1] Which royal connection had 'done wrong' is impossible to ascertain.

and to do here all the good that I can. My children are most grateful for your remembrance, dear Brother, and they ask me to offer you their respectful homage. Alexander and Henry are developing more and more favourably. Their qualities of heart and mind make me happy, they have *noble* characters. And Sophie, who no longer feels the effect of her illness at all, becomes more interesting every day. The expression that permeates her whole being makes her agreeable; although she is not beautiful or even pretty, her bearing promises well. I recommend them to your friendship, dear good Brother.

I was pleased to learn that the work on the beautiful Winter Palace is progressing so well,[1] and wish that you will be able to sing Easter Matins in the great church restored as it used to be.

THE GRAND DUCHESS ANNA PAVLOVNA, THE PRINCESS OF ORANGE, TO TSAR NICHOLAS I:

The Hague,
1 March 1839

Dear good Brother,

. . . I am very grateful for your friendly wishes for me; retain these sentiments for an old friend who recognises them from the depths of her soul.

I would like to say thank you once more for the materials that came to me from you, and which I suppose is from Moscow. As you do not say anything about it in your letters I attribute this consignment to an old promise that you made me at Töplitz. They are very beautiful and I shall deck myself out in them for the arrival of your dear Sasha, whom I thank you a thousand thousand times for sending to us. He will be received with open arms by us all, and William and I are pleased to be lodging him under our roof. May he like it here, that is all that we wish. Yesterday the Turin *Gazette* told us of his arrival there and the details of the stay that he made. He appears to have left – as everywhere he has been – the most favourable memory of his friendly manner. I am only afraid that the solemn time at which he is coming to us is hardly suitable for giving him an agreeable impression, and I regret it only in this respect;

[1] The original palace had been destroyed by fire in December 1837.

we can hardly offer him a good dinner in the middle of the austerities of Holy Week. Is it necessary that the one for this country immediately precedes ours this year? At least we shall pray to God together with a good heart and we shall think of the re-occupation of the Winter Palace, wishing that Heaven continue to grant you happy days there. I am amazed to know that it is so far advanced, and thank you very much, dear friend, for the details that you give me on it. I read them with infinite interest. I see that my last letter crossed yours because I asked you the same question that you asked me with regard to the admission of the Polish warrior to the service of the magnificent Belgian nation. That serves to show what goes on there, although in my opinion, much stranger things have happened which have not incurred so much anger. Liniofski, former Gentleman of the Bedchamber at the Polish Court, and given the mission by the revolutionaries of inciting the Turks to take up arms against you during the war against the Polish insurgents, has been admitted for a number of years to the military service in Belgium. It is difficult to estimate the result that the confusion which reigns in that country can bring. Our country shows an aspect of complete tranquility. The safety measures necessary on the frontiers are carried out actively, they are indispensible. William divides himself among his different duties with an admirable perseverance, calm and activity, and he still finds enough freedom of spirit in these circumstances to receive the general public and to rise to little social obligations. The rest is in God's hands, in whom we trust completely, strong in our good conscience. We venture to hope that He will deign to watch over our destinies.

THE GRAND DUCHESS ANNA PAVLOVNA, THE PRINCESS OF ORANGE, TO TSAR NICHOLAS I AND HIS WIFE:

The Hague,
19 March 1939

Dear Nicholas, dear Alexandrine,

I am writing to you both, my dear friends, to tell you that I have just embraced your dear Sasha [the Tsarevich Alexander] who arrived this afternoon at six o'clock. We were all delighted to see him and find him looking so well; he seems to me to have put on weight since Coblenz, and I find him taller. It is truly a pleasure for us to have him under our roof. May God bless him here! and allow that he should like it a little *chez nous*. William and my sons went to meet him, and I waited here with Sophie to receive him. His room is immediately beneath mine, so that I can almost hear every step he takes. Soon after he arrived William took him to the King and from there to Fritz and his wife, where they are while I am writing to you. On their return we shall have tea together peacefully, for he will need a rest. Sasha was charming in his Cossack uniform which suits him marvellously; the little moustache has prospered, and as for his appearance I can tell you that I find him a very handsome boy. I have seen Orlov but I have not seen the other gentlemen yet. For several days we have had dry weather and sun which will suit Sasha better than humidity, although the air is still sharp. A thousand thanks for your letters of 22 March, which the courier gave me today. I have already embraced Sasha in your name in his room before the picture of St Alexander that I had from Mama and that I placed in his room this morning. Your good Ollie has also written me a charming letter. Until tomorrow for the rest, my dear friends.

23 March 1839, Maundy Thursday

Dear friends,

Your son has just taken communion with us in my chapel! And I have had the happiness of carrying out this sacred act with him and the numerous compatriots who accompany him and whom Providence has gathered here on this solemn occasion. William and my three sons were present at the ceremony. My soul is filled with gratitude towards the Almighty who has allowed your child to be among us, and that, not being able to be near you to fulfil these religious duties, he should take communion with us. This sacred act, carried out with him, is going to form a new bond between us, that of the dearest and most sacred memory that solemnities and religion can form. At 8 o'clock we all gathered together in my chapel. Divine service lasted for an hour and a half and you can imagine the emotions that succeeded one another in my heart; thinking of you, my dear friends, and uniting my prayers for Sasha, for my own family and for you by invoking Heaven to help me to appreciate worthily so many acts of kindness – these were the sentiments that absorbed me. May Divine Providence bless your excellent Sasha and bring him back to your arms as well as he is at present. He was very moved, this good young man, and yet so much master of himself and with such a pure and serious expression of a young and beautiful soul on his face. I am certain that the differences of places and objects have not distracted him from the principal goal which was to occupy him, and that is a lot in so young a man. He has completely justified the impression that he made on me at Coblenz. In coming back from the chapel he said to me, 'And now my parents are at church and fulfilling the same duty as us.' It was half-past nine; I took Sasha into the study where I pray and in which I bless my children, to embrace him and bless him there too. Then we had breakfast together, surrounded by William and all the children. Sasha recalled many memories which formed the subject of our conversation, after which he retired to his room to write. I would have written you a few lines every day if I had not been prevented by headaches which, thank God, have gone today, leaving me in a condition to do my duties very fully. You know from Sasha that we dined with the King and all his suite the day after his arrival, and then we were left free to ourselves until Saturday. All the gentlemen who accompany Sasha come to dine with us in frockcoats,[1] and William and my sons do likewise in order to leave everything according to your daily habits. At 7 o'clock in the evening we go to prayers in my chapel, which is adjacent to my apartments, and when we come back Sasha takes a cup of tea with his old aunt; we talk and drink tea until 10 o'clock and at 10 o'clock we retire. Just as we think of you I am sure that you also think of us and that these days are spent in following our thoughts what each is doing in the others' home. Accept my best wishes for the consecration of the Great Chapel at the Palace and the re-occupation of this family dwelling which is so dear to us. What Alexandrine was kind enough to tell me about the ceremony which will take place on Easter evening interested

[1] Tsar Nicholas dined at 4 o'clock *en famille* and generally wore 'the frock coat of the Horse Guards with the collar of deep pink'. Constantin de Grunwald, *Tsar Nicholas I* (New York, 1955) p. 138.

me greatly. I wish you all possible happiness and long and happy years. And so, my dear friends, '*Christ has arisen*'! greetings from the bottom of our hearts! I embrace Michael tenderly, thanking him for his letter, as well as good Olinka and all your dear children. May God bless you all and preserve you. I shall reply to Mikki and Ollie at the earliest possible occasion. And now I must close my letter, embracing you again tenderly, dear Nikki, and you, dear Alexandrine.

THE GRAND DUCHESS ANNA PAVLOVNA, THE PRINCESS OF ORANGE, TO TSAR NICHOLAS I:

The Hague,
16 April 1839

Dear friend,

. . . The pleasure that we have in seeing your Sasha amongst us is very natural, and the wish that he should like it here, also. It appears to us now as if he had spent his life here, he has such an easy and agreeable character, adjusting to everything and always favourably inclined. I feel tenderly devoted to him and I can assure you that he is generally liked here. He has a great deal of tact, grace and dignity, with a naturalness which charms; qualities and advantages that are rarely found together to this degree. Tomorrow we shall be celebrating his twenty-first birthday. It is a happiness which I had not dared count on, but it is giving us all a great deal of pleasure. Receive in advance, dear Brother, all the wishes that I make for your excellent Sasha, for this distinguished person whom I love as a son. May God preserve him for you and shower him with His most precious benedictions. I would have written many details of his stay if I had not been prevented by the consequences of a blow that I so clumsily gave myself on the head in the cottage of Emperor Peter I. It was a happy day and an imperishable memory when I saw your Sasha and so many compatriots, distinguished for their service and their merits, in the modest dwelling from where so much glory spread over Russia.[1] – My head has remained tender and I still have pain in writing. For the rest, the whole of Sasha's stay has been, as it were, blessed

[1] The event was commemorated in a painting by C. J. L. Portman, and it belongs to H.M. Queen Juliana.

by Divine Providence, and it was successful in spite of the weather which is not favourable, for we are still without greenery. Now that I have given you an account of the essentials for your father's heart, let me thank you for the magnificent shawl that you sent me jointly with the Empress. It is a new form that you have given to Easter eggs; it is so beautiful, this shawl, that I look at it and admire it without ever tiring of it, and it has spent twenty-four hours beside me for the pleasure of looking at it, as if I were fifteen years old! Now I must congratulate you with all my heart on the re-opening of the beautiful Winter Palace which was so successful both as to the day and the occasion which you chose for this re-occupation of the dwelling-place of our ancestors. May Heaven grant you happy days in it! I was delighted to learn all the details and I thank you a thousand times for having sent me the commemorative medallion that Prince Volkonski[1] gave to me. It is beautiful, honourable for those who have deserved it, and gives a proof at the same time of the sentiments of your heart which are so precious to receive. Dear friend, I embrace you as tenderly as I love you but I cannot write much. This evening we shall felicitate and bless Sasha on the eve of his birthday according to our good Russian custom, and tomorrow we shall try to make the day as agreeable for him as we are able to.

The journey to England can only have a good effect. I understand your reasons, which I approve – if you will excuse me the expression – as a decision completely worthy of you. Henry will accompany Sasha, which makes him very happy.

THE GRAND DUCHESS ANNA PAVLOVNA, THE PRINCESS OF ORANGE, TO TSAR NICHOLAS I:

The Hague,
10 May 1839

Dear good Brother,

Having promised Alexandrine in a letter I wrote to her through Monsieur de [Wildsmet ?] that I would give her news of your

[1] Prince Peter Volkonsky was Court Minister and had charge of all of the grand functions involving the court as a whole. Thus the reopening of the Winter Palace would be one of his responsibilities.

dear Sasha as soon as I received it, I am about to acquit myself of my promise, and I am sending these lines to you, dear friend, because I did not write to you on this last occasion. My son Henry informs me that their crossing was so uneventful that they made the journey from Hellevoetslyis to Deptford in twenty-two hours, and he adds that Sasha was marvellously well. More recent news that has arrived here speaks of their deeds and exploits, of the soirées and the dinners which they attended, and the things that they have seen. I was glad to learn what has come to me from a good source, that your young man is much liked in London where they admire his appearance, his manners and his courtesy. He has gone out several times on horseback and his bearing was found to be charming. As you will have directly all the details which can interest you, I will only note what I know – not wishing to neglect anything – to keep you abreast of what I have learned about the son whom you cherish and whom we all love. We hope to see him again here shortly on his return and we are looking forward to it very much. I only regret that he should have seen this country in such poor weather, for it was only after his departure that it started to be fine, while our beautiful flowers, which he did not see, are now in all their glory! It is now the time of the fair, which usually appears lively, but this year it seems to us very quiet in comparison with the eventful life and the pleasures which helped to entertain the stay of our dear guest. Our wishes accompany him and I would like to express them to you for him, dear Brother. A thousand friendly greetings from me to Alexandrine and your children. I embrace our excellent Michael, to whom I am writing. William, who has come in and found me writing to you, asks me to send his loving and friendly wishes.

TSAR NICHOLAS I TO WILLIAM, THE PRINCE OF ORANGE:

Tsarskoe Selo,
11/23 May 1839

Dear good William,

You must have found me very ungrateful for having taken such a long time to reply to your kind letters, to thank you for showering our boy with so much kindness; you were really so obliging, so affectionate for that boy that it goes beyond words, or rather, it is worthy of friend William. If both of us here are sincerely grateful to you, I can assure you too that Sasha, who always liked you especially, is deeply attached to you who were like a father to him. I am so happy that the boy was able to deserve your goodness; he really is an excellent young man and I do not doubt that this big trip will broaden his character a great deal and will give him the poise he was lacking.

It seems that in England they want to treat him with the same indulgence; and from the Queen and the upper classes right down to the lower orders everyone is receiving him with incredibly kind attentions. Chance had him arrive and be present at an unusual time in England; and it is difficult to observe that it is the *petticoats* who have perhaps decided the fate of that beautiful England; what will come out of it? In any case I thank God to have inspired me to demand that my son go to England; and it is singular that it was only my *wife*, my *son*, and *myself* who stood up against the unanimous advice of all the others. You tell me nothing, dear friend, of your plans; are you coming or not? What has persuaded Anne to travel, and where does she want to go?

It seems that the idea of William's marriage is still nibbling away at her; it is extremely sad; and Sophie must be very careful to know how to make herself loved and do justice to Anne; I am not despairing of that, however, as Sophie has enough wits for that. How will William do at his husbandly duties? So mine too has found his lady-love; let us see what will happen; thus far the pretty English girls have not yet prejudiced Darmstadt. In a few days we are expecting Marie;[1] pray God that everything may succeed according to our wishes and our hopes, and I dare to hope it from all His goodness! We have had a month of May such as is rare to have in June and July; 38 degrees in the sun and 25 degrees in the shade. Sasha spoke to me about all your kindness to him at Tilburg, and he was very astonished at the good condition of the troops, especially the grenadiers, and the beauty and orderliness in the artillery. The day before yesterday we had a review of the guard with

[1] Of Hesse-Darmstadt.

which I was very satisfied, and which I very much want to have you inspect. So do come if possible, or your Alexander. Farewell, and thanks again many times over, dear Good William Yours for life, your old friend embraces you with all his heart. . . .

THE GRAND DUCHESS ANNA PAVLOVNA, THE PRINCESS OF ORANGE, TO TSAR NICHOLAS I:

Buitenrust, nr The Hague,
10 July 1839

Dear good Nicholas,

I would like to recommend my Alexander to your kindness and to your friendship as an uncle. You have already greeted him graciously with so much affection, when he had the good fortune to be presented to you in Berlin, that he has retained a deep memory of it. He is looking forward very much to the journey he is undertaking to reach his mother's native country and to see the relatives again to whom he is attached. Michael, on his two sojourns with us, showed him a great deal of friendship, and dear Sasha, during the stay that he has just made, made very warm ties with him so that Alexander is following his heart in going to Russia. May he deserve your approval, dear friend, and please you. I venture to say that he is such a good son and is so dear to us by virtue of the qualities of heart and mind with which he is endowed that he is already a friend to his parents. I am happy for his sake that he is undertaking this journey because it is such an interesting one and most instructive. Alexander sees and judges with discernment and he possesses reasoning powers older than his age, of this I have many proofs. This winter, left to himself by the departure of Major Rigot for Switzerland, he surprised me by the superior good sense which he showed in voluntarily continuing to take lessons and complete his instruction even though his education was regarded as finished. I can assure you that I cannot find any fault in him, and that I have often been agreeably struck by his caution and tact. Please, dear friend, guide him and enlighten him with your advice on this scene which is completely new to him, and of which the proportions surpass anything which he has seen previously. He will appreciate your goodness and will be grateful for the advice that you may wish to give him. I hope that you will allow him to see establishments and things that may contribute to his instruction. He asks no better than to extend his knowledge and fix his attention on useful objects. You have already learnt from the newspapers that Henry was promoted to the rank of Frigate Captain. He is going to the Mediterranean at the beginning of September under the command of Captain Arriens, and this time Henry will be his First Officer on board. He owes this honour to his examinations.

And now my son William is married! And he arrived here with his wife eight days ago. I waited until they were here before replying to your letter of 8 June, dear Brother, the contents of which gave me a great deal of pain. I think that it is to them that you could have addressed the advice that you give me, for certainly the whole of my life, for the twenty-three years that I have been in my husband's family and in this country, show sufficiently that I have striven to maintain harmony with my kin–having gone through the most difficult times with the help of God–knowing the affection and respect of the family into which I entered. So it is not for me to receive these counsels of conciliation but, on the contrary, it is to her who is newly arrived that I would ask you to address them, as well as to my son of twenty-two who has great need of them. I do not know how you could have come to doubt me, dear Brother. I did not think that I had deserved that from you. The first painful moment of the arrival of the young married couple has passed and better, thank God, than I could have hoped for, although in the first moments my son was icy towards me. I leave you to think what that makes a mother feel. The next day, in presenting his wife to me, he embraced me and I suppose that his conscience finally awoke, because he did it effusively although without saying anything. I like to hope that it was a movement of remorse and, as I have become accustomed in my difficult and thorny position to making sacrifices at all times to harmony and keeping the family peace, I have acted from the first with a cordial simplicity that I put in all my relationships. The rest will come or will not come, according to the feelings that I find in the young household; I find them very cold together for such a newly married couple. My husband, who was a witness of stormy beginnings in Stuttgart, finds that she acts with tact towards William whose abrupt character and irascibility jar incessantly. But up to now one can judge nothing, in my opinion. Towards me, Sophie is good and very accommodating. But I am struck by how much older and more of a complete person she is than my son who seems to be a little boy beside her. Certainly there is no liking for him on her side, but indeed a good dose of ambition which makes her swallow him with an eye on a brilliant future. If you could see things you would share this opinion. Today, 11 July, I am finishing these lines and going back to town where, yesterday, we gave a ball for the newly married couple; I think it was a success; I went to bed at 3 o'clock this morning and so I am allowed to feel tired. However, as Alexander must leave tonight I am continuing this letter, wanting to add good wishes for you, dear Brother, as well as for everything which can contribute to your happiness. Now it is precisely the time of our reunion last year at Töplitz. I often think of it with gratitude and satisfaction, remembering the friendship and trust that you showed me there. After having opened my soul to you and laid bare the sentiments that have always inspired me, how could you have come to doubt me? That is what I cannot conceive! This might crush my soul for, if it is not through actions when one's character is put to the test, by what then can one best prove what one is? I hope, dear Brother, that the weather and the season will favour your numerous plans for Moscow and Borodino. I have a proof of friendship to ask of you for Alexander, it is to take him to the fortress in St Petersburg so that he may pay homage to the remains of our parents and that of our late Emperor who was our benefactor; his memory and that of our mother are often the subject of my conversations with my children. They have learnt to revere it.

THE GRAND DUCHESS ANNA PAVLOVNA, THE PRINCESS OF ORANGE, TO TSAR NICHOLAS I:

Buitenrust,
31 July 1839

Dear good Brother,

. . . At the present time, dear friend, my Alexander will be near you already, bearing so many letters and news from us that I restrict myself this time to writing only a few lines to you in order not to delay in expressing how appreciative I am of being remembered by you in this circumstance, which is so dear to you. I recommend our young man to you again, I wish with all my heart that he should deserve your approval. It would have been indeed a little late, as you say, to send him to you only for the reviews of Borodino; you see that it is to you and to your home that we have sent him, and not simply with the aim of curiosity, however instructive that might be. He wished very much himself to see you in Petersburg and, for preference, in those places in the country where you live, in order to enjoy the happiness of being close to you more often and for a longer time than if he had come to join you only at Moscow. Russia, indeed, deserves to be known, and my son is imbued with this feeling for his mother's native country which he has only heard spoken of with affection, gratitude and regret.

I send my friendly and loving wishes to the Empress, recommending myself to her memory; I add wishes for her health, may God strengthen it. A thousand affectionate regards from me to all your children, but most particularly to your excellent Sasha, you know how devoted I am to him. I tell myself too that he retains a little remembrance of us, at least he is warmly remembered here where he was so much liked. I embrace my Alexander, my Sashika as we call him in the familiar language of the home, may Heaven watch over him!

THE GRAND DUCHESS ANNA PAVLOVNA, THE PRINCESS OF ORANGE, TO TSAR NICHOLAS I:

Buitenrust,
16 August 1839

Dear good Brother,

. . . Alexander is most grateful for the friendship with which you deigned to receive him and I thank you most tenderly for it, dear Brother, as well as for having sent a courier to us to announce his arrival at your home. I am most flattered that he had the good fortune to please you straight away, may he continue to deserve your approbation; this approval would be precious to him and like a passport for life. I have nothing really to tell you from here which could interest you. On the subject of the young household – it seemed to me that it was to him and not to me that your advice should be addressed. My age, my position as mother and the conduct that I have pursued in the most difficult times as well as in the most delicate situations in which one can find oneself, have shown sufficiently that I have made sacrifices for my duties and for family peace as well as for public propriety. I consider that I told the truth conscientiously in the affair of this marriage to those who were most interested. I was not listened to. My son does as he wishes and he left to get married without even asking for my blessing. His wife only wrote to me to announce her marriage three weeks afterwards so that I received this letter only a few days before her arrival here. However, I received her with cordiality. She praised it to her father, and I have the proof in a letter the King of Württemberg wrote to me, in which he thanked me for it. Here, dear Brother, is my reply to this unfortunate expression of *fait accompli* that I find in your letter. If ever – from which God preserve you! – one of your children did some regrettable things which would have cause to incur your displeasure, would you accept and condone everything by the sole motive of *fait accompli*? It is a deplorable principle, because it tends to demoralise by inviting action to gain one's end by no matter what means, through the sole idea that necessity or success can legitimise and sanction it.

The young household finds me such as I can be, cordial and

natural. It is all that can be expected from a mother whose heart one does not mind breaking. It is difficult to be reassured about their future when one sees that already there are frequent storms between them at the end of two months of marriage. One will recall that I told the truth when there was still time, and it was not perhaps their true friends who wished and pressed for the conclusion of the affair. It was ambition that was at the back of it all and that they wished to cling to at all costs. These lines will find you as you leave for Borodino. I wish you fine weather and all the pleasures which exalt the soul by memories of glory and honour. I congratulate your Sasha on receiving you on such a terrain. May this noble glory always rest on your flags and perpetuate itself in future generations. There, dear friend, are memories and feelings which will always make my old heart beat, and it is under these auspices that I embrace you tenderly, begging you to retain memory and friendship for her who will never cease to be your most sincere friend and very affectionate and devoted sister.

THE GRAND DUCHESS ANNA PAVLOVNA, THE PRINCESS OF ORANGE, TO TSAR NICHOLAS I:

Buitenrust,
3 October 1839

Dear good Brother,

What thanks do I not owe to you, dear friend, for all the kindnesses which you have showered on my son, Alexander, and for the flattering distinction which you graciously granted him in naming him head of a regiment of your army. May he one day deserve such a great honour as to be counted in the ranks of such an army! May he be worthy of it! It is the wish of my heart, which was deeply moved in learning of this news. Dear Brother, you have added one more honour to this distinction by granting it to him on the field of the battle of Borodino. *I cried with one of those joys that one rarely experiences.* I thank you from the depths of my soul and I am profoundly grateful to you. Your letter of 23 August reached me in time, and it is only from discretion that I did not reply sooner, knowing and seeing in the *Gazette* how busy you were. I followed with the most sincere interest all the details that I found there and I am looking forward to questioning my Sasha on his return. We have just come back from Amsterdam where we spent eight days in celebrations. Everything went very well and I had the rare satisfaction of seeing two compatriots there, Count Panin and Admiral Korsakov. The latter, who is returning immediately to Russia, can give you some of our recent news, although I did not have the time to write to you through him, but as he has been the eye-witness of many things it will be equivalent of a letter. Our dear little sailor put to sea on 28 September after having awaited a favourable wind for twelve days. May God watch over him and bring him back to us safe and sound in His own time. I am sure, dear friend, that you join us in our wishes for this dear child. . . .

My friendly greetings to the Empress, to your excellent Sasha and all the family. Your Order of the Day to the Army, given at Borodino, caused a great sensation in Amsterdam.

THE GRAND DUCHESS ANNA PAVLOVNA, THE PRINCESS OF ORANGE, TO TSAR NICHOLAS I:

Buitenrust,
15 October 1839

Dear good Brother,

. . . You would not believe how much pleasure your opinion of Alexander gives me. You confirm the one I had of him and I am delighted to see that it was not a maternal illusion on my part. May God grant, dear friend, that he shall always be worthy of the good opinion that you have of him and that he may be able to deserve the infinite bounties which you have heaped upon him, and for which he is so grateful. I thank you for it a thousand thousand times, dear good Brother. I am glad Alexander will have the pleasure of meeting your excellent Sasha again during his trip to Warsaw; that will make him happy, for my son is really attached to him. I assure you that I also love your Sasha tenderly and above all I esteem his character, for he possesses very essential qualities. We have heard nothing of our dear Henry since 20 September, new style, when the pilot left him at Brighton cliff. As the weather has been remarkably fine and calm I hope that his voyage will have been agreeable. The rumours that have reached you and which you do not give credence to are only too true.[1] I can imagine that you did not want to believe in them, they are only too much of that nature. '*It is really revolting. Please excuse me, dear Nikki, for not writing much to you about this, but you will understand our and my position. I can only tell you that it is a great misfortune for us and this country. Inhabitants of all classes do not hide their discontent. The consequences may be disastrous considering her origin and faith.*' I thought of you, dear friend, at the exhibition of pictures, you who are so fond of the arts, there were so many fine things, and I acquired a sea-scape by the son of the famous Schottell representing the [frigate *Bellona*] with Henry on board when he went to Russia.

THE GRAND DUCHESS ANNA PAVLOVNA, THE PRINCESS OF ORANGE, TO TSAR NICHOLAS I:

The Hague,
20 December 1839

Dear good Brother,

Not being able to write to you on your name-day nor the day after, it is only now that I express to you my congratulations and wishes on this occasion. May Divine Providence retain for you all the truly good things with which it has heaped you, and grant you health to enjoy them as well as everything that can contribute to your happiness. I suppose you were happy to have been able to spend this day in the Winter Palace again according to your usual custom. We celebrated it by a dinner we gave in which we were joined by the Legation and the little Russian colony established here. It was on this occasion that I had the pleasure of seeing Alexander for the first time in the uniform of a Russian general. It suits him marvellously and I believe myself to be seeing you at this age; a sweet illusion I

[1] The proposal of King William I to marry the Countess Henriette d'Oultremont, who was a Roman Catholic and a Belgian. The project did not please the Dutch, considering the events of the previous decade.

owe to your friendship, dear Nikki, for reuniting thus the dearest memories of the past with the present. Alexander bears you a true and deep gratitude. He often speaks to me of the time that he spent near you as a time of happiness. You will perhaps have learnt already that he has received command of a brigade of cuirassiers stationed at Leiden, where he is about to take up his post. You will understand it is not exactly what he would have wished, while having enough reason to say that the word 'agreeableness' is not known in the vocabulary of the Army. He has gained still more during his stay with you, his reserve, his tone and his manners show benefit from it, and this boy, this little boy shows me a touching confidence. It was a consolation, dear Nikki, in the midst of the sad time in which we are living and of which I suppose you know the details, so I shall abstain from mentioning them to you although they are public. The distressing projects which you did not wish to believe in have produced a totally deplorable effect which could have been foreseen, and it is probable that the gravest consequences will follow.

At present our winter is very mild. This morning it is raining and it is so dark that I can hardly see to write to you. Since William's birthday the balls have followed each other in succession, each one of us gave one in proportion to the premises which we own. Your beautiful apartment is never opened without it bringing back vividly your dear and excellent Sasha, who is remembered by everybody in such an agreeable way and who left here so many good memories. Everyone asks me for his news with interest. Alas, we regretfully received here the Belgian Minister.[1] The envoy of the dirtiest of revolutions with the neighbouring vermin. Except for what indispensable propriety dictates, I never address a word to him, neither to him nor his family, and I expect always to maintain this line which seems to me the only fitting and possible one towards such people. I can assure you that the Dutch public does not approach them and they are completely abandoned because nobody

[1] Joseph de Riquet Carman Chimay (1808–86) was the first Belgian envoy accepted at The Hague. Ironically, his father, Francis Joseph Philippe de Riquet Carman Chimay (1771–1843), was a member of the Dutch government. Thus the son was an envoy of 'the rebels' while the father was a valued councillor of the King.

wishes to speak to them, and they are openly shown all the contempt that the people feel for them. This generally has the effect that the Belgian Minister takes refuge beside the Minister, his father-in-law, but as the latter is very small in size and the other very large, it is as though they are making a parody of their countries, and the Belgian appears to be in authority over the other one. I must confess to you also, dear friend, that it is for much that is Polish in Belgium being the basis for the deep aversion that I feel and in the disgust that it inspires in me. To add another detail to this picture, you will know that they are contesting William's possession of his house at Brussels and his estate at [Tervueren ?] starting with a lie, that is to say, that these two donations were made to the Prince Royal and must return to the domain, while in fact the donation was made to William, Prince of Orange, for signal services that he gave to the state at Quatre Bras and at Waterloo. From this you can see clearly the bad faith and the lies which characterise them every time their interests are at stake. Admit that this is infamous!

1840–55

In part as a consequence of increased dissatisfaction with his policies, and in part as a result of hostility to his proposed second marriage, King William I of the Netherlands abdicated in October 1840. At last the Prince and Princess of Orange gained the first position in the state. King William II was more enlightened than his father, more progressive in outlook and for the nine years of his reign the Dutch were tolerably happy. Nevertheless, despite some general improvement in government and in the economic situation, there were still areas of discontent. The February Revolution in France, followed by similar outbreaks elsewhere, caused King William to instruct Thorbecke, a liberal jurist, to draw up new constitutional arrangements. The consequence was that the Netherlands obtained a democratic constitution. Indeed, one of the last public acts of King William II in 1849 was to appear at the ceremony arranged for him to swear to uphold the new system.

The 1840s saw the hey-day of the Anglo-French *entente*. Its creation was largely the consequence of the isolation of England and France from the policies of the conservative eastern and central European sovereigns. The *entente* collapsed in 1846, however, when the son of Louis-Philippe married the sister of Queen Isabella II. The English had opposed the marriage, and its accomplishment destroyed the harmony between the two countries. The disruption of the *entente* weakened English and French influence on continental politics.

Russia under Tsar Nicholas, Austria under Emperor Ferdinand, and Prussia under King Frederick William IV, remained bulwarks of autocracy. Even so, in the Swiss crisis of 1847, the eastern powers could not intervene to prevent the creation of a more liberal constitution the next year.

The 'February Revolution' of 1848 in Paris overthrew the only monarchy of Louis-Philippe and precipitated a whole series of upheavals all over Europe. Only Russia of the great powers escaped unscathed, and even her satellite Poland remained quiet. Austria, Prussia and indeed all of Germany were involved in violence; Italy exploded into civil war; Hungary declared its independence of Austria and the old Germanic confederation was dissolved. England remained a bystander, not displeased to see Europe in chaos and her enemy Louis-Philippe in distress.

After a short time the forces of reaction regrouped. The Hungarian revolt was crushed by Tsar Nicholas, who sent in troops to assist the young Austrian Emperor, Francis Joseph, regain his authority. The Frankfurt Parliament's election of King Frederick William of Prussia as Emperor of the Germans failed to achieve success when the Prussian monarch declined to accept the crown. The whole project then collapsed completely, and within two years the old Germanic Confederation was restored. The Austrians not only regained their authority in Germany, but recovered their position in Italy as well. The Italian states, who had united to eject the Austrians from their country, were defeated and virtually all of the gains of the liberals were lost. Only the Kingdom of Sardinia retained its liberal constitution. Italian confederation was not to result for another generation.

The last years of Tsar Nicholas I saw the outbreak of the Crimean War. England, France, Turkey and Piedmont joined together to thwart the ambitions of Russia. The Allies were successful and the Russians made peace in 1856 at Paris, but before this occurred Tsar Nicholas I died early in 1855. With his death the last great exponent of the old Europe vanished, and new actors took the stage to control the affairs of nations.

Tsar Nicholas I to the Grand Duchess Anna Pavlovna, the Princess of Orange:

St Petersburg,
7/19 January 1840

. . . The news which comes to us from your world is not very reassuring, so I guarantee to you that frequently our thoughts turn to you and the future which is in preparation. May God keep you from all mischance! Recent events in your country are so extraordinary, so unexpected, that one does not know what to say or to think of them; so we must limit ourselves to praying God to keep you from all danger and to trust in Him for the outcome . . . [indecipherable]; but I confess that I cannot be calm. Everything makes any possibility of seeing you again more and more remote for a long time to come, and I confess that it is very sad, for we are getting old and the years have been passing very quickly for some time, I assure you!

I have nothing very interesting to tell you from here; the care which my wife's health demands makes us live in a very retired way and in the most absolute quiet. Only rarely do we attend the theatre in the evening, and I have been in society only two or three times. My wife is better but her strength is very slow in returning. My son is starting out during the next month for Darmstadt; what will come out of that is what God in His mercy will decide and inspire in him; it is only there, and after having become more intimate, that he will make a definite decision, the direction of which we in no way wish to influence, but it would delight us a great deal if the decision was affirmative. In general they say the Princess has a charming face and is even better for qualities of heart and mind. There, dear Anne, is all I had to tell you for the moment.

TSAR NICHOLAS I TO QUEEN ANNA PAVLOVNA:

Tsarskoe Selo,
11/23 October 1840

I am writing you today not to congratulate you, dear good Anne, but to send you all my good wishes for you and our dear William. I cannot be delighted for you both at your change in position for the trade is neither easy nor pleasant; but your hopes in God and your trust in His mercy will make you triumph over the difficulties which surround you. Your tenderness for William and the care with which you will surround him will ease his difficult moments, and it is this sweet and holy obligation which will be the purpose of the rest of your life. William, obsessed with cares and serious preoccupations, will need more than ever serenity of soul and peace of mind; it is up to you to keep from him all family problems by using your heart, your example, and your influence with the children.

Since the King has deemed it necessary to decide upon the serious step he has just brought about, it would be very much to be wished that he leave the country, for his presence can only be a very serious impediment for the whole course of the new reign; we must hope that his reason will tell him to do so.

Queen Anna Pavlovna to Tsar Nicholas I:

The Hague,
4 November 1840

Dear good Brother,

. . . I have scarcely the time to write to you more than a few lines today, dear friend, and I restrict myself to telling you that everything up to now has been happy and agreeable. That from all sides in the country the most affectionate and excellent feelings have been shown us; may Divine Providence keep them for us all.

Today the little new-born boy[1] will be baptised in the Dutch church. The King, his great-grandfather, has given us the pleasure of coming to The Hague to be present at this ceremony. He will spend approximately three weeks here before going to Berlin where he expects to go to see Marianne. Except for the indispensable receptions and numerous dinners, I give thanks to God for the simplicity of my past life and my daily habits, this sanctuary of private life so necessary to my soul and my feelings. I am personally very touched by the devotion with which I am surrounded and that has been shown me on all sides. Conceive our happiness in seeing our Henry again in perfect health, returned safe and sound in this dangerous season, returned after an absence of more than a year! I thank you, dear friend, for speaking to me of your family happiness wich interests me a great deal.

Queen Anna Pavlovna to Tsar Nicholas I:

The Hague,
9 December 1840

Dear good Brother,

. . . Everything[2] took place to the great satisfaction of all and was beyond anything one could have hoped for, even allowing

[1] Prince William, the eldest son of William and Sophie.

[2] The Dutch do not have a formal coronation but rather an official ceremony in the New Church in Amsterdam, where the king swears to uphold the constitution (Organic Statute). William II's inauguration took place on 28 November 1840.

for the best. We can never thank God enough for it and be grateful for the infinite grace which He bestows on us. You can understand how happy I am to see William so generally loved, and his titles, as well as his past services, appreciated by a whole nation which adopts his glory as its own, and shows it with an almost unparalleled effusion. By now you will have received from our legation details of the entry into Amsterdam and the august and imposing ceremony of William's inauguration. He was himself an edifying sight because of the expression of profound piety prevailing in his face and because of the combination of dignity and a totally chivalrous bearing which characterised and distinguished him. The manly and exalted way in which he read his speech and then pronounced his oath; then covering himself, he raised his right hand to heaven, invoking its assistance according to the customary formula, with an expression so touching in its faith and hope that he moved the whole congregation which expressed itself by long and lively acclamation. We all got up at this solemn moment and remained standing during the taking of the oath by the presidents of the States General, who wish to recognise him as the legitimate and constitutional king according to the wishes of the nation. He received the oath seated and covered, and as soon as it had been made I sat down, while the princes and princesses, as well as all those present, remained standing while the members of the two Chambers of the States General came individually to make the oath to the King before the throne, and then to bow to me. During this time the two [Kings of Arms ?] and the Heralds proclaimed him outside, throwing little inauguration medallions among the people. Cries of joy could be heard right into the church. This civil ceremony was followed by a sermon given by the Protestant preacher from the pulpit and by a prayer for William and for me, and the whole was terminated by chanting a verse from the Psalms. William rose and uncovered himself, and we all rose to sing it standing with the thousands of voices which composed the congregation, it was very touching; then the preacher gave us the blessing [prescribed by the ritual ?] and William, after kneeling in front of him, covered himself, bowed to me, then to the assembly, and returned with the same cortège to the Palace, to the sound of fanfares and of music composed for the occasion which was very beautiful and imposing. After he had left I bowed to the assembly and also retired to the cortège which accompanied me as far as the state coach; then, accompanied by an escort of cavalry, I drove home with the princesses. I joined William in his apartments and we appeared together on the balcony of the Palace, where thousands saluted us with cries of joy. William had chosen for his inauguration costume that worn by the volunteer corps bearing arms from 1830 until the time when they were disbanded – this uniform is similar to the costume worn by the members of the Russian militia of 1812 – and who had been through the Ten-day Campaign with him. It is a dark blue cloth, decorated with embroidery of gold oak leaves on the collar and sleeves; his Marshal's epaulettes, which he had himself put on his royal coat so that they were very clearly seen, and all the crosses that he won in battle – that of [Spain ?] of St George, of Maria Theresa, the great William, and the Cross of [— ?] of '30 and '31 – covered his chest, while the Waterloo sabre hung at his side. For headgear he wished to retain the cap that he always wears in the army and on working days, ornamenting it with embroidery of oak instead of the usual narrow braid, and with a [— ?] for a plume. This simplicity does him honour for it is the man entirely. His aides-de-camp carried his mantle of crimson velvet embroidered with [lions ?] of gold holding a naked sword, trimmed and lined with ermine, with a large collar falling over the shoulders. I was present at his toilet and when he was ready we went together to the great drawing-room of his apartments in which is hung the picture of the naval officer Van Speÿk, showing him dedicating himself to death to save the national flag from the hands of the rebels. On a table in front of this picture were placed the royal insignia, the crown, the sceptre, the orb, the constitution, the Sword of State, and the standard. In the cortège, William was immediately preceded by the Standard of State, followed by the princes as the first called upon to defend him, and for the whole length of the ceremony it [the Standard of State] as well as the Sword of State was held up on the steps of the throne that he twice defended by his valiance. The ceremony lasted three hours in coldness which would have been perceptible if the soul had not been raised above physical sensations by the feeling of this important and august ceremony, the memory of which will be for ever dear to me and which appears to have made a profound impression on all those present. I shall not describe to you, dear Brother, what I experienced on embracing William on the moment of leaving for the church, nor what I felt on entering it and seeing myself *alone* opposite the throne prepared for him, to pronounce there the most solemn of oaths! And in the sight of thousands whose eyes at this moment were fixed on me, I who have never aspired to anything other than my duty and the honour of my husband, I who have only lived with the aim of seeing him respected and loved; if God had not sustained me I should have been prostrated, so moved was I, and after having bowed to the assembly and placed myself on my rostrum to the right of the throne, I already saw William's cortège advancing and he himself beneath the dais carried by two Major-Generals and two Rear-Admirals. General Fuchs [?] whom you saw in Russia, was among them. I am writing to you of these details, thinking they might interest you. Tell yourselves, dear brothers and friends, that I thought of you indeed and prayed for you during the ceremony. Lobanov[1] had arrived just in time to be present, and I was pleased to see there the good and worthy Maltief [?], as re-accredited minister, as well as his wife, a Russian countess. As for myself, I was wearing a coronation costume, the surcoat was of silver cloth bordered with ermine, a mantle of cloth of gold with long sleeves all trimmed with ermine, also, underneath to keep out the cold, there was a heavy gown of silver lamé; I wore my diamonds, the ribbon and order of St Catherine, and a diadem of diamonds and pearls of the 'pavolnik' style. As soon as I was dressed, I sent for my priest and for my chanters to read me the prayers and the *memento mori*, followed by the [special] blessing with the cross and holy water, so that our church should be blessed on that day together with William, otherwise there would be no happiness for me; and immediately afterwards I went to join William for the ceremony. On our return from the church there was a huge dinner for 180 persons in the beautiful hall of the Palace, the States General *en masse* were admitted to it. William wished to have Lobanov at the banquet – the sole foreigner – but because of a confusion he was not there. During

[1] The special Russian envoy for the occasion

the dinner William toasted the States General and the prosperity of the nation; the President of the Upper Chamber toasted William, the newly inaugurated King. After a moment of silence William got up and, turning towards the two presidents and addressing himself to the representatives of the nation, he toasted my health in the most touching way and afterwards embraced me. God alone could grant me a moment like that! It was one of the sweetest of my life, for it was saying to the nation, 'I love you' and 'I respect you'. You all know, my friends, that it is to that that I attach the highest price and you also know what I have passed through. When one has known the year 1830, then one rejoices only in God, but it always seems to me that something of my joys come back through memory of former good times in which everything was shared between us. On the evening of that day we went to see the illuminations which were magnificent. The next day, Sunday, I went to the Chapel of Peter the First to have a Te Deum sung to give thanks for the official ceremony. This was followed by a large dinner for the *corps diplomatique* at the Palace, and in the evening there was a respite which was a blessing as well as a need. On Monday, there was a '*court de felicitations*', we received in the throne room, then dinner, and in the evening a Dutch gala.

In the course of the celebrations there was a ball for 1300 guests in the beautiful hall of the Palace which is truly marvellous in proportions and detail. Lobanov was quite enchanted with it. We came back here on 5 December, the day before our dear William's birthday; we had a reception and lunch at Haarlem, and a solemn entry to receive William here as inaugurated King. It was very touching and I was personally very moved to hear myself greeted by the people by the name 'Mother'. We only arrived home at 4 o'clock in the afternoon. Lobanov dined with us, and in the evening we congratulated William and gave him our presents, as always, on the day before, according to the good Russian custom. We then went to see the illuminations which were so beautiful that they recalled those of Peterhof. It was as though there were [bands] of fire in two avenues in front of our house; the principal buildings, the residences of foreign ministers and those of many local inhabitants, were magnificently lit up. As the day of the celebration was a Sunday, I went to Mass at 9 o'clock and then went to the Dutch church. We gave a great luncheon in the ballroom, where the two beautiful vases stand that you were kind enough to send me this summer, and I pointed them out to Lobanov. The next day there was a great ball in the Palace, in the salon and state apartment, following the wish of King William Frederick himself who wanted his son to make use of it. This setting evoked many memories as the salon had not been used for balls since the year 1830. It was very crowded and lively, although small in comparison with the proportions of the palace at Amsterdam. Since that day we have been resting, which we were in great need of to recover from the fatigue of that brilliant period which will always leave me with a dear and precious memory of the sentiments that were shown us. It seemed that the heavens wished to favour those solemn days by granting us magnificent weather, which set in on the eve of our departure for Amsterdam.

I have been writing this little journal to you for several days, scarcely able to write consecutively because of the frequent interruptions and because of a cold which, very happily, only came over me after all the celebrations, having for the rest admirably borne all the fatigues of that time.

I am writing these lines with the intention that they should be read by the Empress and Michael; it would be useless and tiring to repeat the same things in every letter. I embrace them and thank them tenderly for their letters, to which I shall reply as soon as I am able, having neither the time nor the faculty to write to each through Lobanov; at the most, I shall send on my letters to him at Berlin where he will be stopping for several days.

May God bless the rest of the reign of our William who starts under such happy auspices, and if the feelings that people have for him can increase still further the devotion and confidence, I shall have attained the dearest goal of my existence and of my care. My daily prayer to God is to grant me an affection for him which surmounts the difficulties and problems, so that my duty, based on religious sentiment, makes me triumph over everything that I might feel otherwise. It is only in this way that one should love, without blinding oneself to what might be greatly improved. . .

The choice that you made, dear Brother, of Prince Lobanov gave us great pleasure; he is so *comme-il-faut*, so sensible and so steady that nobody could be more suitable here on this occasion. I wish to thank you exceedingly for it, and I had a lot of satisfaction in talking to him. I told him of the way in which the King of Württemberg spoke about the treaty.[1] Preoccupied as I was in my last letters with the happenings here, I forgot to tell you about it. He said that the conduct of Lord Palmerston on this occasion was an act of the *greatest inconsistency*; and that it was unbelievable that a Whig minister *should separate himself from alliance with France*. He repeated this without stopping in our family conversations and, not content with that, he repeated it at table surrounded by servants who all understand French. I leave you to judge the man after that. . . . Rest assured that he was greatly galled by the rapprochement between Russia and England, and that although he does not like France he is not very fond of Russia either. Keep an eye on him so that he does not play a trick on you all to help to extend his own influence in Germany where he is only seeking to gain terrain and power. His daughter has her head filled with Belgian ideas. . . . Holland is too small and too ugly for her and she finds people there very boring. Her health is in the most pitiable state and she complains a lot about the climate which counts for very little because she herself arrived with a ruined physique. She will need a great deal of care all winter. There, dear friend, is the reverse side of the coin, but I think that you set store by the truth and not by romances which is why I tell you about things as they are. How much I thank you, dear good Brother, for your friendship and your wishes, and I also thank the Empress for her friendly remembrance and everything that she said to me, which I feel and appreciate infinitely. Our good Mikki's letter, which came late, also gave me pleasure and I thank him for it. Ollie wrote me a charming letter and your Sasha also; I shall reply to them

[1] The Treaty of Twenty-four Articles which finally resolved the whole Belgian question. King William accepted the treaty signed on 19 April 1839. Why Palmerston should be accused of acting inconsistently is a trifle unclear. Perhaps by the insertion of Clause VII which recognised Belgian independence and neutrality, thus thwarting for ever the ambitions of Louis-Philippe and the French in the desire to annex the little kingdom. Yet England had always sought to prevent French expansion to the north-east into the Low Countries, and this policy of Palmerston was in keeping with this – *not inconsistent* but rather *consistent*.

all as soon as I can. I am sending the Empress a hat trimmed in the old Dutch fashion. I wear similar ones on great public occasions. It will perhaps have in her eyes the value of novelty or originality, for what can one offer one who has everything that she can possibly desire? I entrust it to her indulgence. I embrace her tenderly as well as your dear children, and I recommend myself, dear excellent Brother, to your friendship and your memory, in short, to all your old feelings. . . .

I am finishing these lines today, 12 December.

Tsar Nicholas I to Queen Anna Pavlovna:

Alexandria nr Peterhof,
7/19 June 1842

Our friend Henry gave me your letter yesterday, dear good Anne, and he did not need its recommendation to be received with open arms. We are sincerely delighted to see him again, he has grown enormously and developed greatly to his advantage. I am very grateful for your consideration in sending him to us for our twenty-fifth anniversary; and I thank you sincerely for your wishes for us on this occasion. God grants that my wife's health is progressing well; without being able to say that it is completely satisfactory, I am pleased to recognise the improvement she has made in comparison with last year. The failure of her health is the only thing that has been missing from our happiness during these twenty-five years. Once the critical time is over the doctors have promised my wife a complete recovery. Henry left this morning to see Michael in town and is coming back here for dinner. We are expecting William of Prussia tomorrow and the King around the 20th. The Duke of Nassau, Archduke Charles and his son, are also to come here shortly so that we do not lack friends for the occasion. I only hope that we shall be able to make their stay agreeable. It is the season of army exercises and manœuvres so that there is continual motion which is somewhat tiring for those taking part. For the rest there is nothing new, which is what I like most. I shall try to give you news of Henry as often as possible, but excuse me in advance if I am not very prompt, I am often short of time to be able to do as I please.

TSAR NICHOLAS I TO QUEEN ANNA PAVLOVNA:

Alexandria nr Peterhof,
7/19 July 1842

. . . The visit of the King[1] of Prussia and the crowd of children of all sorts which fell upon us have taken up my time so much that I have scarcely been able to perform my various duties. This has completely prevented me from keeping myself informed about what concerns our dear Henry, as I would have keenly desired to do; but you will excuse me, I am sure, for having missed doing this considering the complete impossibility of it.

I know that he often writes you and he will probably tell you that his time is spent quite gaily with Anne [?] and the others of his age. It remains for me to add only that, in general, he is pleasing because of his modesty, his politeness, and his bearing. This will not be distressing for you to learn, and you know that we all heartily love him. This morning, at the naval review, he was on board his ship and he is setting sail this evening to cruise near Hagland where I hope to go and meet them the day after tomorrow. The party season is over, luckily, but the weather is very uncertain and unfortunately often turns to rain. Now it is time for the field exercises so that I am scarcely able to be everywhere. My wife tells me to send you many kind regards; she stood up very well under all her wearisome duties and will reply to you at the first opportunity. I am delighted that she can come down to meals again and devote the rest of the summer to work which is so good for her. Marie Alexander is soon to return to Tsarskoe Selo to await her delivery, which should be – as far as we suppose – towards the middle of the next month. May the good Lord bless that solemn moment. Immediately afterwards I must start out to make my usual rounds which this time add up to more than 4 verstes. You see, dear friend, that in spite of my forty-six years I must still be fairly mobile – as long as that lasts!

[1] Frederick William IV and brother-in-law of Tsar Nicholas I.

THE EMPRESS ALEXANDRA TO QUEEN ANNA PAVLOVNA:

Tsarskoe Selo,
18/30 May 1843

A thousand thanks, dear Sister Anne, for your remembrance of 21 April. The day was spent with the usual court duties; a mass diplomatic reception, kissing of hands, parade of the *guardes au chevalier* which I witnessed from a balcony. Since then the temperature has been continually dry and sometimes too fresh because of the north wind, but it has been fine for the last two weeks already and we are fully enjoying Tsarskoe Selo. (25 May) Because it is as hot as July, I feel incapable of writing my letter in a consecutive manner. Spring is well on its way. The lilacs are in bloom – it is the moment I love most in nature. I am expecting my sister Louise with her handsome Fritz in a week from now. It will be a treat for me to have them here. It is a great pleasure to be united with my dear sister and although there is quite a large distance in age between us we enjoy ourselves together like twins. Nicholas has also gone by water to Schlüsselberg. Strange to say he has never seen it, but our son Alexander visited there five or seven years ago. My daughter-in-law is starting to get quite noteworthy with her rotundity which is increasing in a prodigious manner. Good old Countess Lieven used to say to me on these occasions, 'you look like a *Bürgermeister*'. I confess that I am very pleased that I no longer find myself in similar condition.

TSAR NICHOLAS I TO QUEEN ANNA PAVLOVNA:

Tsarskoe Selo,
3/15 October 1843

I have only been back from my long journey for five days, dear good Anne; that is the reason for my long silence; but I have been wanting for a long time to tell you about all the real pleasure I had in finally making the acquaintance of your lovable Sophia, whom I found such as she was depicted to me by Marie and Michael. She delighted me with her charming bearing and by the goodness and spirit shown in her face; I had very few hours to spend with her and I regret it very much; however, they were enough for me to develop for her an affection and a true interest, for she is captivating; may she always be as happy as she seems to be at this moment; her husband loves her a great deal, it seems, and my sister holds her very dear. While I was coming here from Moscow I received your letter, dear Anne, about the birth of Sasha's little one;[1] it is a wonderful happiness for us and for the Empire, may God preserve this dear child for us. . . .

My trip was very long and wearing because of the horrible state of the roads; the bad weather is already well advanced. We stayed for a few days in Moscow where my wife surprised me by arriving without my knowing anything about it.

I was very pleased with everything I saw but am even happier to find myself back at home surrounded by my children and grandchildren who give us so much joy and delight. Michael spent a few days with us. I hope that on his return from London he will let himself be easily persuaded to stay longer; I only have news of his arrival at Windsor, where it appears that the Queen welcomed him very kindly.

Many thanks to William for his thoughts in your letter to my wife; I send you tender greetings and congratulate you both on the birth of your second grandson; it is time for Sophia to do the same.

TSAR NICHOLAS I TO QUEEN ANNA PAVLOVNA:

Alexandria nr Peterhof,
2/14 September 1844

I could only be truly touched, dear good Anne, by the sympathy that you showed with our misfortune.[2] It is not on earth that consolations can come to us after such a blow, but at least the friendship of those to whom one is attached softens what one feels, and I am deeply grateful to you for the friendship that you have shown us. Our grief is lifelong, it is an open wound

[1] The Grand Duke Nicholas Alexandrovich.
[2] The death of the Grand Duchess Alexandra Nicolaievna in July 1844.

we shall carry to the grave; one single thing, one single idea consoles when one can tell oneself that the dear person whom one has lost must be happier where she is than she would have been down here in what we call the height of happiness. In loving one must inure oneself to the idea of the happiness for the person and rejoice in it. This dear Angel was so excellent, so pure, her patience and resignation so exemplary and her end so sublime and edifying that we can hope that it goes well with her up above; she belonged there more than on earth. God has sustained us in these frightful moments and He still sustains us for He sees that the very thought of complaint does not come to us. We abase ourselves before His Divine will saying: *'May Your will be done.'*

THE GRAND DUKE MICHAEL TO QUEEN ANNA PAVLOVNA:

St Petersburg,
5 February 1846

Dear good and excellent Anne,

I could not write you on the very day of your birthday because it fell this year on a Sunday when one is all day topsy-turvey, and yesterday, Monday, was Council day; so it is not until today that I have succeeded in offering you my wishes and congratulations. Thirty-two years ago today, in 1814, the Emperor and I left for the army for the first time, after having all spent your birthday together; when one looks back it is frightening to think how time passes and how many things and happenings one has seen since. This winter is a very harsh one here. For a month now we have continually had between 10 and 20 degrees of frost. May I ask you, dear Anne, to tell Prince and Princess Frederick of the sympathy that I feel for the dreadful misfortune that has just struck them. This must have grieved you also, as well as our excellent William who has such a good kind heart. Embrace him for me and remember me to your children. I embrace you in my mind with heart and soul, and I am for my life your most faithful brother and friend.

TSAR NICHOLAS I TO QUEEN ANNA PAVLOVNA:

St Petersburg,
28 February/12 March 1846

My dear and excellent Anna,

. . . After one of the liveliest of seasons, we have re-entered perfect calm with Lent, which is very agreeable for people who have regular occupations. I spend my life between the duties of military service and my family, a way of life which suits me in all respects for, in my opinion, the only true happiness in in an agreeable home life. The rest is only illusory. After six weeks of hard winter, we are now having a complete thaw. You will certainly have heard of the events at Cracow[1] and all this new revolutionary intrigue in Poland in general. It seems that it is over for the time being but that only proves once more how little all the governments owning part of this country can count on the attitudes that prevail there and how watchful one must always be. What is unfortunate for the country is that every similar blunder naturally rebounds on itself and on its prosperity. Otherwise, dear sister, I have nothing interesting to acquaint you with. Everything here is following its usual course.

TSAR NICHOLAS I TO QUEEN ANNA PAVLOVNA:

Tsarskoe Selo,
26 September/8 October 1846

For nearly a month now I have been holding two of your good letters, dear Anne, but various obstacles have prevented me from thanking you for them earlier. The departure of my daughter Olga[2] especially took up our time, and the emptiness it leaves with us is quite painful. May she be happy in her new homeland! I know that you are at Genoa and so one of your

[1] The Republic of Cracow, which had been occupied by the Holy Alliance in 1836, but which continued to be a centre of subversion in the eyes of the eastern monarchs, was annexed by Austria in 1846. England protested, but very mildly, and the Russians were pleased that it all came off so easily and with no real violence.

[2] She married the Crown Prince of Württemberg in July 1846.

fondest wishes has come true; it was just a year ago that, through the strangest set of circumstances, for once in my life I too was able to see that interesting region. Lombardy is curious, Genoa is certainly very handsome, but I am sorry that you are not going to *Naples* – the only place which surpassed what I imagined of it; it was the opposite for the rest of Italy, which scarcely lived up to my expectations and often did not do so at all, especially Rome. – You almost arrived in Genoa in time for a very sad event; it appears that, thanks be to God, there is a momentary amelioration in the condition of charming Louise and may this continue so. We have another reason for being greatly worried about Michael's eldest daughter, who seems to be strongly afflicted in her chest; our latest news is of the most troubling kind; this would be a frightful disaster, and it reawakens only too much the one which struck us so short a time ago. I am waiting for news from Michael with extreme anxiety. May you finish your trip happily, and I am delighted for your sake that you have your Alexander near you; give him many kind regards from me, and if Henry comes to Genoa, give him, too, my tender affection.

My wife's health is continuing fairly well, and the good from her cure at Palermo is visible. She has continued it here during one of the most extraordinary summers for our climate we have ever had in its beauty and constancy. William has been very near us, and I had hoped for a while that he might have the idea of coming to give us the pleasure of his company; unfortunately that did not take place.

QUEEN ANNA PAVLOVNA TO TSAR NICHOLAS I:

Nice,
13 November 1846

Dear good Brother,

. . . It was very pleasant for me to receive your news and to learn how you and the Empress were after your separation from Ollie, whose departure must have caused so many emotions and left such a large gap. May God sustain you, as her, for the duration, as He has fortified you in the first moments. I am writing these lines to you just prior to leaving Nice, counting on setting out on 15 November to join my husband and return home after a voyage of three months which was entirely successful. I was favoured by the finest weather almost the whole time and I have very agreeable memories of the countries that I stayed in. Genoa and Rome particularly left me with both interesting and noteworthy ones. I enjoyed myself there very much, everything was done to make my stay agreeable, the season was particularly fine, the settings superb, particularly at Genoa and Rome which are so imposing and attractive, both through their artifacts and what one feels. Not having seen Naples, I cannot make a comparison but, surrounded as I was by the most friendly attentions, I confess that I fell in love with Rome and left it with regret. The view of Rome from Mount Pincio is one of the finest that can be imagined, I never tired of it and I used to go there when I wanted to enjoy myself. You have already learnt, dear friend, how well received I was by the Pope[1] and all the attentions that surrounded me on his orders during my stay in Rome. I saw him twice, on my arrival and at my departure, and it would be difficult to combine more pleasant manners and greater amiability. I made the acquaintance of Monsieur de Brotieuv [?] who was very friendly and most obliging, and I was equally pleased to see Russian compatriots in Rome and to be present at the Mass with them twice. The Pope was good enough to name Monsieur Vincente to accompany me on drives and visits to museums, and I often had the pleasure of hearing him speak of you, dear Brother, for he retains a profound memory of you and speaks with gratitude of the kindnesses that you heaped upon him. He is the only agreeable scholar whom I have ever met, and he unites worldly ways with extensive scholarship and brilliant elocution. Thanks to the commentaries which he gave me, the stay in Rome doubled in interest. As for my Alexander, he was on the move from morning till evening; everything interested him and I think he made good use of his stay to instruct himself. I also went to see the studios of modern sculptors and at [Bienaccini's ?] I saw several statues that you had ordered and which seemed to me very well done. Under the auspices of the good General

[1] Pius IX.

[indecipherable] I also visited the studios of Russian painters where I acquired a charming view of the environs of Rome. I received some very fine presents from the Pope, among others a picture in mosaic from the Vatican representing the Herodiad of [Guido ?]. His Holiness extended his munificence to my son and even to my entourage, who are all taking away souvenirs of their stay in Rome. I came here by sea from Civita Vecchia and I was very ill during the crossing. I have been here for more than two weeks and I shall need as much again to return to The Hague, where I hope to be in any case around the King's birthday. I must go through France as the other routes are impracticable. I have heard nothing for a long time of our poor Michael for whom I feel inexpressibly sorry; may God grant that there is still a chance of recovery for his poor daughter, Marie! It would be too terrible to lose two in less than two years.

The climate at Nice, although good, seems to me somewhat inconvenient in its sudden transitions from sun to shade in which you feel a clammy cold [?], but the air is pure, the Mediterranean the finest sapphire blue, and the orange-trees in flower. I shall say good-bye to them tomorrow. I am finishing these lines on the morning of 14 November and I wish to embrace you in my thoughts, dear good Brother, as well as the Empress.

Queen Anna Pavlovna to Tsar Nicholas I:

The Hague,
30 March 1848

Dear good Brother,

It is only today that I feel strong enough to write a few lines telling you of the terrible misfortune which has struck us. Our Sasha is dead![1] and we have survived this blow! God has sustained us and will grant us help in bearing a loss as immense as it is irreparable. His decrees are inscrutable, we resign ourselves to feeling the total extent of our misfortune! He is at

[1] Prince Alexander died on 20 February 1848; news of his death only reached The Hague on 17 March 1848.

peace but we are without him in this world in which he was the friend of all, and for me the most loving son and the most faithful friend! God grants us the consolation of seeing the King well, full of courage and activity in these difficult circumstances, and the country peaceful, united around the throne to maintain order and to provide by its strong nationalism a bulwark against the spirit of subversion and the attempts at disturbance.

As for me, dear friends, I seek all my strength in bed, praying to God to help me carry my cross and to fulfil the rest of my task down here in a manner pleasing to Him. Pray for us as we pray for you; may God preserve you from all misfortune in these terrible times! May God watch over Russia.

QUEEN ANNA PAVLOVNA TO TSAR NICHOLAS I:

The Hague,
7 April 1848

Dear good Brother,

I should believe myself failing in a duty of friendship if I should let slip a safe occasion to write to you in the sad circumstances in which we all are because of the deplorable events[1] that must afflict your heart, and which would risk compromising everything were it not for the calm and energetic firmness with which you have already opposed the devastating torrent. Your noble and touching manifesto has just reached us. May God come to your aid, dear friend! and bless you and Russia! I am asking Monsieur Mehran [?] to bear these lines to you. I shall hand them to him myself so that he can tell you that he has seen me and how he found me at this terrible time in which we are expecting, from one day to the next, the cherished remains of our dearly beloved Alexander. All that I can say is that I live, I live in God and for those to whom I have obligations, but it is only through God that I live! feeling each day my own weak-

[1] The revolution which broke out all over Europe following the overthrow of Louis-Philippe on 24 February 1848. The evening that the news was received in Russia, Tsar Nicholas stated to his court, 'Gentlemen, saddle your horses: the Republic is proclaimed in France!'

ness and His power which sustains me and helps me. Thank God, William is well; he spent a day in Amsterdam, from which he came back in good health, extremely pleased with the good spirit prevalent there in all classes. The great merchants and well-to-do people bear the trials of the moment with resignation, courage and hope in God. The *bourgeoisie* is in a perfectly good mood and lends a strong hand to the communal guard, which in its turn gets on marvellously with the troops, in maintaining order and peace which has not been troubled again since the authorities and the police jointly took effective measures to put down an attempted riot two weeks ago by some workmen; it had been stirred up by a communist club of German workers that was discovered and the men arrested. You see that they spread their ramifications everywhere, using everywhere the same means. Apart from that, our country at present offers no sign of difficulty because of the peace that reigns here; in the towns as in the country, energetic measures are taken to keep order, and it is fine to see this unanimity in their ranging themselves around the constitutional throne of their sovereign to defend the rightful order against the spirit of subversion. The same sentiments that I saw appearing in 1830 are revived at the present time. We too *are putting our hope in God.* May He inspire us and guarantee us freedom from the contagion of the subversive doctrines of any social order in granting us the just liberties which a country organised according to the law can enjoy. William has carefully picked his moment for the measures[1] on which he has decided and they, having the general support of the country, have satisfied people, calmed agitation and in a large part motivated the tranquillity of which the nation offers such a remarkable example at the moment. It seems to me, dear friend, that I owe you these details at a time in which you are afflicted by so many distressing events. What can one think of this Germany, *this Prussia,* making almost common cause with the Poles? There is something *impious* in this thought when one remembers 1813 and 1814! But God does not permit everything that man plots in his wickedness. Perhaps we shall

[1] An indication, perhaps, that King William II intended some alteration in his powers as king. Discussions on the matter had been going on for some time before the events in Paris; therefore, it cannot really be said that King William II made 'concessions' in a revolutionary situation.

see these plans thwarted by the spirit of dissension. I recognise no nationality in united Germany other than this spirit of folly that their dreams and their philosophical systems have brought on. Always jealous of countries, however small, who prefer a strong nationality, they seek to create one founded on all sorts of iniquities. Dear friend, retain for me your friendship and remembrance. Pray for us as we pray for you! and remember me to the Empress, to Michael, and to the Grand Duke your heir, as to all the family.

QUEEN ANNA PAVLOVNA TO TSAR NICHOLAS I:

The Hague,
14 December 1848

Dear good Brother,

. . . I am writing these lines to you to make use of a sure occasion – that of young Schultz's return prior to the 6th – which will prove to you, dear friend, how my thoughts are near you – from afar as close at hand. Perhaps you will allow this young man to hand you this letter himself, it would be a great kindness; I venture to say that he does honour to the education that he has received in the establishment founded by our nephew, Peter of Oldenburg.[1] Not having written to you since Costy's marriage,[2] I cannot take up my pen again without expressing to you my congratulations on the subject of this family event, as well as my wishes for the happiness of the young household who announced to me earlier in very friendly letters that the marriage had taken place. I replied to them immediately, but I thought to put off expressing congratulations, of which you could not be in any doubt, until my next missive to you. I was still suffering a great deal at that time with rheumatism in the right wrist which made, and still makes, writing very difficult for me, although it has been getting better recently. I cannot praise enough, as you have already heard from Monsieur de Maltik, the stay that I made in Gueldere this summer and the good it did my health, and the truly touching sentiments that

[1] The son of the Grand Duchess Catherine Pavlovna by her first marriage to Duke George of Oldenburg.

[2] To the Grand Duchess Alexandra of Saxe-Altenburg.

I received there. I saw the Imperial Russian Flag flying there and that of the Navy also, and on several occasions I heard your national anthem played. At this time, and so close to the frontiers of Germany, one cannot appreciate these feelings enough. I am glad to tell you so, dear friend, in the midst of so many things which must have pained your heart, and it is the bouquet that I am sending you for your celebration. Accept it with friendship, enjoy the high opinion that people have for you in this country, and think of my gentle satisfaction in being a witness of it. Everything continues to be peaceful here and the King receives the fruits of his troubles and his indefatigable cares. Henry is always the faithful child who surrounds us with affection and consolation. Our news of Sophie has been, thank God, good until now. I congratulate you on the presence of Olga whom you have the happiness of having near you.

Queen Anna Pavlovna to Tsar Nicholas I:

The Hague,
6 February 1849

Dear good Brother,

. . . You will easily understand that these days have been for me mixed with sad feelings, although softened by the affection and kind gestures of William and the friendship of the family, as indeed has been shown me from all quarters in everything on this occasion. A few days afterwards, the news of Sophie's safe delivery[1] came to gladden us and to cause a ray of happiness and consolation to shine on us. It was on the very day after my birthday that she presented us with a little girl, well received by everybody. We bless God for it and all that I wish is that this little girl should be for her parents what her mother is for us, the best and most loving of daughters. The news since then has continued to be most satisfactory and we know she is up already. For the first ten days my sister had the goodness to write to us regularly to reassure us, and it is an attention for which we are most grateful.

The season is very mild already, we have had up to 9 degrees

[1] The birth of her daughter Marie Alexandrine.

Réaumur; snowdrops, honeysuckle and green rosebushes. Everywhere in the country they are planting and working, to the great advantage of the poor who are very numerous. I hope that by now the cholera will have stopped with you where it appears to have caused such great havoc. I cannot thank you enough, dear Brother, for the gracious reception which you accorded young Schultz, the bearer of my letter. He wrote to his father in a flood of gratitude which made his father very happy and has given me great pleasure because of the interest which I bear this deserving young man and his family.

Our eldest son is in England where he has been very well received. May God grant that this journey should be advantageous to him in all respects! Now we expect to face the most harrowing reminder of the loss of our dearly beloved and unforgettable, *worthy* Alexander, whom we miss constantly, and the loss is immense to the family and the country which respected and loved him and had a high opinion of his capabilities. The ways of God are inscrutable and it is only in the most complete resignation that one can find some consolation.

TSAR NICHOLAS I TO PRINCE HENRY OF THE NETHERLANDS:

St Petersburg,
24 March 1849

It was with a broken heart, dear Henry, that I received your letter and the few lines from Mama to confirm officially the news we had received a few days before.[1] The loss for all of us is immense, for us who loved him so tenderly, and for you in particular, my dear Henry, who held so dear the most tender of fathers! But such serious duties remain to you that they must turn your rightful grief towards situations worthy of your noble heart; you have a mother to care for who no longer has anyone but *you alone*; you have your King your brother to serve with heart and soul, and in his person you must serve your country at a time of extreme difficulty. Knowing you, dear Henry, I have no doubt that you will always travel the road of honour and duty.

[1] King William II of the Netherlands had died at Tilburg on 17 March 1849. His wife and his son Henry were present and beside him at his deathbed.

That will certainly be your vocation which you will know how to fulfil as much by duty as by affection; and may God second you in it. It is with unchanging attachment and sincere friendship that I shall always be your sincerely affectionate uncle and friend.

Count Stroganov must be with you; I had entrusted him with a letter for Mama but before yours arrived; I do not want to renew her grief by writing her again.

QUEEN ANNA PAVLOVNA TO TSAR NICHOLAS I:

Tilburg,
31 March 1849

Dear good Brother,

I am still writing to you from here the lines that Arriens will give you; I wished to spend near the cherished remains of our dear William all the time he still had on earth, to see them every day and pray for him by his coffin. It is the only place for me, to be near what remains to us of him as long as he is still on earth. In a few days I shall accompany his remains to Rotterdam, and when the sad funeral ceremony is finished, I shall go to the church at Delft where I shall go down into the vault where he will have been placed, to see his coffin in the spot which he chose himself beside our Alexander, and bless them both and pray there for these two dear beings whom death has reunited, and after having carried out this sacred duty and done for my William everything that I could for him and his dearly loved remains, I shall continue my sad journey to The Hague and shall go and live in the house of my late Alexander, which has become my property. May God have the goodness to sustain me in carrying out these sad duties during these two cruel days, as He has graciously sustained me until now. God grants me a deep feeling of resignation which softens the bitterness of my just grief. I tell myself unceasingly that *Thy Will be Done*, even though I do not understand my future. My faith in God sustains me and tells me that He does not abandon those whose hope is in Him! Divine bounty has also already shown itself towards me in the affectionate sentiments and tender behaviour of my son William, who has shown himself the best of sons. My Henry gives me very dear consolation, and Heaven has sent us in a daughter, my Sophie,[1] an angel of consolation. We mingle our tears and our thoughts and thank God for having reunited the fragments of our family at this cruel moment. William has begun his reign well, he is in the place for which Heaven destined him and he does everything to honour the memory of his father. His behaviour foils the plots to blacken his character which appear, most regrettably, to have been planned and to which, unfortunately, his wife is not a stranger. The bearer of these lines, the worthy and honest Arriens, will be able to give you some information on this subject which it is necessary for you to know. It seems that she had entertained only too frequently, ideas of a guardianship of the children and even of regency, and that to attain them she had to blacken the reputation and character of her husband. God did not allow her plots to succeed, and certainly the journey to England saved William from ruin and the country from the greatest calamity that could have overtaken it. The nation has grouped itself around its lawful sovereign and shows itself very respectable in the midst of the general grief which has placed the entire country in mourning. I have reason to be deeply touched by the sentiments of devotion and interest that have been shown to me from all sides and which offer me a gentle consolation in my irreparable grief. But now sad and harrowing details are going to follow, those of dividing the estate between my children. We already know enough to be certain of the unfavourable outcome ahead. Perhaps you will allow me, in this moment of urgency for my two youngest children, to call on the same generosity of which you gave so many proofs to their father, for they will lose almost everything in this initial period when what they received annually comes to an end, before the division of property has taken place, and very serious consequences are beginning to make themselves felt. This is why I venture to call openly on your affection to come to their aid for the time being. The present time is very grave for them all as regards their fortunes. I am reduced to my own means, and they suffice for me, but that is all, and I wish to have sufficient to live modestly and decently

[1] Note, *not* her daughter-in-law, Sophie of Württemberg, the wife of Anna Pavlovna's eldest son.

while waiting for the state to give me what has been fixed by law. But, having of necessity to be sufficient unto myself with all that that entails, I can no longer avail myself of my resources in favour of my younger children as I should be so happy to be able to do. Please, dear Brother and friend, dismiss any idea of complaint on my part, I accept my fate, I find what is taking place at the moment completely natural, but my heart suffers to see my poor children reduced to having almost nothing on which to exist, without being able to help them as I should like! My only thought is to act honourably and to cover up anything distressing as far as I am able. It is why I turn to you who love the honour of your family.

Dear friend, do not blame me but retain for me your old friendship, and please have compassion on the situation of my younger children. My wishes and my sentiments for you are invariable. May Heaven watch over you. But your heart will be profoundly affected by our loss which is as terrible as it is immense. You also have lost a tried friend. Pray for me, for us. I recommend my son William to you, love him and help him with your counsel. Retain for me your affection and believe in the unchanging devotion of your faithful and old friend and sister.

A thousand friendly wishes from me to the Empress and to all the family.

QUEEN ANNA PAVLOVNA TO TSAR NICHOLAS I:

Boschlust nr The Hague,
20 April 1849

Dear and excellent Brother,

I was deeply touched by your excellent letter of 30 March that you had asked Count Alexander Stroganov to give to me. Your regrets for our dear much-loved William and everything that you said about him moved me greatly. I was expecting it but I wept on reading them, written by your own hand with an overflowing heart. He loved you so much and had given so many proofs of devotion to our family in all past and present circumstances that I was sure of your grief and your regrets. I see how much this terrible news has struck you. As for me, after having written to you twice already, I shall not even try to describe what I feel nor to give details of the event, that is beyond me! I only see that we have the same way of feeling and thinking, and that brought up together, having drawn from the same source our principles of action, we feel and act the same when near or far, and I believe that, seeking our strength in God, it will never be otherwise. I have never looked for any strength except in God, and my motto has always been 'God and my courage'. He has sustained me and deigned to fortify my courage, perhaps I might even say inspired me, for I have done and had already done everything that you advise me to do. I see things entirely as you do and I shall try to do my best in this direction with tact and discernment, for to show too clearly that the young sovereign, my son, needs my advice could alarm him and turn him away from me as from an unwelcome guide. His heart is very affectionate towards me as soon as he is himself and left to the impulse of his good and generous heart, but he has beside him a corrosive and pernicious element in the haughty and sly character of his wife, his greatest scourge on this earth. Unfortunately, I have already been exposed to her bad ways since the death of our William, and to describe her in a word, since she became Queen she no longer kisses my hand and no longer comes to meet me when I visit her. She received me with the most insulting arrogance on the first visit that I made her, and that was on the day after the burial. What will you say when you know that with regard to a court arrangement, in which I had even taken the initiative by voluntarily sharing my palace ladies with her, that is to say, the cream of society, she sent me a most imperious letter which was handed to me at 11 o'clock at night when I had already retired and had just prepared for communion and confession in order to fulfil this sacred act the next morning, for the first time since my misfortune. What will your good and noble heart say to all that? What will you say when you know that after a discussion between Sophie and William about this minor subject, my son sent the Grand Chamberlain with a message for me which was nothing else than to tell me that between his wife and myself his position could become too difficult? When I learned from my Grand Master that a message was destined for me from my son, I replied at once that I should never admit any intermediary between my son and myself and that I expected to speak directly to the King. I saw my son again, I explained my position to him in the most friendly way in the world; I found him affectionate towards me, and the proposed message – which concealed without any doubt the spiteful designs of his wife – was foiled as completely as I could wish. I sent word by Baron de Fagel, my Grand Master, to Grand Chamberlain Van Doorn that, never having been accustomed to admit third parties in my family relationships, I had absolutely no intention of admitting any either now or in the future, but as an individual I should continue to see him with pleasure. In this way I believe I have thwarted a wicked trick which had been considered a clever ruse to importune me and probably to get rid of me. I do not know, however, whether I shall be able to stay for any length of time beside the inventive wickedness of Queen Sophie, with her character so unworthy of wearing a crown, and the weakness of character of my son who lets himself be imposed on by her. She would need to be kept on a tight rein and be overruled so that she realised that she cannot do as she pleases with impunity. As to my son's public actions, everything leads me to think that people are happy with his behaviour and, as no one hoped for anything from him, they are favourably surprised by everything that he has done thus far. What I feel is to his credit is the way he honours the memory of his father in all things and on all occasions. I hear from all sides that people are satisfied with him. May God grant that this continues, and I am doing everything that depends on me to show the loving interest that I have for him and how I wish to see his reign prosperous and happy. It is not I who will fail him but beware of the character of his wife. If I could see one of you, one word of conversation would explain to you on what my fears are based. Some very distressing things have happened, and when good news of William came from England she always appeared vexed by it. Will that show you how much she loves her husband and what one can expect of her?

As for my future existence, I am in God's hands, remembering only these years spent with my William, occupied with him and for him. I accept with gratitude the consolations that Divine Providence grants me in His mercy, the affection of my son Henry, that of my daughter whose presence at the moment is a true blessing for my heart. But the emptiness of the future will be terrible. I am established in Alexander's old house which has become my property, and I expect to stay here for the first little while as I prefer the country. Dear friend, as for the souvenir that you asked for, the ring, it is buried with the souvenirs to which he was attached, I cannot restore it to you. He always wore it on a ribbon around his neck with many souvenirs from Emperor Alexander. I have had them given back. *He* had recommended that, if he should die suddenly, one should not forget to put on him his military greatcoat, his little cap and his Cross of Saint George, which cannot be given back to you either.

Dear friend, how I loved to see him like that, with an expression of profound serenity on his features. Dear friend, how peacefully our good William slept. I liked so much to join him and to pray near his remains. I followed him until the last possible minute and I even went down into the vault, where I saw his coffin in its last resting-place beside that of my Sasha. Permit me, dear friend, to rest beside them also; tell me that you will not oppose it, that our rites are not against it. I set such store by it. If you would like some other souvenir of our dear William, indicate it, I beg you, so that I can send it to you, or perhaps I may choose something to send to you when it is possible to do so.

21 April

I am continuing these lines today, the anniversary of the burial of our Sasha, a terrible day which moves me deeply. Our weather has been so bad recently, it has done nothing but snow here, and there is a foot of snow everywhere; everything is white as it rarely is in winter. It is very sad, and Count Stroganov will take away a dreadful idea of our climate. I cannot praise him enough, he has shown me such affectionate interest that I cannot thank you enough, dear friend and brother, for having sent him to us. He will be able to tell you how he found my establishment, how my children behave towards me; he has been a witness of their love and attention for me. It will surely give you pleasure to know that I have a very good entourage, thanks again to the offices of our dear and well-beloved William. I have at the head of my house Baron de Fagel, a man of noble and distinguished character who was Chamberlain to us for ten years and to whom my husband had this winter granted the rank of Grand Master, leaving him to serve me, and two Chamberlains, both of them worthy men. At my request, my good Madame Nagel, whom you knew, has just been named Grand Mistress to me by my son. I shall live tranquilly and modestly, availing myself with gratitude and moderation of the good feeling that has been shown me from all sides. I am about to remake my will completely, dear friend, so the old one which is in your hands has now no value and please destroy it. But in the one I am about to engage on I still look to you to carry out the duties of executor and beg you to be so friendly as not to refuse this last proof of affection. Interrupted so much as it is, I have had a visit from Count Stroganov and we have talked about my son William and about many things here. He will probably be able to tell you what would take too long to mention in a letter. There is one thing, however, that I think too important not to mention to you. It is, I am afraid, that William does not sufficiently consider things as a whole and comprehend the gravity of his position, and he lets himself be absorbed too exclusively by his predilection for military matters down to the most minute details concerning them. As this country is not and can never be a military monarchy, and as civil institutions form the basis of it, it seems to me imprudent to act in a way contrary to the spirit of the country and its institituons. If you were good enough to say a word to him you would probably accomplish more in this respect than anyone because of the high opinion he has of you and the fondness he bears for you. It is also very much to be regretted that William has so little notion of restraining his temper. I have earnestly begged him not to act in his first moment of irritation. I also deplore that he should have received a deputation from Luxembourg so badly. This country showed an exemplary fidelity and devotion to its late King, and its delegates came bearing the same sentiments to his son, in whom, unfortunately, they did not find the same attitude towards them as in his father. It is much too unreasonable of William not to accept with goodwill a state of affairs that his father had allowed and that he had, moreover, to recognise by taking the oath of the Constitution, which he did. It is very distressing and may God grant that the consequences of his behaviour will not be regretted. However small Luxembourg may be, its position is important, and troubles in this country could bring about very grave results.

My letter has become very long, dear friend, I am only finishing it today, 22/10, the day on which Count Stroganov is getting ready to leave us. I shall regret his going and I thank you for having sent us someone of such a noble and loyal character, who inspires confidence and deserves it in all respects. Please, dear friend, communicate this letter to Michael and to your heir, the Grand Duke, whom I embrace and thank for his good letter without being able to reply on this occasion. A thousand affectionate regards from me to all the family.

QUEEN ANNA PAVLOVNA TO TSAR NICHOLAS I:

Biljoen en Gueldre,
15 September 1849

Dear good Brother,

. . . Another cruel loss this year! Our Mikki[1] also lost to us, it is too dreadful! Since I heard of his illness I have been in mortal terror which has been realised only too well in the event. I understand completely everything that you say, dear good Brother, that one cannot always resign oneself, and that one only feels the total extent of the bereavement. Who knows it better than I, who am mourning a son such as my Sasha, a husband such as our William! And now a brother such as Michael! His ring is on my finger and will never leave it again. Thank you, a thousand times thank you for this dear souvenir from you, I know it is to you that I owe it. What tears I spilt when I received it. You have both been faithful to the motto on the ring. May God sustain you, dear Brother and friend, in this cruel misfortune, in the moments that still await you, and later one must accept life itself without the brother, the friend of all time. It is a whole past which is ending with him, with so many intimate memories which no longer have either a witness or a confidant. One falls back on oneself! But in giving one's soul to God, in asking Him for His help when our strength is at

[1] He had had a stroke early in the summer.

an end, one feels upheld, one carries on, and the hope of rejoining them sustains one. But, dear friend, you have such dear bonds around you, your angel of a wife, your numerous and excellent children, a whole country which loves you and which venerates you as a father. Michael also was a witness of the glory of your arms. But also what a blow in the middle of such grand and pure glory. Everything reminds us of the fragility of this world, even the most substantial and most desirable things it offers. The blessings of Heaven have rested on you in all that, dear good Brother. May it sustain you and keep you for our affection. Henry, who was beside me when I received your dear letter, was most grateful for your remembrance, and asks me to send his loving respects to you. You will hear, I think, of everything that is happening here. I have no thought of imposing on you at such a moment but I have a heartfelt desire to tell you what care, affectionate attention and regard I have been surrounded with in this last sad trial. Without much circumspection I was told of the illness of our dear Michael and the cruel catastrophe. I have asked the good M [?] to give you the details but I cannot pass over in silence the name of Baron de Fagel, whose devotion never fails, and that of my good Madame de Nagel who ran to my side as soon as she learnt of our misfortune. In absence of my children they have given proof of the most touching devotion.

QUEEN ANNA PAVLOVNA TO TSAR NICHOLAS I:

Biljoen en Gueldre,
1 October 1849

Dear good Brother,

You will understand, dear and excellent friend, that it needed motives of extreme urgency to interrupt our shared grief by speaking to you of material interests. But, dear friend, I thought that as the honour of the family is at stake and the memory of our dear William, whom you loved so much, I should address myself to your heart and call on your affection. You are not ignorant, dear Brother, of the condition of our William's estate.

The whole work of the commission appointed to see to this affair and use the time for deliberation, was spent in gathering facts and totalling up the estate and the available assets and in establishing the amount of debt. This amounts to a total of *four and a half million florins!* It has been found necessary to sell all the landed property, estates and houses in this country, and our eyes turn towards you, dear Brother and friend, to ask you in this cruel need to consent to acquire William's gallery of pictures that you set such store on owning and which is already mortagaged to you. And if you should decide not to keep it, to please give orders to life the mortgage so that the heirs, my children – for I am not one of the interested parties – may avail themselves of its value by selling it. I may well say that their fate is in your hands; by taking it you will save my children! You will save the honour of the family! Time is pressing and the period of deliberation, which has already been prolonged, expires on 17 November next, that is, then, in almost six weeks. I am sending you a letter that Baron Van Doorn has just addressed to my secretary Schultz, which will show you the importance that one of the principal members of the commission of succession attaches to seeing you make this acquisition. Baron Van Doorn is a man of merit and probity. He was Vice-President of the Council of State and he is now Grand Chamberlain. I give this information on him in order to show you that it is the opinion of a man of weight. I would also like to inform you, dear Brother and friend, that, seeing how urgent the affairs of succession are, I believed it my duty to do what depended on me to come to the aid of the heirs and to give a last mark of devotion to the memory of him for whom I lived, by acquiring the estate of Soestdijk – given by the nation to our William on the occasion of the Battle of Waterloo – so that this gift of national gratitude would not run the risk of falling into the hands of heaven knows whom. As the sum which I have to draw on Lombard for from my capital is considerable, I did not want you to learn of it from anyone other than myself and to explain to you the motives that your heart will approve without any doubt. There are material sacrifices that must be made for the honour of one's loved ones and there is not a moment to lose, in these compelling circumstances, if I wish to assist my children in helping to save from the shipwreck one of the finest and noblest portions of their inheritance. That is the present state of affairs, dear friend. I am sending you a copy of the letter that Monsieur Schultz addressed to the House of Hope and Company, in order to give you a true idea of the situation with regard to acquiring Soestdijk and at the same time of the urgency of affairs.

QUEEN ANNA PAVLOVNA TO TSAR NICHOLAS I:

Biljoen en Gueldre,
8 November 1849

Dear excellent Brother,

Be forever blessed and tenderly thanked with a feeling of gratitude that words are too weak to describe for having contributed to saving orphans and consoling a widow and a sister. It is enough to tell you that I received this very morning your precious and important letter from Gatchina of 17 October, containing the decision you had taken to accept in the place of the sum that you had advanced to William his gallery of Old Masters. I shall take care to communicate your letter to Fritz whom I shall have occasion to see here tomorrow; and as to my children, at least the two for whom I can answer, Henry and Sophie, I think I can assure you in advance of the profound gratitude that they will experience for the outstanding service you are doing the honour of their name. Dear friend, I repeat it, be a thousand times blessed in everything that is dear to you for coming so affectionately and generously to our help, in letting me know just in time your decision so that I can communicate it to whom it concerns before the date when the time set for deliberating the affairs of the succession will expire. How happy I am that you approve my decision to obtain Soestdijk. Your opinion in this respect is like a moral support in upholding my courage. You have in every respect given such great consolation by the contents of your letter that I cannot repeat to you enough the good that you do my soul, and it is with this pleasant impression that I finish these lines, to take up my pen again as soon as I see my children.

TSAR NICHOLAS I TO QUEEN ANNA PAVLOVNA:

St Petersburg,
23 December 1850/4 January 1851

Thousands of thanks, dear good Anne, for having remembered me on the day of my celebration and for all your good wishes for me. It is indeed pleasant for me to be assured that, in spite of our separation, you retain a happy memory of me and give me proof of it on all occasions. I assure you definitely of the same sentiments for you despite my lack of promptness in replying to you; it is scarcely possible for me with my kind of worry, which leaves me little leisure. That is also the reason why I was not able to thank you sooner for your good letter that Fritz sent me from you, from Warsaw. You know everything that has happened there. Since my efforts have not been lacking, may at least the result of the Dresden conferences[1] put an end to this time of confusion of all kinds and restore a little peace. Marie told me in her letters, with much pleasure, of the good times that she spent near you and of the restfulness of your stay. I would wish you to enjoy some [peace] at The Hague, too, where you say you wish to go. As for us we are also leading a very peaceful type of life. It is the only one which suits my wife's health and our age. The theatre is our only pastime. However, Cathy's approaching marriage is going to take us out of this uniformity for a short while but I do not know the date precisely. As to novelty, we have two things which make one more fine amusement; the major bridge over the River Neva has been opened to the public and is producing a very good effect, but it is above all the new Hermitage[2] that I think you would like, given your taste which is so artistic. It is really a most beautiful thing and makes the treasure of our museums of even greater value. The old Hermitage was almost in ruins

[1] A series of meetings following the negotiations between Prussia and Austria at Olmütz. The Dresden Conferences were to consider the constitution of Germany with representatives from all of the states present. The meetings lasted from December 1850 through March 1851, with no real decision being made, and the old Germanic Confederation was re-formed as it had been prior to the revolutions in 1848. This was a great victory for Austria.

[2] Designed by the Bavarian architect, von Klenze; begun in 1840, it was part of the reconstruction of the Winter Palace following the fire.

and is going to be fully restored while retaining its primitive character, for we have more than 1500 pictures for which there is no space; we shall only be poor in statues. A thousand greetings to Fritz and Henry. Goodbye, dear good Anne. Retain for me your friendship and believe in the older version of your old friend and brother.

TSAR NICHOLAS I TO QUEEN ANNA PAVLOVNA:

St Petersburg,
7/19 January 1851

. . . We are on the eve of celebrating the wedding of our niece Catherine[1] and everything leads one to hope that her choice has fallen on someone perfectly worthy of her. They seem to suit each other perfectly. We have had a completely mild, uniform and good winter for the first time in thirty-two years. The ceremony of the blessing of the waters was able to take place with all the pomp formerly used, which gave great pleasure to the onlookers. As for me, I found I was the tenth in the ranks of thirty to forty men who figured at the last review – a strange impression. May God keep you, dear Anne.

My wife sends you a thousand regards. She has been suffering with influenza which has taken hold here, and she is still not going out.

TSAR NICHOLAS I TO QUEEN ANNA PAVLOVNA:

Alexandria nr Peterhof,
6/18 July 1851

A thousand thousand thanks, dear good Anne, for your good letter and your wishes on the occasion of my birthday. I accept them with great joy for I like to believe in our old friendship. Sophie and Charles have been with us for some days and I have had sweet enjoyment in embracing dear Sophie in our home. I found her gentle, witty, lovable and full of good sense. In a

[1] The daughter of the Grand Duke Michael. She was the only one of the latter's five daughters to marry; of the other four, two died in infancy and two in their early youth.

word, remarkably developed since I last saw her. I read her the part of your letter that concerned her and this pleased her. This morning I took them into town by water in order to give Sophie a first impression of Petersburg from its most favourable side. The weather was superb and the town shining with beauty. They are going to stay two days in town to see what interests them and then will return here. Our summer is very beautiful and we are fully enjoying our delightful stay. Peterhof continues to grow more beautiful as well as the whole coast. Strelna has been renovated and Cathy's household is already established there. For the rest, everything is following its normal course and I spend my time divided between my diverse duties with a few moments given to rest here. Nothing new to tell you. My wife embraces you, and I do as much from the fullness of my heart.

THE EMPRESS ALEXANDRA TO QUEEN ANNA PAVLOVNA:

St Petersburg,
7/19 January 1853

. . . Nicholas was very ill with gout in the foot and I was in bed for several days and ill for a long time. Nicholas has been improving in the last two days. However, his voice is so weak that one can see in it certain signs that he has escaped a grave illness from which Mandt brought him out triumphantly. Violent sweatings were a salutary crisis but they exhausted him, and with that, all this agreeable news from Paris and London – this *goodwill* on all sides. You are so good, so open, and so true in these difficult times. It makes us very happy, I assure you, dear Anne.

THE EMPRESS ALEXANDRA TO QUEEN ANNA PAVLOVNA:

Gatchina,
4/16 May 1853

Dear Sister,

I received your good letter and as a first reply I have hastened to send you the ribbon of the order of St Catherine that you asked for. I hope that it will have reached Weimar in time. Now I thank you very much, dear Anne, for your remembrance and for all the kind friendly things you say on the occasion of my celebration. I think a great deal of you and my good Henry; Cathy and I make very warm wishes for his happiness.[1] I embrace him tenderly as well as his wife. We have been at Gatchina for several days but we are scarcely enjoying the country. After having had fine weather for nearly two weeks it is now cold again. May you have better luck than us where you are. Not being able to work, we are keeping to our winter habits and we have gathered around us a little society. The young amuse themselves, as in Mama's day, in the same arsenal which you, dear Anne, will certainly remember. The accommodation in which we are living since the reconstruction is comfortable, elegant and tasteful. Let me embrace you while saying good-bye. Think sometimes of your Alexandra.

TSAR NICHOLAS I TO QUEEN ANNA PAVLOVNA:

Tsarskoe Selo,
20 May/1 June 1853

Welcome, dear good Anne! You will be received by us all with real joy and particularly by me, your old friend and comrade. Everything will be ready to receive you and to this effect I am sending Baron Budgberg, my general aide-de-camp, to receive you at the frontier of the kingdom to take your orders and accompany you here; but hurry, I beg you, to let the marshal know by telegraph – 1. When you wish to be met at the frontier, 2. Who is accompanying you, 3. How you wish to be received, with or without ceremony, 4. How long you wish to stay in Warsaw, and 5. Whether you accept for the journey the usual accoutrements which normally follow my wife. I beg you to inform me of all that as soon as possible by return courier. You will also tell me what reception you would like here. Whether you would accept a great court following, ladies and maids of honour, or whether you do not want that. With all of this settled, everything is under control.

[1] He was married 19 May 1853. His wife was Princess Amalia of Saxe-Weimar.

Now I must warn you that the cholera has been increasing for some time so that yesterday the figure reached 57 new cases for the day and past that number dead. On the 15/27 June manœuvres for entering camp begin and they last until 18/30 July or 19 July/1 August. After that I have about fifteen days with more freedom and on 22 July/3 August our exercises begin and they last until 10/22 August. During this period I must go to camp or follow manœuvres from the surrounding neighbourhood, so that I have little time at my disposal. This year two corps – that is the guard and the grenadiers – are together. My care is doubled, for that makes nearly 100,000 men. Of course all my free time will be divided between you and Marie, who also wishes to come here, as you probably know, and I warn you in advance so that you are informed in time.

Our unhappy quarrel with the Turks has had such a deplorable issue – thanks to the infamies of Stratford Canning – that war is imminent. I still do not know what the English are preparing for us. All this takes an infinite amount of my time, so be indulgent towards me and above all towards my wife whose health requires conditions of existence which she cannot escape.

Sasha's wife is in her sixth month of pregnancy and cannot be of use as a hostess as she has to take care of herself, so I am most afraid that we shall not be able to do much for you here. The Grand Duke of Oldenburg and his wife's sister will be here also, so that Sanny [?] will be busy with that. My boys are all doing their military service so there is only me who can do you the honours. I beg you to be satisfied with that, and I recommend myself to all your indulgences and hope that you will accept at least the wish and the desire that I cherish to make your stay as tolerable as possible, and I shall be happy to let you see what there is new here. I forgot to say that you would probably find Louise and the Fritzes already arrived here. I honestly beg you to take care of your stomach when getting near here for this wretched cholera attacks new arrivals who are the least bit imprudent. One must avoid indigestion and keep one's feet and stomach warm. The [?] that you ask for are leaving any day now but I do not know who is accompanying you and taking the carriages back to Holland. If they are not enough, some can easily be found at Warsaw. Anne, I have very little time to write. I beg you to embrace Marie and to beg her earnestly to inform me as soon as possible of the route she is taking; of fixing the day of her departure; who is accompanying her and if she is arriving by water, as I suppose; what day and where the steamer should wait for her. The time is pressing to make all these arrangements.

TSAR NICHOLAS I TO QUEEN ANNA PAVLOVNA:

Tsarskoe Selo,
7/19 October 1853

I am making use of the courier, who is bringing you the announcement of the happy delivery of our good Marie, to thank you at last, dear good Anne, for the letter that you wrote to me when leaving Russia and for the one from Weimar. I was unable to reply prior to this time, for in exactly one month I went to Moscow, spent three days there, and then journeyed for a day and a half to [indecipherable], from a day and a half there journeyed for a day to Brest [Litovsk], one day's journey to Warsaw, two days there; fifteen hours to go to Olmütz,[1] four days there, fifteen hours to return to Warsaw, five days there with their Majesties, to receive them, and one day to get to Potsdam, two days there, and return here in three days and eight hours. That is enough, I hope, to show you that I did not have time to write. Thank you a thousand thousand times for all the nice things you say to me about the good time that you had with us. I am more than happy to hear your own statements that this stay did not leave you with any disagreeable impressions. I had no other fears except that I foresaw the contrast with the past which it is not in our power to revive, and so it needed all your indulgence and your goodness to be satisfied with the present, but that which was offered to you was done with a good heart, I assure you. So we are happy to know that the object of our common desire obtained its goal and we thank you for it from the bottom of our hearts. I found my wife quite well on my return. I never imagined that Marie would

[1] Here Tsar Nicholas met Emperor Francis Joseph of Austria. It was all part of the diplomatic negotiation to resolve Russo-Turkish problems.

continue her pregnancy until I came home, and I am happy to have been able to be present. Everything happened quickly and well and allows one to hope for an uneventful recovery. Little Marie[1] is a very pretty child – very plump. My journey went very well. The reunion of the three of us had the aim of showing to the world that we need none other and that in a moment of danger they will find us together. The blind hate of the English knows no limits. It seems Louis Napoleon has condemned himself to march at their bidding. These follies take us straight to war. I do not look for it but I shall not flee from it. All this is pitiable, for it is revolution that has taken on this disguise. We shall do our duty, submitting to God in complete confidence. Good-bye, and thank you again a thousand times, dear good Anne, for your friendship and I count on the continuity of it.

TSAREVICH ALEXANDER NICOLAIEVICH TO QUEEN ANNA PAVLOVNA:

St Petersburg,
3/15 January 1854

. . . I was sure of the joy you would feel about our latest victories on land and sea. Let us hope that God will continue to bless our just cause. While waiting the course of events, the governments of the two maritime powers were base enough to send their fleets into the Black Sea under the pretext of protecting the Turkish ports against our aggression, but that which occurred at Sinope was like a blow on the nose and it is only what they deserve. If they think they will intimidate us by this [latter] demonstration they are greatly mistaken. The whole of Russia will arise rather than give in to these threats. I tell you that the sentiments of 1812 are not extinct in the hearts of all those who bear the name of Russians.

[1] The Grand Duchess Maria Alexandrovna, who later married Alfred, Duke of Edinburgh, the second son of Queen Victoria.

TSAR NICHOLAS I TO QUEEN ANNA PAVLOVNA:

St Petersburg,
3/15 February 1854

. . . I appreciate with a full heart everything that your friendship dictates for us on the occasion of the painful circumstances[1] that we are facing and which are certainly very grave, but our confidence is in God, in our good right, and in the character of the nation to which I take pride in belonging. They will not see us flee before danger or threats. One single sentiment dominates us – that of our duty and as a holy vocation to which Russia is called once more. Everyone thinks only of doing his duty. The conduct of England and France cannot be described; shame will rebound on them forever, and it remains a matter of doubt whether they are still Christians when they ally themselves to the enemies of Christianity against a nation which is fighting for the privileges of its fellow co-believers.

I understand neutrality for those who are alien to the conflict; they can remain spectators at the fight, but I do not admit indifference as possible for any truly interested Christian soul in the face of such infamous actions. We are preparing here to join together our troops as best we can. The universal spirit is touching and edifying; our confidence in God is unlimited!

I am stricken with worries and cares, and I have already paid for it by a first attack of gout which stayed with me for fifteen days and from which I am only recovering slowly; it is the sad privilege of my fifty-eight years, which is truly too many, and it is a matter of starting the painful years again, but in that, as in all things, I place myself in the hands of Divine will.

TSAREVICH ALEXANDER NICOLAIEVICH TO QUEEN ANNA PAVLOVNA:

St Petersburg,
3/15 February 1854

. . . What can I write from here? While the political horizon grows more sombre the national sentiment increases in pro-

[1] The disruption of diplomatic relations with England and France and the prospect of war to follow.

portion to it and with it, hope in God. *'We trust in you, oh Lord. Let us not be put to shame for ever!'* Such is the prayer that every Russian heart pronounces, and God will not abandon us as He did not abandon us in 1812. The Emperor's health has, thank heaven, recovered completely after a small attack of gout. As for Mama, with the exceptions of her palpitations, which come back to her from time to time, she feels quite well. Our winter is passing peacefully as far as mundane pleasures go. No one has the heart to seek enjoyment at a moment when Russian blood is flowing.

THE GRAND DUCHESS HELENE TO QUEEN ANNA PAVLOVNA:

St Petersburg,
16/28 February 1854

. . . According to what he tells me Ribeaupierre gives you news of what is happening here. You can imagine that the state of affairs is grave, some people showing a lot of enthusiasm and others showing no depression. There are even some people who are still hoping for peace, but I believe that the preparations for war in England and France are too considerable to have been made in vain. You must expect disagreeable news from the Black Sea where our ports will probably receive a visit from the fleets; Sevastopol alone is fortified well enough to keep them at a distance. Once war has begun, I believe that it will last a long time, for national honour on both sides will wish to make good its rights. The town is very quiet; at the court there are no entertainments, for the Emperor has no inclination in this direction. Moreover, the Empress is more than ever subject to palpitations of the heart which recur every three or four days. One lives very much at home having the pleasure of seeing together those who normally do not frequent our establishment. The only worldly pleasure that one allows oneself – really quite eccentric at the moment as things are – is the Italian and French theatre where Rachel[1] is all the rage. Her acting is astonishing;

[1] Madame Rachel (1820?–58), a French actress, performed on the stage at an early age, but her first true success did not come until 1837. She particularly excelled in plays by Racine and Corneille. She made many tours and was acclaimed everywhere. It is indeed 'ironical', as the Grand Duchess noted, that Rachel was having such a triumphant season in St Petersburg performing French plays, while Franco-Russian relations were totally disintegrating.

thanks to her we have seen splendid and beautiful things on the stage and rediscovered the fine sentiments that one is no longer accustomed to meeting in the French theatre since Corneille and Racine. She has gradually created a public, and even those who are otherwise not of a literary bent have finished by hastening to her performances, filling the hall to overflowing. I have given some soirées which have been successful. At the moment I am resting on my laurels and my expenses, leaving it to Thérèse[1] – would you credit it, she is sick again? – to take the trouble to give balls. Mary[2] does the honours and Thérèse helps at the back of a little box which she has set up at the entrance of the dance hall. Her condition, unhappily, is no less precarious than before, and her spring trip is questionable.

Cathy puts herself at your feet. Sea bathing has had the salutary effect, and we have all reason to believe her pregnant. Her health is reasonably good and let us pray for God to keep it like this, for she is very much afraid at the moment of giving birth in the summer. My sister[3] is very grateful for your regards; she is staying with me till spring, but my brother[4] is leaving me tomorrow, to my great regret. Since I started this letter so many events have occurred; also, here we are on the eve of war. A letter from Louis Napoleon was certainly not intended to bring peace. I think that you will be as pleased as we are with the Emperor's reply which is fine, dignified and clearly makes the point. If the party is strong against us I hope that God will come to our aid. There is unanimity in the country, and as you know it is not a storm in a tea-cup and the insults to the Emperor and to Russia re-echo in the Russian hearts. From all sides come offers of money and men, etc. – from carts yoked with bullocks, to corn. At this very moment the governments in the south are providing ten thousand bullock carts to nourish the troops and bring provisions. As a land-owner in Poltava I have a small part in it. The Baltic provinces are equipping the young nobles who are entering the army in crowds. Finally, the Marshal[5] himself has been

[1] Duchess Theresa of Nassau, the wife of Duke Peter Georgevich of Oldenburg.

[2] The Grand Duchess Maria Nicolaievna, who married Maximilian, the Duke of Leuchtenberg.

[3] Princess Pauline of Württemberg, who married Duke William of Nassau.

[4] Probably Prince Frederick.

[5] Paskevich.

called here, and, according to what is said, is going to unite under his orders all the troops from the south and Poland as far as the Danube. What will come of all that in your country? Will they leave you in neutrality? You are so close to your enemies that I am afraid the difficulties of the situation will finish by also touching peaceful Holland which is so little interested in a Turko-Russian conflict. I am finishing this over-long letter and asking you pardon for my accursed writing, but you know the state of my eyes. I know that every detail interests you when it is a question of your native country.

TSAREVICH ALEXANDER NICOLAIEVICH TO QUEEN ANNA PAVLOVNA:

St Petersburg,
29 April/11 May 1854

Dear good Aunt,

It is from the bottom of my heart that I thank you for your two good letters. Be assured that the recollections of 1839, when I had the happiness of spending my birthday with you, will never be erased from my memory! Oh God, how many things have happened since! How many *dear* people no longer exist! Thank you a thousand times, dear Aunt, for the two portraits of our beloved Alexander. I note that the one which shows him on horseback gives a particularly good likeness. What should I say to you from here? We live in expectation of a visit from allied fleets. It seems that their brilliant feat of arms before Odessa has not exactly given them more assurance for their undertakings. In any case, we hope, with God's help, to receive them here in the same way.[1]

[1] On 23 April 1854 (N.S.) a combined Anglo-French squadron of 9 ships bombarded Odessa and destroyed its port facilities completely. The British losses were 1 killed and 10 wounded; the French lost 2 killed and 2 wounded. Few, if any, inhabitants of Odessa were killed, but 'the Tsar made it a great subject of complaint that they should be thus disturbed on Easter Day'. (B. F. Mayne, *Life of Nicholas I, etc.*, London, 1855, p. 233.) The Tsarevitch's comments to his aunt are a little strange since the Russians certainly did not cover themselves with glory, and the Allies accomplished their aims.

The Empress Alexandra to Queen Anna Pavlovna:

The Cottage,
30 May/11 June 1854

. . . I joyfully tell myself that in this last journey here and to Moscow your heart was rekindled and felt itself vibrate, and it reawakened the sentiments of your native country and religion which were almost dormant. These are the treasures of the soul which lead it to God. These transports which elevate us above the daily round are so easily lost by the preoccupation of our individual lives. In 1812 you were young and enthusiastic and present here, now it is like an echo of those days – unanimity of patriotic sentiments without ostentation, arms in hand, trusting to God and to the Sovereign. (7 June) It is a year since your arrival here, dear sister Anne. It is the same fine weather, the same blue sea, the same lilacs and yet everything is so different.

Tsarevich Alexander Nicolaievich to Queen Anna Pavlovna:

Peterhof,
2/14 July 1854

Excuse me, dear good Aunt, for not having replied until now to your last letter, but owing to our present grave circumstances I have almost no time at my disposal.

That has not, however, prevented me from thinking of you often, dear Aunt, remembering that it is exactly a year since your stay among us.

How many grave things have occurred since that happy time. Then our peaceful Peterhof was so calm, now the enemy is at the door. For several days the entire enemy fleet was clearly visible from the balcony of the Cottage. Ten days ago it disappeared again without having made any attack on Cronstadt.

As for the life we lead, everything is following its habitual course and no one would ever guess that the enemy was so close. The Emperor's health is, thank Heaven, perfectly satisfactory.

TSAR NICHOLAS I TO QUEEN ANNA PAVLOVNA:

Ropscha,
13/25 July 1854

At last, dear good Anne, I can make use of a few moments of liberty to write a few words in thanks for your affectionate letters and your wishes for my fifty-eighth birthday. I assure you that I am most sensible of, and very grateful for, the good sentiments that you show me on all occasions and that I repay you for it by the deepest and most sincere gratitude.

If you sometimes think with pleasure of the moments when you were with us last summer, I assure you that we often think of them. Periodically, as if by habit, I wanted to go to Peterhof and pay my morning visit to you. In every way everything here is full of memories of you but it is a long way, alas, from last year and from what brought us here then to the motives that have caused us to return here now. We are here to say good-bye to the division of the Cuirassiers of the Guard who are leaving so as to have some of them in the place where we might be attacked at any moment. We have already had the news of the sailing into the Baltic by the French expedition and we must expect to see the enemy fleet reappearing one of these mornings. May the God of mercy bless us and permit that their appearance shall be as harmless this time as it was the first. The infamous conduct of Austria towards us has completely paralysed our operations on the Danube and I still do not know what is going to happen. There is every reason to believe that the ingratitude of the Emperor of Austria will lead him to attack us, which will make opposition to the enemy even more difficult. But we do not let ourselves be disheartened and everyone is indignant about it. Everyone is courageously going to meet the dangers that threaten us from all sides without concealing them from ourselves, but also without being discouraged. The confidence of all of us is in God. May His will be done!

I have not thanked you, I believe, for your superb pheasants which, so far, have been bearing the climate well – indeed it has been quite tropical. I do not remember a summer which has been magnificent for so long; unfortunately, one can only half enjoy it; it is still very hot.

Anne, I would like to send you some good news shortly. Let us pray to God and submit ourselves to His care.

THE GRAND DUCHESS HELENE TO QUEEN ANNA PAVLOVNA:

Gatchina,
12/24 October 1854

The first detailed bulletin of the fight on the Alma and the march of the two armies after this affair has just appeared and I hasten to send it to you, adding the news that arrived yesterday of the bombardment of Sevastopol. It lasted two hours with the allies having no real victory. We have lost up to 800 men, and unfortunately General Kornilov of the Black Sea fleet was killed on a battery by cannonball. It was a great loss, for he was a man of superior capabilities and the Emperor regrets his death a great deal. The bombardment took place both from land and sea. It seems that the enemy fleet suffered, but we have no concrete facts about this. Probably the allied efforts are going to begin again shortly. They are preparing to intercept our reinforcements which are expected. You know that the true fortifications are those on the land side, and are earthworks constructed during the course of the summer. Do you not realise that all our thoughts are in the Crimea! In the midst of these preoccupations we are very calm, following in that the example of the Emperor whose attitude is firm and serene. Our army is moved with the best spirit and our soldiers fight like lions.

TSAREVICH ALEXANDER NICOLAIEVICH TO QUEEN ANNA PAVLOVNA:

Gatchina,
24 October/5 November 1854

Dear good Aunt,

If I have delayed replying until now to your kind letter of 9/21 October about poor Kayso [?], it is because I was hoping to be able to tell you something consoling. I am now happy to announce that, according to the Emperor's decree, he is to be exchanged for an English officer, Lord Dunkeln, the son of Lord Clanricard, who was taken prisoner at Sevastopol. All the necessary arrangements have just been made by the Minister of War for this exchange to take place as soon as possible. As for the consequences which Kayso's misfortune could have on his career, I assure you, dear Aunt, that there is nothing to fear for he has already shown his colours in the Caucasus and his wounds give proof of it. Moreover, the spontaneous way in which he came back from abroad to serve his country in the hour of danger is the best proof of his noble sentiments. We are now waiting for decisive news from Sevastopol. On the 13/25 October, General Liprandi was involved in a splendid affair when he seized four redoubts on the right of the allied position. By now all the reserves have been united under Prince Menshikov[1] and it is probable that he will have taken the offensive again. May the good God bless our loved ones. You already know that my younger brothers have left for the Crimean Army but we still have not received any news of their arrival there. The Emperor and Empress are well despite the anxious times in which we live. They ask me to send you a thousand friendly regards.

TSAR NICHOLAS I TO QUEEN ANNA PAVLOVNA:

St Petersburg,
7/19 January 1855

Dear good Anne,

Accept all my wishes and congratulations on your birthday, and allow me to add to it all my deepest and sincere gratitude for the faithful and constant friendship that you never stop showing me in each of your letters. I see with true emotion how your heart comprehends everything that we are experiencing here in spite of the distance that separates us and the domestic concerns that interest you. Your memories of your homeland have not weakened, and you know now how we all felt in the memorable days of 1812. It is a joy to me, I can assure you, that

[1] He had replaced Paskevich as Russian commander in the Crimea.

our country shows itself at this moment as it did then. Nobody has any illusions of the dangers that threaten us, but everyone is ready to make all the sacrifices that the welfare of the country appears to demand, and it will be done fully and spontaneously when the moment arrives. I have rather the task of suppressing an excessive eagerness, which is still not needed, than of letting it have free rein. Soon, perhaps, the moment will have arrived, for I cannot believe in the sincerity of the negotiations that are being entered into,[1] following everything that had been uttered against us and the immense preparations that are being taken to redouble efforts against us, and so, I repeat, I place no hope in the success of these self-starved negotiations. I see in them only a trap for throwing on us their lack of success because of the humuliating demands that they intend to force on us as a sign of the good faith of our proposals. I shall be conscious too of having done everything to avoid the calamity that it is easy to foresee [will result], and I could wish to have as much resignation to bear the burden of responsibility of defending my country against the baseness of those who attack it.

That is enough of this subject for the moment. My wife can scarcely get up from her long and grave illness, and she needs a great deal of care. However, our younger sons have left again to return to their duty and to share the dangers of those defending Russia. May God keep them from the enemy as He has deigned to assist them miraculously until now.

Tsar Nicholas I to Queen Anna Pavlovna:

St Petersburg,
3/12 February 1855

Accept, dear good Anne, all my wishes and congratulations on your name-day. I can only repeat those that I always make for you with a full heart and thank you for the friendship which you show for me on all occasions and which makes me very happy.

[1] Continued negotiations from 8 August 1854 on the so-called Vienna Four Points; these discussions were perhaps unique in that the hostile parties continued to negotiate despite the war. After Inkerman, Nicholas agreed to accept the Vienna Four Points, but the war continued. Further problems for Nicholas resulted when Austria allied herself to England and France on 2 December 1854.

It appears that the influenza that you had is the same which has taken hold here. I have been near to it for a few days[1] and my wife was seriously ill with it, having scarcely recovered from her long illness. She is spending a very sad winter. Nothing that is happening is of a nature to gladden us. I have done everything in my power to show my constant desire to put an end to the misfortunes of war by a reconciliation with acceptable conditions. It is now up to the others, according to the degree of good faith they bring to the conferences.

If I believe my presentiments, these are only pretences to gain time and wait for a favourable season for starting operations again. I foresee no true desire to stop hostilities. At least, I am aware that I have done what I should, and we shall defend ourselves if necessary with all the more energy. Our national spirit has started to rise throughout the Empire and to pursue a single identical sentiment with all our will, and I have rather to hold back the spirit than to stimulate it. My younger sons are at Sevastopol – may God keep them! We are now waiting to see how far Austria's baseness will push her. If the danger from this side continues to threaten us I should shortly be joining the army and see what God will decide for us. You see, dear friend, the state things are in now and how little peace our future appears to present. However, we are most resigned and resolute, and that cannot be otherwise, as you understand. God will do the rest!

[*Tsar Nicholas I died on 2 March 1855. This ended nearly half a century of correspondence between the Tsar and his sister the Queen of the Netherlands.*]

[1] Apparently Tsar Nicholas caught a cold while attending the wedding of the daughter of Count Kleinmichel to Baron Pilar. The next day he inspected a Guards regiment about to go to Lithuania. He did not seem to realise the dangers of influenza.

Genealogical Tables

The Romanovs

Paul I (1754–1801) + Sophia Dorothea of Württemberg (Maria Feodorovna) (1759–1828)

Alexander I (1777–1825) + Louise of Baden (Elizabeth Feodorovna) (1779–1826)

- daughter b. 1799
- daughter b. 1806

Alexandra (1783–1801) + Archduke Joseph (Archduke Palatine)

Julia Henrietta of Saxe-Coburg (1781–1860) (1) + Constantine (1778–1831) + (2) Joanna Grudzinska (Jeannette) (1781–1831)

Helen (1784–1803) + Frederic Louis of Mecklenburg-Schwerin

Paul Frederick (1800–42) + Alexandrine of Prussia (1803–92)

Frederick Francis II (1823–83) + Marie of Schwarzburg-Rudolstadt (1850–1922)

Henry of Mecklenburg-Schwerin (1876–1934) + Wilhelmina Queen of the Netherlands (1880–1962)

Juliana Queen of the Netherlands (1909–) + Bernhard of Lippe Biesterfeld (1911–)

Beatrix (1938–) + Claus von Amsberg (1926–)

3 other daughters (see *House of Orange* pp. 360–1 below)

Willem Alexander (1967–)

The Romanovs (*continued*)

PAUL I + SOPHIA DOROTHEA OF WÜRTTEMBERG (*continued*)

Marie (1786–1859) + Charles Frederick of Saxe-Weimar (1783–1853)

Marie of Saxe-Weimar (1808–77) + Charles of Prussia (1801–83)

Frederick Charles (1828–85) + Maria Anna of Anhalt (1837–1906)

Louise + Arthur of England (1850–1942)

Elizabeth + Frederick of Oldenburg

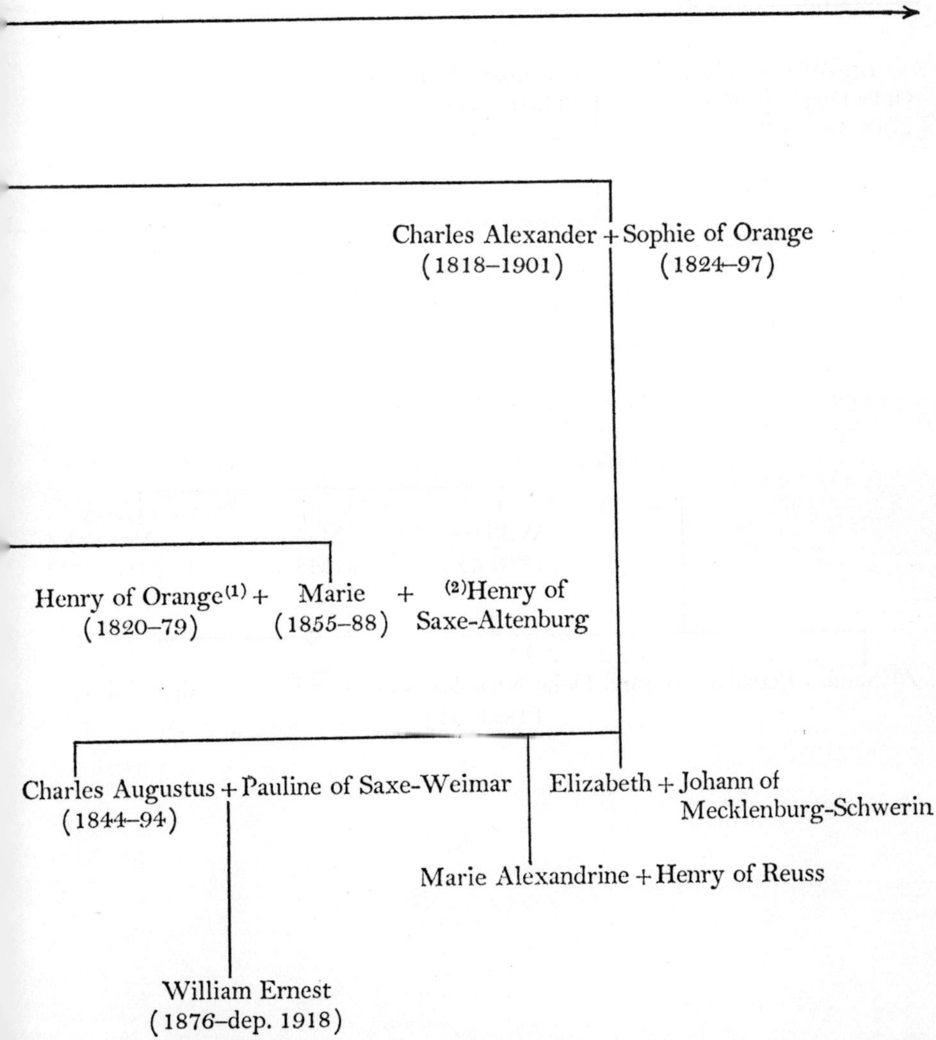
Charles Alexander + Sophie of Orange
(1818–1901)
(1824–97)
Henry of Orange(1) + Marie + (2)Henry of Saxe-Altenburg
(1820–79)
(1855–88)
Charles Augustus + Pauline of Saxe-Weimar
(1844–94)
Elizabeth + Johann of Mecklenburg-Schwerin
Marie Alexandrine + Henry of Reuss
William Ernest
(1876–dep. 1918)

The Romanovs (*continued*)

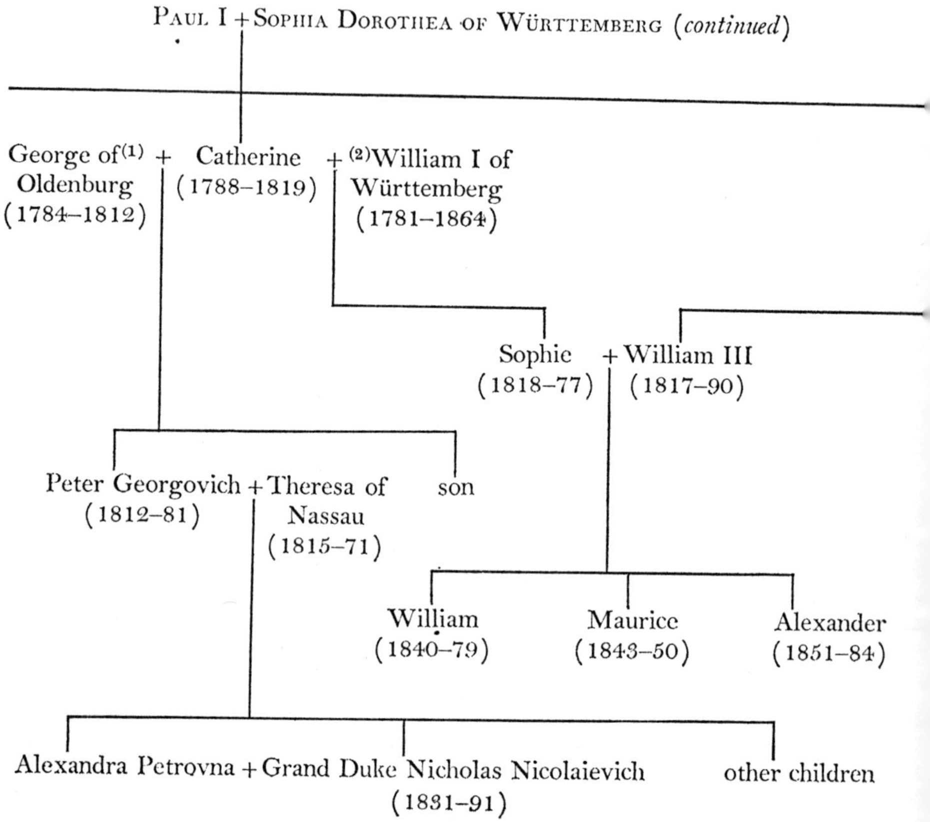

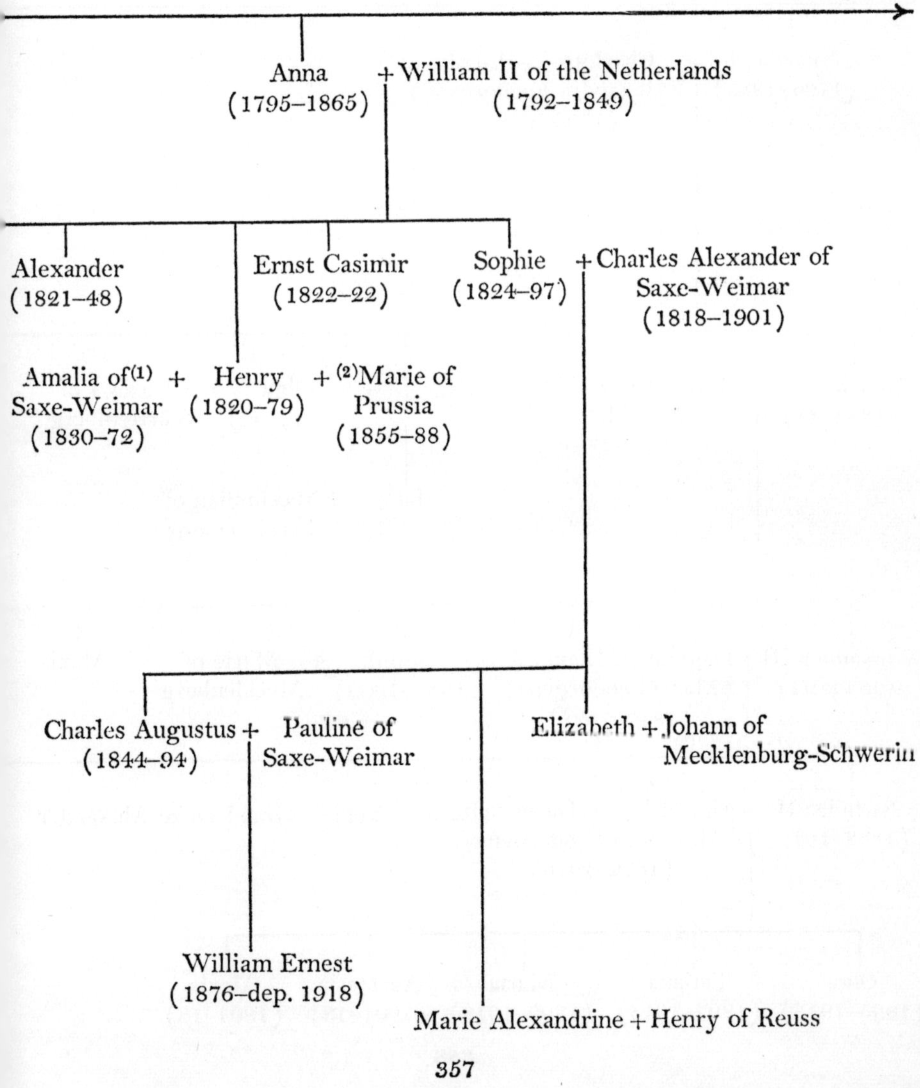
Anna
(1795–1865)
+ William II of the Netherlands
(1792–1849)
Alexander
(1821–48)
Ernst Casimir
(1822–22)
Sophie
(1824–97)
+ Charles Alexander of
Saxe-Weimar
(1818–1901)
Amalia of[1] +
Saxe-Weimar
(1830–72)
Henry
(1820–79)
+ [2]Marie of
Prussia
(1855–88)
Charles Augustus +
(1844–94)
Pauline of
Saxe-Weimar
Elizabeth + Johann of
Mecklenburg-Schwerin
William Ernest
(1876–dep. 1918)
Marie Alexandrine + Henry of Reuss

Paul I + Sophia Dorothea of Württemberg (*continued*)

- Nicholas I (1796–1855) + Charlotte of Prussia (Alexandra Feodorovna) (1798–1860)
  - Alexander II (1818–81) + Marie of Hesse-Darmstadt (Marie Alexandrovna) (1824–80)
    - Alexander III (1844–94) + Dagmar of Denmark (Maria Feodorovna) (1847–1928)
      - Nicholas II (1868–1918) + Alix of Hesse-Darmstadt (Alexandra Feodorovna) (1872–1918)
        - Olga (1895–1918)
        - Tatiana (1897–1918)
        - Maria (1899–1918)
        - Anastasia (1901–18)
        - Alexis (1904–18)
      - Xenia + Grand Duke Alexander
    - Vladimir (1847–1909) + Marie of Mecklenburg
    - Alexis
  - Marie (1819–76) + Maximilian of Leuchtenberg (1817–52)
  - Olga (1822–92) + Charles I of Württemberg

Michael (1798–1849) + Helene of Württemberg (1806–73)

Catherine (1827–76)

4 other daughters died in infancy

Constantine (1827–92) + Alexandra of Saxe-Altenburg

Michael (1832–1909) + Olga of Baden

Alexandra (1825–44) + Frederick of Hesse-Cassel

Nicholas (1831–91) + Alexandra of Oldenburg

Marie + Alfred of England

Serge + Elizabeth of Hesse-Darmstadt

Paul (1860–1918) + Alexandra of Greece

Michael (1878–1918)

Olga + Peter of Oldenburg

The House of Orange

WILLIAM V (Stathalter) (1748–1806) + WILHELMINA OF PRUSSIA (1751–1820)

Louise (1770–1819) + Charles of Brunswick (1766–1806)

Wilhelmina of[(1)] Prussia (1774–1837) + William I King of the Netherlands (1772–1843) +

William II (1792–1849) + Anna Pavlovna of Russia (1795–1865)

Frederick (1797–1881) + Louise of Prussia (1808–70)

Louise (1828–71) + Charles XV of Sweden (1826–72)

William (1833–34)

Louise + Frederick VIII of Denmark

Danish Royal Family

Sophie of[(1)] Württemberg (1818–77) + William III + [(2)]Emma of Waldeck-Pyrmont (1858–1934)

William III (1817–90)

Alexander (1818–48)

Amalia of[(1)] Saxe-Weimar (1830–72) +

William (1840–79)

Alexander (1851–84)

Maurice (1843–50)

Wilhelmina* (1880–1962) + Henry of Mecklenburg-Schwerin (1876–1934)

Juliana* (1909–) + Bernhard of Lippe Biesterfeld (1911–)

Beatrix (1938–) + Claus von Amsberg (1926–)

Willem Alexander (1967–)

Johan-Friso (1968–)

* Queen of the Netherlands

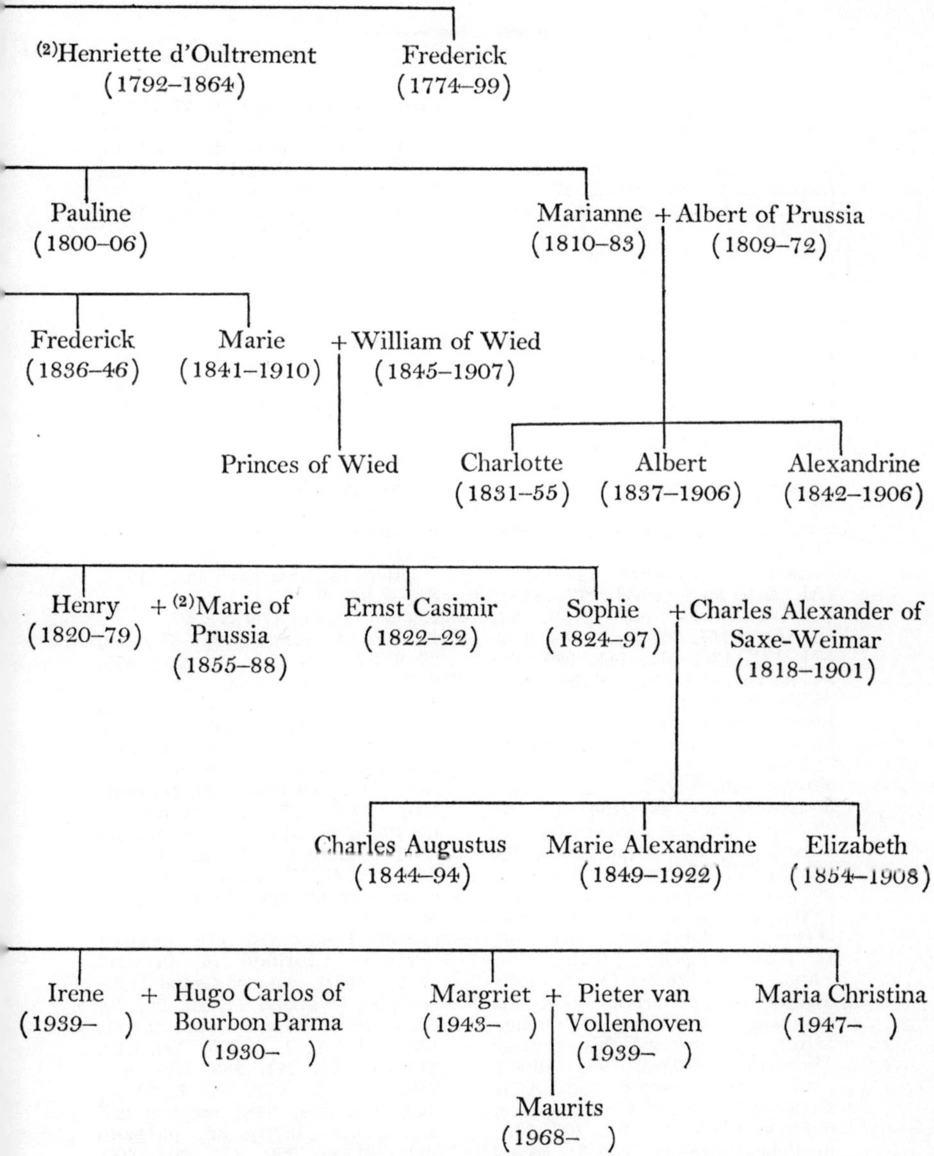
(2)Henriette d'Oultremont (1792–1864)
Frederick (1774–99)
Pauline (1800–06)
Marianne (1810–83) + Albert of Prussia (1809–72)
Frederick (1836–46)
Marie (1841–1910) + William of Wied (1845–1907)
Princes of Wied
Charlotte (1831–55)
Albert (1837–1906)
Alexandrine (1842–1906)
Henry (1820–79) + (2)Marie of Prussia (1855–88)
Ernst Casimir (1822–22)
Sophie (1824–97) + Charles Alexander of Saxe-Weimar (1818–1901)
Charles Augustus (1844–94)
Marie Alexandrine (1849–1922)
Elizabeth (1854–1908)
Irene (1939–) + Hugo Carlos of Bourbon Parma (1930–)
Margriet (1943–) + Pieter van Vollenhoven (1939–)
Maurits (1968–)
Maria Christina (1947–)

Index